POLITICS AND
SCRIPT

STANLEY MORISON

POLITICS AND SCRIPT

Aspects of authority and freedom
in the development of Graeco–Latin script
from the sixth century B.C.
to the twentieth century A.D.

THE LYELL LECTURES 1957

EDITED AND COMPLETED BY
NICOLAS BARKER

OXFORD
AT THE CLARENDON PRESS

OXFORD
UNIVERSITY PRESS

Great Clarendon Street, Oxford OX2 6DP

Oxford University Press is a department of the University of Oxford.
It furthers the University's objective of excellence in research, scholarship,
and education by publishing worldwide in

Oxford New York

Athens Auckland Bangkok Bogotá Buenos Aires Calcutta
Cape Town Chennai Dar es Salaam Delhi Florence Hong Kong Istanbul
Karachi Kuala Lumpur Madrid Melbourne Mexico City Mumbai
Nairobi Paris São Paulo Singapore Taipei Tokyo Toronto Warsaw

with associated companies in Berlin Ibadan

Oxford is a registered trade mark of Oxford University Press
in the UK and in certain other countries

Published in the United States
by Oxford University Press Inc., New York

British Library Cataloguing in Publication Data

Data available

ISBN 0–19–818146–9

1 3 5 7 9 10 8 6 4 2

Printed in Great Britain
on acid-free paper by
Bookcraft Ltd, Midsomer Norton, Somerset

LIST OF CONTENTS

INTRODUCTION

T HE following pages are the print, with some expansions, of the third series of Lectures delivered at Oxford in 1957 in accordance with the provisions of the Lyell Readership in Bibliography.

Study of the symbols intended to convey meanings, as they have been applied, at various periods in various shapes on various surfaces, is a necessary department of bibliography. Without it the accurate description of anything written, engraved, or printed for the purpose of being read cannot be complete; nor bibliography discharge its duty. The historian of politics needs to possess information that will enable him to control the date of the authentic text of this or that enactment or treatise; the critic of literature wishes to have the facts that will do the same for the play or poem in which he is interested. It is to the bibliographer that the historian and critic turn for exact information about the authorship, place, and date of writing of a piece of script. It is the task therefore of the bibliographer to control documentation. Hence the accurate description, ascription, and dating of texts is part of the service that the bibliographer renders to the historian of religion and politics and to the student of the history of civilization.

Furthermore, the form of the symbols, principally those which are alphabetical, may signify to the bibliographer much whose relevance is not obvious to the historian. The grammatically or philologically accurate transcription of a set of alphabetical signs may not always exhaust the suggestions of the text; though it may adequately reveal its purpose to declare a law, commemorate an event, narrate an experience, convey an instruction, communicate intelligence, or offer something for sale; and so on.

Hence, bibliography is more than the study of variations in the graphic outlines that correspond with sounds of speech, and the response of these outlines to changes of the materials available and the tools used, in various times and at various places. The bibliographer may be able, by his study of the physical form of an inscription, manuscript, book, newspaper, or other medium of record, to reveal considerations that appertain to the history of something distinct from religion, politics, and literature, namely: the history of the use of the intellect. So far, that is, as intellect has made its record in script, inscription, or type. This, however, is for the future of bibliography. That the study is active may conveniently be seen in the jubilee volume that celebrated the foundation of the Bibliographical Society in 1892. It may be admitted, on the other hand, that however high bibliography stands in point of exacting standards of accuracy, there may remain questions of definition and method, upon which bibliography needs to reflect; or, perhaps, even to speculate.

So much is advanced by way of apology for the infliction of a series of lectures which fits somewhat uncomfortably into the contemporary range of bibliography, wide as it is. Most bibliographers are in a sense Galtonians; they respect measurement of type, collation of signatures, sequence of editions, etc., and they strive always to secure proof that is the equivalent of demonstration. Hence, it is proper for a still deeper apology to be made for the intrusion here of a mass of hypotheses that may well seem outside the widest definition of bibliography.

There is this to be pleaded by way of personal excuse for the prank of giving freedom to the imagination in a study which is rightly devoted to the principle of verification.

The founder of this Readership in Bibliography viewed that study as embracing both the manuscript and the printed book. Furthermore, as the preceding series of lectures dealt with a textual problem of the typographical age, it was requested that its successor should relate to an aspect of the book in the pre-typographical age. With the consent of the Electors the present lectures concern a prime factor common to the written and the printed word: the script used in both. The whole is offered as a set of remarks on an aspect of a subject to some extent unexplored. As in other explorations, the imagination has been called into play. I use the word 'play' with some complacency, for it is proposed to formulate questions rather than to settle them. And it had better be said immediately that there has been no fixed resolution to avoid rash inference and no settled determination to forbid slight irrelevance.

These lectures were announced as concerning themselves with 'Aspects of Authority and Freedom in relation to Script, Inscription and Type'. The attempt will be made to say something about the origins of some of the changes in form that have occurred in the alphabetical medium of Western civilization, written, inscribed, and printed. A more appropriate title might read: 'Drafts of Notes upon Inferences from Observations on Developments to be seen in certain Aspects of Authority, etc.', or something even more tenuous and suggestive of a string of apparently casual guesses.

I say more or less 'casual guesses', because what follows is not a consecutive outline of the subject such as you expect to find in a manual of palaeography. It is, rather, a detection of some of the causes outside the artists' and workmen's shops that have changed the alphabetical lettering employed in the West for literary and other purposes. These causes may be seen arising out of changes in the nature of the belief and authority, at times sacred and at other times secular, that protected the chief forms of script. In antiquity, the City, the City-State, the State, and the Emperor successively supervised the scripts which the municipality and the empire needed for purposes of local and national administration. At the opening of the middle ages scriptorial authority was divided between the emperors and the bishops of a Church that was then more Greek than Latin in theology, if not in language. In the later middle ages the ambitions of the Carolingian and Ottonian dynasties entailed calligraphical changes. Towards the end of the middle ages the work of architects and artists became implicitly authoritative. In the renaissance, literary preference manifested its power in a calligraphical revolution, to which the Latin Church was a consenting partner. The forms of our letters were thus fixed.

The breakdown in 1453 of the great effort at reconciliation between the Greek and Latin Churches, which had been intermittently the object of popes and emperors since 1054, made finally impossible the assimilation of Greek and Latin letter-forms and the creation of an alphabet common to a united Church. What had been possible in the sixth century and later was made impossible in the fifteenth. Moreover, there was to be no renewal of ecclesiastical authority over script; though the papal chancery was able to exercise the influence of example. Taste, a combination of literary authority and scholarship, archaeology and science, was destined to fill the place formerly occupied by Church and State.

It was not by authority but by taste that Athenian, Pompeian, and Gothic styles were successively revived. The Industrial Revolution exploited all those elements in the interest of a new class, who were rich enough to afford what they liked, and undiscriminating. But abuse of liberty and excessive commercialization inspired an aesthetic counter-revolution that sought to restore not only pre-industrial but pre-renaissance standards and methods. The Arts and Crafts Movement appealed to the authority and discipline of tradition. For Morris, the middle ages was the great period of honest creation. Honesty, not taste, was his authority. It cannot be the purpose of these lectures to select the most 'honest' forms of letters that have descended to us; or to discuss them, or any one of them, in terms of taste or beauty.

It is proposed, rather, to select the forms that are in common use today and to show that much of their long career has been conditioned by movements in religion and politics, friction between Church and State, and schisms between Eastern and Western Christendom. The last lecture concludes with an endeavour to deal with the situation that has developed in the age of typography. As closely as possible chronological sequence has been adhered to. Exceptions have been unavoidable, but it is hoped that some continuity of material may become visible as the thread is seen to unwind.

At this point, the text of the introduction breaks off. It was the author's intention to conclude by thanking those who had helped. His chief debt was to the late Dr. E. A. Lowe, who had guided and shared his palaeographical researches since 1928. It is a debt which, had he lived, Morison alone could have estimated. Now Dr. Lowe too is dead, and I can only regret that he did not live to see what is (among other things) a monument to the friendship of two of the greatest palaeographers of this century. Dr. S. H. Steinberg too is dead. For thirty years he had supplemented and sometimes corrected Morison's historical and theological inquiries, and, while he did not always agree with his conclusions, he shared his enthusiasm for the subject of these lectures. Morison also wished to express his thanks to Miss Ruth Barbour, late of the Bodleian Library, who corrected many of the references, especially those relating to Greek manuscripts.

But besides the text, Morison had many debts to acknowledge over the illustrations. The first of these was to the late Victor Lardent, whose steady hand and keen eye Morison first learnt to respect when, with Lardent's help, he prepared 'The Times New Roman' type. To him is due the brilliant and accurate 'restoration' of those illustrations in which the script is described as retouched.

3

His work had a quality which makes most other reconstruction look like amateur's work. As much and more is due to Arnold Bank, who shared Morison's research into the earlier medieval hands, discussed their construction with him and, finally, analysed and reconstructed them, in ink on vellum, with understanding and rare calligraphic skill. Besides these special debts, there were countless other acknowledgements to be made to photographers, to publishers who allowed reproductions to be made from other books, and to the curators and directors of museums and libraries where the originals are preserved.

In addition to expressing his gratitude to those who had helped him, Morison also intended to try to explain the long delay between the delivery and publication of these lectures. It can only be accounted for if it is realized that the theme was the work of a lifetime. It was in 1921, in *The Craft of Printing*, that Morison first addressed himself to the explanation of the causes of change in the shape of letter-forms, although his interest in the subject even then went back ten years or more. He originally proposed this subject for the Sandars Lectures at Cambridge which he gave in 1932, and from then on it absorbed much of his time; for its sake he constantly rejected more time-consuming tasks, some of great distinction, which were offered to him. When he was planning the lectures and after he had given them, he came to realize that this was not only a subject of great importance; it was also, in a sense, his *apologia pro vita sua*.

For this reason, he constantly reworked and elaborated his text, increasing the length substantially. The selection and improvement of the illustrations, with the addition of many further examples, was also an extremely time-consuming occupation. In the end, he realized that he would never finish it to his own complete satisfaction, and there was indeed a certain amount of work still left to be done when he died on 11 October 1967.

I have done my best to add these finishing touches, in the light of my own seven years' experience of working with Morison on the book. I should like to add my own thanks to Dr. Lowe, Dr. Steinberg, and Miss Barbour; to Dr. R. W. Hunt, Dr. A. C. de la Mare, and Dr. J. J. A. Alexander, of the Bodleian Library; to Mr. J. C. T. Oates, Mr. James Mosley, Mr. J. B. Trapp, and Mrs. Harry Graham; and, finally, to Mr. C. H. Roberts of the Clarendon Press. I believe no further word of explanation or apology is needed to introduce the author's last and in many ways greatest work.

NICOLAS BARKER

March 1971

4

1

FROM THE GREEK INSCRIPTION AT MELOS OF THE SIXTH-FIFTH CENTURY B.C. TO THE LATIN INSCRIPTION AT ROME OF THE FIRST CENTURY A.D.

To scrutinize Western script with any degree of consistency, it must first be observed that the letters we now use are an inheritance which originates in Greece, some twenty-five centuries ago. As it seems profitless to push this inquiry back to Phoenicia, we may recognize that the alphabetical forms, whatever their remote origin, are found in Greece in the sixth century B.C.; secondly, that they were appropriated by Rome two or three centuries later. If the print now before the reader needs to be thought of in accurate terms, it is correct to say that it is a composition using the 'Graeco-Roman' alphabet.

Starting from this point, it is proposed, by way of outlining the career of this alphabet, to comment upon upwards of a hundred and eighty specimens of inscriptional, calligraphical, and typographical lettering. They place in their historical setting, it is hoped, certain significant varieties of Graeco-Latin script. Their significance lies in the fact that they illustrate the action and reaction of Greek upon Latin script from early times until now; and it will be inferred, in conclusion, that the lettering in the form of printers' type most widely diffused in this country and elsewhere is, in point of design, more Greek than Roman.

The first illustrations cover the period from the sixth century B.C. to the second century A.D. The specimens comprise Greek scripts engraved on marble and on stone and written on papyrus; they are monumental and literary; formal and informal. They exemplify the primary distinctions applicable first to the script of the Greek and next to the script of the Latin language.

The first example (Plate 1) is an inscription of the sixth century (B.C.) carved on marble, now in the State Museum at Berlin. It comes from the Island of Melos and the shapes of its letters are those upon which all others depend. It will be seen that they are 'square'. That is not to say that the letters are all perfectly square, but they may be said to be generally 'square' in comparison with handwriting. This is the only sense in which it can be said that Greek, and for that matter Latin, letters are 'quadrate'. It must be noted that, although in the still earlier inscriptions this could not be said, from the sixth century and throughout the classical period it became the rule.

There are four primary characteristics of early Greek letter design in the classical period. First, the apparent squareness of the shapes; secondly, the uniformity of the stroke; thirdly, the consistency of the complete structure; lastly, the rationality of the shapes as having no unnecessary parts and nothing

5

superfluous. Thus the script is square, uniform, rational, and perfectly functional. To these will relate all distinctions in lettering, whether Greek or Latin, to be subsequently mentioned in this book. The squareness, uniformity, and rationality of this original Greek, and later Latin, monumental script are qualities that appear, disappear, and reappear in the course of this examination.

In describing the scripts and letterings of later periods, different places, and other languages, reference will be made to relative plainness of design and equality of width of stroke. If the stroke in the Melos inscription appears to us as 'thin' it must be considered that it looks so to us because we are accustomed to a thicker stroke. Among Greeks of the sixth or fifth century B.C. the stroke that we may

1. Melos. A gravestone. Second half of 6th century B.C. Incised lettering.

Berlin, Staatliches Museum.
I.G. xii. 3. 1130.

Monumental square capitals; thin monoline; unserifed; between incised rules.

Otto Kern, *Inscriptiones Graecae* (Bonn, 1913), pr. 4; E. S. and E. A. Roberts, *An Introduction to Greek Epigraphy* (London, 1889, 1905), i. 33, no. 8c.

2. Priene. Dedication of the Temple of Athena Polias by Alexander the Great. 334 B.C. Incised lettering. British Museum, no. 339.

Monumental sculptured capitals; monoline with thin strokes; serifed with primitive, irregularly and illogically designed terminals to heads and feet, with exceptions as in the perpendiculars of B and E (see next plate).

Kern 31, *supra*; F. Hiller von Gaertringen, *Inschriften von Priene* (Berlin, 1906), no. 156; M. N. Tod, *Greek Historical Inscriptions* (Oxford, 1948), ii, no. 184.

consider thin was normal. The Latins, as will be seen, used a different method of stroking. This does not yet concern us except to remember constantly that it is the Latin stroke that is normal to us in the West. The main element in the design, however, is not the stroke's width but its uniformity. The Greek stroke is not merely thin (for it can be thickened) but it is invariably uniform. This is the first great distinction of fundamental importance to the criticism and classification of Graeco-Roman scripts.

The next distinction of equal importance comes from the following century in an inscription which records the dedication by Alexander the Great of a temple at Priene (Plate 2).

The distinctive feature of this inscription consists of a consistent thickening towards the ends of perpendiculars and horizontals. This thickening is often very slight in dimension but obviously always deliberate—despite the evidence in this example that the sculptor, though a first-class workman, was hurried in his execution. His deliberation is more clearly visible in a rubbing (Plate 3) of certain characters which display this distinction (it may be rash to describe it as an innovation) to as clear a degree as possible. His speed is suggested in the lack of precision. In many respects the lettering has the appearance of a free hand rather than a geometrically regulated inscription.

Whether the sculptor was over-conscientious in following the model given him, perhaps by a court scribe or grammarian of repute, can only be guessed. The obvious fact is that the stroke throughout abandons the principle of

7

3. Priene. Details of five letters in the preceding inscription, from rubbings made by Mr. Arnold Bank. The original letters are about 2⅛ in. high.

uniformity of width. This is more evident in the taperings to the horizontals of the semitic Ξ (Plate 3) to be seen in the rubbing, which broaden at their terminals so as to require a sharp, nearly vertical, cut-off. In the instance of the top stroke, this results in the sudden spreading out of the taper until, as at the right end, the effect of a bracket is suggested.

It would be an exaggeration to say that in this inscription a bracket is actually present. There is no additional stroke; the taper does not spread up and down so far as to become attenuated to the extent we shall later encounter. I think we are justified, however, in arguing that this inscription of Alexander, which is one of the earliest datable examples, is important—as possessing the finished taper and incipient bracket. So far as may be learnt, it first appears in the fourth century, and that after the Greeks had been without it for fully two hundred years.

It is not easy to justify abandonment of uniformity of stroke. However, the abandonment was by no means general; rather, this 'finisher' was recognized as a contribution to style which, while never of the *esse* of legibility, did eventually establish itself as of the *bene esse* of script. The script was agreeable to readers and pleasing to carvers and to the public in general—who, together, discerned in the fine examples of lettering a quality that deserved the degree of consideration due to a minor decorative art. And this was true not only of sculptured but of written script.

In the course of centuries, scribes with the task of producing a visually impressive manuscript began to like the consistent use of the finisher. Our term 'serif' is of late and uncertain origin, for which no Greek or Latin equivalent is known, and no better vernacular word has been found [1] It is a typographical term and bibliographers find it convenient to use it for the most important distinction in letter formation after contrast of strokes. The serif is not essential to the formation of single sculptured Greek letters, but the passage of time, combined with the increase of writing, led to the recognition of such finishers or serifs as being decidedly convenient in easing the combination of separate letters into whole

[1] Since these words were written, it has been plausibly suggested that it is derived from the Dutch 'schreef', a scratch or flick of the pen (Harry Carter, *A View of Early Typography* (Oxford, 1969), p. 48). The word is first found in British typefounders' catalogues, *c.* 1820-30, when the early 'sans serif' types were put on the market. The widely different spellings then used—'serif', 'serriff', even 'surryph'—suggest an aural tradition. Holland was, until well into the eighteenth century, the main source for the supply of types to printers in Britain.

8

4. Priene. Fragment of a letter from Lysimachos. 286–281 B.C. Incised lettering.

British Museum I, 402, lines 8–12.

Monumental sculptured capitals; square; monoline with thicker strokes; serifed with heavy wedges.

From a squeeze.

F. Hiller von Gaertringen, *Inschriften von Priene* (Berlin, 1906), no. 15.

words. It is easier for a chiseller to give full value to perpendiculars with them, than without. When omitted, as in I, or at the ends of the crossbar of T, a weakness shows itself either at the head or the foot, and often both, and consequent loss of legibility arrests the speed of reading. Its function as a sort of grace-note followed. As an embellishment it conferred a ceremonial and ornamental aspect which may be considered particularly appropriate to an imperial inscription. We have not the right to say that the serif was invented for Alexander the Great's inscription, only that this is its first datable appearance.

Nor was this of Alexander's the only form of the serif. It is to be borne in mind that his serif, while decorative, was not assertive. Plates 4, 5, and 6 exhibit inscriptions that make the serif essential to the design. The best example I have encountered is the inscription from Iasos, shown in Plate 7. Any Babylonian letterer or carver might have recognized the wedges affixed to the perpendiculars

5. Knidos. A gravestone. 3rd century B.C. Incised lettering.

British Museum I, 828, lines 1–4.

Monumental sculptured capitals; monoline with thin strokes; B with separated bows; serifed with heavy wedges.

From a squeeze; the top line only, retouched.

6. Iasos. Decree of Rhodes about negotiations with Philip V of Macedon. 202/1 B.C. Incised lettering.
British Museum I, 441, lines 83–94.
Monumental sculptured capitals; square; monoline with thin strokes; serifed with heavy wedges.
From a squeeze.

7. Iasos. Dedication. Early 2nd century B.C. Incised lettering.
British Museum I, 443.
Script monoline with light strokes logically serifed with heavy wedges, giving excellent effect.
From a squeeze.

and horizontals of this inscription from Knidos in the third century B.C. The Greek cities of Asia Minor had for centuries possessed close commercial and less close political contact with the interior as far as Mesopotamia. Is it rash to guess that the serifs found in inscriptions along the Ionian coast are akin to the cuneiform legends which the merchants of Knidos, Priene, and elsewhere must have seen in their travels in Hittite, Babylonian, and Assyrian lands? And, since these examples are later by some years than Alexander's inscription, may not the original impetus have been misconstrued by craftsmen familiar with the aspect of cuneiform lettering?

It cannot be said that the manifest departure from Greek rationalism here illustrated was happily inspired. The earlier Priene serif has far greater aesthetic justification in our eyes. Fortunately, and perhaps not fortuitously, the Priene, and not the Knidos serif, as transmitted by Rome, descended to the late Carolingians. It was deliberately revived in Florence at the turn of the fourteenth into the fifteenth century; won respect as a feature absolutely essential to the literary man's idea of correct calligraphical and later typographical form; and so remains. That is to say, every publishing house in the Latin and Anglo-Saxon world uses characters whose strokes terminate in the fashion to be seen in this monumental commemoration of the visit to Priene of Alexander before, it is believed, the spring of the year 334 B.C., when he set forth to invade Asia.

An important question: if the serif was not invented to honour Alexander, could it have been applied without official approval? Without going so far as to say that the serif was so ordered, we may suggest that it may have been deliberately chosen. The undeniable fact is that such serifing is equivalent to a ceremonial embellishment. This fact should be borne in mind until the period of Augustus, of Constantine, and the Ravenna period of Galla Placidia is reached.

Perhaps, however, we had better inquire how early Greek formal, inscriptional, lettering looked in comparison with contemporary writing on papyrus. This may be seen in one of the plates in Mr. C. H. Roberts's *Greek Literary Hands* (Oxford, 1955).

Plate 8 is the oldest surviving papyrus of any Greek text; the *Persae* of Timotheos. The writing is not consistently upright, as a whole it presents a slightly slanted aspect. The letters are conscientiously made according to the plain, unadorned pattern accepted by the grammarians of the period and, though the scribe does not imitate some of the forms used by the carvers of inscriptions, he retains their proportions. The interlinear spacing is regular. It is also economic, since it amounts to half the height of the letters, which is on the ungenerous side.

Next we have to notice a small papyrus from the third century B.C. (Plate 10). As a schoolboy's exercise, the serifs are not very clearly made, but the specimen is important as being the only extant example of the decorated style from this early period. It illustrates the early appearance in handwriting of the ceremonial termination of strokes that we studied in the inscription of Alexander, which dates from the previous century. The papyrus remains the earliest sufficiently clear example of the serifed, scriptorial, style which, we may prudently believe, originated in first-class inscriptions. Serifing, so far as we can tell from the

8. Abusir. Detail of a portion of Timotheos, *The Persae*. Third quarter of 4th century B.C. Lettering on papyrus.

Berlin, Staatliches Museum, P. Berol. 9875.

Formal book-script; square; monoline; unserifed.

Roberts 1; Schubart 1; Ulrich von Wilamowitz-Moellendorf, *Timotheos, Die Perser*, with separate complete photographic facsimile (Leipzig, 1903).

papyri that have come down to us, was not practised in calligraphy so early, or with the same consistency, as in epigraphy. The serifed style of writing is clear enough from the papyrus of the second century B.C. (Plate 9) from Egypt. It is a portion of Deuteronomy, and its first editor, Roberts, describes the writing as 'heavily ornamented'.

That the scribe responsible for a biblical text should take special care and give extra solemnity to the writing would be natural. That he should do so in this example does not, of course, prove that the *serifed* style had become general in the first half of the second century B.C. Indeed, this was not so, for 150 years later, as may be seen in Plate 11, the *un*serifed style remained in favour; but it is not impossible that serifed, rather than unserifed, letters were considered more suitable for a revered text.

The next example (Plate 11), a papyrus from Fayûm, represents an early and dated (A.D. 88) example of a large round hand. The strokes are thin and still monoline. The script is partly cursive (note the alpha), and partly inscriptional (square M). The square E appears to have lost its position in the third century B.C. This is a point to which we shall revert (see p. 16 below). For the moment serifs are under

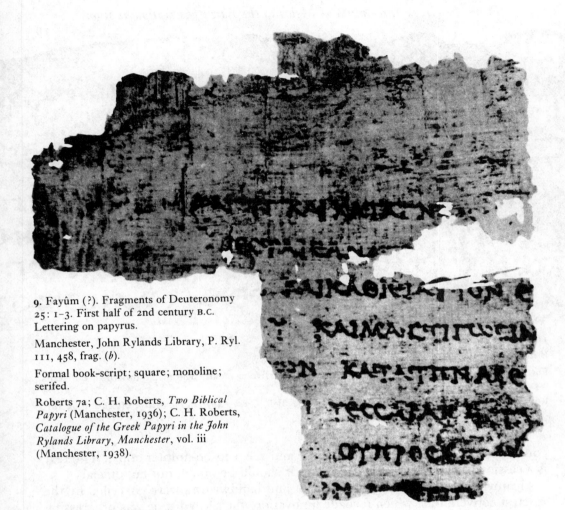

9. Fayûm (?). Fragments of Deuteronomy
25: 1–3. First half of 2nd century B.C.
Lettering on papyrus.

Manchester, John Rylands Library, P. Ryl.
111, 458, frag. (*b*).

Formal book-script; square; monoline;
serifed.

Roberts 7a; C. H. Roberts, *Two Biblical
Papyri* (Manchester, 1936); C. H. Roberts,
*Catalogue of the Greek Papyri in the John
Rylands Library, Manchester*, vol. iii
(Manchester, 1938).

10. Fayûm. Schoolboy's exercise. 3rd century B.C.
Lettering on papyrus.

Cairo Museum, P. Cair. Zen. 59534.

Formal book-script; square; monoline; the top two
lines unserifed; the bottom line serifed; 'the only
clear example of the decorated style in the third
century B.C.' (Roberts, p. 4).

Roberts 4c.

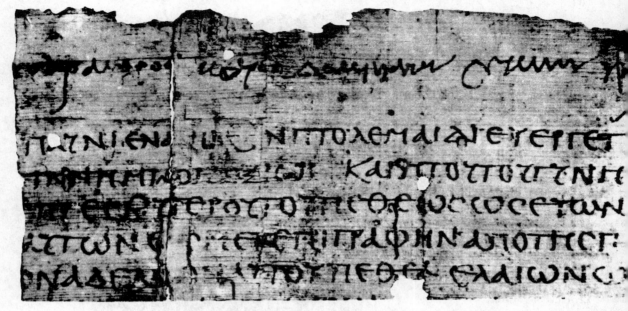

11. Fayûm. Cession of land. A.D. 88. Lettering on papyrus.

British Museum, P. Lond. ii. 141 (p. 181), part of lines 1–6.

Formal book-script; mainly square; monoline; slight cursive element; in principle unserifed, but serifs occur unintentionally.

Roberts 12a; Pal. Soc. ii. 146; F. G. Kenyon and H. I. Bell, *Greek Papyri in the British Museum*, ii, p. 181; *Facsimiles* ii (London, 1898), pl. 31.

consideration. Here they are occasional and seem to be unintentional. The text is a cession of land; a formal document, it should be noted, but not official.

Meanwhile, whereas sculptured script and handwriting were governed by the strictest conventions, which forbade innovation, the serifed style was progressing with infinite slowness, no doubt as the style most appropriate for first-class work.

The centre of the authority which repressed private judgement or artistic innovation in the formal shapes of Greek script cannot be specified. Its strength and effectiveness over many centuries are obvious. No doubt the authority was in part a social convention gradually established, but that it had some quasi-jurisdictional sanction can hardly be doubted. Craft-custom in the engraving of inscriptions inevitably depended upon architectural disciplines; and any use of lettering, upon or within a governmental and religious edifice, necessarily contracted a certain sacred or municipal charge. But Mr. R. P. Austin is unable to point to any official recognition of the establishment of inscriptional engraving in the stoichedon (the vertical alignment as well as the horizontal) style, or for its abandonment.

The acceptance of the serifed style may be seen from the work of a writer, highly skilled, of a Homer belonging to the first half of the second century A.D. Plate 12 exhibits this scribe's finely controlled and serifed stroke. It has to be borne in mind that sculptors and scribes do not always aspire to, or cannot always

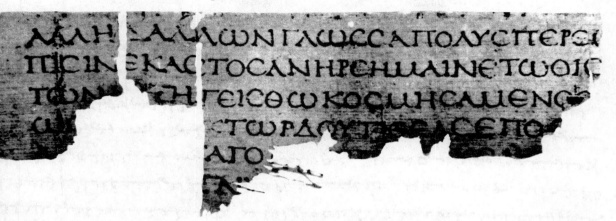

12. Fragment of Homer (*Iliad* ii. 804–9), discovered at Hawara. First half of 2nd century A.D. Lettering on papyrus.

British Museum, Oxy. i. 20—P. Lit. Lond. 7, frag. (i).

Formal book-writing; square pre-uncial; monoline; fine; regular and stylish; fully serifed.

Roberts 12b; Steffens, *Proben aus griechischen Handschriften und Urkunden* (Trier, 1912), pl. 3; Pal. Soc. ii. 182.

reach, a high calligraphic standard. They, or their customers, cannot always afford the time or the expense; also skill may be lacking. In fact, such writing as that shown in Plate 8 must be rare in the nature of such things. Also, in criticizing Greek scripts, it should be remembered that our examples are far fewer in number than are needed for the documentation of the details of calligraphical evolution. If it should seem strange that the lettering of the *Persae* and that of the Homer are separated by so long a period as 500 years, we must reflect, first, that what remains to us is a tithe of what was accomplished; secondly, that, so far as first-class book-work was concerned, scribes were not free to innovate. In this respect the metal workers, especially the engravers of lettering on coins, were less strictly ruled.

But below these classes of formal script there is a common hand suitable for less important literary, domestic, or commercial use. And this more common hand falls into several categories that can be classed in respect of their relative speeds of writing. There is always much more elementary writing than there can be calligraphic. Business is always business; speed is always important and its effect upon quality of writing is always of profound consequence, whether practised B.C. or A.D. Plate 13 is a specimen of early writing in which speed was a main object, but not the sole object. As will be perceived, the hand is designed to be speedy without prejudice to regularity and rhythm. It is a script that does honour to the administration of Ptolemy Euergetes III (246–221 B.C.).

The writing has many of the qualities that would fit it for a certain kind of book-work. If this, however, does not seem to have occurred, it must be due to the fact that the letters are joined. This was not done in book-work. Even in this class of writing care was taken to separate the letters and thereby to manifest

15

13. Egypt. Official epistle in respect of a sale of oil from Horos to Harmais. 242 B.C. Writing on papyrus.
Oxford, Bodleian Library, Gr. class C 21 [P].

Early documentary cursive; monoline; ligatured and linked; unserifed.

Petrie ii. 386.

Plate from Maunde Thompson 19, retouched and bleached.

their 'capital' structure, whereas the script of Horos might easily have given rise to primitive or pre-minuscule. Why did this not occur?

Probably because, although the script is a true cursive, it is too strongly governed by both vertical and horizontal controls. Thus the bodies of the characters are suspended as from a ruled line, a convention still observed in some oriental scripts. We need not be surprised that this device failed permanently, or even for a period, to establish itself as an official hand—so far as we can see from the existing material. It requires more calligraphical cunning than any administration could afford. Nevertheless, we are entitled to show it, for the script illustrates a principle of writing that is essential to cursive and of permanent significance whenever and wherever speed of writing is a paramount necessity. This is the principle of running letters together, as we see it in this third-century-B.C. specimen. This principle underlies all future 'popular' and 'current' writing throughout East and West—and still does.

The *skólia* here shown (Plate 14) are datable as before 283 B.C. The papyrus was found at Elephantine, and is an excellent specimen of an accelerated script in which the letters are well but rapidly made. Notice the round epsilon, which was retained by the later Greeks and the Byzantines. The Latins, too, were to use it in the circumstances that we shall notice in due time. This is the earliest extant papyrus in which the round epsilon appears.

In this connection it is well to remember that the scribe uses a square M. The serifing is informal, and so largely haphazard as to exclude positive intention. Although the scribe intends to preserve the vertical structure essential to his conception of such writing, he does not always attain his standard—see the

14. Elephantine. Skolia. Before 284/3 B.C. Lettering on papyrus.

Berlin, Staatliches Museum, P. Berol. 13270.

Semi-formal book-script; square; upright; irregularly monoline; generally well-controlled and speedy cursive element; casually serifed.

Schubart 3; *Berliner Klassikertexte* v. 2, pp. 56–7.

ends of the last four lines. The explanation is that the last lines are written at greater speed. Is this to say that hasty writing means sloped writing? The answer, nearly always, is yes; although the slope is not necessarily voluntary. A scribe may not intend to slope his letters, but may be compelled by the shape of his tool and the pressure of time. This fact is of profound importance to the form and quality of writing whenever and wherever performed.

Plate 15 shows a hand with an increased, though unintentional slope. It is from a dialectical treatise written before the year 160 B.C. Its script is a slightly but definitely inclined form, whose columns are not justified (i.e. aligned vertically) on the left. The writing is also important as having an alpha which reduces the crossbar from high formality almost to insignificance. There is, in fact, an equal tendency towards sloping and curving. The serifs are more regular and less casual than in the *skólia* in Plate 14, but, consistently with the general style, they avoid formality. We are, in effect, in the presence of a piece of regularly stylish and moderately informal script, written on a scale, half that of the *Persae* of Timotheos (see Plate 8), which must have fitted it for a fair share of good general literary work. This kind of speedy script enjoyed a considerable success and a long career, which ended in its elevation, and consequent assumption of a very high degree of formality.

15. Memphis. Detail of a portion of Chrysippus, *Dialectical Treatise*. Before 159 B.C. Lettering on papyrus. Paris, Musée du Louvre, P. Par. 2. This photograph needs to be reduced to bring it to original size. See Maunde Thompson, p. 112.

Informal book-script; square; slightly sloped; controlled cursive; cursive alpha; round epsilon; casually serifed.

'Les papyrus grecs du Musée du Louvre et de la Bibliothèque Impériale' in *Notices et extraits des Musées de la Bibliothèque Impériale et autres Bibliothèques*, edited by W. Brunet de Presle and E. Egger, vol. xviii, part 2 (Paris, 1865); Roberts 6a; Maunde Thompson 3 ('the hand is altogether uncial', p. 113).

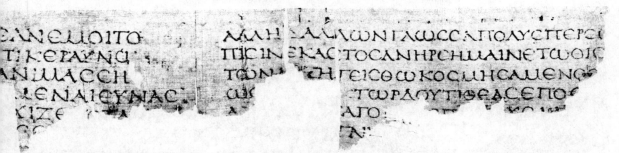

16. Oxyrhynchus. Homer, *Iliad*. First half of the 2nd century. Lettering on papyrus.

British Museum, P. Lit. London 7.

Intentionally serifed, and beautifully. This is the complete fragment of the Hawara Homer of which a part was shown in pl. 12.

Roberts 12b.

According to Maunde Thompson (with whom some may disagree), this script is to be classed as Uncial, a title which, in view of the later pedigree of the letter-form, seems more or less justified; or at least convenient. In our eyes the script ranks as 'Capital'; but of course to the Greek scribes of that day words such as Uncial and Capital would have meant nothing. Nor is it easy to say exactly what the word Uncial should signify to us today. However, as nobody seems to have a better word in this connection, we may use it. We shall have something to say at a later stage about the design.

What this Uncial category of writing looked like when practised much later than the second century B.C. by a skilled Greek calligrapher, who had the support of a well-endowed customer, has already been seen in Plate 12. A further observation upon this specimen from the second century A.D. may now be made. This is from the Homer discovered in 1888 at Hawara, of which other fragments were later found at Oxyrhynchus. The script is thin monoline, delicately serifed and fully formal (especially alpha), though mu and omega are rounded in the form which is basically cursive. It is not suggested that these round forms are new, only that they are handsomely made. The epsilon is also rounded, a point to be remembered. It will be appreciated that by the first and second centuries of our era the serif had secured a firm position in literary work of the finest class.

This papyrus was written in a period of expanding Roman domination over the whole of the Eastern Mediterranean, while Rome herself was increasingly influenced by her eastern peoples. Relations with Magna Graecia, which began as early as the third century B.C., had brought Rome into contact with Greek culture, and her unflagging appetite for Greek literature had inevitably led to the imitation of everything Hellenic—including her letter-forms.

Three or four centuries later calligraphic influence went in the reverse direction. Rome brought its influence to bear upon Greek as written by the scribes of the subject peoples in the old Hellenic Mediterranean colonies and, most notably of all, in Egypt. Accordingly, Greek writing of the first century A.D. exhibits tendencies some of which are certainly not Hellenic but almost certainly Roman.

It has been seen how, from the beginning, Greek writing required an even

17. Provenance unknown. Hesiodic Catalogue. 1st to 2nd century A.D. Lettering on papyrus.

Berlin, Staatliches Museum, P. Berol. 9739.

Informal book-script; condensed; monoline; upright; stylish cursive; serifed.

Berliner Klassikertexte v. 1, p. 28; Schubart 19a. His note compares it with another fragment, 11b, which is an anapaestic poem, particularly in point of the 'lineolae quibus ornantur calces litterarum' (p. xvii). The suggested date of 11b is the first century B.C.

stroke irrespective of serif. In the second century A.D. the even line still prevailed in all Greek writing, and the letters were still square in the general sense. In point of shape, a second specimen of this period, a Hesiodic fragment (see Plate 17), is important.

This fragment on papyrus is a decorative, as well as a flowing, piece of writing. The serifing is highly deliberate and the movement is so well kept under control that its informality is cleverly disguised by decoration. The scribe was a particularly clever fellow who combined speed with elegance. There are one or two details to observe. While the alpha is lapidary in form, the epsilon is not only round but sometimes the top half is closed: an important innovation which has descended to us. The omega is round, and so, too, is mu.

But the really significant point to notice in this script, *qua* script, does not lie in the detail but in the proportion of the width to the height of the letters. The characters here are narrower than in any previous specimen. Another point of some significance is that it comes from Egypt at the time when Rome dominated the land.

There are several specimens of narrow or condensed writing on papyri of the last century B.C. and first century A.D., that is to say shortly before or shortly after the conquest of Egypt by Augustus in 30 B.C. That is the important point; for, while the proportions of these letters are new in Greek, they are not necessarily as new and original as they surely appeared to Greeks who, even then, were averse to innovation. In the writing of Latin, condensed or narrow writing may be found in the first century A.D., as will be seen presently.

Meanwhile, we have to notice that this Greek literary specimen deserts the square that had been preserved, generally speaking, for nearly six centuries. Since a narrow proportion had been adopted, possibly earlier, for Latin, is it possible that Latin influence may have affected the conventions of some writers of Greek working in Egypt? It would be untrue to say that no condensed lettering can be found in Greek before the first century, but certainly true to say that, before then, it had not acquired the status it had attained in the fragment here seen: that of a highly estimable, narrow, semi-formal, book-hand.

There is, perhaps, other evidence of external influence upon this script. In this Hesiodic piece examination of the alpha and lambda, and the omega and the mu, may reveal symptoms of a change in the relationship of their constituent strokes. In some instances where the scribe bears downwards, his stroke is thicker than when he lifts his stroke upwards. No doubt this sort of thing was tolerated earlier, even much earlier than the second century A.D. But toleration of the thick and thin strokes to the extent here seen is a point to be noticed. However, it has to be admitted that distinction of stroke here is not explicit and can only be adduced as a tendency, and not a settled convention, in Greek. As a convention, a contrast between the thickness (or thinness) of strokes within sculptured or written lettering is first apparent in Latin. We shall return later to this point.

Meanwhile, we need to remember, first, that the standard letter of this Hesiodic fragment is oblong in the body and not square; secondly, that many of the strokes are stressed to the prejudice of uniformity; and thirdly, that all the letters, in whatever combinations, are separated.

So far as we have looked at Greek in its formal and semi-formal aspects. Really fast writing is another matter, as was seen above in Plate 14 of the third century B.C. Specimens of rapid Greek writing do not occur before then; but naturally, fast cursive had developed its own conventions long before then. However, there do not exist specimens written with greater rapidity. But they need not be exhibited in the present undertaking, for their only point so far as we are concerned is that they carry further the principle of linking and ligaturing. It is sufficient to say that, while acceleration tends to increase the slope of a cursive, an increased slope does not add to the categories of script anything more distinct than those illustrated so far.

We have now seen the several distinctions that may be counted in Greek script in the period from the sixth century B.C. to the second century A.D., as in use for public buildings, books, and business correspondence. They are, in fact, the main varieties of structure which the Greeks originated and which descended to Latin, and are observable in the vernaculars of our own day. The narrow, compressed, or condensed letter, such as may be seen in the Hesiodic fragment (Plate 17), it seems correct to say, is also found in Latin manuscripts.

Nothing, so far, has been said about the tools used by the carvers and scribes whose work we have been examining. This is a highly technical aspect of the general business of lettering, but it requires mention in connection with such changes in penmanship as derive from changes in the nature of the pen or its cutting, or in the manner of its deployment. You will remember that all the distinctions in script which we have marked as being essentially Greek remain, over a period of six or seven centuries, uniformly monoline: all the strokes are of even width. The partial exception was the Hesiodic fragment, in which some variation in width of stroke was implied.

18. Provenance unknown. Callimachus, *Iambi*. Last half of 2nd century A.D. Lettering on papyrus. Cairo, Museum of Antiquities, P. Oxy. iv. 661.

Formal book-script; square; contrasted strokes; unserifed.

Roberts 16a.

In his Plate 16a (our Plate 18) Roberts shows a fragment of the *Iambi* of Callimachus written on papyrus (in the latter half of the second century A.D.) rather later than the Hesiodic fragment, and discovered also at Oxyrhynchus. Roberts makes the important observation that the scribe aims 'occasionally at achieving a contrast between the light and heavy strokes'. That is to say, in his opinion, this second-century writer achieved this result because he intended it. Here, then, is the highly significant script which renders explicit the contrast in stroke that was noted above as implicit in the slightly earlier Hesiodic fragment.

As to the basic form of the script, it should be noticed that the alpha and epsilon and descending rho are found in a Latin inscription at Timgad (in Algeria) datable as of the first quarter of the third century. As a whole, the *Iambi* script is a fine, square, unserifed letter (whereas the Hesiodic piece is serifed), having marked thick and thin strokes. The contrast between the strokes is firm in the pi and the curved omega. Had the scribe been working on vellum instead of papyrus the contrast might have been stronger. This contrast, surely, must be the result of employing a pen different from that held by the scribe of, say, the Hesiodic fragment (see Plate 17), or the Hawara Homer (see Plate 12). Our Callimachus is written with a broader instrument, held in what the calligraphers call the 'straight' position: that is, with the pen pointed over the shoulder, and so held that the nib is horizontal and parallel to the base-line. That this is the way the Callimachus was written is evident from the vertical omicron as well as the pi with heavy verticals and light horizontals.

The absence of serifing in this papyrus is noteworthy. It must have been due to deliberate preference for a style that had acquired great literary prestige by the second century. In a sense the decision against the serif represents a break with tradition. We should be fortunate were it possible to say that the script was backed by *authority* instead of our merely being able to say that it had acquired great and traditional *prestige*. Certainly, the exclusion of the serif was occasioned by a cause other than a private choice by an individual scribe. The subsequent career of this unserifed script confirms that it possessed a degree of reputation that could be achieved only by its regular use in Greek calligraphic schools. Alexandria, with the largest library in the world, its university, its scholars, critics, and grammarians, had the prestige necessary to establish and propagate such a script. It may be argued, therefore, that the authority of the script derived from the artistry and learning of its sponsors.

The point is of the greatest importance for, as Roberts says, the Callimachus ranks as the earliest datable example of the script that was adopted—two centuries later—for the great vellum codices of the Greek scriptures provided for the Church under Constantine. The surviving copies, too, are written in a script which is generally unserifed and has contrasting strokes—as may be seen in Plate 19. It is necessary to remember that unless the writer's attitude towards the use of the serif is consciously intolerant, its occasional presence may be expected. It is one thing to determine on a general exclusion of serifs, another to make exclusion a dogma, and another thing still, to enforce it. In some scripts of the Callimachus type the exclusion is partial and not complete.

Plate 19 reproduces part of a folio of the Codex Sinaiticus, showing a square letter, with thick and thin strokes usually left unserifed. According to Milne and Skeat, this Codex was written not much later than 360. There is little to remark —except the fineness of the work; or to emphasize—except the contrast between the strokes (which is assisted by the use of vellum) and the general repression of serifs. The adoption of contrast, not only for the Sinaiticus, but also for the Alexandrinus and Vaticanus codices, is as significant as anything in the history of Western script.

Apart from whether the Sinaiticus was written in Caesarea Palaestina, as Milne and Skeat believe, there are other interesting questions involved; as, for example, those arising from the belief of experts that its scribes were also employed on the Vaticanus. But these questions may not detain us. For us the main fact is that these great vellum codices are standardized in monumental upright Greek script, rendered with a special pen which, when held in the straight position, made thick and thin strokes. The structure of the design is foreshadowed in the Hesiod and the Callimachus of the second century. The thick-and-thin stroke had evidently established itself in Egypt, and is known to have been practised elsewhere. If so, the lack of evidence prevents our being able to point to the place.

The serifing by the several scribes of these codices varies. Generally speaking, the scribes omit serifs, or permit them—without making it a practice to do so. It would take us too far off the main road to try to deal here with the problem of consistency. It must be sufficient to say that in the Sinaiticus and Alexandrinus

ΠΟΛΛΑϹΚΑΙΕΠΙ·Ν
ΠΩϹΕΠΕϹΕΝΑΥΝΑ
ΤΟϹϹΩΖΩΝΤΟΝΪ·Χ
ΚΑΙΤΑΠΕΡΙϹϹΙΑΤϳῶ
ΛΟΓΩΝΪΟΥΛΑΚΑΝ
ΤΩΝΤΠΟΛΕΜΩΝΚ
ΤΩΝΑΝΑΡΑΓΑΘΙΩΝ
ΩΝΕΠΟΙΗϹΕΝΚΑ
ΤΗϹΜΕΓΑΛΩϹΥΝΗ·
ΑΥΤΟΥΟΥΚΑΪΓΕΓΡΑ

19. Codex Sinaiticus of the Bible (1 Macc. 9: 20–2). First half of 4th century A.D. Lettering on vellum. British Museum, Add. MS. 43723.

Monumental (Biblical) book-script; square; contrasted strokes; mainly unserifed.

K. Lake, *Codex Sinaiticus* (Oxford, 1911–22); H. J. M. Milne and J. S. Skeat, *Scribes and Correctors of the Codex Sinaiticus* (London, 1938); Roberts 24b.

deliberate and heavy serifing occurs at the ends of the horizontals, and in the Alexandrinus there is accidental and light serifing to verticals. This trick of limiting the serifs to the horizontals should be kept in mind.

Plate 20 is the fifth-century Alexandrinus and Plate 21 shows the Codex Vaticanus (Thompson No. 44). Here the serifing, while much reduced in frequency, exists to an elementary degree.

It has been desirable to exhibit all three of these very similar works in order to show the degree of standardization of the basic letter design, and to illustrate variations in detail. Compare, for instance, these fourth- to fifth-century Greek codices with Plate 22, also Greek, which shows the Ambrosian *Iliad*. It is written with firmly contrasted thick and thin strokes. The difference between the script employed for this Homer and for that of the Bible is conspicuous, apart from scale. The *Iliad* is fully and regularly serifed while the Bible is not. Why is this? And how do the dates fit in?

The *Iliad* was dated by Ceriani and Ratti in 1905 as of the third century,

20. Codex Alexandrinus of the Bible (1 John 5: 15–17). First half of 5th century A.D. Lettering on vellum. British Museum, Royal MS. I. D. V–VIII. Plate from Maunde Thompson 46; bleached and retouched. Monumental (Biblical) book-script; square; contrasted strokes; serifed at heads of some letters. *Facsimile of the Codex Alexandrinus* (London, 1879–83).

21. Codex Vaticanus of the Bible (1 Esdras 2: 2–3). First half of 4th century A.D. Lettering on vellum. Vatican, MS. gr. 1209. Monumental (Biblical) book-script; square; contrasted strokes; semi-serifed. Maunde Thompson 44; Cavalieri and Lietzmann i. Plate enlarged, bleached, and retouched from Thompson.

ϽΑΤΟΤΗΟΗϹΕΝΔΕΒΟΗ ΑΓΑΘΟϹΔΙΟΜΗΔΗϹ
ϽϹΙΕΝΚΑΤΕΠΗΞΕΝΕΠΙΧΘΟΝΙΠΟΥΛΥΒΟΤΕΙΙΙ
ΡΟΜΕΙΛΙΧΙΟΙϹΙΠΡΟϹΗΥΔΑΠΟΙΗΕΝΑΛΛΑΩΝ
ΙΥΜΟΙΖΕΙΝΟϹΠΑΤΡΩΙΟϹΕϹϹΙΠΑΛΑΙΟϹ
ΥϹΙΑΡΠΟΤΕΔΙΟϹΑΗΝΜΟΝΑΒΕΛΛΕΡΟΦΟΝΤ
ΕΝΙΜΕΓΑΡΟΙϹΙΝΕΕΙΚϹϹΙΝΗΜΑΤΕΙΥΖΛΟ
ΛΙΑΛΛΗΛΟΙϹΙΠΟΙΟΝΖΕΙΝΗΙΑΚΑΛΑ
ϹΙΙΕΝΖΩ ΤΗΡΑΔΙΔΟΥΦΟΙΝΙΚΙΦΑΕΙΝΟΝ
ΟΦΟΝΤΗϹΔΕΧΡΥϹΕΟΝΔΕΠΑϹΑΜΦΙΚΥΠΕΛΛ

22. Ambrosian *Iliad*. 3rd or more probably 5th to 6th century A.D. Lettering on vellum.

Milan, Biblioteca Ambrosiana, F. 205 inf.

Monumental script; square; contrasted strokes; fully serifed at heads and feet.

'Ilias Ambrosiana' in *Fontes Ambrosiana* xxviii (Bern and Olten, 1953).

Plate from Maunde Thompson 43, bleached and retouched.

because they saw in the letters structures which resembled the Hawara Homer of that date (Plate 12). This resemblance being undeniable, the date was accepted by Maunde Thompson. However, when Gerstinger edited the Vienna Genesis he rejected the third century given by Ceriani and Ratti and argued for a date two centuries later. Gerstinger gave his opinion in 1931. In 1954 Bandinelli of Florence published his elaborate monograph on the paintings in the Ambrosian Homer, and came to the conclusion that they indicated a date later than the third century. For an opinion of the writing he applied to Bartoletti of the Papyrological Institute in Florence, who answered that he adhered to Gerstinger's date—of late fifth, or preferably early sixth, century.

Comparison of the Ambrosian Homer with the Hawara Homer shows that, as Ceriani and Ratti said, the scripts of both are indeed similarly square in proportion and large in scale. Both scripts terminate all vertical, horizontal, and diagonal strokes in deliberate serifs made consistently with the convenience of the scribe. They occur where it is natural for them to occur. So far the two Homers are very similar. There is one highly important detail, however, in which the Ambrosian Homer departs from its Hawara predecessor: its strokes contrast in width.

Now the fact must be appreciated that while the lettering of the Hawara Homer is on papyrus, that of the Ambrosian is on vellum. At the same time, the change in material was combined with the different use (I do not say the invention) of the writing tool. An instrument similar to that used for the Ambrosian Homer was probably in the hand of the scribe of the Callimachus shown in Plate 19. It will be remembered, of course, that the Callimachus fragment was a papyrus.

Such a change of tool, supposing it to have occurred, must have been a momentous event in the history of calligraphy. And there is evidence for the belief. If the omicron of the papyrus Homer is compared with the omicron of the vellum Homer it will appear, that although both are circular in structure, they are totally different in design. The instrument employed for writing on papyrus, down to the second century A.D., was cut and held so as to realize the intention of the scribe to secure uniform width of stroke in accordance with a tradition of six centuries. The intention of the scribe (or more properly, perhaps, the school to which he belonged) that lay behind the choice of instrument for writing on vellum in the fourth century was different. By habit (of holding it in the 'straight' position) and selection of tools a circular omicron was produced for the Hawara Homer—in which the line is by intention uniform. In the fourth-century Codex Sinaiticus a different tool, held in the same position, also produces a circular omicron, but does so with a line that is thicker at the sides than at the top and bottom. Thus we have in the Codex Sinaiticus a thick and thin omicron, accompanied by other curved letters which also have their thicks in a state of *vertical* balance. This obvious fact proves that in the Sinaiticus the writing tool was held in the 'straight' position.

Secondly, inspection of the omicron and related curved shapes of the Ambrosian Homer suggests that the scribe has held his pen in a position different from that adopted by the scribe of the Hawara Homer or of the Codex Sinaiticus—or, for that matter, of the Vaticanus and the Alexandrinus. By holding his pen as he does the scribe of the Ambrosian Homer produces an omicron that is in a state of *un*-vertical balance. So we have this situation: the three biblical codices of the fourth and fifth centuries are written with the pen held 'straight', with its edge horizontal to the base-line. A vertically balanced omicron is thus determined. The omicron and related letters in the Hesiodic and Callimachus fragments of the second century are also marked by a stress that is vertical, whereas in the Ambrosian Homer, of possibly the sixth century, the balance is diagonal.

This diagonal balance is a very useful pointer in connection with any inquiry into the writing implement used, the way it was held and the effect upon the round letters. The new method gives the Ambrosian omicron what may be described in one word as a 'tilt'. Hence, inasmuch as the other round characters (B C Ɛ P) partake of the same tilting movement, the design and appearance of the script as a whole are radically affected.

There are other codices of this and later periods in which the round characters are seen to retain their vertical balance. Yet we have to spend time on the problem of the tilted omicron because, after various interruptions, that letter, in terms of capital O and minuscule o in the writing of Latin and the vernaculars, retained its tilt until the eighteenth century. As we shall have occasion to see, it was rejected by the Age of Reason and revived by the Arts and Crafts Movement, from which it has descended to us in Europe and the United States. And the tilt is a factor more fundamental in the pedigree of script even than the serif. If we were to remove all the serifs from the script of the Ambrosian Homer its tilt would still make it look different from that of the Codex Sinaiticus.

This being demonstrable, the problem remains: whence came the tilted omicron? How did it win acceptance into the calligraphy of such a piece as the

Ambrosian *Iliad*, a first-class Greek codex in every sense? If we accept the dating by Bartoletti, Gerstinger, and Bandinelli as late fifth to early sixth century, or by Calderini round about the fourth century, the problem becomes no easier. Certainly it could only have come from a school of very high repute. Is the tilt the product of a scriptorium of Greece, Italy, or Africa? Bartoletti holds that the Ambrosian codex could 'as well have been written in southern Italy as in Constantinople or Alexandria'. He adds that 'its lovely uncial script tells us nothing on this point'.

Suppose we ask whether this particular and 'lovely' omicron of the late fifth or early sixth century A.D. is the first appearance of the tilted type of lettering? Is it ancient Greek by origin? The answer is 'certainly not'. Is it conceivable that it began in Constantinople under Justinian? In Ceriani's opinion the scribe was a Latin who may have written from dictation. Bandinelli is fully convinced that the codex was executed in Constantinople. He has in mind, of course, the minia-tures as well as the script. It is difficult to account for the production of so sumptu-ous a manuscript except on the hypothesis that it was executed in a centre rich in money, materials, and artists. A city that satisfies all these requirements in the fourth to sixth centuries is Constantinople.

To answer the question how far the tilted omicron is Greek we need to see what was being done for Latin; and, moreover, to abandon script for epigraphy and to leave Sicily, Constantinople, or Alexandria for Rome. There, in the first

23. Rome. Sarcophagus of L. Cornelius Scipio Barbatus, consul 298 B.C. Probably made *c.* 200 B.C. Incised lettering.

Rome, Vatican Museum.

Monumental incised capitals; mainly square; monoline; unserifed.

C.I.L. i². 6, 7; Diehl 4.

28

24. Delphi. Votive Latin inscription of L. Aemilius Paulus, 167 B.C. Incised lettering on marble. Rome, Vatican Museum.

Monumental incised capitals; square; monoline; thin strokes; uniform thickness according to Greek canon; serifed slightly but consistently.

C.I.L. i². 622; Diehl 6a.

25. Delos. A bilingual dedication. 112 B.C. Incised lettering.

Monumental capitals; square; thin monoline strokes in both Latin (left) and Greek (right), and cut ? by different masons. Serifed; the Latin slightly but generally with occasional wedges, Greek strongly and consistently with wedges.

Bulletin de correspondence hellénique, 1909, p. 404; Diehl 7b.

century A.D. or even before, the *ordinator*, the man who prepared and penned the text for the *marmorarius* to cut on his stone or marble, was employing the 'tilted' o, with the round characters B C D G Q R S to correspond. Thus the tilted omicron of the Ambrosian Greek codex is later by several centuries than the tilted o in Latin inscriptions. This adds point to Ceriani's opinion that the scribe was a Latin.

The earliest Latin inscriptions whose forms are sufficiently regularized to possess consistency are of the third century B.C., the period of the aggrandizement of Rome. In the archaic Roman inscriptions (see Plate 23) the ○ is a perfect circle and all the characters are monoline—strictly according to Greek example. The linguistic changes necessitated by the process of assimilation of the Greek alphabet to the Latin language do not concern us; we have only to observe those details which some aspect of authority and the hand of time passed on to the vernacular.

The first signs of Greek influence may be detected at least as early as the first half of the second century B.C. A votive inscription of Lucius Aemilius Paulus at Delphi (Plate 24) attracts notice. Its strokes, while according with the Western standard of the time, are given slight serifs in the style of Alexander's inscription at Priene (Plate 2). Heavier serifs are found in a bilingual inscription at Delos (Plate 25) cut towards the end of the second century. The difference of style between the two languages is marked: the Greek recalls the deeply incised wedges seen in Plates 4–7; in the Latin, occasional use of the lighter wedge-serif may be seen, notably in the first three lines. Delos, at this period, lay towards the eastern limit of the penetration of Roman influence.

At this point it will be convenient to return to the late Greek serif and examine it as fully developed at Pergamon in the second century A.D. Plate 26 is a four-line inscription on marble in the shape that the Romans adopted for Latin.

The basic Latin ground-plan of their alphabet became that of the contemporary Greek inscription, having square, monoline capitals without serifs. No change

26. Pergamon. Statue base. 2nd century A.D. Incised lettering on stone.

Berlin, Staatliches Museum.

Monumental sculptured capitals; square; monoline; slight but carefully bracketed serifs.

Max Fraenkel *et al.*, *Inschriften von Pergamon* (Berlin, 1894), no. ii. 452.

27. Rome. Boundary stone from bank of River Tiber. 55/4 B.C. Sculptured lettering.
Rome, Vatican Museum.

Monumental sculptured script; square, but with pre-Rustic cursive trend (see next plate); generally mono-line (see especially A, C, M, V); serifed.

C.I.L. i². 766ᶜ, vi. 31540ᶜ; Diehl 8e.

appeared until the serifs, first found in Greece in the fourth century B.C., began to appear in Rome.

The career of the serif in Rome is difficult to establish. No calligraphic standard of such serifed lettering can be dated before the first century A.D. Yet craftsmanship in the next hundred years achieved a height of excellence that has won recognition, universal in the West, as the unsurpassable aesthetic rendering of the Latin alphabet. Notwithstanding this acclaim, some qualification might decently be urged upon aesthetic grounds. This, however, need not be argued here since aesthetic qualities of lettering, as such, do not concern the present examination. It is to our purpose, however, to notice that for Rome, it was in the first century A.D. that the uniform stroke gradually yielded to the contrasting stroke. This convention was adopted primarily for large-scale inscriptions and spread from slight to the greater contrast, and from the more to the less splendid category of inscription.

Coincidentally, perhaps, the contrasted and serifed letters we now call 'Roman' begin to appear with the genesis of the imperial power which made them its symbol. Plate 27 is from the time of Julius Caesar and is datable to 55–54 B.C.

VALERIVS

28. Enlargement, retouched, of a word in monumental sculptured capitals from line 3 in plate 27, showing cursive traits. Note that the horizontals of E are slightly thinner than in A, but that the serifing is regular.

It is a fine inscription bearing already the full-tailed R that was to be typical of the Imperial style. Any variation in width of stroke is hardly perceptible and contrast does not quickly develop—as may be seen from the specimens in Hübner. Plate 28 shows a word enlarged and retouched in order to show the formation of the serifs and the balance of the strokes. Under Augustus and his successors the contrast of strokes becomes greater than had hitherto been seen. The practice became standard all over the Empire and continued down to the time of Constantine and beyond, the contrast gradually increasing in sharpness and developing from a vague tendency into a strict convention.

As it is difficult to observe the effect of this process in a direct photograph, it is necessary to show it by a drawing that is believed to be accurate. Plate 29 shows the alphabet of the celebrated column set up to commemorate the Dacian victories of Trajan during the years 101-6. The lettering of this inscription was cut in the years 112-13. Its quality led to its being imitated by the generation of revivalists during the Italian Renaissance. It is, assuredly, difficult to find a better specimen of Roman sculptured calligraphy as governed by imperial standards.

For first-class work the standard rules required thick and thin strokes, with decorative, bracketed serifs, finely chiselled and deeply engraved. The second-century alphabet, as canonized under successive Roman emperors, partook of both drawing and geometry, though not on equal terms. This matter, however, is not relevant to the present inquiry, though we might, in anticipation of the attitude of Renaissance epigraphers, bear it in mind. The more important point to remember is that the Roman sculptors fixed upon a thick and thin, but relatively slight contrast, while Greek sculptors retained the monoline, and relatively thin, structure of the same shapes. It is to be recalled, however, that some Greek calligraphers, as witness the writer of the Callimachus of this period (second century A.D.), were using the contrasted stroke. Whether such Greek scribes, working in Egypt, side by side with their Latin fellow workers, picked up the thick-and-thin system and other Latin customs cannot be said. It is not unlikely.

The possibility of Greek-Roman assimilation is suggested by an inscription of some relevance, as may be seen in Plate 30. Here is a fragment of Greek, cut in the mid second century A.D. The engraver's Imperial style is full Latin as it had developed by the reign of Antoninus Pius, A.D. 138-61. The Emperor is addressing the people of Ephesus and his text is given the benefit of finely bracketed and thinly tapering serifs of such length that an almost ceremonial aspect is imparted to the inscription. Secondly, the engraver introduces a contrast between the perpendiculars and the cross bars of E, and other letters, including A, which is of the forked type.

The language is Greek, but that the authority was Roman is made calligraphically evident by the contrast of stroke. This, apparently a small point, is, however, worth notice, and may be compared with the detail of Plate 31 which, too, is a fragment of the period of Antoninus Pius. As an enlightened ruler and a promoter of the arts of architecture and the sciences of building, it would not be surprising if he encouraged the crafts of the sculptors of letters.

The bilingual inscription here shown enables comparison between the two letterings then considered appropriate in first-class work. The serifs have been assimilated last. Apart from this the languages are rendered and kept distinct. The Latin and Greek are both correct. The Roman A occurs in the Latin, and the forked A occurs in the Greek, while the canonical Roman N appears in the Latin and the long-middle stroked N appears in the Greek. It needs mentioning that while this Greek N never occurs in the Latin inscriptions of Rome, it

29. Rome. The inscription at the base of the column in the Trajan Forum. A.D. 114. Sculptured lettering.

Imperial sculptured capitals; square; slight but significant (because systematic) deviations from monoline in curves and horizontals; bracketed and tapered serifs.

Drawings by the Revd. Edward M. Catich of St. Ambrose College, Davenport, Iowa; reduced from the set printed as Chant No. 4 in 1951. See also his *Letters from the Inscription in Rome* (Davenport, Iowa, 1963) for detailed drawings, rubbings, and photographs, all made direct from the inscription.

ABCDEFI
GLMNOP
QVRTSX·I

appears in Latin manuscripts, having come into the West through Byzantine influence. Thus the Greek N appears in the Book of Kells, is frequent in manuscripts, and occasionally in inscriptions of the fifteenth and sixteenth centuries. Engrafted upon early humanist script it makes its appearance in the first book in Roman type, the Cicero of Sweynheym and Pannartz, printed at Subiaco in 1465.

This N is doubtless of less formal origin. It makes sporadic appearance in papyri even of the first class, but as it so seldom appears in inscriptions there is no certainty that it ever achieved canonical status. Hence its appearance in a bilingual inscription of official status in the second century A.D. is a matter for remark.

According to the rules observed by Roman sculptors in the Augustan age, a formal inscription requires all the characters to be built up out of mainstrokes

30. Ephesus. Portion of an imperial inscription in Greek of Antoninus Pius, A.D. 140–4, to the people of Ephesus. Sculptured lettering.

British Museum, no. 489. Photographed from a squeeze. The top line retouched.

Imperial monumental square Greek capitals in Roman style. Contrasted strokes; elongated serifs of bracketed type.

which are thick and substrokes which are thin. As already noted, in the Trajan inscription the contrast is relatively slight; that is to say, relatively to later practice, which increased the contrast. Theoretically at least, the strokes are of equal height, i.e. their heads and foot touch the upper and lower lines of the two parallels.

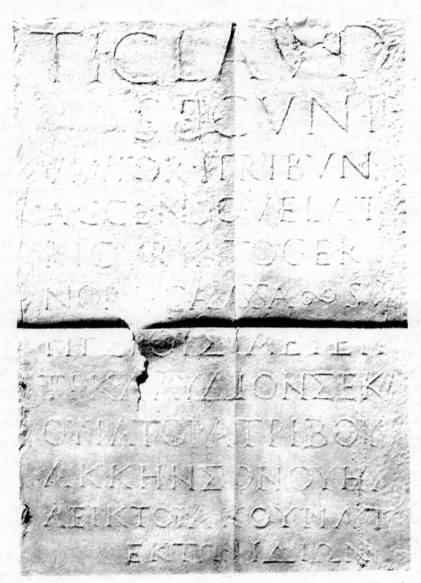

31. Provenance unknown. Monumental bilingual inscription. Antoninus Pius, mid 2nd century A.D. Incised lettering.

British Museum, no. 544. Photographed from a squeeze.

Latin and Greek Imperial incised capitals. Six lines of Latin (in three descending sizes) in pure Roman style, i.e. with contrasted strokes; six lines of Greek (in three descending sizes below the second size of Latin) in pure Pergamon style, i.e. with uncontrasted strokes; forked A; N with low middle stroke; elongated serifs common to both languages.

As to the width, most of the Roman letters, like their Greek predecessors, were drawn on the basis of the square.

To sum up, we may say that in the best class of Roman inscriptions the heads and feet of all the perpendiculars, and many terminations to curved strokes, were finished off with finely modelled, delicately bracketed, serifs. This became the invariable rule for first-class inscriptions throughout the Roman Empire. The Greek serif, which we saw in the inscription of Alexander of the fourth century B.C. is primitive in comparison with that of Augustus. But it is there, and although, and perhaps because, it was cut for a noble purpose, the Greeks appear not to have used it frequently.

The practice occurs most impressively at Pergamon. In this city of splendid architecture, which became so pro-Roman and indeed half-Roman, a different attitude prevailed towards the serif. Fine bracketing is to be seen here as a con- vention in the first and second centuries A.D.—which includes the period during which Pergamon was protected by Rome and in return gave her support (Plate 26). That the Hellenization of Rome was powerfully assisted by Pergamon and its example cannot be doubted. The erection there of a Greek temple on the Acro- polis at Pergamon, dedicated to the worship of Augustus, might have interested Roman builders. Did its inscription influence Augustan lettering? By then Pergamon had been faithful to the bracketed serif for four centuries and it must have been familiar to the Roman governing class. As was remarked earlier, to some Greeks the serif was an accidental adjunct to the letter, justifiable because it grew naturally out of some strokes; to other Greeks it was justifiable when regularly applied to all strokes because it then imparted a desirable degree of family likeness. Moreover, it could be contended, without the serif the letters would fail to harmonize so well, or to combine so easily into groups recognizable as words. In the course of time the architects of Pergamon perceived that this was so and designed accordingly. Plate 32 shows an inscription from Pergamon with stronger serifs. This inscription is cut on marble.

The appearance on Latin inscriptions of the 'Alexandrine' Priene-Pergamon serif may be no more than an additional, and accidental, aspect of the general process of Hellenization that had been permanent in Roman life, art, and archi- tecture since the third century B.C. On the other hand, the 'Alexandrine' Priene inscription may have been the inspiration of later engravers.

However it may have been, the planners of the Augustan inscriptions of the first class knew their task; it was to impress especially the citizens of the con- quered provinces. The engravers were careful, therefore, to see that their letters were worthy of emperors to whom divine honours were given, first by the Romans and afterwards by the subject peoples. The Romans followed and extended a particular Greek example as to serif. In so doing the motive must have been carefully considered. To achieve the dignity and legibility which any sensible embellishment could confer, it was necessary to avoid the absurd cuneiform serifs favoured by some of the Greek states. Equally, it was inconvenient to canonize the abnormally extended and thinly bracketed design. Such a refine- ment required high skill and was very expensive of time. The design shown at

32. Pergamon. 2nd century A.D. Sculptured lettering on marble.
Pergamum Museum.

Monumental sculptured capitals; square; monoline; serifed. With vertical O.

Kern 50, *supra*.

Plate 29 from the Trajan column remains a fine specimen of the orthodox Roman sculptured letter of the first to second century A.D. It is a practical as well as an imperial design.

Later, Roman engravers carried further the refinement of Greek example. When the administration decided to use inscriptions for the purpose of imperial propaganda they increased the height of the letters and the width of the main strokes. Moreover, the thick strokes of Rome, like the height of the letters, greatly exceed in contrast of stroke and size of letter anything that had before been seen there or elsewhere. The later imperial width of stroke, as between thick and thin, can sometimes be 9 to 1 or 10 to 1. Hence the thin strokes required in Rome exceed the measure of those found in Pergamon. As the height of the letters, also, was unprecedented, a necessary consequence was a serif refined and elongated beyond anything hitherto seen. There had been nothing in Priene or Pergamon like this; indeed, earlier Greek sculptors would probably have considered the imperial monumental script as a vulgar propaganda innovation. It is certain that the inscription of this class was highly organized.

The making of a major Roman inscription was the business of highly efficient and professionalized guilds. The significant document in this connection is an advertisement in the form of an inscription of the first century A.D. This inscription (C.I.L. x. 7296) was in Palermo in 1885, but the writer has failed to trace its present location and is unable, therefore, to show a photograph. In Latin and Greek, the advertiser says that in his premises titles were laid out and cut: *Tituli heic ordinantur et sculpuntur*. Here, as M. Jean Mallon suggests, the verb *ordinare* must mean that the advertiser had an '*ordinator*' who undertook the responsibility for the *mise-en-page* of the text, and the designation of the type of lettering, and it was he who traced on the stone the *ordinatio* of the text, which the *sculptor* exerted himself to follow with exactitude.

There were two main types of capital, that made geometrically, and that drawn freehand. A plurality of tools was involved in the process of cutting both scripts, as may be seen from certain surviving inscriptions described by Hübner, Cagnat, and others, which include representations of the square, chisel, compass, rule, curve, hammer, and plumb. All this organization lay behind the inscriptions which then included the largest capitals the world had ever seen.

The Romans were not a squeamish people. The extra publicity they gained

33. Monumental sculptured capitals. Square; contrasted strokes; serifed. Erected A.D. 70–80. The letters are set between parallel guide-lines.

Walter Kaech, *Rhythmus und Proportion in der Schrift* (Olten, 1956), pl. x.

by increasing the dimensions of their capitals and by contrasting the heavy and the light strokes was considered justifiable by the aesthetic standards reached by the best sculptors. Exactitude was achieved by the help of geometrical and mechanical aids. That the text was first written out by a professional *ordinator* and then carefully chalked, brushed, or painted on the stone, is certain. That the letters were braced between parallel guide-lines is evident from an inscription now preserved at Naples (see Plate 33). The lettering is in honour of Vespasian, who reigned from A.D. 70 to 79.

Before leaving the Roman Imperial inscription it is desirable to say by way of summary that a tendency toward contrast of stroke is observable in Rome about the middle of the first century A.D. It should be said that the data available for a study of both serif-formation and contrast of stroke do not justify confident statements about the career of these basically important elements in Roman lettering.[1] But some conclusions must be attempted.

First, we have to notice that the angle of stress, shading, or contrast in the o in the imperial style is slight, accidental, but destined to increase. That the original intention was to keep o vertical, a perfect circle and monoline, is obvious. Departure from this intention in an inscription is only to be explained if the pen-made, slightly contrasted character, including the tilted o, had already established itself as canonical in the eyes of the ordinator, and that it kept its form and balance under the chisel of the sculptor. The monumental alphabet in its highest state of sophistication, as it is in the inscription on the Trajan Column, is therefore to be considered as a geometrical and mechanical formalization of an originally calligraphical model. This being the course of development, and as we have the intentionally tilted o (and Q) on the Trajan Column, should we not expect to find the calligraphical tilted o in a papyrus of the first or second century A.D.?

It is fruitless to search for a tilted omicron in any early or late Greek papyrus, informal or formal, even of the fourth or fifth centuries. The scribes had no intention of varying from monoline, and no question of tilt, therefore, could arise. How, therefore, does it come about that the tilted omicron is standard in the script of the Ambrosian *Iliad*? Experts say that the Ambrosian work is the most remarkable of its time, whatever century it was. But this is in dispute. Contemporary writers argue that it is of the *fourth*, *fifth*, or *sixth* and not of the *third* century, as was formerly claimed. As to comparable Latin manuscripts (comparable in script, that is) the authorities insist that the Square Capital Virgils, which (as we shall see shortly) also show the tilted o, are of the fourth century at the earliest.

---

[1] The engravings used by the Berlin *Corpus*, while copious, neat, and beautifully drawn, remain drawings and lack the degree of accuracy desirable in minute scholarship. The Berlin technique in 1861, when Mommsen produced his first volume, was then the only as well as the best means available, and all epigraphic scholarship is based upon these drawings, inevitably deficient in accuracy though they are. In particular the drawings tend to exaggerate the delicacy of serifs and to falsify the relations between thick and thin strokes. The photographs reproduced by collotype in Ernest Diehl's *Inscriptiones Latinae* in 1905 represent an enormous advance in accurate representation of inscriptional material but, as those who have tried it are aware, the camera can sometimes distort proportions and details. The more certain method is to secure rubbings or, preferably, squeezes.

Are these dates really correct? You may doubt it; yet that is what is conveyed by the little evidence available. So far, opinion leads to the conclusion that the tilted inscriptional O anticipates the calligraphical tilted O by three centuries. Is there anything more to be said?

Possibly—if it be assumed that the tilted O, when it occurs in the inscriptions, must be a lapidary translation of an originally calligraphic pattern. The reason for the existence in calligraphy of a tilt is plain enough: it is easier for a penman, writing in a comfortable position, to permit a circular letter to tilt than to keep it vertical. Moreover, the easier the form is to make, the more it was bound to become familiar. We must not assume that it was the only form, however, nor should we think that the tilted O was standardized to the exclusion of the vertical O. From the beginning there appear to have been two practices current among the best engravers. Some preferred to accept and reproduce the tilt and others to organize and standardize the vertical. The fifteenth-century revivalists, artists, and mathematicians like Feliciano, Moille, Pacioli, and Dürer, perceived this. They elected to follow the majority and preferred the tilt. Why did Dürer go so far as to ignore the vertical O?

The answer can only be that he enjoyed an aesthetic preference for the tilted O. And it is possible that aesthetic considerations such as rhythm moved the lettering artists of Rome to give priority to the tilted O even while the vertical O remained imperative in Greek sculptural lettering. In sum, it seems certain that while the tilted O is older in Latin calligraphy than the second century, and gradually thereafter became the preferred shape, the vertical O maintained in Greek the position it had held since the sixth century B.C. Our first Pergamon Greek inscription (Plate 26) from the second century A.D. shows how well the carver in Pergamon has preserved the outline of his model, which was evidently a fine piece of work, very 'imperial' in style—regular and geometrically consistent. The vertical and tilted forms being both equally circular or square in shape are both equally submissive to the circle and the square of the *marmorarii*, *lapidarii*, and *quadratarii* responsible for carving the inscriptions. We know from Petronius (*Sat.* 29) that the shapes which made up the words CAVE CANEM were known as *litera quadrata*. But not all public or domestic notices could have been set up so formally. For a variety of lesser inscriptional purposes the Romans used a style of lettering that is called 'Rustic'. As an alphabet that is informal and more or less upright, it corresponds only in part to our idea of 'Italic', for it was not intentionally inclined or sloped as the modern italic would be.

The shapes of these Roman Rustic capitals when used for public purposes were free-hand with brush and paint, without resort to any other aid, save the straight-edge which, in the Monumental Sculptured Capitals, ruled the two horizontal parallel lines needed to preserve alignment, and regulate the spacing between the lines. The consideration of the Rustic Capital will occupy our attention in the next chapter.

2

FROM RUSTIC TO HALF-UNCIAL

THE most conspicuous, though not the most important, fact about the Latin
script called 'Rustic' is that, like one of the contemporary Greek scripts
written in Egypt upon which report has already been made, it is serifed (see
the Hesiodic fragment of the first to second century A.D. in Plate 17). Obviously,
the Greek lettering is designed to combine speed and elegance—but obviously,
too, the average measure of the letter differs from what it had been in Greece
since the early classical period. Moreover, as we know, when the Greek capitals
were imitated (the word is not too strong) in Rome, the so-called 'Square' measure
was retained. Contrast between thick and thin, and extension of the serif, are
the only Latin innovations observable up to the first to second century A.D. That
is what appears to be the fact. And it would be demonstrably true if the proportions of the lettering of the Hesiodic fragment originated in a school of Greek
script; say in Egypt, where this first- to second-century papyrus was discovered.
And why press the inquiry further?

The answer lies in the fact that the Greek script of the Hesiodic fragment of
the first to second century is not 'Square' and because lettering of unsquare
proportion also appears in Latin inscriptions cut not later than the first century
A.D. Not only so, but the script of unsquare measure is to be observed, as a pen-
form, on an early Latin papyrus: some fragments of the poem *De Bello Actiaco*.
The papyrus (see Plate 34) was discovered in 1752, but although the text was
transcribed and the lettering copied, no photograph was made until 1938 when
E. A. Lowe included it in the third volume of *C.L.A.* He believes the papyrus
to have been written in Italy between 31 B.C. and A.D. 79. It is presented here
as the earliest datable specimen of 'Rustic'.

Rustic is a condensed, thick-and-thin letter with serifs that vary in direction,
dimension, and emphasis, though they always remain, as in the Square Capitals,
a conspicuous feature of the design. The two basic elements of Rustic are its
freedom of movement and its economy of width. In the *De Bello Actiaco* fragments you see frank free-hand lettering—something written that looks like
writing and does not disdain a varying degree of casualness. And this freedom
is of the very essence of Rustic. Seen at its height in this written specimen, in
a lesser degree freedom runs undiminished and consistently throughout the
Rustic alphabet, whether it is written by the pen, or inscribed by the brush on
stone, or even cut on marble. In other words, freedom and the condensation in
Rustic Capitals constitute a convention as regular as the discipline and the width
in Square Capitals. It is, therefore, correct to describe 'Rustic' as the first of all
calligraphic designs which, in the typography of many centuries later, was to be
known as 'Italic'.

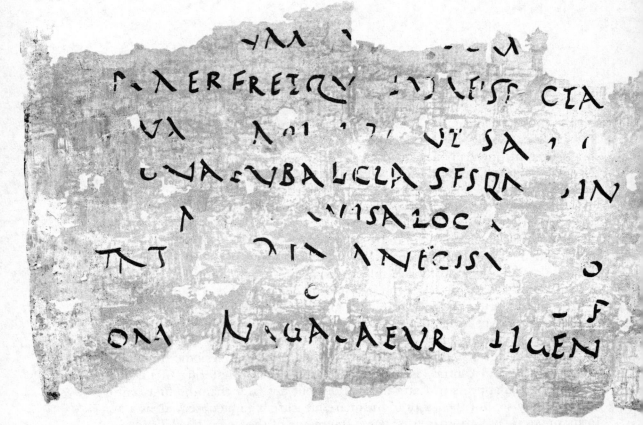

34. Naples and Paris. *Carmen de bello Actiaco.* 31 B.C.–A.D. 79. Freehand Rustic book-script on papyrus. Naples, Biblioteca Nazionale, P. Hercolesi 817, col. i. There are other fragments in Paris (Louvre).

Mixed square and condensed; generally monoline; on occasion cursively serifed.

C.L.A. iii, no. 385. The present photograph is enlarged, bleached, and retouched from Lowe's facsimile from Naples.

The Rustic script is never geometrically perpendicular; rather, as a piece of capital lettering performed at speed, it effects a nice reconciliation of the need for economy in time and material, with the preservation of order and shape. Accordingly, a certain cursive element, kept under control, is essential to Latin Rustic. Inevitably the o is always tilted and the other curved characters follow suit. An important character is G, the final swing of which terminates in a pure curve—an important point to which we shall return, because it retained its form long after the other constituents of Rustic had shed their characteristics. This Ç is the one novel design in what we may call the 'fount'.

It is not in the least surprising that informality should be found on papyrus, or on vellum. The work of the world cannot be expeditiously carried on exclusively in formal script. On the contrary, the most domestic of all scripts and most familiar to the greatest number was, and must inevitably be, informal. Even so, the systematization of a domestic script, and its fashioning into a public epigraphic instrument fit for communal purposes, while retaining at the same time its originally informal character, was a remarkable achievement. It was developed as a second-class epigraphic script between the first century B.C. and the first century A.D. The absolute novelty of the design, apart from its informality, lies in the consistent reduction of the average width of Rustic letter to between half and three-quarters of the first-class Square Capital.

It is true that the so-called Square Capital is less square than generally appears; but—and this is the point—the Rustic was functionally determined as an oblong, and finally became a very narrow oblong. Thus, besides having a great economy in writing at speed, Rustic also makes a notable saving in lateral space. The speed was achieved by holding the pen or brush in the most comfortable, i.e. the slanted, position; the saving in lateral space necessarily followed from the reduction of the width of the average letter. The gain was compound and unprecedented. There is another important collateral advantage in Rustic. Not merely did it save time in making, and space in writing; but, because it saved space in the setting out, it automatically saved material. Altogether, therefore, Rustic is a supreme invention of the Latin mind in the field of practical lettering.

It may well be asked, therefore, whence came the impulse to desert the quadrate proportions that had enjoyed sacrosanctity for Greek monuments during six or more centuries?

The calligraphers say that it is impossible to write Square lettering as rapidly as the type that is content to reach a vertical or diagonal oblong. Now, as has been observed, the Greek scribes used a speedy and inclined capital, which, however, failed to achieve inscriptional status. But it did perform for the writing of Greek some of the functions that Rustic performed for Latin. The Greek lapidary letter remained Square, though it would be too strong a statement to say that Greek writing never departed from the Square. There are many examples of Greek book-script which do so. It is true to say, however, that departure from the Square was not tolerated in any official and public promulgation until the era with which we are now concerned, and then only in areas under Latin influence.

Latin Rustic probably began its career as a rationalized version of official and popular writing, fused with a loosening version of the Square Capitals, the whole written with a pen cut specially for speed. It secured a measure of public approval in Rome during or before the first century B.C., though the evidence is slight. The *De Bello Actiaco* fragments have been shown as the earliest datable specimen of the design, but hardly show its virtues.

As proved by the specimen here shown (Plate 35), taken from the graffiti in Pompeii and written in the first century A.D., Rustic was easily made and perfectly legible. As the most familiar of the high class writings, its prestige for higher classes of literary work was not weakened by its success as a publicity script. How the classical Greeks promulgated the legal enactments of the city-state we know from the numerous, formal, long inscriptions that remain. They appear to have conducted their municipal politics without anything analogous to Rustic.

D

CCVSPIVM · AED

SIQVA·VERECVNDE·VIVENTI·GLORIA·DANDA·EST
HVIC·IVVENIDEBET·GLORIA·DIC·NA·DARI

35. Pompeii. Election notice. A.D. 79. Public Rustic painted capitals.
Condensed; cursive; contrasted strokes; heavily serifed.

Matteo della Corte, *Notizie degli scavi* (Naples, 1911), p. 472, no. 31; V. Federici, *Archivio paleographico italiano* (Rome, 1932), v, pl. 21, no. 7; Jean Mallon, Robert Marichal, and Charles Perrat, *L'Écriture latine de la Capitale romaine à la Minuscule* (Paris, 1939), pl. 4.

It is reasonable to believe, therefore, that the Latin preceded the Greek in this style of writing and that some Roman anticipated the Alexandrian, or whoever it was, who used it for his Hesiod.

The earliest, more or less datable, equivalent of inscriptional Rustic in Greek occurs among Christian inscriptions. We have a fine inscription engraved in Greek Rustic for the church of Autun, itself a daughter of the Graeco-Asiatic church of Lyon. This was cut, perhaps, in the first half of the third century, while an early example of the principle of Rustic applied to Greek in Rome occurs in the fourth century. The Autun inscription is a prayer signed by the petitioner, PEKTOR, or Pectorius (see Plate 36). The letters are highly condensed, in a fashion that would have been considered intolerable in mainland Greece in Classical times.

Curiously enough, the late Hellenes and, as will be shown, the Byzantines, came to think very differently from their forebears about capitals, and reversed the proportions of their Greek Square Capitals in favour of those of Latin Rustic. The process may be seen developing among the Byzantines in the sixth century. Obviously, the adaptation of Rustic to Greek was a highly practical measure for a language in which, unlike Latin, long compound words were common. This does not mean that the adaptation came speedily. Calligraphical changes are never sudden, and nowhere so slow in their developing as in Greece. Even so, such changes were by no means rapidly digested in the West.

The change of dimension from the 'antique', set, Square Capital, to the 'modern', free, condensed, oblong, Rustic represents a truly significant scriptorial invention of the Romans. Yet the design, with its fundamental virtues of time-saving, space-saving, and material-saving, made its way in the West only after many set-backs. Neither among the Greeks nor among the Romans was calligraphic innovation encouraged. The right and natural resistance to any

36. Autun. Epitaph of Pectorius. 3rd century A.D. Greek public Rustic sculptured capitals.

Highly condensed; monoline; strongly serifed.

F. Cabrol and H. Leclercq, *Dictionnaire d'Archéologie et de Liturgie chrétienne* (Paris, 1907), i, s.v. 'Autun'.

meddling with script in the first four centuries of our era yielded only to the revolutionary political and religious changes that marked the ascent of Constantine. Before then, apart from Rustic, the prime standard remained the Square Capital. Rustic had the force of domestic familiarity, but remained a second-best medium. It never acquired full authority in classical times, possibly because it was known to be an economic device, a cheap and easy version of the monumental capital.

No special action for or against it was necessary so long as it looked what it was, and the position of the Imperial Square Capital was not challenged. Thus the Rustic Capital needed to appear unofficial and hence, even when engraved, it exhibited its character as brush- or pen-made. Yet this distinction may not have been equally obvious everywhere at every time. A fine inscription from Tunis shown by Cagnat proves that a condensed version of the Square Capital, stylishly serifed, was used. No such capital seems to have appeared in Rome, nor can it be plausibly suggested that this highly condensed type of fully serifed capital influenced the Greeks.

In any case, what is certain is that prestige remained with the Square Capital. Prejudice against condensed lettering was revived at the Renaissance, and it is disallowed to this day in what is considered 'sound' book typography in England. In Germany, Holland, and France, however, the proportions were changed to correspond with those of Rustic. Thus, it was not until the eighteenth century that the Latin world reaccepted the narrow, Rustic, proportions that Rome developed between the first century B.C. and the first century A.D., and passed on to Greece in the sixth century.

For us the essential point is that the Square Capitals were authoritative in the plenary, imperial sense. Their size, shape, and expression were calculated to symbolize what we mean by the word 'official' when we use it to imply 'requiring obedience'. Of course, they were extended to non-official uses. Rustic Capitals were authoritative in the lesser municipal sense, and their use was maintained in decent domestic or personal use.

From the second century A.D. lettering on all formal inscriptions, whether first or second-class, was still fundamentally Square, and strictly governed. After the time of Trajan (98–117) M is serifed at both heads, which is a logical development and not a merely gratuitous departure from the Augustan canon. In first-class inscriptions towards the end of the second century, however, the toleration of the Rustic G with a curved or bearded lower half does amount to a serious deviation from the Augustan canon. It is present in Rome under Diocletian (284–305), but seems to have been excluded under Constantine. The sculptors of the great Arch with which the pagan Senate honoured the Christian Emperor whose brilliant generalship brought victory over Maxentius and peace to Rome, saluted him with a handsome inscription in Square Capitals, serifed. The inscription is monoline in structure, very thick in the stroke, deeply cut, and the letters, especially A, D, and E, are notably broader than the Augustan model. (Plate 37.)

But this was not without precedent. The inscriptions on the triumphal arches

37. Rome. Arch of Constantine. A.D. 315. Monumental sculptured capitals.
Square capitals; thick monoline strokes; serifed.
C.I.L. vi. 1139; Hübner 702; Diehl 26d; L. Voelkl, *Der Kaiser Konstantin* (Munich, 1957), pls. 30, 31.

(e.g. that of Titus, erected in A.D. 81) were also engraved in a squarer-than-usual type of Augustan letter. For Rome, therefore, thickness and boldness of the strokes must have set off the inscription as a 'conscious' Imperial design, and, as such, enjoyed protection from less august types of lettering.

The presence of the bearded or curved G in the Square Capital inscription of the period of Diocletian represents aggression of a second-class upon a first-class design. It marks an early sign of a weakening of the Roman canon—from within. This is always a risk when two scripts, one first-class (the Square Capital) and the other second-class (the Rustic Capital), are practised side by side. If the first-class is written slowly and the second-class swiftly, competition must ensue. Either the race will go to the swiftest or a compromise, a mixture of forms, will emerge. This is the more certain if, as the greatest scribe of our time, Edward Johnston, was accustomed to say, 'Every formal script is at its best when it is written as fast as it *can* be written.'

The canon of a given script inevitably faces risks if it should by nature be a carefully articulated structure, and for geographical reasons be made to serve two languages, both spoken in the same community. Calligraphical purities are even more likely to be contaminated when a common religion is simultaneously practised by diverse language groups, as was especially the case in Rome and in the Christian cities of the Roman-administered East. We shall see in due course that the effect of a mixed population upon a given canon, whether Greek or Latin, was highly corrupting. In Rome itself, at times, some sculptors seem to have forgotten which alphabet, Greek or Latin, they were engraving, or to remember which canon they were supposed to respect.

In ecclesiastical circles of the second century the prestige of Greek apologetical literature necessarily stood high, and, outside those circles, Greek secular literature was staple reading. The degree of canonical purity in Greek and sculptured lettering and in book-script seems to have been high and continuous.

47

Greek superiority in calligraphy, as the Hawara Homer (Plate 12) proves, developed out of respect for a canonized literary author. Thus an *édition de luxe* was a close transcript of an earlier text of the same class. Hence the letters of the Ambrosian Homer of the sixth century are no less square than those of the Hawara Homer of the second. Both may have been so written by way of homage to an author, and to an original for which, as may reasonably be thought, scholars entertained a regard corresponding to that felt by the humanists of the fifteenth century for early 'editions'. It does not seem absurd, therefore, to conjecture that, as the Hawara Homer was in Square Capitals, the best Homers that lay between it and the Ambrosian were similarly lettered. So we may say that even if the Ambrosian Homer in Square Capitals is of the sixth century, the convention is far older; and all the more certainly since, for a contemporary scribe writing out a Greek text, his only alternative was Cursive, which would have been an impossible choice. Hence Square Capitals were bound to be the rule for the great Greek literary authors.

In the great Latin literary texts from the first century, however, the scribe could perhaps choose between Square Capitals and Rustic. To say that this was certainly so, would enlarge too far the option available in the first century. The copies in Square Capitals that we have, which present Virgil in the calligraphical majesty previously accorded to Homer, are all ascribed by the authorities to the fourth century. They usually dismiss them as 'imitative' and as lying outside the main stream of scriptorial development. Whether this be a correct judgement or not, the use of Square Capitals for such texts seems to be intelligent. The interest of Augustus in the *Aeneid* is well attested, and obviously any copy prepared for him would need to be written in a style at once appropriate to the poetic genius of the author and the imperial dignity of the owner. Such a great Latin text, therefore, would hardly be written in a style inferior in calligraphic honour to the Greek editions of the epic of Odysseus which already reposed in the libraries of collectors.

Moreover, the bibliophiles of that day, like those of our time, were lovers of books that were written (as they are nowadays printed) in a form that combined the distinguished with the familiar. When parchment was introduced at the beginning of the second century it seems not to have been valued as highly as good papyrus. Perhaps the painters were quicker than the writers to appreciate the greater artistic possibilities of vellum. Weitzmann has described for us how the miniature-painter learned to adjust himself to the new material. The column-width picture, after it was taken over from the roll, developed in size and splendour until it became a half-page and then a full page.

The innovation of the vellum codex is but one special aspect of a general revolution that was then taking effect. The fourth century A.D. witnessed the final persecution of the Christians under Diocletian and Galerius, the conversion of Constantine, the Council of Nicea, the removal of the capital of the Empire from Rome to Byzantium; the transcribing of the great Uncial codices of the Bible (of which the Vaticanus, the Sinaiticus and, from the beginning of the fifth century, the Alexandrinus, survive); and, either then or a little later, the Virgils.

In the fourth century the Roman world was prosperous, and there must have been many Square-text Homers and Virgils produced for the libraries of the rich. We deal with these Virgils before coming to the Bibles, though the latter may have been written earlier.

The most sumptuous and monumental of all the Virgils is the Codex Augusteus, so-called because it was once thought to be of the Age of Octavian (see Plate 38). Only fragments remain. According to Lowe, the Codex was almost certainly written in Italy. The script is the creation of the broad pen whose edge is held parallel to the base line; the position of the arm for which, according to the cut of the pen, gives thick perpendiculars and thin sub-strokes. It is a position, also, that requires to be maintained by a constant effort of the will if the lettering is to remain consistent throughout. Accordingly, when, as often, the O is tilted, it is probably *against* the intention of the scribe.

The Codex Augusteus is regarded by experts as having been written in the fourth century. It is possibly a careful copy of an older Virgil also written so as to bestow on the poet the authority inherent in the highest quality of lettering attainable. It is quite true, as some critics have emphasized, that it recalls to us the impressiveness of the highest class of public inscription; but need it necessarily be taken as being 'artificial', and as having been manufactured with the intention of rendering a facsimile of the epigraphic style? Why should we not applaud the decision to confer on the greatest of Latin poets the highest calligraphic accolade: a form analogous to the script with which the Emperor himself impressed his subjects? Moreover, is it the fact that the calligraphy of all these Virgils in Square Capitals is imitative, reproductive, and therefore artificial? Rather, the letters of the Augusteus seem to be an honest piece of penwork. The letterer is not afraid to flourish the top bar of F in a style that was revived centuries later; he carries the thin strokes of V below the line; the crossbar of H is much higher than a cutter would allow; the capital M is the result of several movements, with the pen held in more than one position. All these deviations from the epigraphic practice are proof that the scribe was not engaged in imitating sculptured lettering. The letters of the Augusteus are a full quarter of an inch in height.

The second Virgil, Codex Sangallensis 1394, is similarly lettered, in characters slightly less than a quarter of an inch high (Plate 39). In some respects the lettering here is better finished than in the Codex Augusteus. It seems clear from the regularity of its appearance that the tilted O is within the intention of the scribe. The St. Gall Codex is regarded by experts as of the fifth century. The G, M, and V have Rustic affiliations. The script as a whole suggests the existence of an even better exemplar, now lost, from which it was copied.

Direct geometrical aid in Square lettering of this sort is limited to the use of a pair of horizontal lines, ruled by a stylus, which govern the levels of the heads and feet. Thus the height of the letters was set, and, to the extent desired, their precision was planned. Both these Square Virgil codices, the Augusteus and the Sangallensis, are lettered between two ruled parallel lines.

Readiness to choose freedom from geometrical precision, and to permit calligraphical dexterity, suggests that the bookseller of the Square Virgils

49

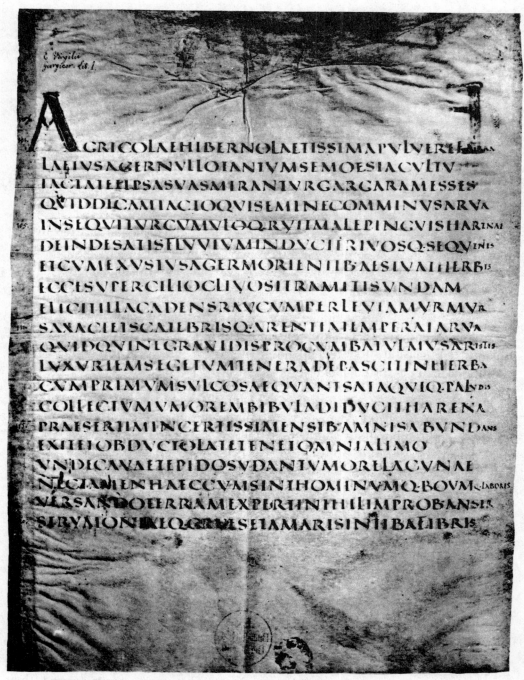

38. Rome. Virgil, Codex Augusteus. Italy, 4th century. Monumental book-script.

Rome, Vatican, MS. lat. 3256; Berlin, Staatsbibliothek, MS. lat. F. 416.

Square capitals (with vertical o); contrasted strokes; serifed.

Complete reproduction: R. Sabbadini, *Codicis Vergiliani qui Augusteus appellatur reliquiae* (*Codices e Vaticanus selecti quam simillime expressi* xv) (Turin, 1926); *C.L.A.* i, no. 13.

VICIT INTER DVRVM PIETAS DATVROR ATVERI
NATETVAETNOTASAVDIREETREDDEREVOCES
ICEQVIDEMDVCEBAM·NIMOREBAAQVEFVTVRVM
TEMPORADINVMERANSNECMEMEACVRAFEFELLIT
QVASEGOTETERRASETQVANTAPERAEQVORAVECTVM
ACCIPIOQVANTISIACTATVMNATEPERICLIS
QVAMMETVINEQVITLIBYAETIBIREGNANOCERENT

39. Italy. Virgil, Codex Sangallensis. 5th century. Imperial lettering on vellum.
St. Gall, Stiftsbibliothek, MS. 1394.
Square capitals; O slightly tilted; G, M, and V with Rustic characteristics.
C.L.A. vii, no. 977.

commissioned less a direct reproduction of inscriptional lettering than a fair rendering of a famous model—itself originally intended to emulate the example of the Square Homers. Let us suppose that the Ambrosian *Iliad* may not be of about the sixth century, as Gerstinger, Bandinelli, and Bartoletti believe, or the fourth, as Calderini says. Suppose it were of the third century, as Ceriani and Ratti claimed? Imagine the existence, then, of a publishing and editorial requirement to accomplish for Latin literature what had been done for Greek—to give Virgil the honour already given to Homer: could such an 'idea' be satisfied irrespective of the antecedent standard set by the Greek Square Capital Homers? Would such an editorial demand be strange? In view of the ascendancy of Greek originals over every aspect of Latin art, it would not appear odd. Moreover, the publishing trade could hardly have disregarded the opportunity to respond to the literary interests of the market. In this connection the suggestion first made by A. S. Hunt and approvingly published by C. H. Roberts deserves attention: that the Ambrosian *Iliad* is a careful transcript executed in the fifth century of an earlier manuscript.

That, conceivably, may have been the trade situation which brought into being these Square Capital Virgils. Alternatively let us ask, if an editor or publisher or bookseller, in the fourth or fifth century, were to instruct an artist to produce a text worthy of the greatest of Latin poets, in the best available Latin letter, would he choose a native Latin letter, should such a script be available and acceptable? Was not the Imperial Capital, which held the unique position of being the authoritative, official script, compulsive of universal obedience in the Roman sense, the only pattern fit to be conferred upon the greatest creative patriot, the most consummate verbal artist that Rome had produced? Did not Augustus himself overrule Virgil's request that the *Aeneid* should be destroyed?

The mass of references to the organization of the book trade collected by Pinner documents the interest taken by the Roman publishers in rare editions. It may be noted that the orator Libanius reports that an allegedly original manuscript of the *Odyssey* was offered for sale by a member of the rare book trade. Nothing is more likely than that the Square Capital was one of the regular settings considered appropriate for a first-class Virgil.

Yet perhaps a publisher could put his hands upon an even more appropriate letter. Was the Imperial Square Capital really as Latin as it appeared? Or was it basically Greek? And was there another letter which had behind it such force of familiarity as might bestow upon it a character, less official indeed, but more national? The answer is that if such a publisher sought for an absolutely native Latin letter, the choice would be the Rustic Capital, which was the Roman calligraphical invention. Indeed, this form, too, was gradually made acceptable for fine book-work.

However, we must finish first with the Square Capital Virgils. Much devotion of time and great expense of material were involved in writing Latin in the old Square style derived from Greek. To write it on vellum needs a broad pen with the writing edge cut horizontally across the nib. The scribe was obliged to hold his pen pointed towards the right shoulder—the so-called 'straight' pen position —in order to form the thick perpendiculars and the thin horizontal substrokes. For letters like A, M, N, and V the hand had to be turned. Easier, as has been said in the previous chapter, is the technique of the so-called 'slanted' pen, held pointing away from the shoulder. This naturally produced the tilted thick and thin, instead of the vertically stressed, O. A convenient combination of the desired effects of the straight pen, with the advantage of the easier direction of the slanted one, can be obtained by cutting the nib at a slight angle to the shaft. The Square Virgils of the fourth and fifth centuries seem to have been written with this obliquely cut nib. The difficulty of continually turning the hand remained, as it does in formal writing generally. Hence, as has been reported, if writing with the horizontal pen held in the straight position is to remain consistent throughout, it requires constant care, strain, and effort, involving a maximum of time, expense, and, it may be emphasized, material. Whatever patriotic respect Rustic might attach to itself, the economic consideration was certainly not less compelling. Economy of speed, effort, and material was bound to effect a change, and, in time, the old Roman Square Capital, as a text script, would first be accelerated and next superseded.

Three other Virgils, all assigned by the experts to the fourth or fifth century, exhibit acceleration in two stages. The Codex Vaticanus (Plate 40) is only just short of formal lettering, and could have been written as a second-best by, say, the scribe of the Codex Augusteus just described. Had such a scribe (be he freeman, or more probably slave, Roman, or more possibly Greek) chosen to hold his pen with the shaft slanting away from the shoulder in the most natural of all positions for writing, and therefore best for fast writing, he would have produced a closely similar piece. The position of the arm, as described, would inevitably produce a less majestic letter than the Square Capital; it would also

40. Italy. Virgil, Codex Vaticanus. 4th century. Formal lettering.

Rome, Vatican, MS. Lat. 3225.

Rustic capitals.

Complete reproduction: *Fragmenta et picturae Vergiliana codicis Vaticani Latini 3225*, ed. F. Ehrle, 3rd edition (Vatican, 1945) (*Codices e Vaticanis selecti phototypice expressi* I); *C.L.A.* i, no. 11.

be narrower, but its gain of economy in space would compensate for loss of dignity. The dimensions of this design, in fact, correspond with the lettering in the first century A.D. papyrus of the *De Bello Actiaco* Fragment (Plate 34) and in the first-century inscriptions on the walls of Pompeii (Plate 35). It is, therefore, the design usually called 'Rustic', which has been described above as the great Roman or Latin invention.

Are these Rustic Virgils to be regarded as 'imitative' of Rustic inscriptions? Certainly the style was increasingly in vogue for inscriptions at this time, yet, as Rustic is frankly a pen or brush letter, it is more just to say that masons cutting Rustic Capitals were imitators of pen or brush work; as, indeed, they were. In any case, as the relatively low cost in time and money, and economy of space and material, made Rustic Capitals for inscriptions the most familiar of public scripts, it is quite possible that the *ordinator* of the inscriptions may have been a scribe also, capable of writing a large-scale script on papyrus or vellum.

The largest letter in all the Virgils is that of the Codex Romanus (Plate 41), which is written in Rustic Capitals of small poster-size, one-third of an inch high. The contrast between the thick mainstrokes and thin substrokes is also strongly marked.

The third Rustic Virgil is the Codex Palatinus (see Plate 42). This is a highly efficient piece of writing, perhaps by a scribe normally engaged on fast work, for his characters are markedly narrower than those of the other two specimens. In the long span of four centuries since the writing of the *De Bello Actiaco* papyrus, Rustic progressed from condensed to extra-condensed, to use typographical terms. It is remarkable that this process was so retarded; for, as all Rustic is fast in comparison with Square Capitals, one would have expected time to have encouraged speed at the expense of dignity. But this was not so. Many

DVLCEM FERRE CIBVM ET CVRVAS PRAEBERE LATEBRAS
QVAE TENVEM EXHALAT NEBVLAM FVMOSQ:LVCORIS
ET BIBIT VMOREM ET CVM VVLT EX SE IPSA REMITTIT
QVAEQ:SVOS EMPER VIRIDIS EGRAMINE VESTIT
NEC SCABIAE IL SALSA EDIT ROBIGINE FERRVM
ILLA TIBI LAETIS INTEXET VITIBVS VLMOS

41. Italy. Virgil, Codex Romanus. 5th century. Formal lettering.

Rome, Vatican, MS. Lat. 3867.

Rustic capitals.

Complete reproduction: *Picturae ornamenta complura scripturae specimina codicis Vaticani 3867 qui Codex Vergilii Romanus audit* (Rome, 1902) (*Codices e Vaticanis selecti phototypice expressi* II); *C.L.A.* i, no. 19.

42. Italy, Rome. Virgil, Codex Palatinus. 4th–5th century. Monumental book-script.

Rome, Vatican, MS. Palat. Lat. 1631.

Rustic capitals. Highly condensed; strongly contrasted strokes; heavily serifed.

Complete reproduction: Sabbadini, *Codex Vergilianus qui Palatinus appellatur* (Paris, 1929); *C.L.A.* i, no. 99.

ILLE AVTEM TV AI EGENITOR TVATRISTIS IMAGO
SAEPIVS OCCVRRENSHAEC I MINATENDERE ADEGIT·
STANTS AL ETY RRHENO CLASSES DAIVNGE REDEXTRAM
DA GENITORTEQVE AMPIEXVNE SVTRAE NOSTRO·
SIC MEMORANS LARGOI LETVSIM VIORA RIGABAT·
TE CONATVS I BI COLLO DARE BRACCHIA CIRCVM
TER FRVSTRA COMPRESSA MANVS ETFVGIT IMAGO·
INTEREA VIDET AENEAS IN VALLE REDVCTA·
SECIVS VM NE AIVS ET VIRGVITA SONANTIA SILVAE·

DEINDESATISFLV
VIVM ABCDEFG
HILMNOPQRSTV
XFLV FIOMNIA

VICIT INTE RDVR
VM ABCDEFGHIL
MNOPQRSTVXY FL
PIETASDATVRORAT

SAEPTIMAPOSTDECIMAM
FELIXETPONERE ABCDEFG
HILMNOPQRSTVXY
FELICESOPERVMQVINTAM

NOS·IN·SCEPTRA·REP
ONIS·OLLI· ABCDEFG
HILMNOPQRSTV·L·
PVER·ASCANIVS·CVI·

43. The scripts of the codices of Virgil of the 4th to 5th century.

(1) Rome, Vatican, MS. Lat 3256 and (2) St. Gall, Stiftsbibliothek, MS. 1934, in Imperial square capitals; (3) Rome, Vatican, MS. Lat. 1631 and (4) Rome, Vatican, MS. Lat. 3867, in Rustic capitals.

Photographs from copies of vellum made on the scale of the original scripts; these are conveniently assembled in Stelio Bassi, *La Scrittura Calligrafica Greco-Romana* (Cremona, 1957), in his section 'Litterae Vergilianae', figs. 118A–121.

generations of booksellers evidently did not consider it decent to accelerate Virgil beyond the point reached in the Palatinus, which, according to Lowe, is of the fourth to fifth century.

The plan of the letterers of this group of Rustic Virgils, therefore, was to use a 'nationally' familiar script in place of the official Square Capital, and at the same time reduce the cost of labour and material without reducing the dignity, size, and legibility of the lettering; that is to say, as compared with the Square Codex Augusteus already mentioned. This Codex is written between pairs of lines $\frac{1}{4}$ in. in depth, while the Codex Romanus, also mentioned above, is written in Rustic between two lines $\frac{1}{3}$ in. in depth. That is to say, the characters of the latter manuscript, though more rapidly written, are taller than those of the Codex Augusteus by $\frac{1}{12}$ in. These two codices of the same text are written in the largest of capitals. While it is remarkable that the letters of the Virgil in Rustic Capitals are taller than those of the Virgil in Square Capitals, the page is so organized as to make the depth of ten lines identical in both manuscripts (see Plate 43). By what means was this achieved? What is the point of it?

The explanation is that the vellum is used with greater economy in the Codex Romanus. How so? Because the space between the lines is less than in any Quadrate Virgil. Thus, to use a modern typographical term, the Rustic is 'leaded' to a lesser degree than the Quadrate. To be more precise, the Quadrate Virgil is 'leaded' to the equivalent of the full height of the character. In other words, the space between the lines is equal to the height of that character. But the scribe of this Rustic codex spaced his lines only to two-thirds of the height of his characters. Moreover, the Rustic scribe made an economy in his technique. He abandoned the practice of writing between parallels. To save time he ruled only one horizontal to guide his levels and control his linear spacing. His eye judged the height of his letter and the space over the head of it.

The influence of the economic factor upon the publishers of such a long text as the *Aeneid* is obvious. But style was equally cared for. The Codex Romanus is, as we have reported, written in the largest capital ever used for a Virgil; it is more—it is the largest capital ever used for the text of any book, a singular tribute to the greatest of Latin poets. It is the work of a scribe aware of his ability —and, perhaps, of his fame. The codex includes nineteen miniatures. There is a border to the first page of the *Aeneid*.

When, later, the Virgilian Rustic format and style were adapted for the collector with a smaller purse, a smaller sheet was used, and a smaller letter. To accommodate a greater number of letters in the longest line it was necessary to compress or condense the width of the capitals. The longest line in the facsimile of Codex Romanus (fol. 61$^\text{v}$.) is $10\frac{17}{20}$ in. long, and consists of thirty-eight full-size capitals, plus two small final characters. The process of compression may be followed in the Plates, especially Plate 36.

The Codex Palatinus is a manuscript of relatively smaller format. It has a long line of forty-two characters ($\frac{1}{4}$ in. in height), brought within $7\frac{1}{2}$ in. The Codex Romanus presents the largest size ($\frac{1}{4}$ in.) of capital (Rustic) with a major line of 9 in. The Square Codex Augusteus has its characters taller by $\frac{1}{10}$ in., but numbering nearly the same in a line 1 in. longer. Thus, all in all, the economic advantages of the Rustic are overwhelming as against Square Capitals. We should expect, therefore, that Rustic, when fully established, would secure the greater use in books; and that is the fact. Traube lists six times as many relics of Rustic as of Square Capitals.

It has been remarked that in writing Rustic Capitals scribes held the pen in the comfortable position apt for semi-Cursive, which results in speedy execution and encourages compression, or condensation. No such elevation of the cursive element, or any such combination of it with formal structure, had developed in Greek lettering, inscriptional or other. The practice was wholly Latin, and, as such, Rustic progressed from the second to the fifth century. It thereafter declined, except for use in *incipit*s and *explicit*s.

Why did this capital script lose favour? Were poverty and shortage of material the reasons? Hardly. For while one can understand that an expensive medium like the slow Square Capital should fail to maintain itself against the faster Rustic, why should Rustic have given place to a new, slow type of lettering hardly less expensive of time and material than the old Square Capital? Why, in fact, did Square and Rustic Capitals both decline from the fourth century, if their prestige and hierarchical relation in Rome were so high in the esteem of *ordinator*s, sculptors, publishers, booksellers, and others? This is not an easy question to answer.

Numerous inscriptions from the first to the sixth century give Square Capitals pride of place in the first three leading lines or so, with the remainder of the text following in Rustic. There is no obvious, material reason why both should not have similarly continued to coexist as media for fine book-work, with the Square Capitals leading a page of Rustics. Such an arrangement being found satisfactory in inscriptions, why did this precedent fail to establish the Square and Rustic system for bookwork in the fifth and sixth centuries? Did authority intervene, and the publishers give way?

Highly organized as the graphic arts had been since the time of Augustus, they ranked as highly respectable and very prosperous businesses. Authors and publishers had all the patronage they wanted. The Emperor himself founded two libraries, each containing separate sections for Greek and Latin authors respectively. Vespasian and Trajan followed the example of Augustus, who, no doubt, had himself marked the precedent set at Pergamon. If there is any substance in the complaint of Seneca that the idlest of men collected the richest of books—which they never read and only used for show—the trade must have been booming, and could easily have afforded a combination of Square and Rustic Capitals. Why, therefore, did fine book-production undergo the change it did? We know that the codex was proving its superiority over the roll at the beginning of the fourth century, but this need not have made Rustic Capitals unsuitable. It is not supposed by experts that the change from roll to codex or from papyrus to parchment necessitated any change in script. What then?

The answer is that a change of attitude in authority occurred which involved changes in texts and scripts. The change in Court calligraphy followed the change in Court religion. Constantine, who had been acclaimed Emperor by the army at York in 306, when he was not much over twenty, encountered considerable difficulty in making his position secure against other members of his family. As Caesar, Constantine belonged to the Herculean dynasty and hence acknowledged Hercules as his official patron; and he so continued as Augustus, when he married Fausta, the daughter of Maximian, a former Augustus of the same dynasty. But the treachery and death of Maximian brought a change. Because something of the kind was politically desirable, Constantine discovered a relationship to the heroic Claudius Gothicus, Emperor in the third century. Thus the man who was in fact the son of a Balkan peasant exchanged Hercules, the official patron of his father-in-law, for Apollo, the god of Claudius Gothicus, his own Balkan ancestor. Thus Constantine chose as his patron the Roman equivalent of the god of light, Sol Invictus. This was in 310. In that year Constantine dedicated gifts to shrines of Apollo in Gaul. Although repression of the Christians continued for another year under his successor Maximian, persecution officially ceased at the death-bed order of Galerius. This was in 311. Having restored Roman authority on the Rhine, Constantine decided to march against Maxentius, son of Maximian, who held Rome in the name of Hercules. Naturally, Maxentius, who had been left out of account at the division of the empire that took place in 305, was ready to stand his ground against Constantine. The death of Galerius in 311 forced the issue. Constantine defeated Maxentius and triumphantly entered Rome on

29 October 312 under a new sacred slogan, a new monogram. He had seen in the sky the Cross outlined in rays of light and having with it words, the exact form of which is in dispute. That they included the Chrismon is certain; equally the combination of alpha and omega therein. As early delineated it showed a forked A, a point to be remembered.

These were the political preliminaries to a revolution that left its mark on book production, in its scriptorial aspect, from the fourth century onwards. Whereas Augustus had established libraries as adjuncts to the temples, Constantine made them annexes to the churches. Naturally, therefore, the collection established by Pope Damasus (366–84) for his parish library at S. Lorenzo in Damaso comprised books different in nature from those collected by Augustus for his public library in the Campus Martius. And Constantine had another duty to perform. The destruction of Christian libraries by Diocletian required, under the new regime, wholesale reconditioning and replenishment. The amount of new writing must have been immense. This was the period in which the Roman Church and its dependants began the compilation of the first unofficial hagiographical 'calendars' and the earliest 'martyrologies'. For writing this mass of new books the appropriate script would clearly not be one closely associated with the persecutors nor with the books which they had honoured, the works of poets and orators, dramatists, historians, satirists, and other favourite Latin authors. The new day was the day of the Evangelists, the theologians, Fathers and Apologists. These, of course, had written in Greek.

Thus, what was looked for by the organizers as the basis of this mass of writing was a new script; one not associated with the honouring of pagan literature and false gods. A new 'contemporary' Christian form was needed for the execution of so much new writing in that new day, when, in Constantine's conception, there had suddenly come into existence 'a world rising triumphant to the stars under the leadership of Christ'.

An official—so to say—ideological or apologetical script, adopted and translated from existing materials, was not difficult to contrive provided that a sufficient number of elements were available and practicable. The situation required these elements to be independent of Square and Rustic Capitals. What, then, were the elements that could be considered feasible by a commission, had there been one, to find a script neither Square nor Rustic, which was not unfamiliar to the Graeco-Roman literary world and was capable of being made apt for the ecclesiastical and ideological needs of that revolutionary day? On the morrow of the Christian revolution the symbols, other than Capitals, that were familiar to the reading classes included a *common* Cursive used for business, and an *official* Cursive for administration which had been in use for 300 years. These were the most seen of all classes of handwriting. We must inquire what they looked like.

From the second century we have an interesting papyrus: an official document in a script of some formality. It is a contract for the sale of a slave, and was written in Syria in A.D. 166. This (Plate 44) is a piece of fast Latin Cursive writing on papyrus. It might be described as in some respects a double-Cursive Rustic, foreshadowing Minuscule. First, a has a descending left stroke; there is an

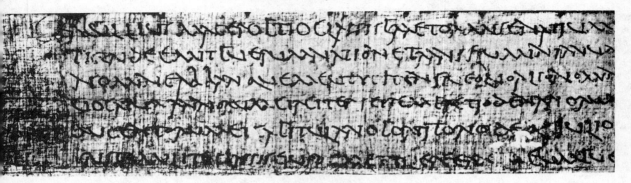

44. Syria. Contract for sale of a slave. A.D. 166. Capitals easily written as a semi-fast documentary script. British Museum, P. 229.

Square; upright with capital, uncial, minuscule, and cursive elements; casually serifed.

Pal. Soc. ii. 190; Franz Steffens, *Paléographie Latine* (Trèves, 1910), pl. 9; Medea Norsa, *Analogie e coincidenze tra scritture greche e Latine nei papiri* (Rome, 1946), tav. II.

ascending b; G has the descending (Rustic) beard; d, e, and u, are round; q, r, and s, are descenders. The document is written with a fine pen in what is not in all essentials a documentary Cursive, for it has distinct affinities with bookscript. Moreover, the document being of eastern Mediterranean origin, it is not surprising that, besides having Roman Cursive traits, it should contain Greek elements such as the round Є.

We may compare a papyrus from Fayûm of the first century, written in Greek, which resembles in scale and in certain other respects our papyrus in Latin (see Plate 11). The conspicuous difference is that the Latin script is nearly half as large again as the Greek. It has already been seen that some Latin inscriptions are larger in scale than Greek. Writing of all kinds seems to have been larger in the West. In fact, the Cursive or semi-Cursive of the present Latin papyrus is the same in scale as that of some of the Rustic Virgils and equals the average size of other scripts that are later found on vellum. Is it possible that those in Rome responsible, during the fourth century, for the establishment of a script for new Latin texts decided in the first place to choose a medium having a size hardly smaller than that illustrated in this contract?

The relation, if any, which the old Roman Cursives of the first century had to the fourth-century Cursives and the chancery hand do not concern us further than to say that the forms, proportions, and dimensions descended to later scripts, and thence, finally, to typography. This transition may be seen at an initial stage in the next specimen, which is a large Chancery hand from the fourth century.

It is a letter on papyrus found in Egypt, which is now at Strasbourg (see Plate 45). The script is very large in scale and most expensive of space and material. Contracted versions were, of course, in official and personal use. From the fourth century, at least, the correspondence hand existed in two forms— both were round and current, but one was broad and open, while the other was

E

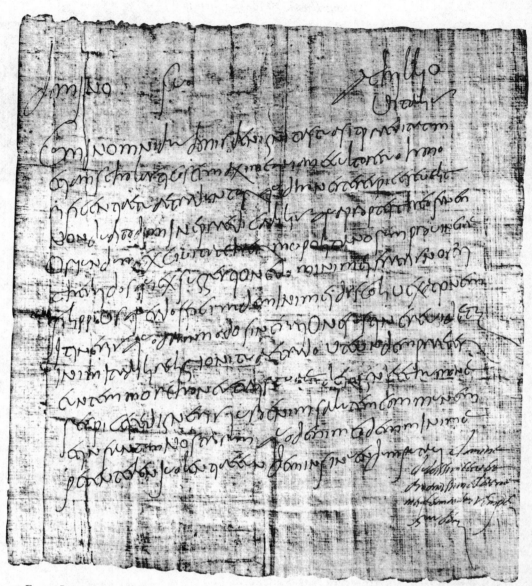

45. Egypt. Letter on papyrus from Vitalis, addressed *Domino suo Achillio*, beginning: *Cum in omnibus bonis benignitas tua sit praedita*. A.D. 317–24. Roman cursive.

Strasbourg, Bibliothèque nationale et universitaire, P. Lat. Argent. i.

Square; upright; large scale; flowing; cursive. Ascending b with bowl on left (distinguishable, however, from d), d, h, l; descending g, p, q, and occasionally f and s. Unserifed except for accidental hooks. Steffens points out that this type of script (which may be compared with contemporary Greek, i.e. Byzantine current writing) is the source of Half-Uncial and Minuscule, and, it should be added, 'lower-case'.

C.L.A. vi, no. 832; H. Bresslau, 'Ein lateinischer Empfehlungsbrief' in *Archiv für Papyrusforschung* iii. 2, pp. 168–72 (Leipzig, 1904); Steffens 13; Maunde Thompson no. 110.

narrow and restricted. It is safe to assume that these hands were practised as a matter of ordinary course by some at least of those who might have the responsibility of guiding the newly established Church in the matter of any calligraphy required for its administration, as well as for the writing of its sacred texts. If such a group, having some instruction in writing and a degree of conviction as to its desirable form, existed (which may be seen as doubtful, though not impossible), they must have taken into account the existence side by side of both Latin-speaking and Greek-speaking communities, for whom the new Codices were to be written. In any case, the calligraphical problem could not be evaded by those responsible for the reading matter of the newly liberated and, it may now be said, newly endowed Christians.

Constantine, who had recognized Christianity as a legal religion in 313, was soon active in every branch of Christian organization and legislation. During the years from the Council of Nicea (325), and before the removal of the capital to Byzantium (330), the Papal and Imperial chanceries could hardly have avoided conferring upon the cost, manner, and probably matter, of the required new books. Could anything else have been the case? When the Emperor appropriated the palace of the Lateran family, reconstructed a part of it to serve as a Christian basilica, and endowed it, the problem of its decoration and furnishing must necessarily have been considered. This was to be the first public place of assembly and worship for the newly emancipated Roman Catholics. We are not concerned with problems of early Christian art, only with the books to be used. The erection of a mighty building such as the Lateran church, which was bound to become the architectural model for succeeding Christian sacred edifices and *ecclesiarum omnium mater et caput*, would inevitably set in motion a whole host of minor enterprises and decisions. Amongst these may surely be counted the choice of an appropriate script for the sacred books accommodated in the library. Would that choice of script have been merely that of the best available scribe of the day? Would he have been allowed to do what he as an individual 'artist' should think fit? Or would he be directed by competent authority?

It was necessary to attempt the difficult task of impressing, favourably, the dissident Roman aristocracy. It would seem axiomatic that in stateliness and legibility the required books would need to be as well written as any Homer or Virgil. Not only so, but, it could have been argued, the script should be an independent design. As to the language of the texts, it would have been partly Greek, perhaps mainly Latin, if C. H. Turner is correct that the latter had been the medium for practical purposes in the Christian communities of Rome since 200, even though Greek was, perhaps, the medium for literary purposes.

It is not suggested that Constantine limited his interest in book-production to Latin-speaking requirements. Greeks, slaves and freemen, had for generations been writing texts for Roman publishers. It was a common complaint that they wrote Latin badly. Nor is it necessary to suppose that the Latin bishops and clergy were made responsible for, still less that they took the initiative in ordering and paying for, the new libraries. In all probability any 'experts' that may have been assembled to decide upon the script most appropriate for the new religion were members of the Imperial staff or had been employed in one office or another of the Imperial bureaucracy. An intelligent secretary could have supplied specimens of the better class of writing practised in Rome and also in Egypt and North Africa.

We may most certainly take it for granted that such a body would have Greek scripts before them. There was one compelling and unavoidable fact before anybody who would organize a new script; that the first text to be considered would be the Bible, and this paramount choice would inevitably set up one more authoritative Greek precedent.

There are inscriptions to be considered and, as Roberts points out, the Chester Beatty papyrus of the Pauline epistles points perhaps in the direction of Latin Uncial. The papyrus is of the third century and is written in a hand that resembles in scale the second-century B.C. Deuteronomy fragment now at Manchester (Plate 9). The important difference is the alpha. In the Chester Beatty papyrus of five centuries later its form is 'Uncial'. Both scripts, it should be remarked, are serifed.

If it is possible that as early as *c.* 313 the Emperor Constantine confirmed the Pope Miltiades in the possession of the Lateran as his episcopal Church, and was ready, as we are told, for the State to bear the expense of furnishing the basilica, among other things with books for the library, it would be reasonable, if a change of script were determined, to expect a script that would respond to the facts of the new society. The bilingual structure of the Church, its constitution as a federation of Greek- and Latin-speaking communities, would be taken into consideration by those responsible. If the new Latin books were to have some brotherly or cousinly relation to Greek, what form would its script be likely to take? A form, emphatically, that would not look barbarous to the Greeks. A letter form, say, used publicly and therefore familiar to the Greeks of the diocese of Alexandria in the third century, might be regarded as legible by both communities, and a Roman administrator could perhaps take it into consideration. A public form of such a script may be seen in two inscriptions from Timgad in Algeria, dating from the third century.

In the first of these inscriptions (Plate 46) the title VOCONTIO and conclusion ALTERI FONTI are in extra-condensed Rustic Capitals, separated by fourteen lines roughly cut in a very different design, built up from a highly syncretic alphabet. Here are to be seen ascending b and d; round E and M; Square C, M, N, and U; Rustic F and G; half-descending P and R; cursive s and t; and L between the two. The letters are all canonically serifed as to the heads in Square Capital style, with one or two exceptions mentioned later. The whole mixes Greek and Latin, Square and Rustic characteristics with a dominant fresh element. Four letters, F, L, R, and S, lie outside the Greek alphabet. As P and perhaps R would be confusing to the Greeks they, like q, half-descend below the normal line, and each tapers cursively at the foot. The presence of ascending b and d, and descending q, should be borne in mind. They have doubtless a long history in Cursive and their elevation to inscriptional status is a manifestation of their vigour.

The subject of the honorific inscriptions found at Timgad has been identified as the grammarian Flavius Pomponianus, who taught and wrote in the first half of the third century. By this time the city of Timgad is the Roman Thamugas, the prosperous place founded by Trajan. It was largely Christian, with doubtless a community, Greek as well as Latin-speaking. Could Pomponianus have taught such a mixed collection of forms? Or could the *ordinator* of such an inscription have been a pupil eager to prove that while he was writing Latin he was well acquainted with Greek? And that although his repertory included every style, he knew how to harmonize them? We cannot prudently say yes, but at least we cannot possibly avoid seeing here some assimilation of Greek and Latin. The P and R point in that direction.

The ascenders b, d, descenders p, q, and half-descender r are the most significant elements of this inscription. Their significance lies, not in themselves (for, as has been said, they had already appeared in Latin Cursive), but in their present

46. Timgad. Inscription of Fl. Pudens Pomponianus to Vocontius. First half of 3rd century. Sculptured cursive capitals. Head-line VOCONTIO in Rustic capitals.

Text in round and cursive version (the late medieval term would have been 'bastarda') of square capitals, with noteworthy sorts such as curved mainstroke to S, E, and head to T, which appear later in Latin Uncial; ascending d, descending m (first stroked p, q, r); all regularly but casually serifed. Tail-line ALTERI FONTI in Rustic capitals. See next plate.

C.I.L. viii. 2391–17910. Illustrated by line-zinco in *Bulletin de la Société nationale des antiquaires de France* (Paris, 1895), p. 135; Cabrol-Leclercq, *D.A.C.L.*, s.v. 'Onciale'; R. Cagnat, *Cours d'Épigraphie Latine* (4th edition, Paris, 1914), *p. pl. SV 4*; H. Degering, *Die Schrift* (3rd edition, Berlin, 1954), pl. 25; Frantisek Muzika, *Krasné Písmo ve výoji Latinky* (Prague, 1958), i. 148 and pl. XXII.

47. Timgad. First half of the 3rd century. The Alphabet constructed from original on previous plate (46). It will be recognized to consist of cursive ('bastarda') capitals. These were later regularized into the form called 'uncials'.

Photographed from the drawing by Prof. Frantisek Muzika.

Muzika i, fig. 98.

situation. When found in a formal script they are of the utmost importance. The text of the first inscription may be described as a formalized Latin Cursive with Greek concessions. The alphabet may be conveniently seen in Plate 47, which Professor Frantisek Muzika of Prague kindly allowed me to reproduce.

Notwithstanding informal Greek precedents, which are numerous, credit must be given to the Romans for the original promotion of ascenders and descenders as elements of a formal, fully calligraphic script. It is necessary to say that by ascenders and descenders is meant the completion of the body of the letter with a head-stroke or tail-stroke. In the inscription to Vocontius the head- and tail-strokes not only ascend and descend, but certain descending characters also project, i.e. they extend and terminate below the normal base-line. This is especially the case with p, q, and R. In Plate 48 the ascenders F and b and d occur occasionally as projectors above the normal height of line.

In general effect the Timgad script as here seen developed for local, semi-official inscriptional use, is as much circular as square, while remaining, as to three-quarters of the script, capital in structure—and as to one-quarter something other than square or capital. The presence of what we call 'Uncial' will be observed. The round Є and round ᛖ (as an alternative sort) are notable.

The quarter that is distinct is absolutely Cursive in basis but so elevated here

48. Timgad. Inscription of Flavius Pudens Pomponianus. First half of 3rd century. Formal sculptured capitals.

Round (especially A, D, E, M, U, with vertical O) monoline; ascending (b, d,) and descending (p, q, r,) sorts. Serifed, and with occasional flourished terminals.

Dessau 8981 illustrated; Cabrol–Leclercq, *D.A.C.L.*, s.v. 'Onciale', illustration no. 9045.

as to preserve the style belonging to the rest of the 'fount' and thus the body of the text is artistically consistent with itself. Not only so, but the movement of the body is consistent with the Rustic headline and final line; which is to say that the whole inscription is uniformly freehand, serifed (triangular heads in b, d, h, i, l and the heads of M, N, and U), with the Cursive element firmly under control.

The quadrate proportion of this type of letter is best seen in Plate 48. It is less Cursive than the inscription to Vocontius, and is in many respects a superior piece. It is serifed according to convenience, but mostly at the heads of letters; m is an exception. There are important minutiae to be noticed in connection with A; E and M are round and serifed.

The canonization (for that is what it amounts to) of ascenders and descenders in this inscription suggests the possibility that the centre stroke of phi and psi in Greek Cursive may not have been without influence in Latin. The perpendicular in these two Greek characters is a double projector; it ascends and descends. This is something unknown to Latin and in the West, which limited itself to single ascenders and single descenders. There are indications that the Greeks had a liking for long strokes and it seems not impossible that a Greek scribe writing Latin may have been happy to elongate his perpendiculars. So far as the evidence is available, the promotion of projectors to formal status is an African development. It is worth remembering the ascending b and d in connection with the Codex Bezae, which will come up for mention in due time; also, in another connection to be mentioned later, the descending q.

Something has been said above about the influences of Africa. Obviously, the critical problems in the production of writing are most likely to arise and demand solution in the area in which most writing of most kinds is most urgently, most continuously, and most massively called for. In the second century this area was the Roman province of Egypt, still Greek-speaking and reading, as to its literate population. Mallon rightly says that the scriptorial analogies between Greek and Latin need to be rigorously analysed. It certainly cannot be denied that the analogies exist. Incontestably North Africa was *par excellence* the region of a bilingual culture. In the second century it reached an extraordinary height of material and civilized prosperity. The mutual influence of Greek and Latin script needs no better explanation. Mallon, in fact, claims that here is the source of everything. According to his argument, present-day Tunisia and eastern Algeria are the places towards which to look for the origin, during the second century, of the important scripts that served the literature of the West from the third century onwards. It is a thesis which finds support in the inscriptions at Timgad. But it may be well to pause before agreeing that the Carolingian Minuscule itself is only a variety of north-east African Regularized Cursive. One thing may be said. It appears certain that the stabilization of a basically cursive b and d, and their use side by side with a cursive but inscriptional variety of Square Capital, which partakes also of the Rustic element, is an Egyptian practice.

It is tempting at this point to discuss the terminology of scripts, and the more so since it will become necessary to trace the development of certain literary and other hands that come to the front in later centuries. But to treat of palaeographical terminology here would be an impermissible digression. It must suffice to say, first, that in terms of current nomenclature the two Timgad inscriptions rank as 'Uncial' and, secondly, that the use of this term is so firmly entrenched by custom that its convenience is undeniable. More exactly, the Timgad inscriptions are to be classed as specimens of Latin Uncial. They are important because they are not only the earliest specimens of this type of lettering, but they are datable. Flavius Pudens Pomponianus is known to have exercised his office of prefect in Aquitania between the period of the emperors Heliogabalus (218-22) and Septimius Severus (222-35).

As will be reported presently, the earliest datable Latin manuscript in this kind of script is much later, 509-10. It has been seen above (Plate 18) that the alphabet of the Greek papyrus fragment of the *Iambi* of Callimachus (assignable, according to Grenfell and Hunt, 'with little chance of error' to the latter half of the second century) comprises ∂, ε, and certain other forms that are echoed in Latin Uncial. It is precisely the presence of these forms in Greek papyri of the first and second centuries A.D. that leads Medea Norsa to state that Latin Uncial was modelled upon Greek Uncial. The writer also states that the Uncial as developed for literary texts was modelled upon the inscriptional forms. Both statements appear to be well-founded, though the second statement is left undocumented.

It is well, therefore, to emphasize the fact that, whether or not Fl. Pomponianus, at once imperial representative and man of letters, had personal responsibility for these inscriptions, their letter forms in the Latin language are recognizable and legible to a Greek-reading population. Hence their choice for public, inscriptional use was politically and administratively sound. If the Timgad Latin Uncial may be said to rank as an official script it could not have been the only one of its kind, either in Egypt or elsewhere on the North African littoral, or even in Aquitania.

It should not pass unnoticed that the Timgad Latin Uncial (Plate 46) is combined with a headline and an end-line, both of which are in Rustic, itself a capital cursive. It may be concluded that the process of assimilation of Latin towards Greek and Greek towards Latin was officially encouraged in Egypt in the early period of the Roman conquest, which coincides with the first and second centuries A.D. We shall see the same process of Graeco-Latin alphabetical assimilation in Byzantium in the fifth and sixth centuries.

Meanwhile we must return to the career of the perpendicular ascending projectors b and d. These can only have begun as constituents of a current official cursive, correspondence, or business hand which, however, was also employed for literary uses. It was, in effect, an all-purpose hand commonly used for all kinds of work, which is why Mallon terms it '*écriture commune*'. On the papyri in the first century the tail of the capital Q is in the curved form, flourishing well below the base line of the body, from left to right. In the second century the tail may be found in the strangest form extending directly well below the body from the base line of the body (not from left to right but vertically), and sometimes ending in a taper.

Caution, however, is necessary here. The career of Uncial exhibits more than one line of development. Unquestionably the script is Graeco-Roman. Equally in its Egyptian form it represents, so to say, the ennoblement, otherwise the capitalizing, of a middle or cursive script. Hence the b and d are usual in Latin Uncial in Egypt. What of Latin Uncial in Italy?, in Rome?

For an early specimen of Latin Uncial on vellum, 'written doubtless in Italy' according to Lowe, it seems well to show the magnificent Cicero thought to be of the fourth century. Three or four centuries later a skilful copyist at Bobbio was instructed to overlay the rich Uncial with a modest version of St. Augustine's commentary on the Psalms. With the Bobbio scribe's (smaller but scrupulous) Uncial bleached out, Plate 49 attempts to suggest the aspect of the original codex, one of the most sumptuous ever executed. It consisted, according to G. Mercati, of some 650 folios of double columns of fifteen lines, averaging eleven letters, whose measure, about a quarter of an inch, equals the space between the lines. The superimposed Augustine in the smaller Uncial is shown in Plate 50. Here also the first script is bleached out.

There were, of course, Christian works that were given similar honour, such as the Quedlinburg Old Testament (now Berlin Theol. lat. 485), fragments of which are written in an interesting, monoline, large, heavy (even black) Uncial, assigned to the fourth century by some, and by Lowe to the fourth–fifth century. It is of the oldest type of Uncial, and retains B in place of b and ascending L instead of l; it has an undulant horizontal. It has round d. The script might be called Square Uncial as emerging from a Square Capital, since it does not have ascending b and l. According to Lowe the writing was executed in one of the great centres of Christian calligraphy. It is obviously the hand of one used to work of the highest class, such as the Square Capital Virgils. Hence the

49. Italy. Cicero, *De Republica*. 4th century. Palimpsest, with the upper script of St. Augustine, *Super Psalmos*.

Rome, Vatican, MS. Lat. 5757.

Square; uncial; contrasted strokes; tilted O; serifed. In the above plate the upper script has been bleached out of the photograph. The text has colophons in large Rustic capitals.

G. Mercati, *M. Tulli Ciceronis De Republica*, edition in facsimile (Rome, 1934); Maunde Thompson no. 87; F. Ehrle and P. Liebaert, *Specimina*, pl. 3, 'Litteris uncialibus elegantissimis et praegrandibus'; *C.L.A.* i, nos. 34–5, 'a bold, beautifully formed expert uncial'; C. H. Beeson, 'The Palimpsests of Bobbio' in *Miscellanea Giovanni Mercati* vi, pp. 171-2 (Vatican, 1946); Stelio Bassi, *La scrittura greca in Italia* (Cremona, 1956), p. 115 and fig. 163.

50. Bobbio. St. Augustine, *Super Psalmos*. 8th century. Uncial.

Rome, Vatican, MS. Lat. 5757 (see previous plate).

Late, small-scale, rapidly-made uncial; minuscule e; majuscule L.

C.L.A. i, no. 34.

Quedlinburg Biblical Uncial avoids all cursive tendency and retains the Square B, L, R, and l.

It would not be surprising if the Old Testament Codex of which the Quedlinburg specimens are a fragment was executed in or near Rome. The script is, in fact, a variety of stately Uncial which suggests that it began as a Rounded Roman Capital. It has been seen that this is not true of Egyptian Uncial and may not be true of Roman Uncial. Obviously, however, a scribe habituated to writing the Square Capital, instructed to write Uncial on the same scale, would inevitably tend to revert to Capital script in optional instances. The Codex Bezae, to be mentioned later, shows an example of Uncial, Greek and Latin, as it had established itself in Italy in the fifth and sixth centuries even for Biblical work. The Latin pages of the Codex Bezae are far from being a first-class piece of writing, but it is consistent in its use of b, d, l, p, and q.

It is necessary here to emphasize the fact that the ultimate adoption into literary work of forms such as were usual in civil service, domestic, and commercial work represents the first stage in the inscriptional and literary canonization of a principle of design. Centuries after the organization of Latin Uncial, projectors made themselves absolutely essential to Western vernacular alphabets, and their use is the source of the unrivalled versatility and flexibility of contemporary printing types. While, as has been pointed out, the Greeks employed projectors certainly as early as the third century B.C., it appears to the present writer that it is in the projectors of Latin Cursive that we have the origin of what is called Minuscule.

An important constructional difference in written Latin Uncial from the antique inscriptional Greek Square Capital is the substitution of curves: F with a flourished top-stroke and descending perpendicular is found in the second century; G has the Rustic curve at the base, but it now ends in a taper, which is new; h has an ascending perpendicular; the perpendiculars of p and q both descend, and both taper. The tapers indicate their humble past, that is to say, a 'common' Cursive pedigree, which may ultimately have originated in the scribble tolerated from a stilus used on the waxed tablets.

A is a relatively irrational character. In its early career as a Latin letter it is hardly to be distinguished from a capital Greek lambda. Later, the inside pocket was emphasized and the left stroke allowed to descend to a fine taper. The specimen shown on Plate 49 is of the fourth century.

The normal Uncial alphabet consists of twenty-one letters. Seven of these, B, C, N, O, S, T, and X, are standard in both Greek and Latin, though not for the same sounds; and two letters, R and U, do not occur in Greek. These nine characters, as they appear in Latin Uncial, are of Square Capital design. The specially rounded characters (those other than C, O, and S) are A, D, E, M, and U. It is curious therefore, that, having retained square N, the designers of Latin Uncial should have altered square M to the round form. Early Latin Uncial kept the initial stroke of M rather closely to the perpendicular, if we may judge from the fourth-century Gospels of Vercelli, or the Vatican Cicero. (See Plate 49.) The rounding of the initial stroke of M can only be explained as a piece of conscious artistry.

It takes time. Hence the rounded M, which was regularly used in manuscripts such as the Hawara and Ambrosian Homers, is largely replaced by the squarer M in Greek Biblical Uncial. It was argued earlier that it would be common sense for Latin script to adopt a letter that would have some brotherly or cousinly relation to Greek. In the main, such a relation clearly exists. Both Greek and Latin Uncial employ thick and thin strokes. This is remarkable. In the Codex Alexandrinus the contrast of stroke is conspicuous compared with the Codex Vaticanus. In the course of time contrast of stroke became a Byzantine fetish. But with these later developments we are not concerned. The differences between Greek and Latin Uncial were inescapable, and therefore became permanent.

The demonstrable birthplace of the ascending b and h is in Latin Cursive. But while Uncial has its ascending h, its B is in the Square Capital form. Why this difference in the treatment of the two sorts? One reason may be that in Cursive the circular bowl of b once came on the wrong side as we should say, and became 'd'—as it did in the *'Cum in omnibus bonis'* papyrus now at Strasburg (Plate 45). To avoid this ambiguity, therefore, it may have been judged well to retain the Capital B form. There was a second ambiguity arising from another source which Latin Uncial needed to avoid. It has been argued above that the establishment of an official Latin Uncial with close physical relations to Greek Uncial was an obviously common-sense decision. It would be an administrative, ideological, political, educational, literary, and economic advantage to design one alphabet capable of serving the two languages. The unity of the Empire would emphasize the appropriateness of using the one letter-form, albeit having local variations for official promulgations. But the common-sense and ideological solution to the problem of communication in two languages with one alphabet created at this period the possibility of serious confusion if the script was organized with regard only to consistency and logic.

The new script needed to avoid the confusion of Latin sorts with Greek. Both kinds of Uncial certainly needed to look familiar and similar, but it could lead to confusion if they looked identical and undistinguishable. There are so many instances on Byzantine coins of precisely this confusion that we must return to the matter at a later stage.

One of the conspicuous details in Greek Biblical Uncial is the length of the descenders of gamma, phi, rho, and upsilon. The phi and rho are longest; they are also the most ancient of all the cursive traits that secured permanence. But the retention, if not exaggeration, in Greek Uncial of a long-descending rho was bound to be a source of confusion as between Greek and Latin Uncial. The overriding similarity of the two scripts when written on vellum lies in the adoption by both of a contrast between thick and thin strokes. This is such a departure from all Greek precedent that it is probably a mark of Latin influence, and suggests that Latin pressure in favour of the canonization of Uncial was strong. Coincidence of form in detail, as in descending Greek rho and Latin P, was seen as a risk to be disregarded in favour of the similarity of form in mass and in the shape of the word. It could hardly have been Imperial policy under Constantine the Great, or his Christian successors, before the Empire was divided, to accentuate unnecessary differences between Greek and Latin script, either for the official Bible or for any other official promulgation. Unity was then the administrative object. Things would have looked otherwise to the successors of Theodosius, at whose death in 395 the partition of Eastern and Western Empires was effected. But in the first half of the fourth century the idea of separation was not politics.

Another descender in Latin Uncial must be given additional mention: the straight-tailed descending q. From an early date it had been preferred by, it may be supposed, Greek scribes writing Latin. For no obvious reason the Latin square capital Q, with flowing tail instead of descending stroke, seemed to the Greeks a strange or unsuitable character. It had no language significance for them, though many of their dialects used it as a symbol for the numeral 90. Its earliest Greek form is a circular head with a descending perpendicular, a form which reaches back to Phoenicia and perhaps beyond. So much for Greek and Latin assimilation in Africa. That a process of this sort existed in the writing schools may well be true. Evidence of influence of Greek upon Latin script on papyri is very slight, but it may be said to have existed.

In Rome the assimilation was occasionally less and occasionally greater. Plate 51 shows an example in which the assimilation is at the minimum.

This inscription exhibits the tailed q, twice aligned with the remaining text. Though to our eyes a minuscule form, it is here rightly treated as a capital.

Clearly, therefore, while Latin Uncial owes some of its inspiration to Greek precedent, the necessity to distinguish Latin from Greek necessitated changes in form. As had long been the case, the implements used for both Uncials were different. The Latins did not use the same tools as the Greeks unless, perhaps, there was a reason for so doing.

Direct comparison between Greek and Latin Uncial is best seen in the Codex Bezae of the fifth century (see Plate 52), which presents the Greek and Latin texts of the Gospels and Acts on facing pages. The two scripts are closely assimilated. B, C, H, I, O, P, S, and T are common to both languages. As usual, M is square in Greek and round in Latin. A and E are round in Greek, and U too in Latin. G is Rustic in Latin. As mentioned above, b, d, h, and l are promoted Cursive forms with the perpendicular mainstroke. This is so peculiar in Uncial that the script is named 'b d Uncial'. It is stated by Lowe that 'the scribe is not expert; he writes the Latin in the Greek manner, but his Greek, too, is peculiar and unlike the usual Oriental uncial'. Plainly we are in the presence of the assimilation process. The place of writing is contested. Egypt is one of the places suggested, and we have seen ascending b and d in the Timgad inscription of the third century. Lowe brought forward new evidence in 1924 that the most probable source was Gallican, and possibly Lyonnese.

From what has been seen it will be judged as reasonable to relate calligraphic Uncial to the script of the Greek Alexandrinus, Sinaiticus, and Vaticanus codices.

51. Rome. Epitaph of Romanus presbyter. A.D. 482 or 461. Popular inscriptional sepulchral lettering. Rome, Lateran Museum.

Condensed; semi-cursive; descending q used as capital; serifed.

De Rossi i, no. 879; Diehl, pl. 35, no. 10.

In view of the familiarity of Latin Square and Rustic Capitals, the round G with a slight beard is an interesting proof of the Rustic consanguinity. If we were to say 'descent' of the bearded G, as seen in this example of Latin Rustic, what should we say of the similarly bearded G to be found in Latin Uncial? Surely here too it is of Rustic origin.

It is notable that in the provincial Timgad inscriptions the round Greek epsilon occurs, and that in the metropolitan Roman inscription it does *not* occur. It does occur, however, in Rome as early as A.D. 236 for the Greek epitaph of Pope Anteros (Plate 53), who resigned some forty days before he was martyred, and it is standard in Latin Uncial. The round epsilon is standard in a Greek literary

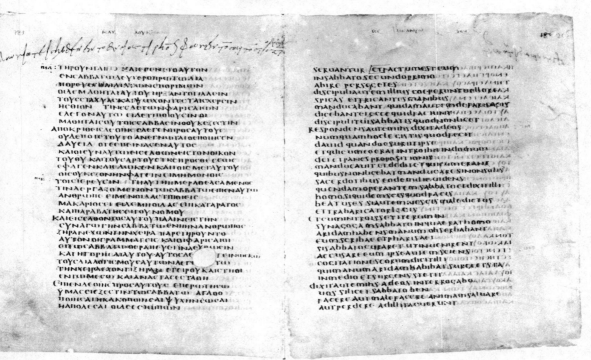

52. Southern France. Pre-Vulgate Gospels and Acts, Greek and Latin, Codex Bezae. 5th century. Greek and Latin uncial book-script.

Cambridge, University Library, Nn. II. 41.

Round; contrasted strokes; ascending b, d, h, l; descending R and P in both languages; descending f, q; descending Upsilon and Phi in Greek; unserifed.

Complete facsimile: *Codex Bezae Cantabrigiensis* (Cambridge, 1899); *C.L.A.* ii, no. 140: 'The scribe is not expert; he writes the Latin in the Greek manner, but his Greek, too, is peculiar and unlike usual Oriental uncial.' Southern France, Southern Italy, and Egypt have been suggested as places of origin. The present figure shows portions of both Greek and Latin texts, which in the original face each other.

hand from the third century B.C. Hence some of the elements, e.g. E and Q of Latin Uncial, are ancient Greek. A too is Greek; also R descends. More could be said on another occasion about the Greek deposit ('basis' is probably too strong a word) in Latin Uncial.

It has been usual since the eighteenth century to say that Latin Uncial is a rounded form of Square Capital. It is true that A, D, E, and M are rounded and that they preserve two of the main characteristics of Latin monumental lettering: the square proportions and the contrasted thick and thin strokes. One 'Capital' convention is missing from Latin Uncial. As we see her written in her youth, she is irregularly serifed. This fact alone is not irreconcilable with the theory that Latin Uncial is, by nature and origin, nothing but a Capital script, retouched and rounded. Had the Square Capital script been modified by the simple introduction of curved sorts the result would certainly have been the domination of the part by the relative whole. As B, C, E, F, G, H, I, K, L, N, O, R, S, and X are

53. Rome. Greek epitaph of Pope Anteros. A.D. 236. Capital sepulchral inscriptional lettering.

Rome, Vatican Museum, Hist. a. 34.

Monumental inscriptional uncial, constructed in capital form; serifed.

De Rossi, *La Roma sotterranea* ii (Rome, 1867), p. 56; Kaufmann, p. 236; Silvagni, *Monumenta* i, pl. I. 2; Montini, fig. 18. C.M.

54. Italy. Hilary, *De Trinitate*. End of 5th century. Uncial.

Verona, Biblioteca capitolare, XIV (12).

C.L.A. iv, no. 485.

CANDUM·NEQUEALI
udquamdmuerum
quiexteuerofatre
Natusestconfiten
dum
Tribueerconobis
uerborumsicnifi
cationemintelle

cositadmettecele
brarenesolum
eteumfraedicare
nefalsum
AMEN

unmodified, they would preserve their formal and probably bracketed serifs. The regular serif in Uncial is a later embellishment; and, when added, was horizontal, unbracketed, and limited to the heads of h, I, N, R, and U. The feet had no serifs, and hence we have the perpendiculars of I, N, R, and M continuing to terminate in Cursive tapers, which is a trick found in Greek Uncial only in Byzantine work.

It is to be noted that, although Uncial had a fashionable career in North African Latin as an inscriptional medium, it fared much less well in Rome in that capacity. In its regularized and standardized form, as adopted as a medium for the renewal of the Christian libraries, Uncial was a prime book-script, fitly reserved for first-class work. The large, handsome form of this script, as practised at the end of the fifth century, is well shown in the Verona Hilary, *De Trinitate* (see Plate 54). The scribe slightly ticks the ascender of L and the head of I; the N is fully serifed at the head; the perpendiculars of f, p, and q descend and taper; the perpendicular and tail of R both descend. Although the script of this Hilary is a highly finished piece of Uncial, it has no more than an emergent serif; a trick permitted, rather than a decoration contrived.

It is otherwise with the Gospel Book written on purple vellum known as the Codex Veronensis. Here is a superfine piece of calligraphy in which the constituent structures are carefully built up from a pen broader than usual, which is employed to add horizontal, carefully formed serifs. They are attached to the heads of all perpendiculars, and in some instances to the feet. The e is in minuscule form and elongates the lateral stroke beyond the body, and thus confirms the view that the serif, as such, is a decorative as well as functional device. It is permissible to consider that this purple codex, assigned to the end of the fifth century (the period of the Hilary mentioned above), is possibly the highest continental development of serifed Uncial. It is certainly a magnificent piece of writing, more highly finished than any other Uncial manuscript. But the serifs, deliberate as they are, never occur in the bracketed form.

It is, however, equally permissible to judge that the Psalter, one half at Lyons, and the other half at Paris, described by Lowe in his *Codices Lugdunenses Antiquissimi*, is finer and purer, as well as larger, in design. Here is a superb Uncial with heavily contrasted strokes, delicately serifed. The scribe is careful to observe the epsilon form of є and to serif the lateral stroke. His ᙏ is beautifully shaped. It seems well to put it forward here as, in fact, the highest continental development of late Uncial, in this case of the fifth to sixth century. (See Plate 55.)

Another interesting seventh-century Uncial manuscript is that of the writings of the Agrimensores, the classical writers on agriculture, now at Wolfenbüttel (Plate 56), whose sectional titles are in serifed Square Capitals of the almost canonical Augustan form, with good Rustic Capitals employed as titles to the diagrams. The Square Capitals used as initials to this manuscript are delicately serifed. The idea can hardly be resisted that the fine serifing of Uncial suggested itself to scribes who were working, or had worked, with Square Capitals. The expert writer of the Uncials in the Agrimensores manuscript does not bracket his delicate serifs, but he is admirable at placing their horizontals.

That is to say, it was admirable to connoisseurs in the seventh century who

F

55. Probably France. Psalterium Romanum et Gallicanum. 5th to 6th century. Uncial.

Paris, Bibliothèque Nationale, Nouv. Acq. 1585; Lyons, Bibliothèque de le Ville, 425.

Square; formal; script of magisterial size and design; strong contrast between thick and thin strokes; careful serifing; Greek Epsilon with serifed lateral stroke.

C.L.A. vi, no. 772.

were satisfied to reserve serifs in Latin Uncial to letters as and when their structure called for them. This is the practice of those who wrote the Greek Uncial Vaticanus and the other Biblical codices. While the serifs to *some* of the Latin Square Capitals are functional, *all* such Capitals are serifed; those in Latin Uncials are wholly functional, and only certain uncial letters are serifed. The limitation in Latin Uncial of the serif where it was functionally justifiable must have been highly deliberate. The 'all-or-none' rule that prevailed in Augustan Capitals was rejected for Christian Uncials; not that there was any theological principle involved. Rather, a dependence upon Greek precedent may be the reason.

In the fourth century there is another script to note as winning recognition for work of literary importance, and as destined for a long and distinguished career. It was originally a rough and uncultivated combination of formal and informal elements. In its later stages, as professionalized by expert scribes, it evolved into a smooth, harmonious regularized medium fit for good bookwork. The projectors in this middle- or lower-class script are more numerous than those in the aristocratical Uncial. The existence of projectors in two scripts, one of which is of better quality than the other, does not prove that the lower is a close derivation or direct deformation of the higher. The lower-class script more probably began quite independently of the higher; that is to say, the script now being examined could have developed earlier, or parallel with, Uncial, and probably out of the same type of writing as the Common Cursive.

Mallon has painstakingly marked out the process by which ascending b, d, h, and l, and descending p and q, were individually regularized, and their positions organized into a Cursive which, it is important to note, is more, rather than

DE ALLVVIONE

CONTROVERSIA EST...

56. Italy. Agrimensores Romani. 7th century. Uncial.
Wolfenbüttel, Herzog-August-Bibliothek, MS. August 2º. 36. 23.
Serifed square capitals and Rustic capitals for titles and initials.
Châtelain, *Uncialis scriptura*, pls. XXIV–XXV; *C.L.A.* ix, no. 137a.

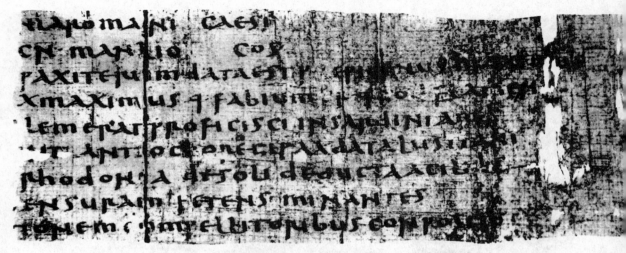

57. Probably Egypt. Papyrus of the *Epitome* of Livy. 3rd to 4th century. Formal book-script. Mixed uncial and half-uncial.

British Museum, P. 1532.

Contrasted strokes; cursive traits; ascending b, d, l; descending f, n, p, r, y; unserifed. It is remarked in *C.L.A.* that b, d, r, m are 'distinctly half-uncial' (ii, no. 208).

B. P. Grenfell and A. S. Hunt, *Oxyrhynchus Papyri* (Oxford, 1904), pl. VI; Steffens, pl. 10; *C.L.A.* ii, no. 208; Mallon, pl. XVII. 3.

less, upright. From it the species of lettering now known by such confusing terms as Minor Uncial or Half-Uncial took its being. This lettering, too, is a Latin development. The discoveries in Oxyrhynchus reveal that as a type of script it is older than had been thought. The relations and connections of the script on some of these papyri are obviously humble. If the implements with which they were written were also humble, when the same lower-class script came to be written with a high-class pen, a great change might result.

That something of this sort occurred may be verified by referring to a British Museum papyrus (No. 1532), a fragment of the epitome of Livy, which was written earlier than the fourth century (Plate 57). If the script is compared with the Common Cursive it will be observed that while it is written with a broad pen, it is, structurally, the current hand of the '*Cum in omnibus bonis*' type (Plate 45), obviously written with a fine pen. By a change of implement the script of the Livy is completely transformed.

To put it briefly, the script of the Livy is a perpendicularized, regularized, and rationalized version of the semi-perpendicular, irregular, and erratic '*Cum in omnibus bonis*' Cursive. The letters in the Livy are separated, as in Uncial. This may or may not be evidence of some sort of link between the two scripts, since both were practised in the same place and the same time each may have acted and reacted on the other. Had this been so, the further probability is that, provided the Livy script was sufficiently superior, economically, to be in greater demand, its influence would be greater upon Uncial than vice versa, and it would be true to say that our Livy script, in this limited sense, is related to regular Uncial. Thereby the title currently given to it of 'Minor' or 'Half-Uncial' would, up to a point, be justified. But once more it would be too much of a digression to argue here about the names of scripts. Everybody knows what is meant by 'Half-Uncial', even if everybody does not agree that it is a satisfactory name for this combination of full and reduced capitals, with ascending and descending sorts.

Expert opinion ranks the script of the Livy as the earliest stage of Half-Uncial. Important similarities as between this Half-Uncial Livy of the third century written probably in Egypt (Plate 57) and, say, the Uncial of the St. Gall Gospels (Plate 58) of the fifth century, written, according to Lowe, in Italy, are that both are thick and thin, and neither has serifs. In the course of time both types acquired serifs, though they were not applied on the 'all-or-none' principle adopted for Square Capitals. Also, both the Egyptian Livy and the St. Gall Gospels hesitate over the descenders and abbreviate them. Some perpendicular strokes were tapered in early Uncial and treated later to a serif. It should be noticed that comparison of this third-century Egyptian Livy papyrus and the third-century Timgad inscriptions reveals striking parallels.

In the West there existed a script for books with a status between the current charter-hands and the Half-Uncial: Burgundian Minuscule. The papyrus (Plate 59) of the Homilies of St. Avitus, Bishop (c. 490–518) of the old Gallo-Roman city of Vienne, was written in the sixth century. Compared with the 'Cum in omnibus bonis' (Plate 45) script the letters are more frequently separated and partly rationalized. The forms that it is usual to call 'Minuscule' are here to be seen progressing towards ultimate emergence and stabilization. Obviously, the script of the Homilies is the result of the long process of pressure by documentary upon literary writing. A slowly made script defends itself by adopting the pose of a smarter, more quickly made script, hence more used and therefore more seen. That is to say, in a period and in an area where writing is increasing in demand and supply, the accent and, so to say, calligraphical slang of a current Cursive will impinge first upon a semi-formal, and next upon a fully formal script. This was one source of calligraphic compromise. There was another.

The demand for a more economic script was met also by decelerating, and thereby improving, an existing informal script, rather than by accelerating and thereby inflating, so to say, the value of an existing formal script. There were diplomatic, notarial, and other special hands with which the ecclesiastical and ruling classes were familiar. These are the special forms that developed out of the originally common correspondence Cursive and later official and diplomatic hand, of which the Ravenna large Charter hand (B.M. Add. MSS. 5412; Steffens 16) and the still larger provincial Charter hand (Geneva MS. [really P] Lat. 76; Bruckner and Marichal, *Chartae Latinae Antiquiores* 5) are examples. The Homilies of Avitus illustrate the later stage of a process of digestion whereby a Cursive originally developed for correspondence and diplomatic use entered into the service of theological literature.

The Avitus is a highly interesting manuscript. Our plate exhibits two sizes of its 'Half-Cursive', as the experts call it. Take away its ligatures and there

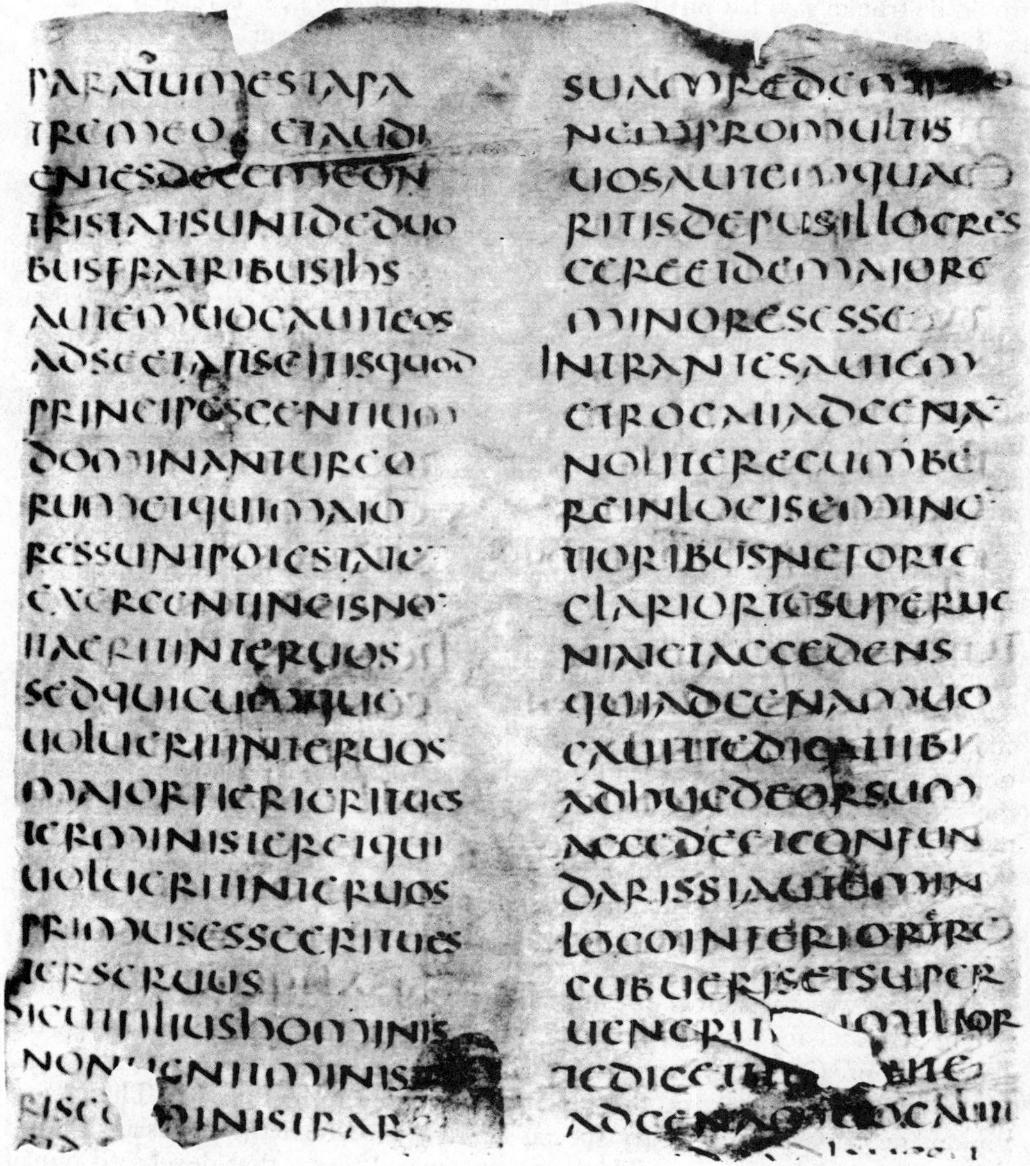

PARXIUMESTAPA
TREMEO · CIAUDI
ENTESDECEMEON
TRISTATISUNTDEDUO
BUSFRATRIBUSIHS
AUTEMUOCAUITEOS
ADSEETAISEITISQUOD
PRINCIPESCENTIUM
DOMINANTURCO
RUMETQUIMAIO
RESSUNTPOTESTATE
EXERCENTINEISNO
IIAERIINTERUOS
SEDQUICUMQUE
UOLUERITINTERUOS
MAIORFIERIERITUS
TERMINISTERETQUI
UOLUERITINTERUOS
PRIMUSESSEERITUES
TERSERUUS
SICUTFILIUSHOMINIS
NONUENITMINIS
TRISCO MINISTRARE

SUMMREDEN
NEDAPROMULTIS
UOSAUTEMNQUAD
RITISDEPUSILLOCRES
CEREETDEMAIORE
MINORESESSE
INTRANTESAUTEM
ETROCAIIADCENA
NOLITERECUMBE
REINLOCISEMINO
TIORIBUSNEFORTE
CLARIORTESUPERUE
NINTIACCEDENS
QUIADCENAMUO
EXUITTEDICAITIBI
ADHUCDEORSUM
ACCEDEFICONFUN
DARISSIAUTEMIN
LOCOINFERIORIRO
CUBUERISETSUPER
UENERIT QUITTIOR
TEDICET AHE
ADCEN

58. Italy. Pre-Vulgate Gospels. 5th century. Uncial.

St. Gall, Stiftsbibliothek, MS. 1394, pp. 51–8 + 172 (frag. at p. 258), and Stadtbibliothek s.n. + Chur, Rhätisches Museum.

Square; unserifed; strong contrast of thick and thin strokes.

C.L.A. vii, no. 978a.

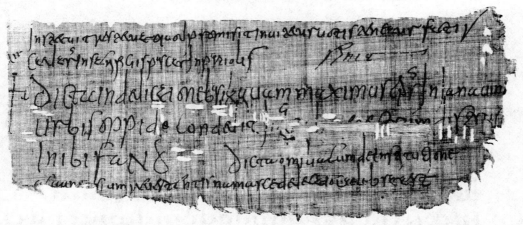

59. France. St. Avitus Viennensis. *Homilia.* 6th century. Merovingian Documentary. Written probably in Burgundy. Cursive as book-script on papyrus.

Paris, Bibliothèque Nationale, MS. Lat. 8913.

Upright cursive; long ascenders and descenders; the large script at foot which begins with ✝ follows with 'dicta', with the &t ligature.

Pal. Soc. i. 68; Steffens, pl. 24; *C.L.A.* v, no. 573.

remains a genuine Minuscule—written in haste by an elderly scribe. Ligatures apart, he has reduced his alphabet to its simplest elements. Apart from the cc form of a, the Avitus alphabet is almost as 'modern' as a piece of contemporary so-called 'print-script' would be—if written at speed. Numerous sorts are, of course, thrown up in the course of the work that do not appear in the fount as here shown, which is limited to the basic characters. These, it should be observed, are all traditional Latin forms and reflect no extraneous inspiration.

The Half-Cursive alphabet, when separated into its constituents, approximates more closely than Uncial, or Half-Uncial, to what printers call 'lower-case', more closely, in fact, than anything so far seen. It will be appreciated that the humble Half-Cursive does not set out to compete with a noble script like Uncial. But it was well fitted to compete on favourable terms with Half-Uncial or any other script that was available for less expensive or more modest book-work. When the Avitus was written, the most superior script, Uncial, had become even more superior by the assumption of regular serifs; also, the same adornment was spreading to the ascenders of Half-Uncial. That was the competitive situation in which the sixth-century Burgundian Half-Cursive found itself. How 'artistic' Half-Uncial became in the seventh century may be seen in Plate 60, from a text of the *Epistles* of Jerome, now in the Library of the University of Ghent. It is a truly grand, a superb, piece of Half-Uncial, written carefully with the straight pen. Interesting are a with a perpendicular vestige at head of mainstroke; g with a long beard; m with third stroke curved; t with curved mainstroke. This magnificently organized alphabet may be ranked as genuine and unique a Latin invention as Rustic Capitals, but it is more original, for

60. Probably S. France. *Epistles* of Jerome, fragment. 7th century.

Ghent, Bibliothèque de l'Université, no. 246.

Round a has a perpendicular vestigial head, g has a long beard, m has a third stroke as a curve, t has an occasional top stroke with a slight curve. Informal serifs to the tops of b, d, h, l.

Châtelain 76; *C.L.A.* x, no. 1556.

there was no Greek Half-Uncial and never has been—whereas there was a kind of Greek Rustic. This will be acknowledged when we arrive at the tenth century.

From the seventh and eighth centuries there are many excellent specimens of both Latin Uncial and Half-Uncial formal writing. There are also specimens of Half-Uncial which were expedited, as I think one is entitled to suspect, by the competition of Half-Cursive of the St. Avitus type. As the machinery of State became settled and the system of diocesan and monastic administration was consolidated, so the activity of missionaries enlarged the population and boundaries of the Church, and hence the need for writing increased. With new demands new scripts were bound to emerge. Even sacramentaries and missals began to be written at speed. The Bobbio missal (eighth-century according to the latest opinion) was rapidly written in business-like fashion by a missionary scribe (see Plate 61). Its rough and ready script partakes of Uncial, and Half-Uncial, and, towards the end of the book, of Minuscule, Half-Cursive, and others of lower rank.

The amount of speedy writing done at this time, though we do not have much of it left, was, of course, greater by any count than the case with the formal. Ephemeral notes and business communications must needs perish. However, a certain amount of fast bookwork remains. It is amazing to see what can happen when the canon of writing loses its force and, in the absence of authority, scripts arise in which degenerate descendants of aristocratic parents are mixed with new arrivals promoted from the servants' hall. The eighth century is full of scripts of dubious ancestry and desperate appearance. As, for people like us, bad art is often more interesting than good art, a book like the Paris Eugippius (see Plate 62) is an inspiration. So is the Lucca Isidore (see Plate 63). Everything is in disorder. Script was scribble. The formal Minuscule had not been evolved. Nobody was in authority.

The final partition of Eastern and Western empires in 395 and the legal separation of their legal systems in 438, the invasions of Italy and the sack of Rome in 455, the deposition of Romulus Augustulus, the last Western emperor, in 476, had extinguished the authority that had backed the Square Capital and the Uncial. Invasions, sieges, and sackings had reduced Rome to nullity. The authority in the sixth century was Justinian, and the West entered upon an age of successive periods of pro- and anti-Byzantinism that was to last nearly a thousand years. The Western scripts reflect this uneasiness and the alternative intrusion and extrusion of Byzantine elements.

From the sixth century, scriptorially speaking, the West was free to develop, without obligation to the East, and to follow any example it chose. In the long period after 633, when no Roman emperor visited Rome, it was hardly expected that the city of Constantine and Justinian would exercise direct official influence upon the city of Romulus and Remus. There was no longer the same incentive to manifest the unity of the Church by the use of an interchangeable alphabet, though the idea had not died, and there were important Greek monasteries in Rome and numerous Greek popes in the seventh and eighth centuries. Something will be said about this later. At this point it is necessary only to say that

61. France. Gallican Sacramentary or 'Bobbio Missal'. 8th century. Mixed informal uncial, half-uncial.

Paris, Bibliothèque Nationale, MS. Lat. 13246.

Round; has minuscule portions; irregularly serifed.

C.L.A. v, no. 653; A. Wilmart in Cabrol and Leclercq, *D.A.C.L.*, s.v. 'Bobbio'; complete facsimile, edited by E. A. Lowe and others, in *The Bobbio Missal*, Henry Bradshaw Society, vol. liii (London, 1917).

62. Tours. Eugippius, Excerpts from St. Augustine. First half of 8th century, probably at Tours. Half-uncial and minuscule.

Paris, Bibliothèque Nationale, Nouv. acq. lat. 1575.

E. K. Rand, *The Earliest Book of Tours* (Cambridge, Mass., 1934): Rand distinguishes hands A–K in this manuscript in Uncial, Half-Uncial, and Minuscule; they occur in no logical order. None has any calligraphic value, but the variety gives the book abundant palaeographic interest. Rand says of hand K that the scribe was responsible for 'an epoch-making experiment' (p. 37). The serifing of the top line in cursive Half-Uncial should be noticed. The plate is from fol. 96ʳ; Rand, pl. XXIII: *C.L.A.* v, no. 682.

63. Lucca. Isidore, *Chronicon*, etc. 8th to 9th century. Uncial and mixed pre-Caroline scripts.

Lucca, Biblioteca capitolare, MS. 490, fol. 214.

C.L.A. iii, no. 303b.

the Common Cursive and Half-Cursive are non-Greek, and that they and Half-Uncial fully justified themselves in terms of speed of writing and quantity of production. The promoted Half-Cursives—such as those known as Quarter-Uncial, Eighth-Uncial, and even Sixteenth-Uncial—are also to be seen in abundance.

While the laws of supply and demand for books during the eighth century raised the speed and increased the number of the minor, swifter, Avitus types of Half-Cursive at the expense of the major but slower Uncial and Half-Uncial, the correspondence hands and documentary Cursives, which are independent of books, naturally continued to be written for their special purposes with their appropriate tools. The whole represented a new Western development conditioned by a history different from that of the East. The West with its wars arising from the invasions, the short range of authority and the long series of schisms with Constantinople, combined to set Latin Script upon a path separate from that which Byzantine Script had taken from the foundation of Constantinople in 330.

The question may well be asked whether, after the denunciation in 482 of Acacius, Patriarch of Constantinople, by Felix, Bishop of Rome—which resulted in the first schism between East and West—the Byzantine style of writing was likely even indirectly to influence Latin Script; whether, that is to say, Latin Uncial would be the final calligraphical vestige of Eastern power. This question can be considered, it would be rash to say answered, only by looking back from the fifth, sixth, and seventh centuries to the second, third, and fourth centuries, in order to discover what evidence there may be of special Eastern influence upon the West. By 'special' is meant the possibility of a definite Eastern exemplar having exercised upon Rome a direct influence, distinct from that afforded by the general opportunity for Greek scribes, working side by side with Latin colleagues, to assimilate certain characters. Had Constantine chosen to stay in the West this assimilation would most probably have increased. We ought at least to inquire to what extent the forms current in the new capital and its dependencies influenced the old.

It has been seen that in the writing of literature after the period during which imperial authority gave prestige to the Square Capital, patriotic piety promoted the Rustic Capital, and religious piety promoted the Uncial, there existed another category of work. The writing of non-literary composition enjoyed great freedom, out of which Half-Cursive and Half-Uncial emerged. It is to be recognized that Half-Uncial was as valuable an invention for its time as the Rustic with which the present lecture started, and an innovation more practical than Uncial for more kinds of work in which a good general, and less monumental, transcription was necessary. It has been seen, also, that these creations were Latin in their inspiration. Does it follow that during the period when Square and Rustic Capital scripts had fallen into disuse in favour of, first, Uncial, and next, Half-Uncial, only Latin forms are to be found in the book-production of the West?

The question requires the consideration of scripts other than those designed for continuous text: those intended and developed for the displayed portions —such as the titles, *incipit*s, or other equivalent of the opening page. Are these, too, purely Latin?

To answer this question we must make the East the point of departure for the following lecture. We shall look back to second- or third-century Phrygia and inspect the inscription of Aberkios. The immediate purpose of the inquiry will be to ascertain what happened after the adaption of Uncial to the titles, chapter-headlines, and initial letters, and to consider whether these elements may be of oriental inspiration, and reflect Imperial authority.

3

SECOND-CENTURY PHRYGIA TO
EIGHTH-CENTURY GAUL

FROM Phrygia comes an inscription of the late second century whose literary form, calligraphical excellence, and impressive dimensions earned it great renown.

Phrygia was a prosperous country and its great saint during the second century was Aberkios, a popular bishop of some means who could afford to prepare luxuriously for his sepulture, and to contrive expensively for the inscription. The inscription was discovered in 1884 by Sir William Ramsay, in response to a friendly challenge from G. B. de Rossi. It made an immense sensation. The reason for the excitement was that the text, long familiar from the quotation in the menology of Simeon Metaphrastes, the tenth-century Byzantine historian, was believed to be entirely bogus and the bishop a wholly hagiographical creation. This was the judgement of Renan. Ramsay's discovery of the stone itself, albeit in fragments, demonstrated that the Aberkios in question was a historical figure and was indeed bishop of Hieropolis in Phrygia. Plate 64 shows a portion of the inscription. In the judgement of Marucchi the inscription may be confidently dated to the reign of Marcus Aurelius (161–80), and is the identical lettering that Aberkios ordered. The present photograph insufficiently displays its merits. It will be rated as an exceptionally fine piece of work by anybody who will inspect the original now in the Lateran Museum.

The extent of reciprocity of Greek and Latin influence in both inscriptional and calligraphical lettering at the time when Christian culture was in process of formation has already been pointed to as a worthy field of inquiry. It would be profitable at this point if the priority of the engraved over the written varieties of this script could be established. As things are, the present observations must be elementary, though the special epigraphic forms which occur in the Aberkios inscription are of considerable point. It will first be noticed, as a generality, that the inscription is perfectly serifed. The particular forms to be observed are the low forked A and the high forked M, and of these the more important is the A. From the late fourth century it is found associated with omega in the Chrismon. What was the authority for the use of the forked A in the Chrismon? Was it new in Rome in the life-time of Constantine? No, it had already been received into Christian usage.

An early appearance (see Plate 65) of the forked A occurs in the Greek epitaph of Gaius (or Caius), who was head of the Church of Rome between the years 283 and 296. The epitaph for a Bishop of Rome can hardly be regarded as a vulgar inscription (in any case Gaius was a sort of distant relation of Diocletian),

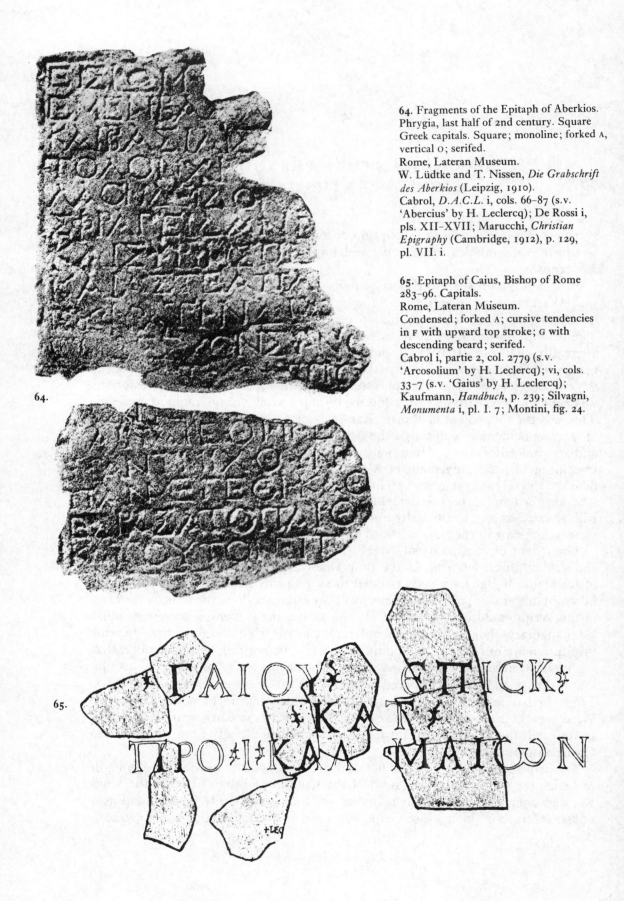

64. Fragments of the Epitaph of Aberkios. Phrygia, last half of 2nd century. Square Greek capitals. Square; monoline; forked A, vertical O; serifed.
Rome, Lateran Museum.
W. Lüdtke and T. Nissen, *Die Grabschrift des Aberkios* (Leipzig, 1910).
Cabrol, *D.A.C.L.* i, cols. 66–87 (s.v. 'Abercius' by H. Leclercq); De Rossi i, pls. XII–XVII; Marucchi, *Christian Epigraphy* (Cambridge, 1912), p. 129, pl. VII. i.

65. Epitaph of Caius, Bishop of Rome 283–96. Capitals.
Rome, Lateran Museum.
Condensed; forked A; cursive tendencies in F with upward top stroke; G with descending beard; serifed.
Cabrol i, partie 2, col. 2779 (s.v. 'Arcosolium' by H. Leclercq); vi, cols. 33–7 (s.v. 'Gaius' by H. Leclercq); Kaufmann, *Handbuch*, p. 239; Silvagni, *Monumenta* i, pl. I. 7; Montini, fig. 24.

64.

65.

66. Letter of Ptolemy VI Philometer. Thera, 164–159 B.C. Capital Greek inscription.
Square, with forked A; serifed.
I.G. xii. 3. 327, plus suppl. to fasc. 3, p. 283; Kern 22 *supra*.

and we may assume that the forked A was sanctioned for Christian use by impressive precedent, not Imperial because it was of a generation earlier than Constantine. How then did Aberkios, a century before Gaius, come by it? The forked A was not new in the days of Constantine, but it was new in the Rome of the third century. Was it new then in Phrygia? Far from it. That it must have been considered orthodox and canonical in Christian Greek will be admitted when it is seen to be used in the Codex Alexandrinus for certain titles. But its origins are far more ancient. The present Plate 66 is from an inscription at the Aegean island of Thera, dated 160–159 B.C. The forked alpha may be seen throughout the text, but it seems well to retouch the first word in the top line for the purpose of improving its visibility. This second-century B.C. specimen is by no means the earliest extant specimen of the forked A. As has been seen above, the form is found in an inscription of the fourth century B.C.

There is no evidence, however, that the forked alpha, though present in early Greek engraving, was used in early Greek writing. The occasional tendency, visible in papyri of the fourth and third centuries, to set the crossbar of A in a downward curve (see above, Plate 8, the Timotheus papyrus, which may be compared with Shubart 3 and Roberts 4) need not be placed in the scriptorial pedigree of this form. Originally, perhaps, it was an epigraphical invention, created to harmonize with the forked M, the centre diagonals of which do not, in Greek, descend to the base-line as they do in Latin. Moreover, the outside legs often spread in M. The variations in both may have been technomorphic improvements on their predecessors. Whatever the cause, the fact is that the forked alpha remained in ancient Greece as a carver's and not a scribe's form.

Similarly, although the forked alpha was used abundantly in Western Greek inscriptions from the third century onwards, it does not appear to have secured a permanent lodgement in continental Latin writing of the first five centuries. But suddenly, so far as we can see, it makes a conspicuous début as an extra-large decorative initial in the Square Capital Codex Augusteus of Virgil of the fifth century, but then, apparently, without echo. It continued, however, to maintain its position in Latin inscriptions. Understandably it may be found very early at Trier, and thence seen spreading to Mainz, Cologne, and all over the Germanic or Frankish West—as may·be seen from the tables in Brandi's *Grundlegung*. To this day the forked A is thought of in Germany as a 'Gothic' or 'semi-Gothic' character.

It seems correct to say that the forked alpha, as an epigraphic character, recognized to be ancient and native, was first christianized in the conservative Church of Phrygia in the second century; and, later, in the Church of Rome in the third century; and thence transmitted to the kingdoms of the Franks, the Egyptians, and hence to the Copts (who made occasional use of it in titles). It was later received by the Irish and English, as will be noticed later in connection with the courage of Offa I, King of Mercia in the early eighth century. This being so, it would be reasonable to expect that some such form would be used by the Byzantine Romans. Yet, although the forked A is to be seen in the Byzantine Greek Chrismon, it occurs very infrequently in Byzantine Latin legal texts. Moreover, in Byzantine Greek, the most usual alpha was the archaic ∧ with left to right upward stroke. Although forked alpha appears occasionally in titles in the Codex Alexandrinus, its career in Byzantium seems to have been arrested in the time of Constantine's immediate successors. As to Old Rome, the forked ∧ appears on Christian Latin inscriptions of all classes from the third and fourth centuries. It is in the Epitaph of Zita dated 391 (Plate 67), which is otherwise interesting, as we shall see later. We thus have the paradox that the fourth-century

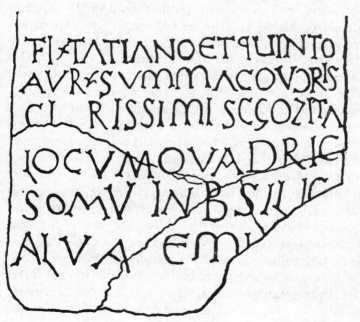

67. Epitaph of Zita. Mixed capital and uncial; Latin inscription. Dated 391.

Square; cursive tendencies; forked A, divided B, G with descending beard; L with descending terminal, spread M alternating with uncial, tailed q.

Kaufmann, p. 26 and fig. 27.

B.C. Greek inscriptional forked alpha became not only Phrygian and Roman, but Insular, early Medieval, and modern vernacular Gaelic.

It is impossible to say whether other Hellenic forms that secured permanent or temporary lodgement in the Roman alphabet began their Christian career in the Old or the New Rome. If it can be shown that any Hellenic inventions first appeared in Old Rome it does not follow that they were the work of Latin craftsmen. The city, as is well known, was full of Greek scribes. This is why the Codex Theodosianus of the sixth century (Rome, Vat. Reg. Lat. 886) came to be written in Latin Half-Uncial but with a Greek pen (*C.L.A.*, i, no. 110). In any case, all designers for the graphic arts, whether in Old Rome or the New, in ancient or modern times, were automatically learning and being inspired from each other's work. Naturally, when Constantine abandoned Rome and took the capital to Byzantium, carting off architects and artists with him, he also took scribes. In 330, when he solemnly celebrated his twenty-five years of Empire and dedicated his new capital under the name of Constantinople, he incidentally, but profoundly, affected the relation of Roman to Greek script. The evolution of the Graeco-Roman alphabet (or alphabets) in the Constantinian age needs study in every medium. Numerous points of interest might attract historians of the minor arts. Here it can only be noted that when Constantine left Rome and established his capital at Byzantium the principle of authority in inscriptional lettering was automatically jeopardized in the old capital and equally in the new. What was to happen in both places to the Augustan Square Capital? Would anybody now protect it? What kind of Imperial Capital Script would gain approval in Christian New Rome? Who would now be the equivalent authority in Old Rome? Would it matter? As far as we can see, no calligraphical consequences followed immediately upon the transfer of the capital to Constantinople in 330.

The first Christian Emperor died in 337, leaving the Empire to be divided by three sons and two nephews, a system which did not please the army chiefs. They massacred most of the near relations except one son, Constantius, who became sole Emperor in 351. The Bishop of Rome from 352 was Liberius. He resisted the Imperial policy of appeasement towards the Arians and was banished from Rome by Constantius, who filled the vacancy with one of the Arianizing party, Felix. In 358 Liberius, having signed a formula (later criticized as unorthodox), returned to Rome and Felix was ejected by the Senate. In 361 Constantius died. He was succeeded by a surviving nephew of Constantine, Julian.

The new Emperor immediately espoused the old religion. The Church of Rome having endured the pro-Arian intrusions of Constantius was now faced with the pro-pagan laws of Julian. The Christians everywhere found themselves deprived not only of their privileges, salaries, and pensions, but burdened with the cost of restoring the temples. The old religion was actively promoted and the new vigorously persecuted. Christians again faced massacre and martyrdom. Only Julian's death in 364, fighting the Persians, saved the faith from a permanent set-back. But as Julian's successor the army chose Jovian, a Christian of the tolerant sort, ready to restore the Constantinian system in principle. Jovian's death within a year necessarily made the Church highly apprehensive. The

G

choice could have been another adherent of the old religion, another Christian of the heretic, Arian type, or one of the orthodox, Athanasian type. The brothers Valens and Valentinian were elected. The first was neutral and the second Arian. They partitioned the Empire into East (Valens) and West (Valentinian).

Some idea of the confusion that reigned in the Church that had only been emancipated thirty years earlier may be gained from what happened in Rome at the death of Liberius. Damasus, the new bishop, had protested against the banishment of Liberius, had then acknowledged Felix, and next supported Liberius on his return. Finally, in 366, Damasus won a majority of votes. The minority, determined supporters of Liberius, proposed one Ursinus and consecrated him. After much bloodshed they intruded him into the See of Peter and extruded Damasus. This, however, did not suit Valentinian. He intervened and recognized Damasus. While the imperial act by no means ended the troubles, the bishop maintained his position and increased the authority of the See of Peter to a degree surpassing that achieved by his predecessors. Fortunately Damasus was no stranger to Rome; he was born there, the son of an ecclesiastical notary and archivist. At his succession the great city was swarming with schismatics, partisans and demagogues, careerists, heretics, and saboteurs of every kind and race. Hence the bloodshed at the election of Damasus. The privileges and pensions attached to ecclesiastical offices were worth fighting for. Damasus was ready for the fight. He was the man of the moment.

Over all, the new bishop was faced with the problem of finding the means to maintain continuity of the official policy whereby the State did not intervene in ecclesiastical tribunals or their judgements, while he himself needed State power to secure order in Church life. Sentences of deposition in the case of heretic or recalcitrant bishops, of whom there were more than a few, were not enforceable by Damasus acting alone, and they were certainly not going to give up their good salaries merely on his request. In such conditions the neutrality of the State would be both a help and a hindrance. With its power behind him, Damasus could have dealt more effectively with the crowd of Arians, semi-Arians, Donatists, Marcionites, Montanists, Sabellians, Novatians, and other heretics and schismatics, many of whom had been protected by Julian. But as it was, Damasus and Valentinian were both ready to let the Church face these troubles by herself. Damasus added to his authority by appealing to the Scriptures, which he was prepared to catalogue, the Liturgy, which he was ready to reform, and the faith of the martyrs, which he was determined to immortalize.

He dealt with the Scriptures by promulgating in 382 the first canon of the New Testament, drafted by his secretary, Jerome, and with the martyrs, by memorializing their virtues in poems written by himself. The work of Damasus on the Scriptures and the Liturgy does not concern us; his work on the martyrs does, for it made its mark on calligraphy.

Before turning to one aspect of his cult of the martyrs, it is well to recognize in Damasus a man to whom the exercise of authority was second nature, and that the eighteen-year rule of this energetic, able, and masterful man brought a notable and permanent access of authority to his See. That See, in his eyes, derived its precedence only from the primacy of Peter, a concept that had political importance from the fourth century. Rome stood at the head of the Church on the basis of the promise of Christ to Peter, not because of any dignity conferred upon Rome by the Emperor or by the State. Rather, he let it be inferred, Emperors had conferred dignity upon Christ and Peter by shedding the blood of his servants. To this end Damasus espoused the cult of the martyrs and composed their eulogies. The quality of the versification does not concern us (Duchesne's sarcasm is doubtless in place); it is the calligraphy that is relevant. There are two points to be borne in mind in connection with Damasus's inscriptions in praise of the martyrs. First, they were engraved on costly marble; secondly, they were inscribed in lettering whose engraving was itself very expensive of time and space. The design of the letters was evidently formed after careful consideration. Only a serious motive could have justified it, and Damasus was not deterred by the expense of creating a design peculiar to, and symbolic of, the sanctity of the victims of the Emperors, and the special position of the Bishop of Rome. The script, devised within two generations of Constantine's proclamation of Byzantium as his new capital, was achieved in the old capital after Damasus exerted himself to preserve the rights of the See of Peter as the primatial See of Christendom, east and west. The intention carried with it a willingness to accept the support of Caesar on Damasus's terms of independence from the State in dogmatic jurisdiction. It is not surprising that the lettering devised to eulogize the martyrs who had perished only fifty years before Damasus was born should be in contrast with the Imperial form used by Decius and Valerian, their persecutors.

Damasus's lettering effectively symbolized a complete independence of the Church from the State, and appropriately illustrated the unique steadfastness of the martyrs. The calligraphy used for the inscriptions is an absolute and unique departure from anything ever seen before in Rome, or, it should be emphasized, elsewhere. In the time of Damasus, Constantinople and Antioch were held to be tainted with Arianism, while Rome, Milan, and Alexandria were upholding the Nicene doctrine. Hence Damascus had every reason for emphasizing the orthodoxy, and with it the precedence, of Rome and Alexandria over Constantinople.

It cannot be denied that the inscriptions of Damasus are ambitious, as he clearly was; distinctive, also—a quality he obviously desired. A non-Christian sculptor of the age of Constantine, used to cutting an Imperial inscription and still working in Old Rome, could hardly admire them, but he would respect the new religion for attempting a Romano-episcopal lettering of its own. Anyhow, he would certainly say it was right for these Christians to possess an authoritative style, and that it was well to care for the provision of a proper inscriptional lettering in the basilicas, novel as it was, like the religion it symbolized. Such a non-Christian but patriotic Roman sculptor might have been glad, also, to see that while the Damasine letter was an innovation, underneath its decorations lay the old Square Capital proportions, and that there was no forked A or other Hellenistic infiltration. In that sense it was pure Roman.

Damasus, dominating figure as he was, had the gift of attracting men of great learning to his side. No less a figure than Jerome was his scripture scholar. Philocalus, his scribe, is famous for his Kalendar of 352, which we know from late copies. It was he who designed the alphabet which Damasus used for his inscriptions in praise of the martyrs. The significant detail is the curved and sometimes undulant serif. The basic form of the alphabet is that of the Square Capital with contrasted strokes; Q is circular and is a pure Square Capital; R has a long tail. In general the alphabet is more regularly square than the traditional Augustan type (see Plate 68).

68. Pope Damasus I, Eulogium S. Eutychii. Rome, 366–84.

Rome, S. Sebastiano.

Square; contrasted strokes; perpendicular O; wavy serif to heads and feet of perpendiculars.

Epigramm. Damas. 21. The plate shows a small portion of the complete inscription, which was repaired in 1615.

Silvagni i, pl. V. 2.

The new script looked authoritative, and so it remained for a century, but if the Damasine script did not affect general style it may have been part of the intention that it should not do so. For the inscription to his mother, Damasus did not employ it, but used a slightly condensed version of the normal Roman capital. Thus it would appear that it was no part of Damasus's scheme that the script of Philocalus should be used for civic purposes; he was careful at all times to make the distinction between the sacred and the secular.

Damasus was a conspicuously able ecclesiastical statesman. He had benefited from the support of Valentinian in 366 and of Gratian, his son and successor, from 375. With Gratian, his half-brother Valentinian II was associated with him in the title. On the death of Valens in 378 Gratian inherited the Eastern Empire. The burden being too heavy. Gratian in the same year ceded the

East to Theodosius, the son of the first Valentinian's great general of the same name.

Though the Pontiff Damasus finally secured the position of his See, and had secured the establishment of the Catholic Church throughout the Empire, the position was less sure than it seemed. The Church perhaps benefited when Gratian was murdered by the army in 383 and Valentinian II fled to the East to join Theodosius. When Damasus died in 384 he left to his successors in the Roman Church and patriarchate an official status and consequent degree of authority it had not hitherto possessed or exercised. He made important and permanent changes in the Liturgy and in the Chant. It has been seen that it is the canon of the New Testament first drawn up at his instance that we still have. The mass of writing occasioned by the authorization of the new text was considerable, and it is certain from Jerome's well-known remark, that he was opposed to a luxury standard of lettering for biblical texts. There is no reason to believe that he was opposed to a size of letter appropriate for liturgical use. It follows that he would not have disapproved a script larger than that of the standard Greek Codex he was in the habit of using; the Codex Sinaiticus, for example. Still less is there reason to think that Jerome would have radically altered the design used for the transcription of his text. He was no innovator. It may be imagined that his influence would be thrown on the side of a good, bold, legible, and dignified hand, of the sort we have in early evangeliaries written in Uncial of the oldest type. It is with full justification, therefore, that Traube can designate Latin Uncial as the 'Christian' script. He could have added Half-Uncial, to be discussed later.

Damasus did not bequeath a calligraphical or epigraphical style of any purity or durability, though, as will be seen, significant vestiges are found in many manuscripts of the eighth century from Luxeuil and Corbie, and even Aachen. Why they then vanished is a question to which an answer will be attempted in due course. It has been mentioned that shorn of their decorative serifs the characters designed by Philocalus are broader and heavier than usual, and that they are comparable in these respects with the letters on the Arch of Constantine. The style, anyhow, is Roman and not Greek. It is true that some inscriptions, apparently Damasine, include the forked A and other Hellenisms, but it has not been proved to universal satisfaction that these particular inscriptions are attributable to the pontificate of Damasus. In all probability they are later.

Twenty years after the death of Damasus an interesting, indeed a fine, or in some respects fine, piece of lettering dignified a second-class sepulchral tablet engraved for a Roman lady—perhaps related to a mason (Plate 69). This exhibit shows the lettering of a highly competent engraver who takes a step towards the policy of adapting the old Augustan Monumental Script to the proportions of Rustic, although the words are not separated by spaces; ivy leaves are inserted as paragraph marks. But Roman as the inscription is in temper, the capital A with the forked cross-bar and the G with the cursive beard (in two forms) exist side-by-side with the long-tailed Roman Square Q. The fork of the M descends

95

69. Epitaph of Constantia. Rome, A.D. 404.

Formal capitals; condensed; forked A; uncial G with descending beard; N reversed in fifth line.

De Rossi i. 529; Diehl, pl. 34, no. 27.

midway, which is a Hellenism. There is a reversed И in SEXAGINTA in the fifth line. Bracketed serifing is consistent throughout. The mason's mallets and knife are an interesting decoration. The date of this inscription is 404. It is important as showing the tendency to extend and establish the relatively modern, narrow, as against the ancient, wide, scale of letter. This is significant when the origins of Byzantine capital titles are considered. It is clear from other work that by the fifth century in Old Rome the Augustan canon of pure, fine lettering for first-class inscriptions had been gravely weakened by the example of Damasus's lettering and the economic pressure of Rustic. The present inscription is a piece of relatively canonical Latin script, but it was doubtless exceptional. The authority behind the script of Damasus had now proved its insufficiency. It had always been expensive in space occupied and in time required. The old standards were vanishing and there were no new standards to take their place. Naturally, this is more clearly seen in the popular inscriptions.

Plate 70 is a specimen of lettering of Rustic proportion from the mid fifth century. The shapes are crude but not cursive, the words are not spaced. The A is forked; M exists in three or more varieties, in all of which the legs are spread

96

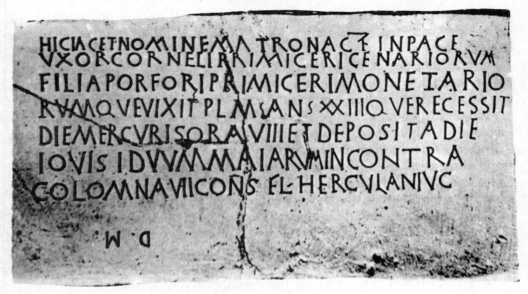

70. Epitaph of Matrona. Irregular capitals. Rome, A.D. 452.

Condensed; forked A; L varies; spreading M; roughly and irregularly serifed.

C.I.L. vi. 8460; De Rossi i. 754; Diehl, pl. 35, no. 5.

and the centre firmly brought down to the base-line; unfortunately G does not occur—but it would almost certainly have been rounded and bearded at the base. The variety of M that occurs twice in the first line NOMINE and MATRONA should be noticed, as it will be referred to later. The inscription as a whole is a very poor piece of design, eloquent of the sad state into which Rome had fallen in the fifth century, prophetic of the condition into which it was destined to remain for generations. The inscription is dated by Ernst Diehl as of 452. It is contemporary, therefore, with the Council of Chalcedon, when the Pope, Leo I, refused to ratify the canon declaring Constantinople to be equal in status with Rome. The state of affairs between Rome and Constantinople was destined to deteriorate still further; the Pope of Rome also had difficulties with the people of Rome. The pride of families and ambition of heretics perpetuated turmoil and strife.

The civil situation of the old capital became more settled towards the end of the sixth century. The arts slightly improved their status. The Bishop of Rome between 561 and 574 was John III. Thus he was a contemporary of the Emperor Justin II (565–78), and it was during John's pontificate that the Emperor bestowed upon the Eternal City a magnificent processional Cross that embodied a fraction of the True Wood. The reliquary was ornamented on one side with embossed plates of gold or silver gilt, across and down which runs an inscription: LIGNO QUO CHRISTUS HUMANUM SUBDIDIT HOSTEM DAT ROMAE IUSTINUS OPEM ET SOCIA DECOREM. As far as I can make it out, the Emperor was the donor of the relic and the Empress the donor of the decoration. Plate 71 shows the head of the Cross, with a central medallion as added by Pius IX. The pendant agates are also modern.

De Waal decides in the negative the question whether it could have been a gift of Justin I, who reigned half a century earlier. In any event the inscription was engraved in New Rome in Latin for presentation to Old Rome. We do not have to decide whether the presentation was made to the city of Rome, or to the successor of Peter. It is the alphabet that concerns us. It consists of eighteen characters. The drawing of Plate 72 shows these more clearly than the photograph of the cross itself (Plate 71). At first sight the script is a chaotic mixture of Greek and Roman, Square Capital, and Uncial forms. Coming as it did from the most illustrious capital, the richest commercial centre, and the most lavishly endowed artistic community in the civilized world of about the year 570, it must have seemed strikingly original to the eyes of the conservative and impoverished Romans. None of the letters could have been altogether strange to all of them, for they had in Rome the epitaph in Latin mentioned earlier as cut for Zita and dated 391 (Plate 67). The carver of this inscription of Zita embodied minuscule q, uncial Ç, and round ꟼ serifed at the feet, alternating with spread M, with several varieties of A with diagonal and forked cross-bar. The carver of the inscription of Justin preserves the Augustan form of A with the horizontal cross-bar, but in addition to the Greek Λ with the forked cross-bar. That both these forms should be present in Justin's inscription might be significant of something more than an artist's whim, or was it the fact that the authority for it was purely 'artistic'?

Zita's Roman inscription, it needs to be emphasized, is dated 391. It may be reconsidered at this point, for it is comparable with that of Pomponianus (Plate 48), which is African, and datable as of the first half of the third century. The point is that the forms in these two inscriptions occur in a similar social and political situation, i.e. the coexistence of Greek- and Latin-speaking communities. It was suggested (p. 62) that the form of the African inscriptions may have enjoyed a measure of official recognition. This, it was guessed, was probably the case in Africa. It is less probable that the syncretical amalgam, of which the Zita inscription, and others of the fourth century, is a degenerate version, enjoyed any official Roman approval. It is equally improbable that such inscriptions derived their inspiration from official African sources. Had this been so, more examples might have been expected to survive in Rome, whereas only one or two are recorded. The awkward fact remains that some of the forms common to the Pomponianus–Zita alphabets were applied in Constantinople in 560 in an Imperial inscription from New Rome, intended to be legible and respectable in Old Rome.

It may be not without significance that, under the emperor Tiberius II, who was appointed Caesar by Justin II in 574 and became his successor in 578, that considerable changes were instituted in the types and letterings of the coinage legends of Byzantium, and of other mints of the Eastern empire. The Uncial forms b, ᴆ, ɢ, m, and u were all introduced during his short reign (578–82). All

71. Precious-jewelled inscribed cross of Justin II (565–78), presented to Rome, then under the pontificates of John III (560–73) and Benedict I (574–8). Constantinople.

Rome, St. Peter's.

Engraved hybrid capitals and uncials, with formalized cursive elements; mainly monoline; the whole serifed.

D.A.C.L. iii, cols. 3110–13, fig. 3411.

✝ LIGNO YUO CHRISTUS
HUMANUM SUBDIDIT
HOSTEM DAT
ROMAE IUSTINUS
OPEM ET SOCIA
DECOREM

72. Lettering on the reliquary of Justin II.

five of these new forms are observable on Justin's cross. Further, in place of the
figure of Victory, the regular reverse type from Anastasius to Justinian, or of
Constantinople, introduced by Justin II, Tiberius (as a result of a vision, according to John of Ephesus) introduced on the reverse of all his gold coinage a cross
on a dais. Among his numismatic achievements were a series of large gold medals,
weighing one pound each, some of which he sent to Chilperic, King of the Franks.
No example is now known to exist, but they are described by Gregory of Tours,
to whom Chilperic showed them in 581, and he chronicles the text of the legends.
The impression upon the sixth-century Franks of these immense gold pieces
with the syncretic alphabet of their legends could not have failed to be profound,
and their desire to emulate their example must have been equally deep. The
attitude in Old Rome to the script of New Rome may have been less reverential.

Certainly the amalgam of Capitals, Uncials, and what-not would have been
rejected by the *quadratarii* responsible for the inscriptions on the Arch of Constantine. Roman standards had decayed in the succeeding two centuries for a
sure reason: Alaric sacked Rome in 410, and the invasion of the West explains
the progressive debasement of Roman inscriptional lettering. The standards of
a Damasus could hardly be expected to be maintained by his successors while
the peninsula and the capital were virtually under siege.

But what of rich and secure Constantinople? Was there no Imperial canon in
sixth-century New Rome? If not, was there a guild of craftsmen that could have
set it? The fact appears to be that it was the metal-workers of the city who

designed, and as a guild sanctioned, the lettering. That it was authorized by the Emperor created the canon. Taking the alphabet into their own hands, and doing what they liked with it, the city's engravers in the mint, the goldsmiths, and other workers in precious metals shaped the hybrid Greek and Roman, Half-Square and Half-Round, Capital alphabet that was engraved on Justin's cross and impressed on the coinage of Tiberius.

The influence of the Byzantine workers in precious metals upon Western scribes is traceable, though with difficulty. It is impossible here to do anything more than mention it as the probable explanation of certain calligraphic eccentricities to be observed in northern writing-centres such as Luxeuil and Corbie. Notwithstanding the high standards in epigraphy and calligraphy of Pope Damasus, and however well Uncial had been written within and without Rome, capital lettering in the West generally in the sixth and seventh centuries was unstandardized and hesitant. Moreover, from the standpoint of a fourth-century Roman, it was un-Latin. The fact remains that the prestige of the Byzantine goldsmiths was amounting almost to authority. It was an authority that arose from the deference paid to them as artists.

Even so, it can hardly be doubted that the authority of the artists extended only to the forms of the letters, not, that is to say, to the idea, if such there was, intended by a Greek and Latin combination symbolizing Imperial unity. This is a point to which attention will be given later.

The fact of the removal of artists to the new capital, with instructions to concentrate upon the task of glorifying the New Rome, combined with the subsequent event of the barbaric incursions upon the West, could only impoverish Old Rome. The wonder of the world, the Cathedral of the Holy Wisdom at Constantinople, was consecrated in 563—two years before the death of the great Justinian and the succession of Justin II, and five years before the Lombards flooded into Italy and made ready to besiege Rome.

The question remains: how was it possible that first-class lettering, executed for an imperial purpose only a few years after the Cathedral at Constantinople was finished, could take the shapes exhibited on the diplomatic gift to Old Rome of what Justin II and the whole Christian world believed to be the True Cross?

There could have been no deeply rooted tradition of fine lettering in a capital only 250 years of age. But had not the artists and sculptors, triumphant in mosaic and in other arts, settled a calligraphic style for the new capital's inscriptions? And if so, what relation does Justin's inscription bear to this settled style, if it existed? To establish an official alphabet in the new Imperial capital as it then was may not have been an easy administrative task to the architects of Constantinople.

Neither the ancient Greek nor the contemporary Roman standards could have made the slightest appeal to Constantine in connection with the plans for his new capital. The old Roman Square Capitals could not mean to the Christian monarch what they had meant to Augustus and Trajan. Their victories had not been won under the sign of the Chrismon. Nor could such Latin lettering appeal to a Greek-speaking populace. It is known that the passion for luxury which so strongly marked Byzantine society in the sixth century found its maximum expression in the metal crafts, above all, decoration in gold. Thus the pulpit in Hagia Sophia was faced with plaques of gold, and the altar-screen was decorated with figures of silver and sumptuous enamels in various splendid colours. Doubtless it was in one of the workshops attached to Hagia Sophia that the Cross of Justin II and his wife Sophia was designed and executed. It may be assumed that the engravers in such a workshop were often in consultation with those responsible for the gold coinage. But was there any authoritative direction given? Apparently not, but in the absence of any official directive the workers in mosaic and metal do appear to have devised their own lettering, and to have done so on the basis of popular understanding, as would be natural, given the demagogical basis of Byzantine political and religious life.

The lettering most familiar to the mass of the people is not that engraved on marble or stone, or engrossed on charters, but that struck on metal. Coinage is the most popularly distributed of all the applications of lettering. In consequence, as Alföldi has brought out, coins and medals are the media most used for propaganda. Hence they are significant for the interpretation of policy. They symbolize more powerfully than any other medium the bilingual structure of the Byzantine dominion and illustrate the social necessity to employ an alphabet effective in the service of a Greek-speaking population dominated by a Latin-speaking administration.

In dealing with this problem, the bureaucracy of Constantine had witnessed the assimilation of the Greek and Latin alphabets in process in Rome before the transfer of the capital. A precedent for Byzantium was the contemporary Chrismon of the Constantinian type with the XP. It was used by Justinian on his coins and objects. These have the forked A as well as the rounded ω. The early influence of the Aberkios inscription is not to be overlooked, and the early and frequent use in Rome of Greek kappa has been noticed among other Hellenic importations. In Egypt the practice could not have been rare.

There is evidence from Constantinople that in this capital, where two languages coexisted, the calligraphers engraved their Latin inscriptions in Greek characters —and their Greek inscriptions in Latin characters. Was this wholly an accident? wholly due to ignorance? Rather, it seems probable that scribes felt that the time encouraged them to intermix Greek with Latin forms, and vice versa. Thus Justin's cross could have been lettered on the principle that a bilingual alphabet was desirable if the political and religious attitudes of East and West were to be reconciled. There was to be no doubt on the point that Old Rome and the New were born to be administered as Christian. Old Rome had her first Christian governor in 325. The previous policy tolerating polytheism was reversed. Old Rome and New Rome were shown how little sympathy Constantine had with paganism when Sopatros the Neoplatonist was put to death sometime after 330. The lettering for the new religion would be new. Thus the successors of the Thirteenth Apostle never gave authority to the Square Capitals of Augustus. By the time of Justin II this had been the practice for two and a half centuries. Just as Graeco-Roman sculpture was pagan, all sculpture was disallowed in the churches of Constantinople. Equally the old Roman lettering standards set up by sculptors had no status and no future.

Hence it may be accepted that the inscription on the Cross of Justin II is evidence that the Byzantine Romans were willing to redesign the alphabet of the Latin Romans (if that is the way to express it); to give Imperial authority to an alphabet that would serve Old and New Rome, Greek and Latin. How great a service this had been to both communities henceforward, could it then have been made operative! The attempt might have been made by Constantine had he never abandoned Rome; not, indeed, that he could have imposed a brand-new Christian alphabet upon Rome, but he could have co-ordinated the administrative alphabets of the Eastern and Western halves of his Empire. That is to say Constantine could have done it then by an act of authority. Evidently he decided rather to tolerate an evolutionary process. Time and art would decide the constituents of the Christian alphabet.

But any intention of Justin II to encourage the use of a Graeco-Latin alphabet seems to have been left implicit. It was not followed up with a sanction of the kind that Charles the Great two centuries later was to give to his Latin alphabet, deliberately purified, as will be seen, from Byzantine accretions. As it was, in pre-Carolingian times, during the sixth century and later, East and West, alphabetically speaking, were in a state of half-hearted though practical reciprocity, which, it would appear, was understood equally by the Roman Bishops and the Eastern Emperors as a *modus vivendi*. A state of equilibrium existed. This the joint alphabetical system appropriately symbolizes. Unhappily it did not become permanent; the Pope had not the executive authority, nor the Emperor the present intention, to impose throughout his dominions a single Graeco-Roman alphabet. Apparently the Byzantine Imperial policy in this respect was one of common-sense *laissez-faire*.

It had never, so far, been part of Roman and papal policy to encourage the slightest separation either from the Imperial Court or from the Eastern Patriarchate. Nor was it the Emperor's policy to put himself, as a Christian, absolutely in the hands of his own Patriarch. Hence, down the centuries as far as the Palaeologi, the Emperors were more receptive of the claims of Rome to ecclesiastical primacy than were the Patriarchs of Constantinople. Thus for Pope and Emperor an assimilation of Greek and Roman forms would equally suit Old and New Rome, and reflect the formal dogmatic agreement of the Western and Eastern Patriarchates. The sixth and seventh centuries presented the last chance of achieving the administrative unity of the Church, of the Empire, and of a Graeco-Roman alphabet as its liturgical, legal, and literary medium. And to this day not merely the alphabet, or only Europe, but the whole wide world suffers from the fact that the opportunity of creating and establishing a Latin-Byzantine alphabet was lost. The prime consequence for a long time to come was that Rome would, in point of inscriptional calligraphy, stand upon the antique ways.

Reversion to an older, and, as the classicists and humanists would say, 'purer', form of lettering first appears in Old Rome as an aspect of the considered policy of one of the greatest successors of Peter. It cannot, however, be said that he initiated the tendency.

Gregory, rightly called the Great, had been ambassador of Rome at the Imperial Court, and, while appreciating the magnificence of New Rome in contrast with the ruination of Old Rome, he, as a son of St. Benedict, distrusted its power, its riches, its luxury, its marvels, and its splendours. For no other cause but Roman pride (it must be supposed) Gregory lived nearly seven years in Constantinople and never learned the rudiments of Greek. He was a very patrician, a Roman of the Romans. From the time he became Pope in 590 his policy was to stimulate pilgrimages to the shrines in Rome, by way of enforcing the lesson that the See of Peter was the first in Christendom; and that not because of any so-called 'unique' imperial, legal, or civic importance but because of the primacy in the Apostolic group bestowed by Christ upon Peter. Gregory, like Damasus, taught that although the chief of the Apostles was Bishop of Rome and martyred in Rome, these were but accidents; what was not an accident was that he, Peter, was the rock upon which Christ had established his Church. It was on account, solely, of Peter's unique authority, transmitted to his successors in office, that Rome was the primatial See. The imperial estate and the commercial prosperity of Constantinople were of the highest importance. The Emperor was the Emperor. But it did not follow that the Patriarch of a capital instituted by the all-powerful Emperor acquired ecclesiastical equality with the See founded by Peter as the Chief Apostle. Damasus refused to confirm the canons of the first Council of Constantinople which gave the Bishop of Constantinople the primacy of honour after the Bishop of Rome, because that city is 'New Rome'. Gregory reaffirmed Damasus's position and protested against the assumption by the Bishop of Constantinople of the novel title of 'Oecumenical Patriarch'; but he took to himself the novel title of 'Servant of the servants of God'. Moreover, Gregory, as a Roman aristocrat, necessarily looked askance upon Byzantine pretensions. There is no reason to think that the Pope, because he could not read Homer, had neglected his Virgil.

It is no surprise, therefore, that the lettering of Gregory's inscription should be as Roman as he could make them. It would be stretching the evidence too far to say that Gregory believed himself justified in appropriating the lettering as part of his heritage as the supreme authority of the Capital City. Even so, the choice was more than a personal whim and his chancery may have thought so. The situation was to have parallel in the pontificate of Gregory VII. In the basilica of St. Paul on the Ostian Way there is an inscription of the year 604, the year of Gregory's death (Plate 73). Its lettering is in the Square Roman antique style that would have been considered 'pagan' in Constantinople.

If it is clear that the antique capitals (see Plate 128) symbolized pre-Christian Rome, there was certainly also a feeling that many Christians in Rome entertained this belief in the early years of their new freedom under Constantine. As has been seen, Damasus acted on the conviction that for inscriptions honouring the martyrs 'pagan' capitals would be inappropriate.

In the time of Theodosius, Damasus was able to profit by the Imperial power

GREGORIVSEPISC·SERVVSSERVORVMDI·FELICISVBDIAC·ETRECTORI·PATRIMONIIAPPIAE
ETOMNIA QVAEHAECA POSTOLICAHABETECCLESIA BEATORVM PETRIACPAVLIQVORVMHONOREETBENEFICIISADOVI
OSINTAVCTORECOMMVNIA·ESSETAMENDEBETINAMMINISTRATIONEACTIONVMDIVERSITA SPERSONARVM VTINADSIGNATISCVIOVI
EBVSCVRAADHIBERIPOSSITIMPENSIOR· CVMIGITVR PRO ECCLESIA BEATIPAVLIAPOSTOLISOLICITVDONOSDEBITACOMMON
ET NEMINVSIIIICHA BER ELVMINARIAISDEMPRAECOEIDEICERNERETVR QVITOTVMMVNDVMLVMINEPRAEDICATIONISIMPLEVIT ETVA
EINCONGRVVMACESSEDVRISSIMVMVIDERETVR VTILLAEISPECIALITER POSSESSIONONSERVIRET INQVAPALMAMSVMENS MARTI
CAPITEESTTRVNCATVSVT VIVERET VTILEIVDICAVIMVSEANDEMMASSAMQVAEAQVASALVIA SNVNCVPATVR CVMOMNIBVS
NDISSVIS IDEST· CELLAVINARIA·ANTONIANO·VILLAPERTVSA· BIFVRCO·PRIMINIANO· CASSIANO·SILONIS·CORNELI
ESSELLATA· ATQVECORNELIANOCVMOMNIIVREINSTRVCTOINSTRVMENTOQVESVOETOMNIBVSGENERALITERA DEAM
ERTINENTIBVSEIVSCVMXPIGRATIALVMINARIBVSDEPVTARE ADICIENTESETIAMEIDEMCESSIONI HORTOSDVO PO
TO SINTERTIBERIMETPORTICVSIPSIVSECCLESIAE EVNTIBVSAPORTACIVITATISPARTEDEXTRA QVOS DIVIDITFLVVIVS
LMONINTERADFINESHORTIMONASTERIISCISTEPHANI QVODESTANCILLARVMDI POSITVMADSCMPAVLVMETAD
NESPOS SESSIONISPISINIANISIMVLETTERRVLAS QVAEVOCANTVRFOSSALATRONISPOSITAS·IDEMIVXTAEAN
EMPORTICVMEVNTIBVS SIMILITERAPORTAPARTESINISTRA VBINVNCVINEAEFACTAESVNT QVAETERRVLAECO
AFRENTABVNOLATEREPOSSES SIONIEVGENITISQDSCOLASTICI ETABALIAPARTEPOSSESSIONIMONASTSCIARISTIQVAE
MNIA QVONIAMDOADIVVANTEPERANTEDICTAEECCLESIAEPRAEPOSITOSQVIPERTEMPORAFVERINTAPRAESENTISEP
IMAINDICTIONEVOLVMVSORDINARI ETQVIDQVIDEXINDEACCESSERITLVMINARIBVSEIVSINPENDIATQVEIPSOSEXIN
EPONERERATIONES IDCIRCOEXPERIENTIAETVAEPRAECIPIMVSVTSVPRASCRIPTAMMASSAMA QVAS SALVIASCVMPRAE
OMINATISOMNIBVSFVNDISSVIS NECNONHORTVSATQVETERRVLASQVAESVPERIVSCONTINENTVRDEBREVIBVSSVISDELEREDEBE
TACAVPERRE ETCVNCTAADNOMENPRAEDICTAEECCLESIAEBEATIPAVLIAPOSTOLITRADEREQVATENVS SERVIENTESIBIPRAEPOSITI
MNIPOSTHOCCARENTESEXCVSATIONE DELVMINARIBVSEIVSITASINENOSTRASTVDEANTSOLICITVDINECOGITARE VTNVLLVSIL
ICVMQVAMNEGLECTVSPOSSITEXSISTERE FACTAVEROSVPRASCRIPTARVMOMNIVMRERVMTRADITIONEVOLVMVSVTHOCPRAE
CEPTVMINSCRINIOECCLESIAENOSTRAEEXPERENTIATVARESTITVAT BENEVALE

DAT·VIIKALFEBRVARIASIMPLIN.HOCARDINE·ANNOSECVNDOPICONSOLATXBEVSANNOPRIMOIND·SEPTIMA

73. Diploma of Gregory the Great. Rome. A.D. 604.

Rome, S. Paolo fuori le mura.

Square; elementary serifs.

Silvagni (ii) 4790; *Monumenta* i, pl. XII. 1; Diehl 37b.

to mark calligraphically the independence of the Church from the State. The Pope could concern himself only with the faith of the people. The defence and provision of the City was not the responsibility of Damasus. Conditions changed as the result of the barbarian invasions and the sacking of Rome in the fifth century and siege in the sixth century. The investment of northern Italy by the Lombards in 568 brought Rome and the Popes face to face with hordes which were not only barbarian but Arian. The City became more conscious of her position as the defender of orthodoxy and of civilization. Insistence upon the distinction between Church and State was less appropriate under John III (561-74) than it was under Damasus I (366-84). The Empire under Justin II (565-78) was not in the position it had been in under Theodosius I (379-95). The defence and provisions of the City by the Imperial Duke of Rome could not suffice when the Emperor, with his hands full of trouble in the East and in the Balkans, was unable to furnish troops. It was obvious to Rome that the conversion of Clovis in 496 was a capital event. Small wonder, therefore, that the resulting establishment of Catholicism among the Franks should determine the policy of the Popes. Hence Pelagius (579-90), desperately struggling with the Lombards, looked to a Western power for the help that he could not obtain from the Eastern Emperor. 'By a special dispensation of Divine Providence', he wrote to a chosen intermediary, 'the Frankish princes profess the orthodox faith', and therefore they, 'like the Roman Emperors, should protect this city.'

The political sense of the reference to the Roman Emperors was understood by the Pope's correspondent, indeed agent, Annarius, Bishop of Auxerre (573–605) and trusted adviser of the Frankish chieftains. Pelagius was a Pope of substance and deserves credit not only as the architect of policy, but for his choice of means and men to make it effective. He chose as his chief confidant and assistant the deacon Gregory, his successor as Pope in 590.

The point for us to notice is that the distance from Rome of the Emperor at Constantinople, the nearness to Rome of the Lombard leader at Pavia, and the incapacity of the Imperial Duke of Rome to provide for the defence of the City, made the Pope its sole defender. It is not surprising in these circumstances that the lettering of Pelagius II should be free from Hellenisms. The papal chancery provided for him a letter that was Roman, Square, and Papal in the sense that it was not Imperial. Pelagius, and Gregory after him, continued the proportions of Damasus, whose capitals, whether for the decorative martyrological inscriptions or for the plain diplomatic inscriptions, were Square, they were never imitatively Imperial. Their closest approximation is to the lettering typical of the best inscriptions of Constantine, which are perceptibly squarer than those of his predecessors.

Damasus's adoption of the Roman Square lettering, its maintenance and purification from succeeding non-Roman infiltrations by Pelagius II, is to be seen as a symbol of policy. There is a fine mosaic in the Church of St. Laurence *extra muros* which portrays Pelagius with the Saint, the inscription upon which is pure Roman (Plate 74). There is also an inscription of his time on marble, the lettering upon which is Roman, but rough. We need, however, to notice Pelagius's conscious 'romanità' and his nostalgia, expressed in his plea to Annarius, for the 'Roman Emperors'. He realized, first, the need of the City for a protector more seriously interested in the prosperity of Old Rome than the Emperors at New Rome could ever choose to be. Secondly, Pelagius realized that such an Imperial protector could only arise in the West. Finally he believed that such a leader would, for geographical and strategical reasons, appear in the North. These were the points of policy which would consistently guide the actions of the Apostolic See (as Damasus was the first to entitle the Church of Rome) for a very long period. This was the policy, too, which much later would bring into existence what we now recognize as Western Europe, under an Emperor crowned by the Pope.

This policy, initiated by Pelagius and supported by his prime deacon Gregory, was carried further when the deacon, in 590, succeeded him as Pope, and (as *de facto* civil head of the City) the temporal as well as the spiritual ruler of Rome. The difference between the lettering of Pelagius II and Gregory's is that Gregory's is more finely wrought. It is well seen on the long diploma finely engraved on marble and shown on Plate 73. It is seen to be notably free from non-Roman elements. The A in the inscription is of the relatively rare antique type with a double serif at the apex. The rejection of the long-familiar Hellenistic forked A was probably deliberate, even highly deliberate. This is confirmed by the reversion to an M with the centre fork reaching to the baseline. An important character

74. Mosaic. Pelagius presenting St. Laurence with a model of the basilica. Rome, circa 580.

Square capitals.

Enciclopaedia Cattolica, s.v. 'Pelagius II', vol. ix, p. 1079.

to notice is Q. It is once more a capital, though the shape of its tail is distinctive, and will later be found at Corbie. The serifs are not pronounced, so we may assume that the craftsmanship then available, though of high quality, was not what it had been before the invasions. Gregory's proportions may be slightly less square than the Imperial models of Augustus and Trajan, but they are by no means as narrow as Latin Rustic or Greek Majuscule. On the whole, Gregory's inscription is a papal design with an Imperial inflexion; as such it is impeccably Roman. For the sake of convenience this type of inscriptional Square Capital will be referred to below as 'Gregorian'; not, it should be understood, that it is suggested that the Pope was its inventor, but that he refined the design, and that his example later promoted its use among the Franks.

Outside the City the process of assimilation of Latin to Greek continued. Naturally it is found in Milan in the fifth century. In Ravenna, in the sixth century, the mosaics give us, among other Hellenisms, the forked A—as may be seen in the inscriptions in San Apollinare Nuovo. Most of the lettering in Ravenna is narrower than would have been usual in Rome, but never so condensed as Rustic.

The gradual disappearance of such a practical design as Rustic from the Christian repertory in Rome is difficult to explain. Traube's list of manuscripts in Rustic contains no Christian text. Perhaps its association with old pagan life and literature, coupled with the later anarchic condition of Rome, hastened its decline. Gregory may have thought it not sufficiently Imperial. Notwithstanding, the need (as the practical and rational Greeks recognized) for a condensed letter remained and would remain. Officials would be bound to see its economic advantage. The later struggle for recognition of a Condensed Capital, in a style more formal than the Rustic Capital, is foreshadowed even in Gregory's time. Gregory's choice of the Square Capital could not satisfy every need, but it did remain the Roman medium for papal inscriptions. The Square Capital much more aptly than the Rustic Capital symbolized Gregory's sense of continuity with the past of Rome, and his determination to suffer no diminution of the authority of the successors of Peter as its Bishop.

Little, however, was stable in this period. Sixty years after Gregory's death the prospects for even a fair standard of craftsmanly lettering could hardly be worse. Christianity itself, suicidally divided by schism, was soon threatened with death by Islam. The Arabs were at the gates of Byzantium continuously from 674 to 678. In Italy the Lombards were still devastating the Papal dominions. That the arts, including lettering, could flourish in such conditions was impossible. The chaos is reflected in popular inscriptions of the seventh and eighth centuries. It could only be in centres outside Rome that Latin lettering might flourish.

It will be well, before examining what in the westward regions may signify something for us, to guard against the belief that because, as will be seen, the principal and permanent factors of Western script were developed in France, therefore no interesting innovations occurred elsewhere. The need for speed in writing and economy in material was felt in all writing centres at one time or another, and sometimes simultaneously. Informal, narrow-bodied, utility hands would inevitably spring up, gain limited approval, be rejected or improved, ennobled, or even embellished. This is the process by which an originally humble hand works its way up to respectability, attains ennoblement, and ultimately succeeds in becoming established; thus it so consolidates its position as to supersede scripts which had from the very begining of their long career been calligraphical aristocrats. For these great scripts expense had been of little account. The process of their supersession by a script of lower rank is of great interest.

The present work, however, cannot aspire to be a contribution to palaeography; it is no more than an effort to trace the effect, so far as it may be done in a few lectures, of ecclesiastical and civil politics upon lettering and script. For this reason it is necessary to spend less time on changes in script and more time upon the power situation that later brought about the coalition of the Frankish

Kings and the Roman Popes: this carried with it a calligraphical evolution of unique significance to European civilization.

Between the sixth and seventh centuries the chief writing centres, in Italy and in Spain, tolerated numerous scriptorial innovations. They resulted from independent experiences, reciprocal causes, or the migration of manuscripts. These national, provincial, or local hands are all of interest in their own right, but few lead on to the kind of writing that ultimately, when given authority for political reasons, became general in Italy, Spain, and elsewhere. It is not to be thought, however, that the early stages of this predominantly Frankish process were independent of Spain and Italy. Rather, all these influences, deriving independently from diplomatic, trade, and literary necessities, became centralized in Gaul. The process was a natural evolution; it owed nothing to ecclesiastical or political direction. There was no authority competent in the sixth and seventh centuries, as there had been in the fourth century, to impose a script for books. At the end of the seventh century there may have existed a wider reading-public, but there was much less consent as to the alphabetical mediums. Rather, absence of uniformity in the style of transcribing first-class Christian texts was tolerated to an unprecedented degree.

Such toleration had no authority behind it beyond local custom. In other words, authority had broken down. Acceptance of wide variety in form and low standard of achievement was a free act on the part of the monasteries and chanceries occupied with writing. Such freedom was a new factor in the development of the Western medium of literary record. The authority that had once been strong enough to make Uncial the standard script for books, even those written in Jarrow, was now only a negative force. A Christian attitude was, however, still evident.

Nothing is more remarkable in the history of Latin Script than the continued disuse of the pagan economic Rustic. Such a suppression (it can have been nothing less) is explicable only by the intervention of an authority higher than that of a well-organized book-selling trade responsible to the pressure of economic forces.

It has been seen that, in the course of time, serifs were added to Uncial, and also to its nearest competitor, Half-Uncial. Thereby additional expense was created for both. An opportunity was open for a future third competitive book-script. This was the Minuscule, whose elements had long existed in fast Full-Cursive and, more explicitly, in the less speedy Half-Cursive on the St. Avitus model. It is to be observed that the original economy of these types of script lay in their speed of production, not in any saving of space. Even Half-Uncial and the best of the Half-Cursive are Square in proportion. It might be expected that even after twelve centuries, the Greek Square Capital of the fifth century B.C. would remain the norm in respect of quadrature, for Latin Capital (except for Rustic), Uncial, Half-Uncial, Half-Cursive, and Full-Cursive writing. Were there any exceptions among the non-Capital Scripts? All curves tend to diverge from the perpendicular and from the square. Did one of the many business or domestic cursives existing in the fifth to sixth centuries influence a script of greater importance than itself? A type of Cursive Chancery hand did so. It was an official Cursive less fast than the common correspondence hand, but it had the merit of saving space by its better discipline and increased narrowness of body.

Plate 75 shows the official Roman and provincial administrative hand of the sixth century in Imperial size. The letters (on papyrus) are grand in height, yet they are mean in width. Some of the Chancery hands officially practised were inclined right to left, and occasionally, as here, left to right. In all cases the narrow set of the letters was preserved. It was, however, the vertical style, which is the less easily and less rapidly achieved, that prevailed.

As practised in Gaul by the Franks as their diplomatic Cursive it remained vertical and increased in narrowness. It can be seen in a number of charters issued from the Merovingian Chanceries in the seventh century, of which the earliest is dated 625. Our specimen comes from the Chancery of Thierry III who, originally a monk of St. Denis, succeeded to the Kingdom of Neustria and

75. Fragment of a charter on papyrus from the chancery of a provincial *Comes sacri stabuli* at Ravenna. Roman official cursive. 6th century.

Geneva, Bibliothèque publique et universitaire, MS. Lat. 75.

Majestic cursive; condensed, ligatured letters, tightly-spaced words, long descenders, and hence plentifully-spaced lines.

Bruckner, *Ch. L.A.* i, 5.

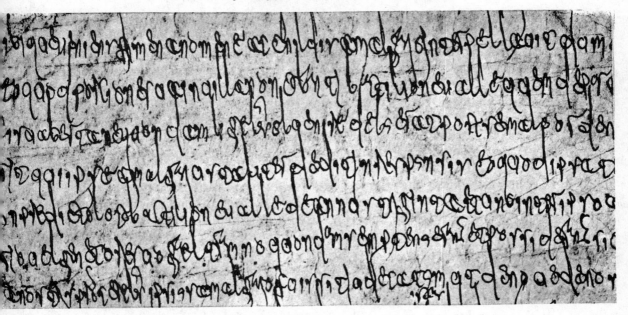

76. Diploma of Thierry III, King of the Franks. Compiègne. 30 June 679.

Paris, Archives nationales, K2, no. 13.

Merovingian current chancery cursive; condensed, intentionally upright but curving very slightly to left; strongly ligatured and linked; elongated ascenders.

E. H. J. Reusens, *Éléments de Paléographie* (Louvain, 1899), pp. 49-50, pl. viii (the original of our plate); *Album Paléographique*, ed. L. Delisle (Paris, École des Chartes, 1887), no. 16; Maunde Thompson 218 (seven lines); Lauer and Samaran, *Les Diplômes originaux des Mérovingiens* (Paris, 1908).

Burgundy in 675, and became King of the Franks in 679-80 (Plate 76). This excessively contracted and graceless script was written in 679. It is not merely condensed like the Ravenna Charter, but extra-condensed, and to all appearances is deliberately illegible and inimitable.

Unlike the Byzantine officials at Ravenna, their Frankish-Gaulish counterparts could not afford grandeur of scale and pomp of style in engrossing documents. The clerks, not having the means to display a script to the most spacious advantage, packed it as closely as possible, heeding only economy of vellum. This material was then new in Gaul. Thierry III was the first of the Merovingian kings to give up papyrus. By running together all letters and words they contrived a utilitarian and, to some extent, a regularized, scribble. Thus they conventionalized a perpendicular script which was far narrower in the body than any that had yet been tolerated in official service. It was by far the most economic script so far seen, perhaps anywhere, in the Latin script of the seventh century. Diplomas so written were accorded by the recipients (including as a matter of course the heads of religious houses) all the respect due to the Royal Chancery. An official script must always do this; but no script ever originated so permanent a change as that employed in

III

the documents dispatched by the Merovingian and Frankish kings from their hunting-lodges at various centres during the seventh and eighth centuries.

The change was the equivalent of a revolution. Its preliminaries need to be outlined. In 585 Columban, formerly of Bangor in Ireland, founded his abbey at Luxeuil, now in the Diocese of Besançon. The output of this house over the sixth to eighth centuries furnishes not only the most advanced writing of the period, but manuscripts of the highest liturgical importance. The finest of these are constructed and articulated with originality and care. They effectively illustrate the momentous change that was to end the long period during which Latin Uncial was the dominant script for such books.

One of the finest of the manuscripts of this style is the Sacramentary, the so-called 'Missale Gothicum', written, say the experts, in the late seventh or early eighth century. The Capital titlings used throughout this important manuscript express a degree of freedom unexpected in an otherwise strictly regulated Uncial manuscript (Plate 77).

An instance is the heading: MISSA IN NATALE SANCTI LAVRENTI. The exaggerated serifs of these capital forms, here seen, recall those of Roman inscriptions of the type employing the Philocalian serif, as copied by a pilgrim scribe with a turn for archaeology, like the compiler of the Sylloge Einsidlensis, who had seen some of the inscriptions of Damasus.

The 'Missale Gothicum' is, we have said, written in Uncial. Hence it is a Roman book. But the employment, even as an expedient, of a line or a page in a non-book hand for such an otherwise imposing work is non-Roman. Rather, such a device is absolutely Gallican or Merovingian. According to Mohlberg's analysis, the use of this new hand, or something similar to it, is not confined to one of the scribes at work on the codex but is common to all. In other words, the new script became the prime script of the calligraphical repertory of Luxeuil at, or before, the end of the seventh century.

The elevation of this decelerated and disciplined Merovingian Cursive for the entire text of a Lectionary (Plates 78-9) symbolizes the response of Luxeuil to the equation of the moment. It was, of all the choices made by a continental house in the whole history of Western script, the most significant. It implied nothing less than the establishment of what printers call 'lower-case', although, as will be seen in the next chapter, it was historically anticipated, but not genealogically originated, in Ireland.

The functional justification for the elevation of this script, humble indeed in relation to Uncial and Half-Uncial, lay in its factor of effectiveness in the conditions of its production. The history of the abbey may discover other factors which contributed to the change of script, so momentous in its consequences on the Continent. One of the aspects of the change is that a provincial script of Merovingian use competed with a universal script of Roman provenance. This was a development that could hardly have been conceived by Columbanus. The austere and particularist Irish missionary was forcibly extruded by Thierry II, the Burgundian King, about the year 610. The resulting divisions within the community were resolved by the intervention of one Agrestius. He had, says

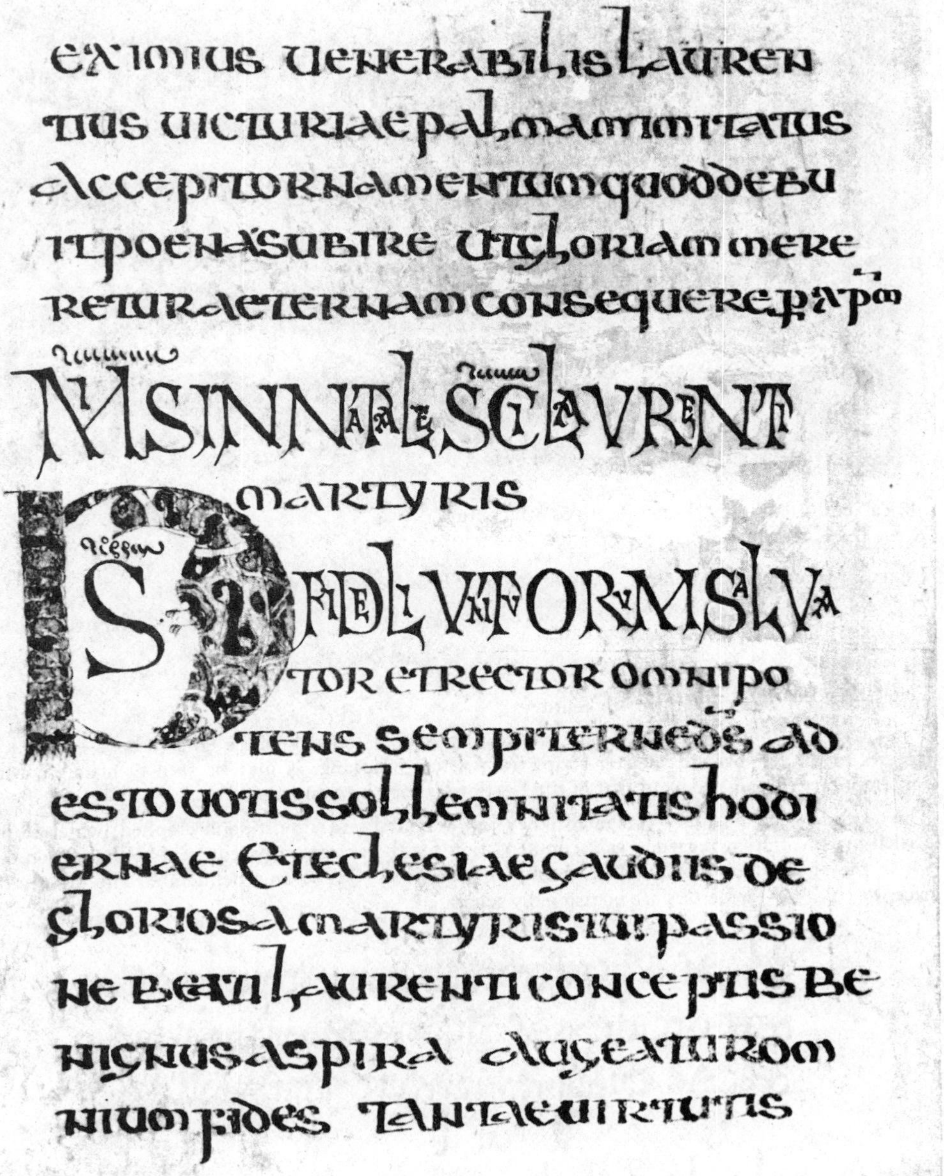

EXIMIUS UENERABILIS LAUREN
TIUS UICTURIAE PALMAM INITATUS
ACCEPTOR NAMENTUM QUOD DEBU
IT POENA SUBIRE UT GLORIAM MERE
RETUR AETERNAM CONSEQUERE p·p̄·m̄

IN SINN̄ALE SCI LAURENT

MARTYRIS

DS FIDELIVM FORMS LVA
TOR ET RECTOR OMNIPO
TENS SEMPITERNEDS AD
ESTO UOTIS SOLLEMNITATIS HODI
ERNAE ET ECLESIAE GAUDIIS DE
GLORIOSA MARTYRIS TUI PASSIO
NE BEATI LAURENTI CONCEPTIS BE
NIGNUS ASPIRA AUGEATUR OM
NIUM FIDES TANTAE UIRTUTIS

77. 'Missale Gothicum' or Sacramentary. Luxeuil, 7th to 8th century. Uncial with Luxeuil Minuscule for conventional liturgical formulae.

Vatican, MS. Regin. Lat. 317.

Titling and heading display script in multi-ligatured, decorated capitals, tricked out with wedge-shaped and bifurcated serifs.

A complete facsimile in C. Mohlberg, *Missale Gothicum* (*Codices liturgici* i), Augsburg, 1929.

C.L.A. i, no. 106; and see *C.L.A.* vi, pp. x, xv, xvi; E. A. Lowe, 'The Script of Luxeuil: a Title Vindicated' in *Revue Bénédictine*, nos. 1-2, 1953, which provides numerous facsimiles of the Luxeuil display captials. The forked A is to be observed as a normal but not invariable constituent.

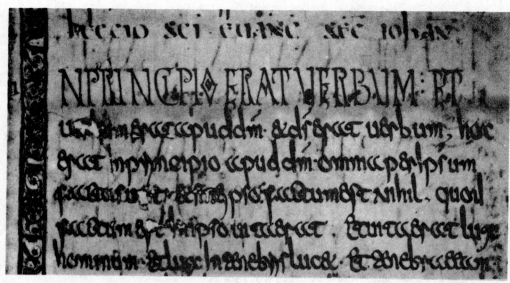

78. Luxeuil Lectionary. Luxeuil, 7th to 8th century.

Paris, Bibliothèque Nationale, Lat. 9427.

Luxeuil Minuscule; condensed; slanted; strongly ligatured and linked.

C.L.A. v, no. 579, and see vi, pp. xv–xvii; Reusens, pl. viii.

79. Lectionary. Luxeuil, 7th to 8th century.

The Luxeuil Minuscule analysed and redrawn by Arnold Bank. While a cursive book-script, it strongly inclines to the left like the charter-script from which it sprang, as may be seen in plate 76, with which contemporary diplomatic hand that of the Lectionary may be compared.

The ascenders are not only elongated; they are weighted and almost semi-clubbed, which is perhaps a scribal ornamentation regarded as a compensation for the absence of serifing. The inclination to the left which may have been accidental in the diploma of Thiery III is now deliberate. The descenders taper, except q; a = cc. The letters are occasionally separated.

Wilmart, been secretary to the King (he died in 613) before he became a monk of Luxeuil. Agrestius was a man of some force of character and led the opposition to Eustace, the pro-Columban abbot. As Agrestius's policy of mitigated asceticism was upheld at the Council of Mâcon in 625, he remained in a position to influence the conditions prevailing in the abbey. His policy attracted noble vocations and substantial benefactions, which, it may be guessed, made possible the firm establishment of a scriptorium at Luxeuil and the foundation of numerous daughter houses.

It is possible that Agrestius was responsible, at least in part, for the introduction into Luxeuil of some of the calligraphic practice which had long obtained in the Royal Merovingian Chancery. To be imaginative, it may have been he who promoted the use of its charter script for certain monastic purposes. In any case the post-Columban settlement at Luxeuil could hardly have avoided a reorganization of the scriptorium and the drafting of a programme of book-production. It may have been by some such means that the contemporary Merovingian Court-hand was not only chosen as the basis for the text of the Lectionary, but, so to say, 'canonized' in its decelerated form as a permanent addition to the abbey's repertory of scripts, even for the liturgy.

No charter of Thierry II is extant. That illustrated in Plate 76 provides a fair specimen of the standard diplomatic hand of the Merovingian Kings, whether of the northern or southern regions. It is written in the style with which Agrestius would have been professionally familiar before he entered Luxeuil as a monk, and which he, or some other Chancery scribe, introduced and successfully elaborated as a book-script. That it could have been used, even incidentally, in a Sacramentary at once elevated it; but, probably, time passed before it won recognition as a satisfactory solution to the problem of providing for the economic transcription of a Lectionary, whether the work was actually done in Luxeuil or elsewhere among the affiliated houses. It must have seemed, at the beginning of its liturgical career, a daring innovation. Was it not fortunate that the script bore the privilege of use in the Royal Chancery? Could it have been used even by a house with the prestige of Luxeuil, without royal agreement?

These are questions for which the answers can only be guessed. It is more than probable that the appropriation by the abbey scriptorium of the script distinctive of the Royal Chancery needed official permission. As this seems almost certain it may reasonably be argued that the adoption and use of the official script for monastic purposes were, in fact, accorded royal authority. In effect, therefore, the old international, ultramontane Uncial and Half-Uncial scripts were to be superseded. This occurred at a time when the cisalpine power was increasing its range and strength. The calligraphical changes at Luxeuil are not limited to the organization of the Minuscule.

The house of Luxeuil also adopted a new system of headlining (Capital, Uncial, and Half-Uncial scripts hierarchically displayed), a 'modern' system of punctuation (with the full point at the end of sentences, followed by an initial letter in Majuscule), and a canon of decorative elements (at the beginnings of chapters, and *initia* of feast days, etc.) in liturgical work. Many substantial and simultaneous changes therefore point to the adoption at Luxeuil of a well-considered calligraphical policy sometime after 610. It is to be borne in mind that the new style was followed, doubtless by order, in daughter-houses in all the Merovingian dominions. We are entitled, as it appears by the evidence, to surmise that the Luxeuil style, including headlines and Minuscule, won approval as a practical medium familiar already to the official classes in Gaul. It has already been described here as the first continental Minuscule to be given effective approval. We can now go further. The Luxeuil script is the first continental script, Minuscule or Majuscule, to be given so high a degree of patronage since the adoption of Greek Biblical Uncial for the codices commissioned in the fourth century. The adoption of Uncial for these texts of the Bible of Constantine's time was, it has been claimed above, an act of the competent Authority. The adoption of Minuscule for the text of the Luxeuil Lectionary was equivalent to an act of the competent Authority, and, moreover, the first of its kind in any cisalpine region.

It remains to notice one or two details in the design of the Luxeuil Minuscule, as practised in the house itself (as we may believe), and in other writing centres (within or without Frankish dominions). The treatment of the ascenders in any Minuscule written anywhere is always significant. The same is true of the ascenders in any Half-Uncial. In the case of the (native) Luxeuil script the ascenders are elongated, which alone is a sure indication of a Charter origin, thickened at the heads and tapered at the feet. It is important to observe that this practice results in all the ascenders being weighted to a degree out of all proportion to the rest of the script. It is not necessarily to be taken as an indication of the Charter origins, though the presence of such tricks may lead to that conclusion. They may have been inserted as a protection against 'passing off', in other words, as a constituent of 'house style'. The most that can be positively stated about this feature in the Merovingian charters of the seventh century is that a tendency to thickening as well as elongation may be perceived, but it is not in the least conspicuous. In the course of time and from place to place ascenders became both elongated and thickened or 'clubbed' to use Maunde Thompson's convenient term. In the Luxeuil script it becomes a fetish, so much so that the example influenced the later Carolingian hand. In the absence of any special investigation of the treatment of ascending and descending strokes it is impossible to do more than point to the emphatic position they occupy in the Minuscule written in Frankish houses during the seventh and eighth centuries, and, secondly, to the practice of 'clubbing', which may be found in Oriental scripts, principally Syrian, for theological texts which were esteemed in the West or at least read there in certain circles.

There is reason to believe that Syrian books were current in Gaul. It is well known that under the Merovingians trade had long been chiefly in the hands of Byzantines, Syrians, and Jews gathered in such centres as Marseilles, Bordeaux, and Orleans. This explains why when Guntram King of Burgundy entered Orleans in 585 he was acclaimed in the Latin, Hebrew, and Syriac languages, and how in 591 one Eusebius was appointed Bishop of Paris. He is recorded to have been criticized for giving preferment to his fellow Syrians. It is possible that a certain sacrosanct quality attached itself to a Syrian codex. What is certain is that the treatment of the ascenders in Syrian is closely paralleled in Luxeuil in the seventh–eighth century and in Italian centres at a later period. Whether there were any Syriac books in the library at Luxeuil is not known, but it is not unlikely. Ebersolt mentions the existence of Syrian codices in Tours and Bordeaux in the sixth century.

This said, we may now turn to the general appearance of the Luxeuil script. It has a strong character. Its curves, loops, ligatures, the double stroke of p and long s are all contrived to make it one that is very difficult to write well. This is one more indication that it originated as a Court-hand. In the interest of 'security' it was never thought advisable to make a diplomatic script easily legible and imitable. With good reason, therefore, Lowe writes: 'It is my conviction that the mastery of a script like "Luxeuil" cannot be acquired outside of the centre in which it was at home.' This is clearly true. While the canon is settled and definite, the script is so volatile and liquid that to write it at all requires great effort and sure control. 'One cannot copy such a script; one must be brought up on it', adds Lowe. 'A pupil may become a master and move to another centre and there write "Luxeuil".' It is impossible to believe that a script such as that shown in Plate 80 could have been developed independently.

80. Gregory the Great, *Regula pastoralis*. Ivrea (suffragan diocese of Turin), 7th to 8th century.

Ivrea, Biblioteca capitolare, MS. I (I).

Luxeuil Minuscule.

C.L.A. iii, no. 300.

The ascenders, while 'clubbed', as has been noted, are often exaggerated and there are numerous variants. The length of the ascenders gives the page a spacious effect which compensates for the extreme condensation of the design and the habit of ligaturing at will. Some words are written without lifting the pen. The brake having been put on the writing speed, the shapes of the letters were standardized and greater care was taken in forming them. The most important stage of all was reached when it was decided to set off the structures distinctly from one another—by unjoining them. It is in this process of separation that the Half-Cursive becomes transformed. It ceases to be a Condensed Half-Cursive and becomes a Minuscule. As in the early career of Half-Uncial, the strokes of this new script (for such it is), were not serifed.

The Lectionary is the most substantial remaining piece of writing in the Luxeuil Minuscule, just as the 'Missale Gothicum' is its greatest monument in Uncial. Now that Lowe has changed his mind about the date of the Uncial Sacramentary (as possibly of the seventh century, rather than definitely of the eighth) it is easier to bring it into relation with the Minuscule Lectionary, and to argue that the Uncial Sacramentary was written contemporaneously, or even first; and, if so, to confirm the hypothesis that Uncial was thereafter deliberately rejected for further liturgical work. That the Luxeuil Minuscule was not adopted out of mere calligraphical curiosity or wholly out of practical necessity is proved by the difficulty of writing it. This last-mentioned point is, however, only one of the reasons why, despite the local authority it enjoyed, the Luxeuil Minuscule fell short of taking the position of a national Merovingian book-script.

The house itself sustained a crushing blow in 731 when the Saracens, who had first crossed the Pyrenees in 720, arrived and massacred the community. Their defeat by Charles Martel in 732 was certainly decisive, but the recovery of Luxeuil must have been very slow, for the Saracens were not expelled from Narbonne until 759. It may be confidently assumed that books in Luxeuil script continued to be written in daughter houses. Nevertheless, it would seem that even a script so well organized and so tenacious of life needed, if it were to become national in its dispersion, to be written in greater quantities than was possible under the conditions prevailing in the southern regions of Gaul in the eighth century.

In any case it is always difficult for any script to make its way only by the manner in which it is made. It needs the backing of more than local authority to become the symbol of a successful cult—as for example the humanist revival of the fifteenth century. In the instance of Luxeuil the script was too well made and, more importantly (for the purpose of these lectures), its authority was too limited. It possessed high authority, but in the existing decentralized administration of the Merovingian kings it was insufficient to establish the Luxeuil Minuscule, or, indeed of any other. This is why the establishment of a national Frankish Minuscule—even one more simply organized than that of Luxeuil— was impossible at the end of the seventh or the beginning of the eighth century.

The requisite authority for such a national Minuscule needed itself to be national.

The ultimate basis of authority is, of course, power. The conquest of power among the barbarian tribes which had invaded the Gallo-Roman regions had pursued a long and inconsistent course, and had not reached stabilization by the beginning of the eighth century. The pressure of the Saracens alone made consolidation an urgent necessity for the Franks. The necessity for some discipline among the tribes, and for unity as the basis for survival, was too urgent to be ignored in the middle of the eighth century, and had indeed been building up for generations. The need for centralizing the power of the Franks was implicit in the baptism of Clovis at Reims in 496. As this policy very gradually became explicit, the Salian Franks gave increased patronage to the orthodox Catholic religion as it had been established by Theodosius I. These Franks appreciated the structure of the clerical estate, though they were in no mind to subject themselves to it. On the one hand they depraved the institutions by appointing bad bishops, and on the other conciliated the Almighty by encouraging good monks. No doubt there were valid political reasons for offsetting the power due to bishops' acquisition of riches by advancing abbots vowed to poverty. They thought it sound statecraft to encourage a third force, and to obtain for the abbeys immunity from the bishops.

As generations passed and kingdoms were divided the country was ravaged by dynastic wars. Rivalries spread to the nobles and the bishops. In 670 the Bishop of Autun succeeded in incarcerating a rival in Luxeuil. It was only when the Merovingian overlords consolidated their hold on the administration under Charles Martel (711–41) that the Frankish regions began to experience the effectiveness of law and order.

Frankish relations with the clergy and the papacy were permanently strengthened in 722, immediately after Boniface, on the admonition of Gregory II, sought the help of Charles Martel. Papal dignity and austerity were recommended to the Franks, and Roman liturgical correctness and musical purity were taken as models. The restoration of Roman culture, Roman Christianity, and Roman education became an integral part of state policy under Charles Martel's successor, Pepin. It led directly to the Frankish ascent to power by way of a supernatural religion, and entailed the assumption by the Frankish leaders of divine sanction. The kingdom made ready to claim the full respect of an authoritarian State. The obedience to be exacted was to be that due to an entity more than dynastic according to Merovingian custom. These kings had from the beginning claimed to be the sons of the gods. Their successors would claim an even greater and more immediate sanction.

Pepin, as a determined seeker after power, and planning in the middle years of the eighth century to usurp the place of Childeric III, who had reigned since 743, needed not only an elective kingship but a still greater moral sanction. To confirm his claims and exalt himself, Pepin needed a legitimation and recognition above that which could be accorded by an assembly of tribal chieftains. Also, what Pepin desired was the continuity of his family in the seat of authority.

Accordingly, he sought the highest sanction recognized by the Western communities. The deposer of the last Merovingian king was duly elected by the Frankish chiefs, and, furthermore, with the blessing of Pope Zachary (a realistic and subtle Greek), was crowned by Boniface. The ceremony at Soissons in 751 ensured to the newly elected monarch and his sons a crown which was the effective guarantee and symbol of the new Frankish king's absolute legitimacy. This, however, did not content Pepin. He required a ceremony even more striking. The new monarch was anxious to impress not only the West but the East: he would be anointed by the Pope himself. So it was that in 753 Zachary's successor Stephen confirmed Pepin the King with holy unction, and together with him anointed his two sons, Charles and Carloman, to the royal dignity.

It is not surprising, therefore, that under the regime of Pepin the strongest calligraphic impulse should extend from a northern house.

The abbey of Corbie in Picardy was the most important of the many daughter houses founded by Luxeuil. It had high patronage from the start. Bathilde, the widow of Clovis II, is celebrated as the foundress of the abbey, in association with her son Clothaire III (657–61), King of Neustria. It boasts a long line of other royal benefactors from Childeric II to Pepin himself, who, in the year of his coronation, confirmed the privileges of the abbey. The abbey naturally possessed a scriptorium. Pepin's ecclesiastical enactments alone would require much work on missals, etc. Various hands would be employed in liturgical, theological, domestic, and perhaps diplomatic writing. It is reasonable to guess that the Corbie scriptorium, in view of its situation, was one of the most up-to-date of its time, and conscious of the fact. The characteristic hands used at Corbie have been described by various experts who have separated them into classes. They are all Minuscules which in general type are distinct from that of Luxeuil, but reached, apparently, by the same process: that of reconditioning the contemporary diplomatic Cursive.

Perhaps the earliest Corbie manuscript is the Gregory of Tours, considered to have been written before the end of the seventh century. According to the experts the script is obviously based upon that used for royal charters of the period. The entry in *C.L.A.* v, no. 671 (Plate 81) indicates that it was 'written probably in North Eastern France in a centre under Luxeuil influence'. This is especially noticeable in the titles and displayed capitals, and in the use of Uncial and Half-Uncial. The Minuscule of the text, as highly characteristic of the contemporary diplomatic hand, is close to Luxeuil. But while this is obvious, it is equally obvious that the Corbie hand shown in the Gregory of Tours is less well controlled and less well suited to the relatively well-made Capitals and Uncials. In both Corbie and Luxeuil these last mentioned are regularly serifed, a fact to be noted. The extent to which the hand in the Corbie Gregory of Tours drew away from the example set by the founding house is interesting. But for the disaster that fell upon Luxeuil in 731, when the Saracens massacred the best part of the community, the house might have maintained its leadership as the great centre of Gallican writing. As the situation was, in the years when Luxeuil was in the state of confusion and stagnation, Corbie was able to experiment with

81. Gregory of Tours, *Historia Francorum*. ?Corbie, end of 7th century.

Paris, Bibliothèque Nationale, Lat. 17655.

Minuscule of strongly current type dependent upon Luxeuil.

C.L.A. v, no. 671.

profound and beneficial consequences to the history of handwriting and, it may as well be added, printing.

The date of this advanced Corbie type of writing is a matter of contention. Comparison of the several scripts known to have been used at this abbey in the eighth and early ninth centuries, in some instances—as it appears—successively, in others concurrently, points to the evolution of the Minuscule as having passed through several stages, under several quite different impulses. In the early stages the formal hands written at Corbie probably resembled those of its parent foundation, which we have observed at their best in the 'Missale Gothicum'. At an early stage, too, there was a less formal hand, the 'eNa' script, which might be described as a Quarter-Uncial; although, being closely written, irregularly spaced between letters, and highly ligatured, it has the appearance of being more cursive than it really is. Thus, like—but independently from—Luxeuil, an attempt was made to produce an acceptable book-hand on the basis of the Merovingian Charter-hand.

At a definite period, which can be associated with the abbacy of Leutchar (744-68), formal Uncial and Half-Uncial were assimilated to produce a basically Half-Uncial script with distinct Minuscule characteristics. The later career of a near-Minuscule script, which reached its prime under abbot Maurdramnus (771-80), constitutes a development of the first importance, which must be considered at length. Before so doing, the development of the third script, based more immediately on the contemporary Charter-hand, into the distinctive

82. Isidore, *Etymologiae*. Corbie, end of 8th century. Corbie 'ab' minuscule.
Brussels, Bibl. Royale II, 1556 (see *C.L.A.* vi, p. xxv).
Upright; formal; round; monoline in half-uncial proportions; curious *a b* forms attest its chancery origin.
C.L.A. x, no. 1554.

Corbie 'ab' script, should be recalled (Plate 82). This script was used for a considerable period, perhaps as well on account of its decorative quality as for its spaciousness. The available dates of its most frequent use suggest that it may have been protected at Corbie by the successor of Maurdramnus, Adalhard (780–826). The 'ab' script is well organized, and its conservation of double, triple, and even quadruple ligatures confirms its debt to a court-hand ancestry.

The Corbie scripts of the Leutchar period show the Minuscule in process of rapid development towards maturity. It is written with a broad pen, held in such a way as to require effort to maintain its formal character. The paucity of ligatures and the regular separation of letters are striking features.

The most significant fact about this script, therefore, is that it represents an early attempt to create a Minuscule independently of precedent, whether of Luxeuil or the Royal Chancery. Whereas the 'ab' script is a broadened and spaced version of the Chancery script, the script shown in Plate 82 is an attempt to reach the same objective by different, indeed opposed, means. The surviving manuscripts do not display the script to high advantage. It is an invention (the word is not too strong) that deserved for its execution a skilful hand. The passage in our plate from Berlin (Theol. Lat. 354) is a far better specimen of the hand than the Leningrad (F.V.I. 6) Ambrose (shown by Lindsay). Until Lowe used the plate (reproduced here as Plate 83) to illustrate his valuable preface to *C.L.A.* vi the significance (and the beauty) of the best script practised under Leutchar could not be adequately appreciated. Its Half-Uncial structure retained considerable authority in Corbie. What did this 'authority' amount to? It has been seen that Leutchar was abbot from 750 until 768. A work of unprecedented dimensions came into prospect within a few years. Some authority would be required for it.

Pepin died in 768. The project of an edition of the Bible may have been determined upon some years before. The paucity of exact dates makes a definite statement hazardous, but the coronation and consecration of Pepin makes very plausible the theory that the Frankish State decided before 768 to spend money on a huge text which was calculated to help ensure the continuity of the regime.

While elective coronation and episcopal consecration were deemed necessary to the recognition of the monarch, more was required for the perpetuation of the dynasty. For this purpose the sacral kingship of Israel offered the most exploitable precedent, as enabling Pepin and his sons to pose as the divinely appointed protectors of revealed truth. It also gave them the option of acting for the bishops against the magnates, for the people against both, and for all against the Pope. For Pepin, anointing signified a status which, while existing within the Church, was moreover, as monarch, superior in degree and distinct from it; and

83. Gregory the Great, *Moralia*. Corbie, after 750.

Berlin, Staat. Bibl., MS. Theol. Lat., fol. 354 (Rose 312).

Half-uncial tending towards minuscule. The Leutchar script. 'One of the most important manuscripts issued from Corbie' (E. A. Lowe). The plate shows how the scribe, being pressed for space, reduces the half-uncial element and practises the equivalent of the minuscule now known as the 'Maurdramnus' type. Leutchar was the predecessor of Maurdramnus as abbot of Corbie.

C.L.A. vi, pp. xiii, xxiv; *C.L.A.* viii, no. 1067a.

anterior to the jurisdiction of the successor of St. Peter. Pepin and his sons could point to Holy Writ with supreme confidence as giving the divine sanction for the hereditary principle.

Events were exceptionally favourable to Pepin when he was the new King of the Franks. In 751, the year of Pepin's coronation at Soissons, Ravenna was captured by the Lombards. They next made ready to attack Rome itself. Zachary's successor, Pope Stephen II, having vainly appealed to the Byzantines, renewed his predecessors' appeals for the help of the Franks. This gave Pepin the opportunity to induce the Pope to perform an additional ceremony, by means of which the King of the Franks was made a sacred as well as a royal personage. By procuring the presence of the Pope Pepin assured the sacrosanct continuity of what came to be called the Carolingian dynasty. The coronation and anointing ceremonies for Pepin were capital acts of policy necessary for a monarch who had won his throne by force. The appeal to the Bible and the writing of a new text were natural corollaries. The theme of a covenant between Almighty God and the House of David, the insistence of the sacredness of the king's person, the sacrilege of any subject who should stretch out a rebellious hand against 'the Lord's anointed', gave monarchs a divine right to personify their people. Moreover, the Lord had sworn never to bring ruin upon David's line, for he had made a covenant promising to keep his lamp unquenched for ever. No doubt Pepin had many learned clerks about him who could be trusted to point out the political significance of these divine admonitions and promises to 'the Lord's anointed'.

Did Pepin like such mitigations of divine punishment upon royal transgression? It is not to be doubted. For 400 years, from the time of David's active interest in the Ark to Josiah's reform, the dynastic Kings of Israel superintended the organization of public worship. Men like Pepin and his successors were bound to regard such a prospect as highly attractive.

Pepin's anointment therefore implied that his commission was directly from Almighty God and to him only would the *Dux et Princeps Francorum* be called to account. As *Patricius Romanorum*, the title conferred upon him by Pope Stephen, Pepin claimed equality with the highest Byzantine and Italian potentates. Any deference to the Roman Pope would be at the Frankish King's discretion, although the liturgical and theological direction of Rome would be admitted. Thus about 754 Pepin imposed upon his dominions the contemporary Roman Sacramentary and Antiphonary. Inevitably a large number of books were required for the achievement of Pepin's programme. Stephen's successor, Pope Paul I (757–67) supplied him with a library: 'I send you all the books which could be found . . . all written in the Greek tongue.' There were liturgical books, grammars, scientific treatises, an Aristotle, and a Dionysius. The consequent demands for new writing must have greatly exceeded the supplies available. The needs necessarily affected the programme of work in every competent monastic scriptorium. In such a situation the shapes and sizes of the letters could hardly remain unaffected. And this was the situation that Corbie faced under Leutchar.

That the books sent from Rome were in Minuscule is impossible. That some were in Uncial and some in Half-Uncial is more than probable. That their example would have been powerful is certain, perhaps equivalent to authoritative. What is demonstrable is that the Leutchar script is not based directly or indirectly upon the Merovingian Charter-hand but upon Half-Uncial. And it may plausibly be argued that Pope Paul's Latin collection sent to Pepin comprised more items in the economic Half-Uncial than in the expensive Uncial. It is hardly to be doubted that by Paul's time Half-Uncial had established itself as the normal book-script, especially for the Christian Fathers, and that not only in Rome. There is an interesting Hilary *De Trinitate* in Rome, written probably at Cagliari before 510, of which the bulk is in Half-Uncial and a portion in Uncial (Plate 84). It contains an inscription in the 'ab' script, which indicates that it was at Corbie before the end of the eighth century. By the time books such as this reached Corbie the script must have been long familiar there. Why had they not turned to it for inspiration before 750 or so? Had the provenance of Rome anything to do with Leutchar's choice? What else had been done, calligraphically, to Rome during the period when Half-Uncial was in the ascendant? And with what authority?

It has been noted above that the old Roman canon of Square Capitals was maintained by Constantine before he abandoned Rome for Byzantium in 330. The innovation of Damasus, still maintaining the Square base, was succeeded by lettering that faithfully reflected the poverty of the City. And this is equally true of Roman inscriptions in the Greek language. As has been pointed out, Byzantine influences are observable in Latin. The best extant inscription of the

84. St. Hilary, *De Trinitate*. Before 509–10.

Vatican, Archivio della basilica di S. Pietro, D. 182.

Half-uncial; very slightly sloped; heavy perpendiculars.

C.L.A. i, no. 1a.

sixth century is that for John II (533-5), but it contains ligatures even in the Pope's name. Though the capitals are neatly serifed their proportions are Rustic. The inscription (shown by Silvagni ii. 5) suggests no highly dignified ancestry, which makes significant the lapidary policy of Gregory I (590-604). His great pontificate has left us an excellent Square Latin capital inscription whose purity evokes the memory of noble antecedents. Gregory's alphabet (Plate 73) tolerates no Byzantine adhesions. It was Roman, and effectively re-creates for us, as must have been intended, the sense of the old Roman justice and discipline. His example gave a new meaning to Rome—but it was not immediately or consistently followed. The square proportions and the serif continued, but even so the square c, round E, coupled with the Hellenic habit of ligaturing, are found in ambitious Roman inscriptions of the end of the seventh century and the beginning of the eighth. The 'classical' canon simply could not withstand, in Rome or anywhere else in the West, the pressure of Hellenic habits and force of Byzantine example; nor, let it be marked, that of the theological and ecclesiastical ideas with which they corresponded.

The principal scriptoria in the Western patriarchate are to be found, notwithstanding the example of Gregory the Great, using Greek symbols, ligatures, or conventions. This seemingly deliberate theological comprehensiveness naturally gave the common-or-garden craftsmen of the period the opportunity to disregard secular precedent and canonical sanctity. The epitaph shown here (Plate 85) is an instance. Minuscule a and e coexist in the same word with capital and Uncial B and T. The clerks responsible could lose control of T and not apprehend its difference from t; use round E and e without discrimination. Remarkably enough the a remains standard, while M, N, O, and R are capitals and d is Uncial. The inscription represents an excellent specimen of very bad work done by an unusually illiterate engraver conscientiously reproducing a uniquely (it may be hoped) bastardized original.

Bastardized as it is, the lettering of this inscription eloquently proves that old and poor Rome, 400 years after the foundation of new Rome, did not separate herself from her rich rival. This must certainly be the inference to be drawn from this inscription. No doubt, too, the high degree of individualism and coarseness in Roman inscriptions of this period are aspects of the poverty and ruin of the former *caput mundi*, plundered, ravaged, and half-destroyed as she was in the eighth century. In 739 Gregory III had fruitlessly besought Charles Martel for help against the Lombards, the Greeks, and the Arabs. Rome was certainly in a pitiful state when the Franks were gaining steadily in power. In such circumstances Rome could hardly be relied upon to stabilize an alphabet of her own.

Moreover, such a mixture of Greek and Latin in Capital, Uncial, and Half-Uncial forms was made the more easy of acceptance by the presence of non-Roman elements. Gregory III (731-41), a great Pope indeed, was a Syrian. The oriental influence upon Latin was at its height at this time. The syncretic Graeco-Latin script for the titles of books and headings to chapters is found not only in Italy and France but in Ireland and England. There is no reason to suppose that

IC REQUIESCIT · IN PACE DOMNA BONU
SA QUIF ANN ꝯꝯꝯꝯ E DOMNO MENNA
QUIFIT MNOS   E ABEAT ANAT
EMA A IUDA SI QUIS ALTERUM OMINE SUP
ME POSUERI ANATHEMA ABEAS DD TRI
CENT DECEM ET OCTO PATRIARCHE
QUI CHANONCS ESPOSUERUN E DA SCA XPI
PUATUOR EUGUANGELIA

85. Epitaph of Bonosa and Menna. Rome. 7th–8th century.
Rome, Lateran Museum.
Mixed square capitals, uncials, half-uncials.
Diehl 37f.

Boniface would have rejected it. He must have seen it on one of his several visits to Rome in the time of this Pope. His reflections upon the divisions between the Eastern and Western Churches could have led him to the conclusion that it was well for Old Rome to conserve vestiges of its Greek-speaking past. Similar writing was to be seen in Fulda. It is not greatly different from that familiar to Willibrord. A syncretic Greek-Latin alphabet was not what the great Gregory would have approved, but while his successors were, not less than he, champions of the primacy of the See of Peter, they recognized that as the Christian Empire was half-Roman and half-Greek the appropriate script, at least for titles and headings in books and for the text of inscriptions, should partake of both alphabetical forms, as was already the case with Latin Uncial.

In conditions of almost constant war with the Lombards, the city of Constantine and Justinian was bound to dominate all 'style' in the West. However much the popes might encourage pilgrims to visit Rome to pray at the shrines of the martyrs, the emperors attracted more to Constantinople to trade at the markets for precious metals, diaphanous silks, instruments, and, no doubt, books and writing materials. The infiltration into the West of Byzantine customs was continuous. When the Irish brought their customs to Gaul, they were already considerably orientalized. Portable objects such as books and textiles, as among the most vendible of imports, would be sources of inspiration to Western artists and calligraphers, as also would be precious objects of gold and silver. Hence Byzantine decorative elements are found in Gallican manuscripts even when the textual basis is native. And this holds good throughout the eighth century and later. A plain set of, so to say, Gregorian capitals, plainly applied, is conspicuously absent from the great centres of writing in Lombardy and Gaul. The open, outline letters (they could be called 'contour' capitals) devised after the example of the Byzantine workers in precious metals persisted. Characteristic examples of such Merovingian decoration occur in the 'Missale Gothicum'. As long as the iconoclastic controversy was unsettled, scribes continued to lavish their skill and ingenuity upon naturalistic ornament and to indulge in tricks with serifs; and, as in the Book of Kells, upon the grotesque and dehumanized images of barbarian chieftains and gangsters.

This, then, was the general situation in the third quarter of the eighth century after Leutchar's period as abbot came to an end (768). Four years later a great enterprise was undertaken. At some time between 772 and 781, when Maurdramne or Maurdramnus was abbot of Corbie, the abbey undertook the transcription of the Old Testament. It was, so far as can be ascertained, the most ambitious setting forth of the text of Scripture that had been attempted on the Continent. The execution and scale were far less magnificent than the codex of the complete Bible written in England under Ceolfrid, abbot of Wearmouth from 682 and also of Jarrow from 688. While abbot, Ceolfrid had commissioned three copies of the Bible, one of which, now the Codex Amiatinus, he prepared for presentation to the Pope. On his journey to Rome, accompanying the Codex, the abbot (he was 74) at last reached Langres on the Upper Marne and died there in 716. The transcription of the Biblical texts at Jarrow-Wearmouth while Ceolfrid was abbot was, apparently, a work of pure piety. The cost must have been enormous. It was largely met by gifts from the kings of Northumbria. There is no evidence, however, that the royal interest in the Jarrow-Wearmouth Bible before 716 was in any sense personal or dynastic or political. Is the same true of the Bible which Corbie undertook after 772? What had earlier been done about the Bible?

Close as the connections of Pepin's Court were with Corbie, the parent house of Luxeuil was still a dominant factor in calligraphical style. It, too, was strengthened by considerable patronage. It is not surprising that eighth-century manuscripts surviving from this great centre should include texts of a Bible known to us in fragments only of Haggai, Ezekiel, Lamentations, and Jeremiah. That these are all Old Testament portions need not at first sight excite remark. It seems so probable that a New Testament was written at Luxeuil, at the same time and in the same style, that it is natural to assume the fact. But there is no evidence of its existence.

There is less doubt, perhaps, in this respect, about the codex of the Scriptures written, a generation later, at Corbie. This Bible, it may be inferred from the colophon, never proceeded beyond the Book of Maccabees. In all probability it may never have been intended to include the New Testament books as part of this text. It must be admitted here that Berger does not allude to this possibility in his description of the work. There is, however, no trace of any New Testament written in Corbie in the eighth century.

There are so many interesting features to be observed in this Old Testament that attention must be paid to it. A conspicuous feature of the work is the scribes' display of Square, Half-Square, Uncialized, and Hellenized Capitals. Thus we are given round ᛞ, Є, and Ц, ᛗ; though not uniformly. Square c is a frequent alternate character. In numerous titles (as for example Leviticus) the letters are narrow. Vowels are inserted in the body of consonants (as in INC.P.T and CAP.TUL.A. The Half-Square Capitals are, apparently, an invention of the house. The small Square Capitals used for the initial lines of chapters are basically pure Roman (in the Gregorian style) and have strokes which terminate in stoutly bracketed serifs. They are, however, variegated with Uncial elements and Greek capital ligatures. The high discipline of all these capital scripts is conspicuous, but it is equally obvious that the scribes, conscious of their skill, were opposed to uniformity and temperamentally inclined to show off. Heavy ornament is applied to large initial letters and simpler decoration to smaller letters. Some of the capitals (as in Genesis 1: 1) are coloured, on the principle later made more familiar by the scribes of ninth-century St. Gall. While the capital writing is of first-class quality for the period, the decoration is unskilful. The large size text Minuscule and the small size Capitular are both beautifully regular in pace of writing, and obedience to a canon is strict, though cc for a appears. The ascenders are regularly perpendicular, firmly headed with a slight taper, and the same firmness of pressure is applied to the backs of f, long s, and its ligatures s-t (in two forms); the script as a whole looks masculine as well as simple, in absolute contrast with the sinuous and complicated script of Luxeuil. The two

86. Fragments of the Gospels (Vulgate). 5th century.

Saint-Gall, Stiftsbibliothek, 1395.

Half-uncial of early type.

C.L.A. vii, no. 984.

Minuscules have nothing in common. The early ancestry of the Maurdramnus Minuscule is Uncial to Half-Uncial.

The Vulgate fragments, 'written in Italy, possibly during the lifetime of St. Jerome, to judge by the palaeography of the manuscript' according to Lowe, are therefore of great interest. They are now at St. Gall and Zürich, and show an early type of Half-Uncial (Plate 86). Had the ascenders and descenders of this script been slightly extended, and had the N been changed to n, they would have borne close comparison, in terms of size, form, pace, and weight, with the Maurdramnus text-script. The latter takes rank as not only the earliest datable 'Carolingian', but the finest Minuscule of the period.

It is unlikely that the Maurdramnus Bible was initiated independently of royal, or at least court, influence. The format began by being generous and the dimensions extensive. Whereas Ceolfrid's was one immense folio of 1,089 pages of Uncial, Maurdramnus's Bible was of smaller folio format, but, according to Berger, arranged to consist of no fewer than twelve volumes. On the assumption that the work occupied several monks for a number of years, and a great mass of vellum, and that it served no liturgical or parish purpose, the cost must have fallen exclusively upon the abbey's resources, unless either (1) the abbot was able to induce a royal benefactor to subsidize the work, or (2) the abbot had himself been induced, at royal instigation, to undertake it. Was there a political reason for it?

A vast political change had been effected a year after Maurdramnus became abbot. He became abbot one year after Carloman, Charles the Great's elder brother, died, in December 771. Charles thereupon seized the sole sovereignty, and for the first time all the Franks in Neustria and Austrasia became subject to one king. A new regime ruling one kingdom with laws in common was thereby constituted. Pope Stephen III (IV), who succeeded Paul I in 768, died in February 772, three months after Charles had seized power. His successor was Hadrian I. This Pope carried further the policy of Pelagius II (579–90) whose situation *vis-à-vis* the Lombards was exactly that of Hadrian, who had, therefore, the same reason for relying upon the Franks. Charles, well able to exploit his advantages, encountered no opposition from Hadrian. The beginnings of what was soon to become a Holy Roman Empire were in sight.

In English the adjective 'Carolingian', or the eighteenth-century form 'Carlovingian', is usually taken to describe what appertains to the dynasty founded by Charles the Great. The term thus ignores the pioneer activity of Pepin, who was the initiator of his son's religious and national policies, and even of the spread of education and the increase of book-production. The programme was now to be pushed forward with unprecedented energy. The way was at last open for the stabilization of a national Frankish script, suitable for all books of religious or other importance. It may have been a question in 772 whether the national Frankish script should be Frankish or Roman, or perhaps both. But in 772 it was too early to decide. What happened was that, soon after, Corbie took in hand the writing of the Old Testament.

It is difficult not to believe that the abbey was assisted at the beginning by royal funds for the writing of this, the greatest Bible so far attempted on the continent of Europe, and that a grant could be justified as an act of state by the nature of the Frankish king's claim and the divine prescription that the holiest of all books gave to it. A Christian monarch who practised divorce, bigamy, and concubinage needed all the sanctions he could get, as nine wives, approximately, could jointly testify. Next, Charles had forcibly taken the sole kingship, and forced Carloman's widow and sons into exile. They, too, could testify to the fact that Charles needed every available sanction. In the Bible for the benefit of all Charles's literate subjects, including the minority of those Frankish chieftains who sided with Carloman and his sons, was the text to which Charles as 'One from among thy brethren' could appeal to justify his seizure of power:

> When thou art come into the land which the Lord thy God giveth thee, and shalt possess it and shalt dwell therein, thou shalt also say 'I will set a King over me like the nations about me' . . . One from among thy brethren shalt thou set King over thee. (Deuteronomy 17: 14, 15.)

This was sufficient; but there are other texts of similar tenor, the propaganda value of which Charles's learned clerks could point out to their master. A book of such tremendous theocratic implications, conveyed with the blessing of Peter's successor, was literally a godsend to the power-seeking self-styled successor of David.

Such a book deserved to be written majestically, not, surely, in a merely elevated

Charter-hand. Instead, the script (Plate 87) of the Maurdramnus Bible is a consistent development of Minuscule, more directly out of Half-Uncial even than the earlier writing at Corbie between 750 and 758 practised under Leutchar. Of this Bible we have five volumes and part of a sixth. It begins on the grand scale for the Pentateuch and was reduced in size as the work proceeded. As the colophon (mentioning Maurdramnus) occurs at the end of Maccabees, it is more than plausible to say that the work consisted of the Old Testament only and that in all probability it was designed as such. The successors of David required no more. Were the New Testament required, and there is no evidence that it was, perhaps the successors of Peter might furnish the funds?

The general calligraphical situation at Corbie in the last quarter of the eighth century was that a fine book-script, appropriate for Biblical and liturgical work, but requiring less time in writing than Uncial and less room when written, was a need that would not be gainsaid. This problem had been faced at Luxeuil in connection with the new Lectionary. It was solved by the use of the form based on the diplomatic Cursive used in the Chanceries. At Corbie the need was met by Leutchar with a new, formal Minuscule formed on the basis of Half-Uncial. Maurdramnus contrived a refined version of the Leutchar script and thereby, calligraphically speaking, made a sound decision in respect of a Bible having some State patronage. The script has a majestic appearance. Beyond question its appearance is far superior for the purpose to any alternative, Uncial, Half-Uncial, the Luxeuil Minuscule, the 'ab' script, or the Leutchar script. But there is a technical objection to the Maurdramnus Minuscule.

The Luxeuil pen, held as it was for the execution of the decelerated Chancery Cursive, commanded an economy of speed and space greater than that reachable by the Corbie pen, held as it was for the accelerated Half-Uncial. Therefore the Luxeuil, as the hand more economic in space and more expeditious in speed, held the advantage.

Yet was that the way to secure respect for Pepin's and Charles's claim to be the *novus David*? This was never a merely temporary or 'picturesque' appellation. It was a monarchist demand intended to be taken by the present and next generation of Franks with the utmost seriousness. Alcuin was already in the habit of publicly and significantly referring to Charles as 'David'. This was Alcuin's propaganda for Charles. Had then 'David', successor to Pepin and Carloman, the greatest monarch in Western Christendom, no vested interest in the appearance of the book from which he derived his authority as 'the Lord's anointed'? Was an expeditious script of the Luxeuil type to be allowed in place of the more expensive hand that would be fit for a special copy of the text of Sacred Scripture? It was not a question of organizing a text for an 'edition' of a number of copies. That was to come. Now only one copy, in a set of volumes, was in question.

When the Latin Christians in the fourth century organized their Uncial and a later generation organized Half-Uncial, they recognized the fact that the Scriptures, the Sacraments, and the Fathers required a letter and a *mise-en-page* that would correspond in dignity with their sacred subject. That recognition was

87. Old Testament. Corbie, 772–81. Minuscule.

Amiens, Bibliothèque municipale, MSS. 6, 7, 9, 11, 12 (fols. 2–192); Paris, Bibliothèque Nationale, Lat. 13174 (fols. 136, 138).

The Maurdramnus script. An elaborate, 'artistic' Biblical minuscule formed on the basis of half-uncial, which is used for *incipits* and *explicits* etc., with weighted ascenders. The diagram below shows the alphabet and lining scheme.

C.L.A. vi, no. 707 for another specimen of the script; two pages shown in G. Ooghe, 'L'écriture de Corbie' in [André Verfaillie, doyen de Corbie,] *Corbie Abbaye Royale Volume du XIIIe Centenaire* (Lille, 1963), pp. 263–82.

strong in the attitude of Luxeuil as represented by its 'Missale Gothicum'. It was weakened by the later decision at Luxeuil to elevate the contemporary Charter-hand into a book-Minuscule for use in its Lectionary. At Corbie under Maurdram-nus the earlier, strong, recognition was restored. The contrast between it and the Luxeuil Minuscule, or some adaptation of it, is unmistakable. Which would survive when it came to the multiplication of texts for an increasingly literate nation?

A boom in writing that might result from an act of Church-State policy would, in the absence of authority, give the race to the swifter script, i.e. the Luxeuil Minuscule. This would be far from dignified if applied to Sacramentaries. Evidently Corbie first appreciated this possibility, when the house evolved its 'ab' compromise, the Merovingian Charter-hand broadened for book-use. Retaining peculiarities unknown to any other house, it is a script that is by no means unsuitable for canon law, for which purpose, indeed, it was used concurrently with the Maurdramnus Minuscule for the Bible. It is not unexpected, therefore, to find the 'ab' Minuscule being continued under Maurdramnus's successor, Adalhard, and much later.

After the rule of Maurdramnus there was, in fact, some reaction at Corbie in favour of calligraphical economy. The abbot's resignation in 781 was perhaps under pressure. His successor Adalhard used a less splendid script on the lines of his penultimate predecessor, Leutchar. Adalhard was a cousin of Charlemagne. In 771, after he had taken objection to Charles's repudiation of his wife, the daughter of the Lombard king Desiderius, he threw up his place at the Frankish Court, entered Corbie, and, after transferring to Monte Cassino, finally superseded Maurdramnus as Abbot of Corbie. He must have been surprised when the Lombard king Desiderius, defeated at Pavia in 774, was brought to die at Corbie. That Corbie should be Charles's choice would not have surprised him. It had been a royal annex and was obviously the focus of scriptorial initiative.

Among the solutions to the problems of finding a Minuscule for general book-work, there now existed at Corbie the Biblical Minuscule and at least two other Corbie sets of Minuscule. A simultaneous development, however, was in process after Charlemagne had united Austrasia and Neustria and had re-established in great style the old, small Court Manor of Aachen as his normal Palace and capital city. He erected his church at Aachen on the model of the two churches of the Holy Virgin in the palace of Blachernae in Constantinople, the churches most representative of Byzantine monarchy; they had earlier on influenced St. Vitale in Ravenna, whence Charles took mosaics and other decorations with the connivance of Pope Hadrian I. Now Charles, By the Grace of God King of the Franks and Lombards and Patrician of the Romans, sought to aggrandize himself as a leader of civilization in the eyes of his barbarous subjects and sought to rival Constantine and Justinian. Charles, too, would create a city of unique splendour, more luxurious than Byzantine Ravenna—whence loads of ornaments were brought north, more powerful than Rome—whose bishop was glad to bestow precious mosaics upon him. To the Palace, as the most sumptuous residence ever seen in cisalpine Europe, were to be attracted every kind of merchant, intellectual, and artist. It was a project that would have appealed to Pepin.

Among the institutions duly attached to the capital, in addition to the offices of state and centres of trade, was an academy to which was attached a scriptorium. It was exceptionally well endowed, and its style and execution as to script, decoration, and material rose to a height of excellence never before seen in the West and hardly surpassed in the East. This standard was reached soon after Corbie had passed its peak of achievement under Maurdramnus. The luxury of the Gospel Book 'written doubtless at the order of Charlemagne' (*C.L.A.* v, no. 681), and the dedicating verses enable the work to be attributed to the artist Godescalc, and assigned the years 781–3 as date (Plate 88). The text consists of the lessons to be read in the Liturgy and is written in serifed Uncials with, it is to be noted, some legends in Rustic. The chapter-titles are in Roman Capitals of Gregorian type, though with round E and other Uncial elements. The whole is written on purple vellum, with much silver as well as gold for the scripts. The dedicatory verses, however, are in a Minuscule of fine formation. At about the same time (i.e. *c.* 780) one Ada (whether a daughter of Pepin is uncertain) commissioned a Gospel Book from the Palace School. The script throughout is serifed Uncial, written in gold on purple vellum. There are also in the *Codex Adae* (Plate 89) leaves in a Minuscule identical with that in the Gospel Book of Charles just mentioned, and therefore attributed by scholars to the hand of Godescalc. It is a well-formed script, written with great regularity, the intention being to produce the most elegant specimen that this kind of writing could possibly attain. The ascenders are carefully tapered from the heads and only sometimes 'clubbed'. The scribe normally achieves a perpendicular effect, even if there is a marked tendency at times to slant towards the left. In short, the Godescalc script is a most admirable secondary book-hand, well fitted to take its place in a royal book in company with the scribe's (or scribes') noble repertory of Square Capitals, Rustic Capitals, and Uncials.

It is not surprising, therefore, that the Minuscule to be seen in these two datable Biblical codices should be universally described as 'the Carolingian Minuscule'. It is not easy to improve on this title, faulty as it may be when the Maurdramnus Minuscule is also labelled 'Carolingian'—as is justified by its form and date.

But are the Maurdramnus and Godescalc hands equally 'Carolingian' in all respects? The dates coincide; the former's Bible was completed between 772 and 781 and the Godescalc Gospel Books between 781 and 783. Both are certainly in Minuscule. There are, in fact, two Minuscules. The difference arises from the fact that the Godescalc hand is the equivalent of a younger branch of the Minuscule family, itself a younger branch of the Half-Uncial dynasty. Comparison of the Maurdramnus and Godescalc Minuscules demonstrates that the former is the more nearly related to Half-Uncial. It is enough to point out the practice of beginning the initial line of a chapter with two or three words in serifed Half-Uncial and following on in Minuscule. The close technical relation of the two scripts is proved by the use of the same pen held in the same 'straight' way.

The most highly finished Uncials and Half-Uncials are very careful constructions. They are made with the pen held in the 'straight', i.e. perpendicular,

88. Evangelistarium, written by Godescalc. A.D. 781–3.
Paris, Bibliothèque Nationale, Nouv. Acq. Lat. 1203.
Uncial and Caroline minuscule.
Steffens 45a; *C.L.A.* v, no. 681.

89. Gospel Lectionary ('Codex Adae'). Aachen, *c*. 800.
Trier, Stadtbibliothek 22.
Caroline minuscule resembling the hand of Godescalc (cf. plate 88). The ascenders are heavily weighted.
K. Menzel *et al.*, *Die Trierer Ada-Handschrift* (Leipzig, 1889); Steffens 45ᵛ; *C.L.A.* ix, no. 1366.

position, while the best Cursives are elevated notations written with the pen held in the 'slanted' position, i.e. pointing away from the shoulder. Uncial and Half-Uncial are both constructions which are possible to write only with care; and the Cursive, whether Diplomatic or Domestic, is a notation capable of being written quickly. It has been seen that the Luxeuil Minuscule is a regularized version of the Cursive in use in the Royal Chanceries. These Cursives, naturally, were written with moderate speed, and with the pen held in such a way as to encourage dispatch. It is to be noticed, however, that the Corbie 'ab' script, which is a broadened version of an original Diplomatic Cursive, is written with a special kind of pen, held in the Half-Uncial position. This practice effectively decelerated the script.

A relationship between the Godescalc Minuscule and the Merovingian Cursive is indicated by the 'rta' ligature which occurs on fol. 39 recto of the Ada Codex. The script has Half-Uncial characteristics, but it is produced by a pen held in a position that permits the letters to be made more rapidly. In other words, the Godescalc Minuscule is a more economic medium. Compared with the Maurdramnus it is an inferior script. Brilliant as the palace scribes were, the results they achieved by their use of gold and purple, the virtues of their Minuscule, were less the majesty and grace of its form than the compactness of its body and the ease with which it achieved its effects.

The adoption of the Godescalc Minuscule for use in such a royal text as the Codex Adae can only be interpreted as a deliberate act of calligraphic policy, the result of a careful estimate of the time and materials available. In judging of the policy responsible for the calligraphy of the Ada Gospels account needs to be taken of the fact that the book also employs expertly made Square Capitals and Uncials for titles and introductions. The design of the Capital is to be noted in view of later developments at Tours. The so-called Palace School practised, at this time, a Square Roman Capital Script whose form would have pleased Gregory the Great—who, it has been remarked above, ejected from his Square Capital alphabet all Byzantine abbreviations and combinations. It was, however, a papal alphabet and not a reproduction of the old Imperial alphabet. Godescalc's, or rather the Palace Capital, alphabet was similar. It is very carefully serifed by an expert calligrapher well aware of the inspired nature of his text and the exalted personage for whom it was to be presented. The whole of this display apparatus auxiliary to the Minuscule is Roman.

A much more sumptuous production of the Palace School is the Psalter commissioned by Charles and executed by Dagulf for presentation to Pope Hadrian I (Plate 90). Here the Godescalc Minuscule is given the supreme honour of being written in gold for the text of the Psalms. The titles are in Square Capitals with Rustic. In both scripts in this Psalter there is a slight tendency towards a decorative serif. In other words, the Palace School had for its Square Roman Capitals a basic proportion and style that the present writer would describe as Gregorian with Damasine vestiges (Plate 91), and therefore appropriate for use in a Psalter designed for presentation by the Frankish king to the Roman pope. 'The manuscript constitutes a milestone in the history of Caroline minuscule' (Lowe, *C.L.A.* x, no. 1504). There is no exaggeration here. In every respect the minuscule of Dagulf is a notable advance upon that of Godescalc. The Psalter, when completed, was not delivered to Pope Hadrian, since he died in 795 before the present could reach him.

The form of the legends in Square Roman (as I venture to label 'Gregorian' for this purpose) Capitals needs to be noted. That of the legends in later Frankish productions markedly differs in detail of style. The difference was deliberate, as comparison will make manifest.

These later legends or titles are best seen (so far as facsimiles are a guide) in manuscripts executed at Tours. It is unfortunate that few of the manuscripts of the period can be precisely dated. We do know that the Admonitio Generalis in which the king of the Franks embodied the directives of his liturgical and other reforms was signed in 789. The scribes of the new books were to be mature and 'si opus est evangelium, psalterium et missale scribere perfectae aetatis homines scribant cum diligentia'. This may have been the starting-point of Alcuin's revision of the text of the Bible. That he would have appreciated the political value of the Old Testament and its immediate importance to Charles cannot be doubted. There is much evidence to prove that Alcuin inspired the 'imperialist' element at the Court of Charles and organized its application and supervised its propaganda.

Alcuin was regularly using the term '*imperium*' from at least as early as 798, and there is little room for doubt that Alcuin had associated the ancient Roman

Aurea dauiticos en pingit littera cantus.
Aornari decuit tam bene tale melos.
Aurea uerba sonant promittunt aurea regna
mansurum q; canunt & sine fine bonum.
Haec meritot abulis cultim decorant eburnis.
quas mire exculpsit ingeniosa manus.
Illic psalterii prima ostentatur origo.
& rex doctiloquax ipse canere choro.
Vt quedecus rediit sublatis sentibus olim.
quod fuerat studio peruigilante uiri.
Aurea progenies fuluo.   lucidior auro.
carle iubar nostrum plebis & altus amor.
Rex pie dux sapiens uirtute insignis & armis.
quem decet omne decens quicquid in orbe placet.
Exiguus famuli dagulfi sume laborem.
dignanter docti mitis & orelege.
Si tua per multos decorentur sceptra triumphos.
dauitico   & demum consociere choro.

90. Golden Psalter of Charles the Great, written for presentation to Hadrian I, f. 4ᵛ. Carolingian minuscule. 8th century.

Vienna, Österreichifche Nationalbibliothek, Cod. 1861.

Dagulf's minuscule written in gold. Unserifed. Uncial versals. The titles are in square capitals with bracketed serifs occasionally decorated (see plate 91); subtitles are in condensed capitals with informal serifs frequently decorated.

The minuscule is perfectly regular in spacing and form. The ascenders are less heavily stressed. The initial forked A will be noticed. It also occurs as the initial to the Gospel of Godescalc (plate 88).

J. R. von Karabacek and R. Beer, *Monumenta Palaeographica Vindobonensia*, vol. i (Leipzig, 1910), plates 17-26; *C.L.A.* x, no. 1504.

91. Golden Psalter of Charles the Great, f. 25ʳ. 8th century. See Plate 90.
Dagulf's 'Gregorian' capitals with Damasine vestiges.
Karabacek and Beer i, plate 19.

Empire with potential Western Empire, and next with the policy of making actual the '*imperium Christianum*' already prayed for in the official Roman-Frankish liturgy. In the words of Levison, Alcuin may, therefore, be said to have made the 'notion of "empire" more familiar to the King'. As Levison expresses it, 'the liturgical texts of the eighth century insinuated the continuity of the "Imperium Romanum" and of his [Charles's] "imperium"'. That Alcuin was the principal organizing force behind the revision of the biblical, liturgical, and other texts authorized by Charles is morally certain.

A digression is necessary at this point as it must be emphasized that the 'continuity' mentioned by Levison carries with it the implication that Alcuin was acting in accordance with a conception already accepted as the basis for the future theocratic Frankish State. Some such conception may be traced as far back as Clovis and lay behind the forcible assumption of royal power by Pepin and the subsequent sacring in 751 by Boniface. This was a significant step in a series of revolutionary acts which culminated in the politico-ecclesiastical Romano-Frankish treaty of 754. One of the main points of the agreement negotiated by the Pope (in person) with Pepin was the legitimization of a dynasty which had obtained power by force. For this only supreme sanction would suffice. The continued weakness of the Emperors at Byzantium in face of the pressure upon Rome of the iconoclast Lombards made the pope desperate, and Pope Stephen II (752-7), accompanied by a train of advisers, journeyed to Pepin's court to conduct the negotiations. During the proceedings he conferred upon Pepin and his two sons the title of 'Patricians of the Romans' and then anointed them. Furthermore, at an assembly of the Frankish nobles Stephen forbade, under penalty of excommunication, any to elect as king one who was not of the blood of Pepin. At the same assembly, the Romans gained a guarantee of the extension of the limited duchy of Rome to a large province, protected by the kings of the Franks and the Lord's anointed, with the successor of St. Peter as undisputed Sovereign.

The plan of buttressing the material power of the Frankish (we may now say Carolingian) State with the spiritual authority of the Roman Church was carefully prepared. There is no reason to believe that the problem of sovereignty was disregarded by the Franks, or that they would accept any ecclesiastical formulas that might in certain circumstances limit the range of royal jurisdiction, and thereby open up the possibility of allowing absolute sovereignty to the bishops of Rome, successors as they were of St. Peter to whom Pepin professed a genuine devotion. But the king was to be the anointed of Almighty God Himself.

The inclusion of unction was new in the Frankish regions (and apart, perhaps, from some Anglo-Saxon and Spanish anticipations) and unknown in the East. The bringing into the coronation rite of the Franks of this Old Testament precedent may have been ordered by Rome but it is at least equally probable that the impulse came from the king's inner circle of policy-makers. It may be taken for granted that they knew their Bible or at least those references which interested them.

That St. Peter in his first Epistle enjoins obedience to the King 'who enjoys the chief power' was doubtless appreciated by Pepin when he was first crowned in 751. The king's chief concern in 754 was for recognition of his family as the sole legitimate heirs to the monarchy. To secure this supreme sanction was to achieve the culmination of Pepin's ambition. And for this sanction the text of the New Testament fell short. The legitimacy of Pepin's line could not be guaranteed by St. Peter alone.

Pepin was surely aware that the King of the Lombards entitled himself 'Agilulf gratia Dei rex totius Italiae'. The Frankish Chancery, therefore, would require Pepin to be recognized as the anointed of the Lord. Hence, the implications of the ecclesiastical ceremonies would be considered with the greatest care by both teams of canon and civil lawyers. They found the texts they needed in the first book of Samuel, whose action towards Saul and David gave Stephen the necessary precedent and Pepin the divine sanction required by the situation. Hence, Stephen's own words to Pepin: 'It is the Lord who through our lowliness consecrates you as King.'

For all these reasons it is the less certain that Alcuin was the creator, though it is evident that he was the agent of the liturgical changes which were intended to lead to the sacral Coronation of Charles the Great as Emperor in 800 by Pope Hadrian's successor, Leo III (795–816). It is important to view the origins of the Carolingian imperialist policy as anterior to both Charles and Alcuin if the consequences in book production are to be understood. To anoint the King of the Franks and invest him with a quasi-sacerdotal character was practical politics. It was certainly no less later for Charles in the time of Alcuin. The means of propaganda was principally the Bible, in which anointing was ordained, and the liturgy, in which the prayers for the Empire were 'insinuated'.

The Old Testament, assuredly, was the primary document. Indeed, Schramm argues that it is possible that, independently of any Visigothic example, the Frankish Chancery adopted anointing under the direct influence of the Bible. It may be more than possible; it is the most probable explanation. How, otherwise, can we explain the fact that the early Carolingian kings and emperors gave such emphatic support to the transcription of the Bible? Why should they encourage Luxeuil and Corbie to execute such expensive texts of it?

These codices, it needs to be remarked, were gloriously decorated, those of Tours less so than those of Aachen. Nevertheless, the illumination lavished on Holy Writ contrasts with the relative simplicity of the display considered appropriate for the Liturgy. The display system practised by the Palace School comprises Square ('Gregorian') Capital, Uncial, Half-Uncial, and Minuscule hierarchy for titles, sub-titles, chapter-lists, and text. A similar hierarchy was standardized at Luxeuil, and next at Corbie. It possessed prescriptive rights for over a century when the leading scribes of the Palace School, such as Godescalc and Dagulf, established the 'house style'—to use a modern publishing term. They kept this hierarchical system. But there was a notable addition. For use as colophons and as secondary titles in the hierarchy, the palace resuscitated the Rustic Capital. No doubt Rustic had been used here and there before 780 but its use in royal books must have been the result of deliberate choice. If Rustic had been discarded as non-Christian in the fourth century, by Charles's time it was policy to overlook its pagan associations. The instructed bureaucrats in Charles's service discriminated in the other direction. What was then significant to them about Rustic Capitals was that they were Roman, and if they were not Christian, Charles's administration would baptize them.

This is the first, modest, sign of the use as insignia of Imperial Roman standards of lettering outside the Rome of the great Gregory. It has been noted above that the Square Capitals which had been used in Luxeuil and Corbie were given decorated serifs as if the original scribe had taken as an example the martyrological inscriptions of Damasus I. The Palace School reduced the ornament of the Square Capitals, thereby shaping them on Gregorian lines. This may seem to have been accidental, but the revival of Rustic cannot be said to have been a scribe's whim. It hints at a more complete restoration of Roman forms, because they were first Roman and later 'Gregorian' (in our sense); it symbolizes a nationalized plan long present in the minds of the policy-makers of Charles's Court. That policy, indeed, was already in process of formation under Pepin; it aimed, eventually, at the appropriation and use as Imperial insignia of the typical Roman scripts. Its objectives under Charlemagne would not permit the Papacy to identify itself with the Empire. The difference in policy between Pepin and Charlemagne was not one of object, but of acceleration in reaching it.

The use for luxury codices, like the Evangeliary and the Psalter, of a Minuscule as a script more compact in the body and needing less time to write, may have been decided upon in view of the plans to proceed with a State educational project, the greatest ever undertaken in the West, or perhaps anywhere at any time in the Roman Empire. For such an enterprise the employment of an accelerated script would become an interest of State, or, to be accurate, of State and Church.

It may be assumed that from the start of his association with Charles, Alcuin was ready to seize every chance to urge upon him a proper sense of his unique importance as the great Christian King, and to impress upon his subjects a proper sense of loyalty to their monarch. As Catholics they would demonstrate their piety and orthodoxy in synods, and as aspiring Imperialists they would prove their literacy and demonstrate their artistry by producing luxurious calligraphy and illumination. Thus the Franks, unlike the Lombards, could show that they were no longer barbarians. They would, after Charles seized his brother's kingdom and thus united Francia, put themselves forward as successors to the Romans by a carefully articulated programme of *Renovatio*. Lettering apparently took a similar course.

When Pope Hadrian I died in 795, the lettering on the epitaph that Charles ordered to be sent to Rome was engraved in Square Capitals, of a calligraphical purity and technical excellence that Rome of that day could not but have admired. As mounted by Sixtus V at the entrance to St. Peter's, the inscription is still to be seen. What purpose it was originally intended to serve will be considered later (see p. 171 and Plate 104 below); in the meantime it may be remarked that the lettering is as Roman and as carefully cut as that of Gregory the Great himself.

Later Popes kept more or less closely to a standard that was Square in proportion and free from Byzantinisms.

Leo III's consecration of Charles as emperor in 800 did not signify a papal policy that was positively anti-Byzantine. Rome did not follow the Council of Aachen when it inserted the clause 'Qui ex Patre Filioque procedit' in the Nicene Creed, nor when the *novus David* ordered the addition to be sung throughout his Dominions. The 'Filioque' was not said or sung in Rome for centuries after Aachen.

It may be accepted that the Romans and all those concerned recognized in the Square Capitals of Charles's epitaph an alphabet that was more Imperial in intention than any that had been used in the West for centuries. It was indeed better disciplined in design and more accomplished in craftsmanship than the lettering hitherto seen in Gaul since Roman times, or, for that matter, since Gregory the Great in Rome itself. But it was not capable, by itself, of continuity. Even in Gregory's time it could not be said that any calligraphy in any medium used in Rome in the service of any pope had more than mere artistic precedence. It is only when calligraphy had political connotation and administrative support that it could become truly significant. For a script to have authority it must be imposed by authority. This is what Charles, inspired it must be believed by Alcuin, effected. A convincing specimen of his Imperial symbolism, as imparted to the new calligraphy, is the early ninth-century copy of Donatus's commentary upon the *Aeneid* (Plate 92) once in the famous collection of Queen Christina of Sweden. According to the best opinion, this fine book was written at Tours. Its Square Capitals, says Rand rightly, 'have the dignity of the Augustan age'.

Here is to be found an excellent array of inscriptional Square Capitals, beautifully serifed, canonically orthodox, except, perhaps, for the top serif to A. The R is especially characteristic of the Augustan period of

92. Tours. T. C. Donatus, *Interpretationes Vergilianae Aeneidos I–VI.* Early 9th century.

Rome, Vatican, MS. Regin. Lat. 1484.

Square capitals; contrasted strokes; serifed.

Rand ii, MS. 89, pls. CX, CXI ('The square capitals have the dignity of the Augustan age'); Rand i, p. 143.

the '*scriptura monumentalis*'. They were a supremely apt choice for the Emperor of the West with supreme ambitions. Dependent as his artists may have been upon Syrian and Greek colours, materials, and models, they knew it would be inconsistent with their master's ambitions to accept inspiration from Byzantine calligraphers, tolerable enough as the practice might have been in Pepin's time. There was no room for any doubt on the point after the Coronation of 800. The emperor's appropriation of Augustan Roman Capitals was a political act of the first importance, and as such intended to impress the literate world.

The lettering for the titles in the several codices of the Bible, the text, writing, and decoration of which were supervised by Alcuin, expressed the same Imperial and Augustan intention. It was necessary to impress Rome, and probably Byzantium, with the capacity of Charles to champion the Christian cause, not only by force of arms but also by his readiness to revive learning according to the example set by the Romans in the days of their power. Thus, in Alcuin's Bibles, the practice of writing Uncialesque Capitals (with round D, E, and U, and with vowels inserted inside the body of consonants) was discontinued. Pure Rustic was chosen for the colophons in these Bibles. The reversion to the Old-Roman canons was not the result of a change of 'taste'. A political ideology underlay the substitution of the Square Latin E for the Round Greek E. Moreover, the new programme suppressed all bastardizing, ligaturing, contraction by inserting, and other Byzantine habits that earlier had been acceptable at Verona, Luxeuil, Corbie, and Tours; and, it is important to note, before Gregory the Great's time in Rome.

It has been seen above, in the account of the inscription on the Cross which Justin II presented to Rome, that an opportunity to fuse the Greek and Latin alphabets existed but was not seized. And some years before 800 when Charles the Great set upon his plan to assume the title of Emperor of the West he appropriated, with calligraphical consequences, the insignia of ancient Rome. Although he attracted artists from Byzantium to work on his building projects, the national policy favouring Rome which had been initiated by Pepin fifty years earlier entailed in Francia the elimination of all Greek and Byzantine alphabetical forms and calligraphical habits from the titles of books and inscriptions on walls. That popes like Hadrian (*d.* 795) and Leo III, his successor, would themselves maintain the Roman standards of Gregory the Great, was proper. It was not for them to imitate Augustus, though they could with propriety follow Constantine —and this is what Damasus and Gregory had already done.

It was not until 812 that Michael concluded the treaty whereby Charles was recognized as emperor by the Greeks. in 814, in his seventy-third year, Charles died at Aachen. No trace of his palace remains, but the Minuscule developed within its walls and passed on to Corbie, Marmoutier, St. Gall, and many other continental writing-centres was destined, with interruptions in its long career, to become after the fifteenth century the universal medium of Western civilization. It is a purely Latin script. It had no Greek elements when it first appeared in the sumptuous Gospel Books produced about 780 at, or in the region of,

Aachen, and it had acquired none since the breakdown of Leo III's plan to unify the Empire and the Church by the marriage of Charles to Irene.

For the time being, therefore, no more Eastern touches would be seen in Western script. The writing in the books produced in Charles's dominions would be wholly Latin and perfectly 'Carolingian'. The Aberkios forked A was extinct in the Francia of the ninth century. Was the situation different elsewhere, say in the North of Europe? Had the Irish and English scripts, after the Uncial and Half-Uncial period, been free from Byzantine influence? If not, how long did it continue? These are questions to which answers will be attempted in the next chapter.

146

4

FROM THE PSALM-BOOK OF ST. COLUMBA, *c.* 561, TO THE GOSPEL-BOOK OF HENRY III, *c.* 1046

THE last chapter emphasized, among other points well known palaeographers, that the first Gallican Liturgical Minuscule was created at Luxeuil out of the existing Diplomatic Cursive. The thickening of the ascenders b, d, h, and l was noticed as possibly due to Syrian influence. It was pointed out that the first datable 'Carolingian' Minuscule, that used for the Maurdramnus Bible written at Corbie, was a construction based upon Half-Uncial and having in its form no inheritance from Cursive, whereas the later 'Carolingian' Minuscule used for the Godescalc codices written at Aachen or thereabouts shows signs of a cursive element in its ancestry. The Maurdramnus and Godescalc Minuscules are identical in their deliberate Western purity, compromised occasionally by the forked A.

It has been seen that the Aachen–Tours script standardized by authoritative ruling was completely Western as to text and Roman as to display. That is to say, the Minuscule was native Gallican, while the Aachen Majuscule was Gregorian, and the Tours Majuscule Imperial Roman. The older, pre-Alcuinian headline scripts used at Luxeuil and Corbie retained a number of Eastern symptoms which were common in Pepin's time. That has been mentioned more than once.

It has now to be considered whether other non-Gallican symptoms, having some sort of authority at an important writing-centre and therefore some permanence, manifest themselves. To what extent is there evidence of external influence upon Gallican writing in the eighth century?

The magnificent 'Missale Gothicum', and the Minuscule Lectionary, both of Luxeuil, have been referred to. There is a third manuscript, also apparently a Luxeuil product, that now requires mention. The text is of St. Augustine's Letters and other tracts. The manuscript has been broken up, and parts are now at Paris, Geneva, and Leningrad. Its script is Uncial and Half-Uncial. Of the Half-Uncial Lowe says that the 'shafts of tall letters have a wedge-like finial strongly reminiscent of Insular calligraphy'. He adds: 'this is, as far as I know, the only visible trace of Insular influence at Luxeuil.' To account for this 'wedge' it is necessary to abandon the order generally maintained so far in these pages. In the development of Minuscule the serif, wedged or otherwise treated, is sufficiently important to justify an interruption of the chronological arrangement. The 'wedge' is a calligraphical phenomenon, so curious and so persistent and so geographically limited in its use that it deserves investigation for these reasons alone.

The dispersion of the wedge among the continental scriptoria is no matter of surprise, in view of the importance of Irish and English foundations in Frankish regions. The wedge-like finial has been pointed to by Lowe as a reminiscence at Luxeuil of Insular influence. It is a feature that is not to be seen in the Minuscule of Luxeuil, Corbie, or Aachen. But it does occur in one of the Half-Uncials of Luxeuil. What is its origin in letter-formation—calligraphic or epigraphic? Eastern, Western, or native Irish?

The wedge-shaped serif as practised, 'probably', according to Lowe, 'in the Luxeuil region', in Half-Uncial for the St. Augustine, was written towards the end of the seventh century, or the beginning of the eighth. The wedge serif in this superb piece of writing is rightly termed a 'reminiscence', for, while it is by no means casual in its formation, its appearance in the script is spasmodic in its frequency.

In Plate 93 the wedge serif may be seen copied and applied to all the letters

93. Alphabet from the Luxeuil Augustine, Bibliothèque Nationale fragment. 7th to 8th century, copied from the specimen in Plate no. 94. Uncial and half-uncial.

94. France. Augustine, *Epistolae*, etc. Probably Luxeuil, 7th to 8th century. Calligraphic book-script.
Paris, Bibliothèque Nationale, MS. Lat. 11641 + Geneva m.I. 16 (97) + Leningrad R.I. 1.

Uncial (the top three lines) and half-uncial; the latter serifed in the Insular manner. Four bi-folia on papyrus
occur within a bi-folium of parchment in the Paris portion. The cursive minuscule of the Gregory of Tours
(7th century) employs roughly-made triangular serifs, as may be seen in *C.L.A.* v, no. 671.

C.L.A. v, no. 614.

of the Luxeuil Half-Uncial alphabet. Plate 94 shows the script as it appears on
one leaf from the Paris portion of the manuscript. The inner parts of some of
the quires of the book are written on papyrus, which may have induced extra
care from the scribe, who was a very expert hand. Whether it was he who wrote
the titles and the red and green initials it is not possible to decide. The display
lettering, however, is of great interest. The shapes comprise Hellenisms such
as the forked A (which is not uncommon on the Continent) and Insular symptoms
such as the diamonded ◊ (which is rare outside Ireland and England). The
only point at the moment is that the Irish-English diamonded ◊ confirms the
'reminiscence' of Insular which may reach back even to the time of Columbanus;
to a St. Augustine surviving from his time. A newly entered recruit from this
side of the English Channel would have been more consistent in his wedging of
the serif—in view of the prestige given to it in Ireland first and England second.

The much-needed monograph on the career of the characteristic Irish, and
later Anglo-Saxon, serif will no doubt be forthcoming some day. The present
remarks are superficial and incomplete, but not, it is hoped, misleading. It must
be remembered that, however important the wedge serif, it is not easy to describe
—no serif is, whether early Greek, late Roman, or early Irish. It is impossible,
however, to avoid acknowledging its significance in connection with changes in
Latin script that originated in the eighth century and whose effects persisted
for centuries—and still do. Slow in establishing themselves in the West, they

never penetrated the East. The unserifed and monoline Greek style competes vigorously today with the serifed Romans, but this is a nineteenth-century English revival, as will be shown in a later chapter.

Meanwhile, trivial as the feature may be in itself, it is needful to say that no attempt to understand why we write and print the way we do can omit mention, however incomplete, of the wedge serif. For a reason at which one can only guess, the Irish made a particular point of their serif. Their Half-Uncial was serifed as Uncial—but, though the Irish scribes adopted this continental system, they particularized this detail, as becomes manifest in the sixth century. At some time during that century a school in Ireland influenced a motion by which what had been found a scribal convenience was now treated as a rigid convention, so much so that the wedge became a fetish. It continued in vigour for so long that it is difficult to believe that it could have happened without appropriate backing from the start. The reputation of the originator of this transformation, therefore, must have occupied a position to which authority was attached. The nature of this authority we shall presently try to define.

Continental scribes writing Half-Uncial were aware at the outset that economy and not allure was its virtue, and therefore that the serif was not essential to it. The serif, as scribes knew, belonged originally and authoritatively, essentially and consistently, to Square Capitals; also, by toleration and option equally consistently, to Rustic Capitals; but not essentially to Uncial—though, as has been seen, it acquired this decoration in the sixth to seventh centuries, though not consistently. It has been reported also that, as the position of Uncial weakened in the seventh century, so serifs begin to appear in Half-Uncial. Obviously such an elaboration, superimposed upon a script whose *raison d'être* was economy as against Uncial, created an opportunity for a new and less ambitious script. Thus the over-embellishment of Half-Uncial placed it in the position of Uncial when Half-Uncial displaced it. Thereby was conferred upon the Documentary Minuscule the prospect of a literary career. What this embellishment of Half-Uncials amounted to is to be seen in the alphabet (Plate 94) of the Augustine just mentioned. Here is a masterpiece of finely serifed Half-Uncial.

It was seen in the first chapter that in Greece in the fourth century B.C. a short, blunt, splayed, unbracketed serif, embellished a monoline inscription cut for Alexander the Great at Priene; how, next, in the Latin inscriptions cut for Augustus in Rome the new principle of contrasting the thin and thick strokes entailed a long, tapering, and elaborately bracketed serif which became canonical and imperative for first-class Latin lettering on stone and marble. Also, it has been seen that the Augustan serif was adapted as a long horizontal, but un-bracketed, termination to the ends of the strokes in Rustic. Next, the same horizontal, unbracketed serif occurs in late Uncial, and finally in Half-Uncial.

Now, the consistent making of a horizontal serif requires care, it does not contrive its existence automatically or spontaneously—or, so to say, create itself as inevitably as a diagonal or slanting serif may. In other words, the horizontal serif, even unbracketed, needs more care than the slanted variety. This is true even of the plain serif which was usual in Rustic Capitals. The fitting of a bracket to a horizontal serif makes the serif as a whole even more of a 'performance'. The decorative serif to the Square Capitals invented in the fourth century by Pope Damasus for purely religious use is distinctly artificial, but it was not bracketed. To say that the bracket was and remained an Imperial 'hallmark' that began with Augustus might be an exaggeration, but it may not be rash to surmise that the bracket came to be held authoritative and official. Hence Constantine's advisers would hardly have tolerated anything less stately for him than the serifed forms that the bureaucracy had thought dignified for Augustus and Trajan.

In Rome, under the popes, there was a lapse from the bracketed serif until it was revived for the Square Capital under Gregory the Great (Plate 73). This, however, was but a temporary reappearance; the bracketed serif of the emperors as appropriated by this pope, great as he was, did not stay permanently. So thoroughly, indeed, was it abandoned that the best papal inscriptional lettering from the seventh to the eleventh century was un-Imperial, and hence unembellished. It had no bracketed serifs. Moreover, the post-Gregorian lettering was mixed with Hellenic forms. That is a matter we have often mentioned and to which we must return. For centuries Rome had been subject to Eastern influence. But not only Rome was so affected. In the sixth century the development of the serif occurred outside Rome and the progress of writing was in motion off the Continent. The initiative in fine lettering passed to Ireland.

In Gaul the example of Insular writing and perhaps the direct labour of Insular scribes produced such work as the 'Missale Gothicum' at the end of the seventh century or the beginning of the eighth, and the Augustine of the same time. The 'Missale Gothicum' is a splendid monument to Uncial. The serifs, while often formally deliberate and sometimes heavily stressed, remain unbracketed, and intentionally horizontal at most heads and at many tails. The second half of this manuscript, or, more exactly, one portion of the second half, exhibits the horizontal serif heavily bracketed. This, according to the remnant of documents available, appears to be new on the Continent and found only in this 'Missale' and in the contemporary Augustine, which, it must be remembered, contains Uncials, although the text is in Half-Uncials. The questions remain: how and why did this St. Augustine 'written in the Luxeuil region' get its wedged serif?

Whether the Irish can be credited with inventing and not merely propagating this serif, and when they invented it, is another important question. They were certainly the most ingenious scribes in all the West in the seventh century. They contributed to Half-Uncial, when they were called upon to write it with care, not only their 'patent' serif, but a peculiar sophistication and artificiality which not only thickened the strokes, but rounded out the alphabet in a special manner that is conspicuous in their treatment of the base of b, d, and l. This process is certainly new, positively irrational, and undeniably Irish. Also, the old Roman cursive flat-headed g is canonized in an embellished form. Moreover, besides the ascenders, the Irish m and n lead with a finely wrought wedge. As applied to a super-de-luxe manuscript like the Book of Kells, this dandified serif might seem to be too 'artistic' and individualistic ever to become important. But it was also applied with equal conscientiousness, if not equal artistry, to less formal writing.

It is fortunate that the Irish imposed such an ostentatious and superfluous decoration upon the originally plain Half-Uncial. Its canonical existence governed the form of the predestined Irish Minuscule and, in due time, the encumbrance saved the cursive script from degenerating as otherwise might have happened. No such appalling scribble as was practised in the Merovingian chanceries is to be found in Ireland. Was it then the one function and only *raison d'être* of the wedge to act as a brake upon too great speed? Was that the sole reason for its existence and consistency of application? If so, how is it that this construction, which inevitably decelerates intentionally speedy writing, was nevertheless applied?

It was first observable in the famous 'Cathach' (Plate 95) of St. Columba, a Psalter (basically in Jerome's Gallican version), dated as of the second half of the sixth century, i.e. a hundred and more years before the two manuscripts from Luxeuil that we have mentioned. According to expert opinion the Cathach was written in Ireland, traditionally, but not certainly, by St. Columba; and though that attribution is doubted by historians, the arguments advanced by Lawlor in 1916 appear to be convincing—the more so as it is Lowe's belief that 'the early date for the manuscript is palaeographically possible'. His remarks upon the script are tantalizingly brief. It represents an 'early stage of Irish

95. Ireland. Psalter (Cathach of St. Columba), second half of 6th century. Semi-formal book-script. Dublin, Royal Irish Academy.

Half-uncial; serifed in the specifically Irish 'wedge' style.

C.L.A. ii, no. 266.

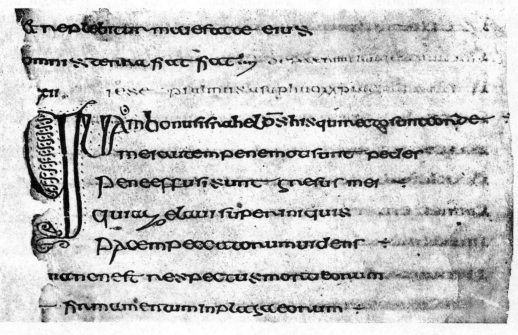

majuscule: typically Irish is the triangular top of all down-strokes'. The influence of the Welsh Church upon the Irish is known to have been powerful in Ireland during the fifth century. Did the Irish script depend upon the Welsh? The dates of existing manuscripts do not favour this hypothesis. In Bieler's opinion the so-called Irish 'Majuscule' must be viewed as the creation in the sixth century of an Irish monastery which had at its disposal a collection of current scripts, chose to base a new book-hand upon Half-Uncial, and added to it traits found in Uncial and Half-Cursive. This seems to have been a very complicated proceeding. Whether or not the form of Irish script was settled by a committee, the result is to be seen in the Cathach.

Columba died in 597, aged 76. The writing is not that of a young or an old man. If written by Columba it must have been finished before he went to Iona in 563. The script of the Cathach is a rapid, unstudied transcription of a familiar text written, perhaps from memory, for individual use. It is, however, a not unprofessional piece of work. The writer is obviously a trained, and in places proves himself a fine, scribe. It is, in fact, a pleasure to look at the surviving 58 folios of this venerable manuscript, though the scribe was in haste and allows himself to fall into Cursive and to 'flourish' as he thinks fit (a, x). The triangular or wedge serif is carefully made and decorates all, or nearly all, perpendiculars, whether they ascend (b, h, l) or not (i, m, n). The original circular basis of Half-Uncial is manifest, though the scale is small. Thus, as a, c, e, and o are all generously curved and serve as a basis for b, d, and p, logic entailed a round-based l. The concluding stroke of d is swung over to the left and is sometimes serifed. The descenders are very short according to Uncial standards, and hence it is not always obvious that f, p, q, and g come below the base-line; g has the flat head. The only exception to the fully mature Irish canon is r, which does not descend. This is remarkable. It is well to postpone any comment upon A.

In sum, the Cathach has the appearance of being a competent piece of writing by a trained scribe not feeling himself on this occasion to be professionally engaged. It may reasonably be held that an ordinary copyist would have ignored such a feature as the wedge, conspicuous as it is; alternatively, that an above-the-ordinary copyist might have invented the wedge for the invention it certainly seems to be in book-script. Nor is it found in any Diplomatic script. Indeed, it is evident that, rather than omit or underrate the wedge, the present scribe will exaggerate it.

In other words, either the wedge serif possessed, already before the book was written, a magisterial sanction which the scribe felt compelled to respect; or it did not exist, and was created by one to whom was soon conceded the authority to make such an innovation. We may surely believe therefore, that whether or not the present manuscript is the autograph of Columba, it is a close copy of what had already become recognized as a magic exemplar. It was made and revered in an age that had been saturated with relic-worship ever since Constantine thought to increase the power and prestige of his capital by collecting pieces of the True Cross, the True Nails, and so on. We need not doubt that the Cathach was 'traditionally' believed to be the autograph of the saint long before it was enshrined, and that it was the tradition which earned it the high honour of being placed in the 'cumdach'. In any case, the Cathach is the earliest datable Irish manuscript of any kind that we have. Its Half-Uncial, wedge serif, and other distinctions set the type of writing for all subsequent Irish first-class book-production—and for inferior work.

What other authority than Columba's could have sufficed to establish it? Could it be the authority of a predecessor superior to Columba, who was himself revered by Columba, or may he have been the writer of the Cathach? If the book was written *c.* 561, such a date would be a hundred years after the death of St. Patrick. Is it impossible that the Apostle of Ireland was the saintly predecessor whose authority was deferred to by the scribe of the Cathach, and by all the Irish scribes for three hundred years? In other words, did St. Patrick invent the Irish script and the Irish wedge in a manuscript now lost? Could he be the authority that led the Irish to make such a fetish of it?

Bieler does not like the suggestion that the great Saint invented anything new in script. 'It would be strange', he says, 'if Patrick the Roman (as he considered himself all his life), or any of his companions or immediate disciples had created a new type of script.' His argument is that the formation of a new style in any field of art is 'normally' the expression of a 'new form of life'; 'normally' is, perhaps, a strong term. While we need not take Minns literally when he says that 'changes in writing are mainly due to laziness', it is to be remembered that the importance of a carefully wrought serif does correct slothfulness in writing. It is conceivable, though one thinks unlikely, that this was the reason for its existence. Bieler points to the great change wrought in the Irish Church by the monastic movement which was so strong after Patrick's death in 461. For this reason, too, he emphasizes the importance of the Welsh Church, which was partly responsible for the increase of Irish monasticism.

It may be doubted, nevertheless, whether the explanation that 'new style' is 'normally' the expression of a 'new form of life' adequately accounts for the surprising uniformity of the Irish serif and its preservation in Irish scripts, no matter how inferior they might be to the Majuscule. It may be questioned whether a single monastery could have possessed enough authority to establish the uniformity, ubiquity, and longevity of the wedge. Corbie did not follow Luxeuil in correspondingly faithful detail. Something, surely, more than local prestige must lie behind this wedge serif, so tenacious of its position even in the humblest cursives. Some greater authority even than custom must be looked for, such as the conviction of the scribes in the abbeys of Ireland that what we think of as the 'typical' Irish serif was the equivalent of the autograph of St. Patrick, St. Columba, or some other renowned saint.

Moreover, if we stop short of saying that the wedge serif was invented by one of these saints, we have to face the simple facts: first that holy men were devoutly revered in Ireland, and secondly that the wedge is unknown in Roman or Western calligraphy. That is to say, there is no continental anticipation of the Irish serif. It is unique. We are left, therefore, to find some explanation for its existence and persistence. In other words, it is necessary to find some place or point of origin, specifically Irish, for this particularity, or, if possible, in addition to a place of origin, a person with whom it originated.

But supposing that there lay behind the wedge serif the authority of a great monastic scriptorium dependent upon a sanctified abbot, is it as certain that, while unique in handwriting, a serif of the wedge form was unknown outside calligraphy? Is it possible that when, 'under guidance' as Bieler suggests, the Irish collected the material from which they developed their national script, they were familiar with media of alphabetical application other than papyri, codices, and charters? Did the Irish also possess works of art such as precious metal vessels, ecclesiastical objects, ritual vestments, etc.? They certainly did have all those which they imported from Rome and the East. Some might have been among the sources of inspiration available to a leading Irish writing-centre in search of an appropriate book-script.

In terms of a general inspection of the serif outside written script, there is not observable on the Continent, it has been noted above, any anticipation of the Irish wedge serif. If it were believed that conditions were against the wedge serif's being native to Ireland, and yet that it was demonstrably un-Roman and equally un-Frankish, what then? Could it be Byzantine? Apparently not, for there is no ivory, stone, or marble from Constantinople that uses the wedge serif before or after it appeared in Ireland.

What, then, about metal? Here there is a notable difference. The wedge serif is markedly evident on the coins and medals of the Roman emperors and Caesars. Short, bracketed serifs may be seen making an appearance, hesitant, doubtless, for technical reasons in the first century, as, for instance, under Nero (54–68). Under Trajan the skill of the engravers and casters had advanced, but while the serifs were longer they were thicker, as, for instance, under Marcus Aurelius (161–80). By the time of Aurelius (270–5) the mainstrokes of the capitals are thicker, but their serifs, while correspondingly thick, are tapered at the ends of the strokes. This process is especially clear in the perpendiculars and horizontals. The treatment of T produces three conspicuous serifs of the wedge type. A gold medal of Constantius I Chlorus (293–305) marks an advance in craftsmanship, and the consequent sharpening of the serif, which at this time reaches its full development as the equivalent of a wedge. Henceforth the wedge serif became an Imperial numismatic convention.

Plate 96 shows a gold medallion of Constans (325–50) which is typical of coins and medals of the age of Constantine the Great.

96. Aquileia. Gold medallion of Constans (emperor 325–50).

Berlin, Staatsmuseum.
Heavy capitals; uncontrasted strokes; heavily serifed with wedges.

F. Gnecchi *I Medaglioni Romani*, 1912, vol. i, pp. 27–8 (no. 12) and plate 10. 3.

The degree to which the wedge serif was later exaggerated may be gauged from the large gold portrait-medallion of Galla Placidia, daughter of Theodosius the Great and wife of the Emperor Honorius. It was engraved during the period of their joint rule (Plate 97), in the first quarter of the fifth century. Here is displayed an inscription in which the serif to all the letters is a construction so carefully made that it is impossible not to believe it was intended to glorify the joint rulers by emphasizing their legitimacy and continuity as Imperial rulers. The serif is clearly a wedge even more deliberately drafted than that on the inscription of Constans. His medallion is datable as of 315 and that of Galla Placidia and Honorius as of 418–23.

We are now left with the question: how did this Imperial serif come to Ireland and make an appearance, the first according to the available evidence, in the Cathach, the date for which is 550–99, according to the experts. The question is not made easier by the fact that as a numismatic convention the wedge was applied to Roman Capitals and that these Capitals were not used in Ireland in

97a. Ravenna. Gold medallion of Constans (emperor 325–50).
Berlin, Staatsmuseum.
Heavy capitals; uncontrasted strokes; heavy serifed with wedges.
F. Gnecchi *I Medaglioni Romani*, 1912, vol. i, pp. 27–8 (no. 12) and plate 10. 3.

97b. Ravenna. Gold medallion of Honorius, 395–423.
London, British Museum.
Capitals; uncontrasted strokes; heavily serifed with wedges.
Gnecchi, i, p. 39 and pl. 19. 11.

the sixth century. The Cathach is, in fact, written in an Insular form of Half-Uncial.

As the wedge serif was never canonically or systematically affixed to Continental Uncial or Continental Half-Uncial before the seventh century, even if then, is it probable that a gold coin or medal of some Imperial source accounts for its appearance in Ireland?

Mention has been made of the donations made by the emperors (Tiberius II was not the only one) and expressly calculated to astonish the barbarian chieftains to whom they were presented. It does not seem too far-fetched to guess that Ravenna under Galla Placidia, as the second greatest city after Byzantium, may have been among the ultimate sources from which the wedge serif came to the notice of some advanced calligraphic school within an abbey whose superior was himself renowned for his sanctity.

Calligraphy does not always and everywhere live by the pen only. The influence of the binder upon the scribe is noticeable at Luxeuil and Corbie. The jewelled cases made for precious codices were bound to stir the emulation of scribes. In the time of Placidia and Honorius the ascendancy of the workers in gold, silver, and jewels was manifest. Such craftsmen would hardly have been content to depend for their style of lettering upon the models used by carvers on bronze or ivory, carvers on marble or stone, or writers on papyrus or vellum.

Gold and silversmiths are naturally proud that their work is relatively more seen than sculpture because it is portable, more admired for its brilliance, and more coveted for its value. The engravers on gold and silver, therefore, may be found acting independently in their lettering from engravers on ivory, stone, and wood. The medals shown in Plates 96 and 97 are not put forward as inventions in point of lettering. It is suggested, instead, that the wedge-shaped serifs were already recognized among workers in precious metals as symbols of the Imperial estate. In any case, the wedge serif is not found in use by the engravers of dies for coins and medals before the fourth century. That it should be developed under Constantine need not surprise us. We have already seen something of the attention which that emperor bestowed on inscriptional matters (see p. 58 above). Earlier emperors had already made impressive the form of inscriptions destined to catch the eye of their subjects. Later emperors might equally give thought to the lettering of the inscriptions on the coins which were to pass through the hands of every one of their subjects. In fact this new wedge form was developed by Constantine's successors and perhaps reached its highest development in the medal of Galla Placidia, engraved at the beginning of the fifth century.

This form of serif, it may be said by way of summary, is lapidary neither in origin nor by adoption, nor is it scriptorial in origin though, possibly, it is by adoption. As to its early appearance, the gold medallion engraved for Constans may be pointed to. The third son of Constantine was appointed Caesar by his father in 333 and given Illyria as one of his provinces in 335. After Constantine died in 337 the three brothers each assumed the title of Augustus. The present medallion so dignifying Constans was therefore cast between 337 and 350, when he was murdered. As has been seen, this was not the end of the wedge serif. Galla Placidia's medal was engraved between the years 418 and 423. Whether any of the medals of Constans, or of Galla Placidia, Honorius, or others came to the remote West cannot be proved, but it is at least possible. Their connection, as examples of royal lettering, with calligraphical tendencies of Ireland, can by no means be established. All that can be affirmed is that the wedge serif appears in the Roman Empire in the fourth and fifth centuries, and that the same wedge is never found in handwriting anywhere until the Psalm-book produced in Half-Uncial in Ireland about the year 561. One may feel disposed to inquire whether any other precedent is known—in the West. That is to say, it would be interesting to know if the wedge appeared west of Babylonia, where it was practised from the first century B.C., elsewhere than in certain Greek City States where it may be found in the fourth century A.D. But to continue this inquiry now would take the discussion in the present chapter too far off course. To return to the remote West, it remains to say that the acknowledged experts offer no explanation as to how the Irish acquired the wedge or why they should make of it such a feature of all their scripts.

It had a singular effect when carried into the modest, small, upright *notula* used for comments in the margin of manuscripts written in their large, round, heavy Half-Uncial. In reality this *notula* is an upright, regular, condensed Cursive Minuscule, developed independently of the continental Charter-hands. Originally designed for use in glosses, it later served for the text of the type of book suitable to an isolated folk bound to economize. Written with a thin, slanted pen the wedge serifs were easily emphasized, and thus preserved for the script an obvious family resemblance to the wide, heavy book-hand, while the lightness of the stroke and the narrowness of the body of the *notula* sharpened the contrast with it. It is obvious too that, in addition to emphasizing the family resemblance to the highest form of script, the application of the wedge to the rapid Minuscule had a decelerative effect. It does not follow that this was the reason for its application.

Before noting the career of the wedge serif in Ireland after its first appearance in Columba's Cathach (sixth century), and while bearing in mind its evolution as shown in the Bangor Antiphonary (end of the seventh century) and the Schaffhausen Adamnan (early eighth century), it is well to refer once more to the upper portion of the leaf of papyrus of the Augustine written in Luxeuil (seventh to eighth century). (Plate 94.)

Here are seen the wedge-shaped serifs applied to the Half-Uncial, which begins at the fourth line from the top. The single-bodied a marks the line at which the unbracketed Continental Uncial gives place to heavily bracketed Continental Half-Uncial, with wedge serifs of the Irish type. The wedges here vary in dimension although they are consistent in design. A curious fact about this manuscript is that the wedge is the only Irish symptom in its make-up. Its presence in Luxeuil at a date such as *c.* 700 suggests the possibility that the accomplished scribe responsible was working from an exemplar that had survived from the age of Columbanus.

Some recapitulation on the origin of the wedge may here be in place. It was suggested above that the goldsmiths who wrought the precious vessels, reliquaries, and medals may have developed in engraving tendencies that are manifest in lettering as early as Nero, and occur probably before his time. It is certain that the fame of the ecclesiastical monuments set up by Galla Placidia and her successors went forth all over Christendom. We even find in the Liber Pontificalis the names of four of the mosaic artists: Cuserius, Paulus, Janus, and Stephanus. It is beyond doubt that wedge serifs were not merely tolerated in Ravenna; they were compulsory for certain purposes. From the evidence of the medals of Constans, Galla Placidia, and Honorius, the opinion may at least be entertained that, in so far as the origin of the wedge serif does not lie in Ireland, it may immediately be Ravennate; and secondly we may consider that its antecedents lie outside the scriptorium.

We can now turn to the kind of capital letter that distinguished Irish and English writing in the seventh and eighth centuries. Everybody is familiar with the complicated, almost arabesque, headings of the Book of Kells, of the Lindisfarne Gospels, and of some continental books, all written in the seventh to ninth centuries. The peculiarity of the titles in these books is the practice of formalizing, interlacing, ligaturing, and combining the capitals. This is a dependable sign of the influence of Byzantine example upon Kells and Lindisfarne writing, and upon that of Luxeuil. Eastern Greek influence is already effective in Frankish inscriptions of the seventh century and in Gallican manuscripts of the eighth century. Moreover, at this time the capitals, which are often badly formed, are also condensed in the body. This matter of condensation is important. Conventional as a narrow-bodied letter is to us now, once upon a time in the West it was novel. Rustic script was the earliest effective Capital example of the invention, and the Merovingian Charter-hand is the earliest effective Minuscule example. But the Capital alphabet used in the mosaics at Ravenna may be seen steadily progressing from wide to narrow in the interval between Placidia and Justinian.

Naturally, Verona felt the impulse, and the process of condensation in the Capital letters used for titles and headlines may be watched in the plates of Carusi and Lindsay's *Monumenti* (1934). Some, indeed many, of the Luxeuil capitals tend to become narrow. The same tendency is observable at Corbie. Moreover, while condensation of width is a factor in alphabetical design that must be recognized for the novelty it really was at that time, there is an additional parallel habit to notice. As innovation in point of condensation increased, so did the creation of new serifs, new ligatures, and new monograms. The scribes during the seventh century, so far as they were at liberty, seem to have been exposed to many ideas simultaneously. Byzantine, Egyptian, Syriac, Coptic, and other oriental patterns, mixed with Norse and Scandinavian influences, were abroad in all the crafts in the seventh and eighth centuries.

Here we have only to deal with the fact that deliberately complicated patterns are formed into Capitals and other sorts. In short, that deliberate complication is the object of the design. This may have been the result, perhaps, of Arabic inscription mediated to Ireland, probably by way of Spain. The turning of letter-ing into a pattern, in disregard of what it is normal for us to think of as legibility, became a conspicuous feature in Arabic calligraphy.

But, as we look at the Irish titles we feel that they, like the Luxeuil titles, were we to deprive them of ornament, would appear in their true nature as a Graeco-Latin syncresis of Capital, Uncial, and Half-Uncial titling script. The amalgam is reminiscent of that on the processional cross presented by Justin II to Pope John III, *c.* 570. (Plate 72.) The Irish titles, for example those in the Book of Kells or the Lindisfarne Gospels, as here shown, consist of a highly eclectic set of letters overloaded with a monstrous profusion of weedy decoration, which, when cut out, leaves an alphabet of which A is a forked capital; B is a capital with a broad lower half; D is Uncial; F is Minuscule; G is Rustic; H is Minuscule; I is Square Inscriptional; M is Half-Uncial; N is Square with low diagonal; O is a diamond; R is Rustic; and T is Rustic. (See Plate 98.) The proportion of the letters is narrow as compared with Square Capitals and even with Luxeuil titling scripts.

Finally it is to be noted that these titling Capitals, as designed for display, are finished off with highly artificial wedge serifs. The result as a whole seems to us the kind of wild absurdity that may have resulted from Irish humour. It was all copied by the prosaic English who, with their Irish masters, took these strange Capitals and huge serifs to the Continent. This was the Irish and Insular contribution to the general calligraphical situation which Charles and Alcuin were striving to latinize. The Irish brought in an Anglo-Erse script in which decoration of oriental inspiration predominated. The basic display alphabet of the Book of Kells is more Greek than Roman; rather it is a Byzantine-Roman syncretic alphabet of the kind that might have been developed by Christians who believed in a Church that was neither Greek nor Roman, but universal. There was nothing strictly 'Latin', in the Byzantine sense, about the headlines and titles that became the most familiar in Gaul, Ireland, England, and, it should be added, Germany. The Capitals are well within the scheme that underlay the alphabet on Justin II's cross. It is otherwise with the text. The so-called 'Irish Majuscule', a typical, if distinctive, Latin Half-Uncial, is a fine, bold, well-contrasted design, finished off with careful and not extravagant wedge serifs, single in i and its relative, m, but double in terminal N, which approximates to the Greek form.

Before proceeding with the criticism of headline design at Luxeuil and Corbie we must scrutinize the evidence for the priority of Minuscule. It is necessary to inquire how the Irish Minuscule stands chronologically in relation to that of Luxeuil, which we recognize as the first Gallican, and most likely the first conti-nental, Minuscule. It has been seen that the earliest surviving Irish manuscript is the 'Cathach', already described as datable between 550 and 597 (perhaps *c.* 560), and it has been admitted above that the evidence for or against its having been written by St. Columba is not conclusive. It was argued that the scribe deferred to what he conceived to be a competent authority, that of a school already recognized as having jurisdiction in calligraphical matters, or of an

98. England, Lindisfarne. *Evangelia*, *c.* 700. Displayed lettering.

British Museum, Cotton Nero D. IV.

Anglo-Saxon titling: Roman or Byzantine capitals (see A with forked crossbar and the ligatures) bastardized with uncials, the whole given a monastic house-style by the inclusion of tricky sorts (such as B). The text is in beautifully formed Insular major script.

Complete facsimile is in T. D. Kendrick, T. J. Brown, R. L. S. Bruce Mitford *et al.*, *Evangelium quattuor Codex Lindisfarnensis* (Olten, 1960); *C.L.A.* ii, no. 187.

outstanding personality whose example was considered paramount. The greatest influence in Ireland from the middle of the fifth century was St. Patrick. He is important as having made Ireland an integral part of Western Christendom, especially dependent upon Rome, and for having introduced Latin as the language of the Irish Church. Unfortunately his writings are only known to us from late copies. St. Patrick as a scholar ranked as inferior to his contemporaries. He was as well aware of his 'rusticity', as of his capacity to organize. That the saint was aware of Ireland's need for books may be taken for granted, and that the patristic texts he collected from Pope Celestine (422-32) were mostly written in Half-Uncial. That the Irish major script was a local and self-conscious version of Half-Uncial is obvious. It is conceivable that even in St. Patrick's time, when the clergy first learnt to write Latin, the distinctive wedge serif was incorporated for no other reason than that it was distinctive. The Irish clergy were proud of their new ability to write Latin Script. Perhaps they were eager to mark their script as Irish? Thus it is possible that St. Patrick introduced or authorized the wedged Half-Uncial. Less speculative is the status of Irish Minuscule. The wedge serif was held to be necessary to all Irish scripts. This included the most rapidly written, where it was least convenient and desirable.

It may confidently be said that the Irish Minuscule is a highly ingenious and truly practical invention. The earliest explicitly dated Irish manuscript originated at least a century after the completion of the Cathach. It is a most remarkable composition, a manuscript called by its first editor, Muratori, in 1713, an 'Antiphonale'. More properly termed a 'Collectarium' or 'Orationale', it is a collection, made at Bangor, of antiphons, hymns, prayers, collects, canticles, and other pieces. They exhibit Gallican and therefore, antecedently, Eastern symptoms. Inserted are some prayers in a semi-cursive Half-Uncial, some in Cursive Minuscule, and others, pages of them, in Formal Minuscule.

The Bangor Antiphonale was completed during the abbacy of Colman (690-1) and is the work of perhaps a score of men. Some scribes wrote Half-Uncial with the pen held in a straight position for their rubrics—which is not remarkable. It may have been the rule that rubrics were written separately, as in the Cathach itself. Of course, the anthems were memorized, while the rubrics were not. But when a large Minuscule (never smaller than a quarter of an inch in height) is employed for the text it seems illogical, for one would nowadays expect the rubrics to be in Minuscule and the text in Half-Uncial. But this was evidently not 'illogical' in Bangor in the seventh century. The hierarchization of scripts had not been made explicit. That is why it is not unreasonable to describe Irish Half-Uncial as 'Majuscule'. The Bangor Minuscule is large in scale and varies greatly in speed of execution and degree of currency. In short, the Bangor Antiphonale presents early Irish Minuscule in wide variety. Hardly any Half-Uncial appears. The only passage of text in Half-Uncial (the anthem *Te patrem adoramus aeternum*) appears on the last folio (35 recto); otherwise Half-Uncial is found only (Plate 99) in rubrics.

The script of the initial nine folios of the Antiphonale or Collectarium is important. Folios 8 verso and 9 recto are especially significant. Here are large, bold letters, a third of an inch high, carefully separated, written with the slanted broad pen by a talented scribe. His economic use of time and space by the practice of slightly inclining to the right and thereby narrowing the body of his letters is prophetic. He has produced a design that anticipates by four centuries the design executed at St. Gall and Reichenau. The scribe of the folio here shown (Plate 100) is one of the best craftsmen represented in the Antiphonale. It has an unusual sense of canonical propriety, as witness his d with vertical mainstroke, not respected by his colleague responsible for folios 1–6 recto. His a is single-bodied. It varies; sometimes he makes it in the style of a Greek alpha, as in the second line of our Plate. This is an interesting deviation. Talented as our scribe is, he is obviously essaying to write Minuscule with a pen cut for Half-Uncial and intended to be held in the straight position required for slow writing. The folio here reproduced exhibits the difficulties encountered by a scribe struggling to execute simultaneously a Minuscule for the text and a Half-Uncial for the titles and rubrics.

The Antiphonale is of the utmost technical and palaeographical significance. A passage that would have interested Leutchar and Maurdramnus, could they have seen it, is the occurrence of the Half-Uncial and the Minuscule on folio 35 recto. This conveniently contrasts the two methods of holding the pen. The collects are written with the pen consistently held in the slanting position, while the hymn is written in Half-Uncial with the pen moving occasionally and very slightly from the straight into the half-slanting position. The consequences of slanting the pen either partly or fully are momentous, and may be seen at their most obvious in the perpendicular and circular characters, which become thinner and lose their monumental character. Also, the original finely wrought wedge-shaped serifs are forced to give way to arched constructions.

Finally, it is important to note that the Antiphonale embodies a script—it occurs at several places—which approaches a cursive so regularized as to reach a near-calligraphic standard. Plate 101 shows the antiphons *Lux orta est* and *Triumphalium memores*. The large-scale writing here seen exhibits all the tendencies that later achieved canonical status in the small scale employed for the economical transcription of Gospel texts.

Intensely interesting as the range of writings is in the Book of Bangor (written, it has been reported, between 680 and 691), the best writing of the period comes from a later production at another house. The difference between Bangor and Iona is that of second best and best. This is plainly seen in Adamnan's *Vita S. Columbae* (Plate 102), written before 713 by Dorbbene, himself Prior of Iona. It is a superb achievement in Minuscule, some passages of which are even comparable with the Minuscule of the Maurdramnus Bible, written at Corbie between 772 and 781, that is to say two generations later. The script of Dorbbene represents the peak of Irish calligraphy in the style of the native invention. It is kept as nearly upright as possible, with the pen conveniently held slightly on the slant, as is plain from the diagonal axis of c, o, e, and other rounded letters. There is a vertical d in addition to the rounded form.

It can be seen that there is an important technical difference between all the

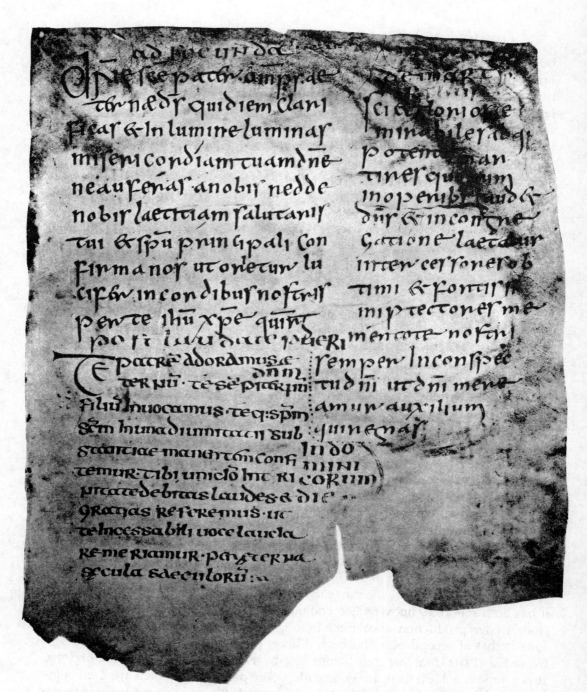

99. Ireland, Bangor. Collectarium or Orationale (Bangor Antiphonary), 680–91 ('The first date in Irish palaeography'—E. A. Lowe). Mixed formal and current scripts.

Milan, Biblioteca Ambrosiana, C. 5 inf.; fol. 35 recto.

Irish half-uncial (lowest portion of the plate); and minuscule (upper portion); the cursive minuscule (left-hand side) is the script in which the bulk of the manuscript is written.

The Antiphonary of Bangor, ed. F. E. Warren, London, 1893–5 (Henry Bradshaw Society iv and x). Warren remarks that the hand (half-uncial) of the collect *Te Patrem adoramus* does not appear elsewhere in the manuscript.

D.A.C.L., cols. 183 ff. (Paris, 1910), s.v. 'Antiphonaire de Bangor' by F. Cabrol; *C.L.A.* iii, no. 311, and ii with plate of fol. 15ᵛ opposite page xii.

Induces plantans eos in monte here
ditatis tuae in praeparata habi
tationis tuae . quod praeparasti
dne scimonium tuum dne quod
praeparauerunt manus tuae
dne tu regnas in aeternum & in sae
culum saecli & adhuc quoniam
intrauit aequitatus faraonis
cum curribus & ascensoribus in
mare & induxit dns super eos
aquas maris filii israhel habi
erunt per siccum per medium
: Benedictio puerorum mane
Benedicite omnia opera dm
dnm ymnum dicite & super
exaltate eum in saecula
& caeli dnm dno ymnum

101. Ireland, Bangor.
Collectarium or Orationale
(Bangor Antiphonary).
Cf. Plates 99, 100.

Condensed minuscule; semi-
cursive but with formal wedged
serifs which, while triangular,
slope from the head.

Right-hand column of
fol. 26 recto.

102. Scotland, Iona. Adamnan, *Life of St. Columba*, before A.D. 703. Semi-formal book-script.

Schaffhausen, Stadtbibliothek, MS. Gen. I.

Irish minuscule; large regularized but serifed with less formal wedges of sloping triangular type. There are variations in style and size in the manuscript.

W. M. Lindsay, *Early Irish Minuscule Script* (Oxford, 1910); *C.L.A.* vii, no. 998, and ii, p. xii (plate opposite).

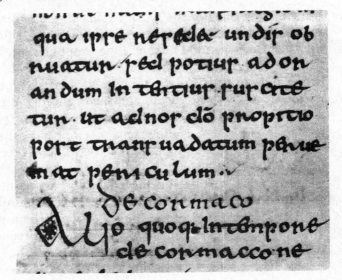

scripts in the Bangor Book and the script of the Iona Life of Columba. The Bangor scripts are informal, being written with the pen slanted to a noteworthy extent, while the Iona script is formal, being written with the pen held in a relatively straight position. Thereby was produced in Iona a more rounded and more dignified script, recognizable as having a natural consanguinity with the Half-Uncial of the Cathach.

The seventh-century informal Minuscule hands in the Bangor Book do not qualify to be classed as accelerated Half-Uncials. Still less do they appear to be promoted Charter-hands. In the Bangor Book their lack of finish is such that they seldom attain calligraphic status. Yet they foreshadow a great change. The merit of several of the Bangor hands, even of the most cursive, is that their writers separate their letters more carefully than the scribes of Luxeuil were to do when they wrote their Lectionary within the next generation. Thus it would appear that the poorer Irish had earlier (thirty years, in fact, before their better-off Luxeuil brethren) dealt with the problem of the expense of Half-Uncial, and had worked out for themselves a Minuscule which was original in form and derived from their own Book-hand, and not from a Charter-hand as at Luxeuil. As this had been done well in advance of the Continent, the Irish are to be credited with the invention of Minuscule. Moreover, the Irish are to be credited with a Minuscule more finished in form than the later continental type. The later and relatively cursive Minuscule of Luxeuil (described above, pp. 112-16) dates from about 650; the purer Gallican Minuscule dates from the next generation. In both these, however, the letters are joined.

This may be seen in the Gospels, written probably by the scribe Moling, who died in 696. The importance of the Iona hand, that which Dorbbene employed for his Life of Columba, is that he separates his letters more frequently than he joins them, and, moreover, that the separations are distinct. The hand of the

St. Moling's Book of the Gospel joins all the letters. The Iona script, therefore, ranks as a basically formal hand, while the St. Moling script ranks as a frankly informal Book-hand. Thus the Iona script makes a basic step forward from Half-Cursive to Formal Minuscule whereas the St. Moling script marks the stage from Half- to Full Cursive. These scripts were practised in Ireland, only, between the end of the seventh and the beginning of the eighth century.

It needs to be remarked that the pen (perhaps too soft for the purpose) used by Dorbbene did not allow him to emphasize the serifs with the weight and angularity characteristic of almost every other piece of Irish professional writing that we have. But the Iona script style remains an unmistakable example of masterly Irish writing, having character, spontaneity, and relative speed, and being neither artificial nor tricky. The Life of Columba was taken to the Continent and later formed part of the library of Reichenau, where it doubtless influenced the calligraphy of the Alemannic regions as a force on the side of regularized and serifed Minuscule. More will be said about this.

The Irish monastic missions to Britain and the continent of Europe carried their scripts with them. Manuscripts written on both sides of the Alps mark the foundations and attachments of the Irish and Anglo-Saxon evangelists. The characteristic Anglo-Saxon Majuscule and the Minuscule were both practised on the Continent by Insular monks and those they taught. The so-called Kalendar of St. Willibrord, with the Martyrologium Hieronymianum and Paschal Tables show strictly written Anglo-Saxon scripts, Majuscule, formal Minuscule, and Cursive, which bear comparison with those in the Bangor Antiphonale. The fine Irish Minuscule portion of this 'Kalendar' was written in the second half of the eighth century.

Summing up the situation as it developed after the sixth century we have the following datable specimens of the seventh and eighth centuries which all use Minuscule:

Merovingian Chancery Cursive, Clovis II	654
Durrow Book	650–700
Bangor Antiphonary	680–91
Mulling Book	*ante* 696
Luxeuil Lectionary	*c.* 700
Iona Life of Columba (Dorbbene)	*ante* 713
Echternach Kalendar	760

Plainly the Irish scribes have a strong lead over their continental brethren in terms of Minuscule. The clear proof of Irish inspiration on the Continent, if not actual Irish workmanship, is, it has been seen, the Augustine, written at or near Luxeuil, partly on papyrus in the seventh or eighth century, a date which is roughly contemporary with that of the Bangor Antiphonary, and something like a century after the foundation of Luxeuil by St. Columban. The Irish influence, however, was limited to Uncial and Half-Uncial, and that temporarily. Thus, while the Irish at Bangor were first with the invention of the Minuscule, they did not exert at Luxeuil the influence upon the Minuscule that one would

103. Germany, Echternach. The Willibrord Kalendar. Second half of 8th century. Anglo-Saxon minuscule for liturgical use.

Paris, Bibliothèque Nationale, Lat. 10837.

Fine specimen of the Insular minuscule for collects.

C.L.A. v, no. 606ª; H. A. Wilson, *The Calendar of St. Willibrord* (London, 1918).

expect. Their contribution was limited to the wedge, which is to be found occasionally applied in the writing of major script.

The reason, doubtless, lay in the events of 731. In that tragic year the Saracens arrived and massacred most of the community, numbering perhaps six hundred. The house, thrown back upon its own resources and rebuilt by a few survivors, faced a poverty-stricken future. Any Irish standards that had survived the exile of Columbanus were forgotten.

The calligraphic career of Luxeuil, in terms of Minuscule, which began with the script best exemplified by the Lectionary described in the previous chapter, was independent of Columbanus, and of late Irish influence. Later the Gallican initiative in Minuscule passed to Corbie, which, as has been seen, was a daughter-house of Luxeuil.

That Insular scribes were among the community at Corbie cannot be doubted, but they do not appear to have marked their contribution to the production of the house. The variety of termination to the ascenders which occurs in the output of Corbie has not been studied as it deserves. It ranges from a sharp chiselled bevel, a characteristic more Arabic-kufic than Irish or Anglo-Saxon, and a soft rounded bevel, to a round horizontal or pear-shaped head. There are no wedges at Corbie. Occasionally, the base of l is rounded as in Irish Half-Uncial. Something will be said shortly about the headlines at Corbie.

The Minuscule in the Gospel Lectionary, described previously as (according to many experts) the product of the Palace School of Aachen, is datable to 781–3 (see above, p. 135). The decree of Charlemagne which entailed the establishment of the Palace Minuscule was, it has been reported, promulgated in 789. This Minuscule has a pedigree different from that of those practised at Bangor or Iona, Luxeuil or Corbie. Whereas the Bangor and Corbie Minuscules are related to Half-Uncial, the Luxeuil Minuscule, as has been seen, is related to Gallican Documentary Cursive. The Palace Minuscule also retains vestiges of the Documentary Cursive. This explains why the earlier Frankish Minuscule, being slower to write than the later version, was superseded by that of the Palace School.

If the Irish and Anglo-Saxon scribes made little contribution to the developments of Minuscule at Corbie during the time of Leutchar and Maurdramnus, they perhaps influenced, directly or otherwise, the form of some of the titling Capitals. Anglo-Saxon scribes were settled at St. Martin's in Tours by the second half of the eighth century, and practised their Cursive Pointed Minuscule. The Egerton Jerome, which is partly in Tours script and partly in Anglo-Saxon Minuscule, was written at Tours. Later a Gospel-book was written, perhaps in a Breton monastery, in which the script is Insular Half-Uncial with wedges after the model of the Cathach. These are probably exceptions. The Insular Minuscule remained distinct and there was no assimilation with the Continental Minuscule. The general rule was that Irish and English calligraphical customs prevailed only in Irish and English foundations.

It is clear by the ninth century that, though the Irish might write in their own style or practise that of Tours, they were not, in doing so, allowed to deviate from the authorized version of Minuscule that is called 'Carolingian'. The wedge therefore remained a purely Insular characteristic. It was not grafted upon the Minuscule as then practised at Tours. Nor did the wedge make any impact on the Minuscule at St. Gall until the tenth century. The Tours canonical Minuscule was before 796, when Alcuin became abbot, at the age of sixty or thereabouts. That he had been a principal instrument in creating the programme of editing and copying Biblical, liturgical, and literary works cannot be doubted. That he had no interest in their form is an impossibility. The hierarchical principle of the use of Capitals, Uncials, Half-Uncials, and Minuscules must have been approved by him, even if the design and layout were not arranged by him personally. Again, that Alcuin loved lettering can hardly be doubted. When Charlemagne ordered the poetical epitaph to be sent to Rome on the occasion of the death of Hadrian I in 795 (Plate 104) and (as De Rossi believed, and Wallach confirms) Alcuin wrote the verses, could so elaborately engraved a monument be set forth in letters to whose form he objected? We may be sure that he did not object.

It seems certain that Alcuin approved the shape of the Capitals of his verses that were engraved and gilded on the great slab of black marble that went to

Rome. Equally, he approved the layout of the books covered by the decree of 789. Are we entitled to go further and assume that he instigated the suppression of the mixture of Capitals long used at Luxeuil and more recently employed at Corbie? What was the general situation after the death of Hadrian in 795 and the election of his successor, the unpopular Leo III?

Alcuin was under no illusion about the realities of power. When Pope Leo III was dragged out of the procession of the long Litanies on 25 April 799, beaten up, left half-dead, but eventually restored to health and returned to St. Peter's, he found there two emissaries of the Frankish king. The upshot was that the pope went to Paderborn where the king was in camp against the Saxons.

Rome had recognized since the great Gregory's time, and the lesson had been enforced upon Hadrian I, that spiritual independence from secular domination was impossible without the exercise of temporal power. Rome had neither spiritual prestige nor physical strength in the ninth or the tenth centuries.

The calligraphical consequences justify a digression. While it would be superfluous to narrate events rightly chronicled in the textbooks, the steps by which Central Europe secured precedence as the calligraphical centre of the West need to be noted in these pages.

The pope's arrival led Alcuin to address Charles. He reminded the king of the Franks and Patrician of the Romans how, hitherto, three persons had occupied the supreme positions in the world. First came the '*Apostolica sublimitas*', who exercised the spiritual power of Blessed Peter, Prince of the Apostles; next the '*Imperialis dignitas*', in the person of the secular power of Second Rome, the emperor at Byzantium. But that emperor had lately been deposed, and not by strangers, but by his own folk. (Alcuin's allusion is to Irene, Constantine VI's mother, by whose orders in 797 her son's eyes were stabbed out so that she could continue to reign.) Thirdly, proceeded Alcuin, there is the '*Regalis dignitas*', in which Christ had set Charles, who, in the capacity of ruler of the Christian people, occupied a station excellent in power, illustrious in wisdom, and exalted in regal dignity. Finally, Alcuin urged Charles to settle quickly with the Saxons and immediately visit Rome. He, Charles, was now the pivot of the whole Christian world: 'Ecce in te solo tota salus ecclesiarum Christi inclinata recumbet.'

Although Alcuin urged Charles to go to Rome, being aware (it cannot be doubted) that the royal visit would achieve a Western Imperial ambition as old as Pepin, he excused himself from accompanying his king. Busy with the text of the Bible and other weighty matters, he was confident that the king would be named emperor safely and legally. Constantine VI may already have been dead. Irene could not be considered the true Augusta. In any case Charles was put forward as the emperor of the Christians and not as emperor of the Romans. The way was clear. Leo III needed Charles, so that he was certain to comply.

It may be accepted, therefore, that Alcuin realized, if he did not design, the later implications of the 'renovatio'. Accordingly, he saw the revived use of the

HIC PATER ECCLESIAE ROMAE DECVS INCLYTVS AVCTOR
HADRIANVS REQVIEM PAPA BEATVS HABET
VIR CVIVS TVDIIS PIETAS LEX GLORIA CHRISTVS
PASTOR APOSTOLICAE SPROMPTVS AD OMNE BONVM
NOBILIS EX MAGNA GENITVS IAM GENTE PARENTVM
SED SACRIS LONGE NOBILIOR MERITIS
EXORNARE STVDENS DEVOTO PECTORE PASTOR
SEMPER VBIQVE SVO TEMPLA SACRATA DO
ECCLESIAS DONIS POPVLOS ET DOGMATE STO
IMBVIT ET CVNCTIS PANDIT ADASTRA VIAM
PAVPERIBVS LARGVS NVLLI PIETATE SECVNDVS
ET PRO PLEBE SACRIS PERVIGIL IN PRECIBVS
DOCTRINIS OPIBVS MVRIS EREXERAT ARCES
VRBS CAPVT ORBIS HONOR INCLYTA ROMA TVAS
MORS CINIL NOCIT XPO AE MORE PEREMPTA EST
IANVA SED VITAE MOX MELIORIS ERAT
POST PAREM LACRIMNS KAROLVS HAEC CARMINA SCRIBSI
TV MIHI DVLCIS AMOR MODO PLANCOPATER
TV MEMOR ESTO MEI SEQVITVR TE MENS MEA SEMPER
CVM XPO TENEAS REGNA BEATA POLI
TE CLERVS POPVLVS MAGNO DILEXIT AMOR
OMNIBVS VNVS AMOR OPTIME PRAE SVLER AS
NOMINA IVNGO SIMVL TITVLIS CLARISSIME NOSTRA
HADRIANVS KAROLVS REX EGO TVQ·PATER
QVISQ LEGAS VERSVS DEVOTO PECTORE SVPPLEX
AMBORVM MITIS DIC MISERERE DS
HAEC TV AN VNC ENEAT REQVIES CRSSIME MEMBRA
CVM SCIS ANIMA GAVDEAT ALMA DI
VLTIMA QVI PIETVAS DONEC TVBA CLAMET IN AVRES
PRINCIP CVM PETRO SVRGE VIDERE DM
AVDITVRVS ERIS VOCEM SCIO IVDICIS ALMAM
INTRAN VNC DNI GAVDIA MAGNA TVI
TVNC MEMOR ESTO TV INAT PAE OPTIME POSCO
CVM PATRE DIC NATVS PERGATE TIST MEVS
O PETER EGNA PATER FELIX CAE LESTIA XPI
INDE TVM PRECIBVS AVXILIARE GREGEM
DVMS OHGNICOM ORVTILVS SPLENDES CITAB AX E
LAVS TVAS CRPTER SEMPER IN ORBE MANET
SEDIT BEATAE MEMORIAE HADRIANVS PAPA
ANNOS XXIII MENSES DIES XVII OBIIT VII KL IAN

104. France. Epitaph of Pope Hadrian I. ? Tours; post 795. Documentary inscription.
Rome, St. Peter's portico.

Carolingian square capitals in Imperial Roman style; but with occasional ligatures and insertions; almost monoline; very slight serifs.

Silvagni i, pl. II. 6; L. Wallach, 'Alcuin's epitaph of Hadrian I', *American Journal of Philology* 72 (1951), pp. 128–44.

Augustan Square Capitals as a political act. Did he understand also (say in 796, when he went to Tours) that the suppression of the mixed Capitals used for titles there, at Luxeuil and at Corbie, signified a clean break with a habit of mind having two centuries of precedent? What was involved was the organized disuse of a dominating Mujuscular script which combined characters that had served both Christian cities: Rome and Second Rome.

Were Charles and Alcuin then responsible for ending all possibility of a calligraphical unity of East and West, in terms of Capitals at least? Does Alcuin share responsibility for reversing the process of assimilating the Capital alphabet of the Latin West to that of the Greek East? It seems that Alcuin did not know that in Constantinople the Augustan Capitals had always been avoided because they symbolized pagan Rome in opposition to Christian Rome.

Charles and Alcuin were therefore jointly responsible for ending the Byzantine influence upon the lettering of the Frankish Empire, and with it the possibility of fusing the Greek and Latin elements in script into one consistent Christian alphabet. Alcuin's defence would have been that his system was a valid Roman '*renovatio*', and the Christian symbolism required was served in the retention of the Uncials for sub-titles and initial lines. The fact remains that, for a high political reason, the pagan Roman Square Imperial Capitals and the pagan Rustic Capitals were given prime place in the displayed Carolingian titling scripts, while the Christian Uncials and Half-Uncials came second and third.

In sum, the notion of a Christian lettering-style appropriate to a Christian Roman emperor was abandoned in favour of an Imperial lettering-style appropriate to a pagan Roman emperor. The pagan Capitals gradually dominated the display pages of manuscripts written in the ninth and tenth centuries. Thus the process of history, despite a reversal (to be chronicled in the next chapter), provides us today with basically pagan Capitals on our title-pages.

However, there is more to be said on this point. Was there no Christianized Roman Capital alphabet whose example could have served Alcuin in place of the Augustan letter? The illustrious precedent of Gregory the Great of nearly two hundred years earlier, which the Palace School reserved for use in the great Codex which Charles prepared for Hadrian I, had but a limited success. Gregory's example was not followed by his successors.

We cannot say what the intervening popes would have thought of Charles's and Alcuin's policy, but their situation was such as to lead them to encourage the Franks. As ever, Rome was in no hurry to separate from Christian custom. When Leo III crowned Charles as emperor, all the correct Byzantine ritual was followed. At that time Irene was still on the throne. She bore the humiliation which Charles's assumption meant for the Byzantine Empire, but refused to recognize his title. In 802 Irene was deposed; in 804 Alcuin died, aged about 70. Twelve years were to separate Charles's assumption of the title of CAROLUS AUGUSTUS A DEO CORONATUS, and its recognition by the Eastern Emperor Michael II (as the result of a deal over the Dalmatian coast). In 814 Charles died, aged 72, having reigned 46 years. He was succeeded by his son Louis the Pious. The

Western Empire began to disintegrate under the dissensions of the sons of Louis. In 843 the Romance-speaking Franks and the German-speaking Franks parted, and on the death of Charles the Fat in 888 the disintegration of Charles's empire seemed complete.

This disunity could not but encourage the enemies of the Cross. Henceforth the would-be autonomous Papacy was to find itself immediately and uncomfortably dependent for protection upon the most powerful ruler, for the time being, of the French, German, or Italian peoples, whoever he might be. The popes were thus obliged to keep in good repair their relations with the Eastern emperors, who themselves needed Western help against the Moslems.

These shifts of power explain why the impetus given to careful lettering in Italy by Charles's conquest of the Lombardy plain, and the inscriptions he there raised, had so little general effect below the Milan-Verona line. Roman stone-cutters may have been antipathetic to archaism; equally it is possible that Rome desired to manifest independence. It cannot be doubted that papal diplomacy preferred the Protectors of St. Peter to keep their distance. The lack of consistency after Gregory the Great may well have been due to policy. Such a strict pope's notion of a strict Roman canon could not have been lacking in authority. Hence it might be less accurately described as neglected, than as abandoned, perhaps in the interest merely of calligraphical freedom. The lettering of Rome in the ninth century conveys a distinct air of liberty, bringing with it a curious absence of authority and uniformity. It is not surprising. Everything was changing in the West; the great days of a single Carolingian Empire were quickly passing and the Papacy, too, was rapidly falling into decay. Weak as the successors of Louis the Pious were, the occupants of the see of Peter had to seek confirmation of their election from them.

The break-up of the Carolingian Empire, which had made such an absolute difference to Europe, made less difference to the Roman bureaucracy, which had long since judged that it could no longer pay the Papacy to take sides. There is only an intermittent calligraphical sign that Rome in the ninth century was anxious to mark her special position, as Gregory the Great had done in the sixth century, by expelling Byzantinisms from her great inscriptions, or to adopt a letter-form that could be interpreted as indicating a challenge to the secular authority. Rome was not in the position to indulge in any trial of strength.

The degradation and weakness of the Papacy were shockingly demonstrated under the rule of Sergius II (844-7). Crippled by gout, 'no doubt', says a clerical historian, 'because he was addicted to the pleasures of the table', this pope was utterly unable to defend Rome from the Saracen attack of 846. The invaders carried off all the treasures of St. Peter's and of St. Paul's. His successor, Leo IV (847-55), was a man of very different stamp from his predecessor, and under Nicolas I the decline was arrested. He foreshadowed the claims enunciated by Hildebrand. Nicolas I supported the wrongly deposed patriarch of Constantinople and excommunicated his successor Photius, whose schism began the open rupture between East and West, the cause of so much disaster. He refused

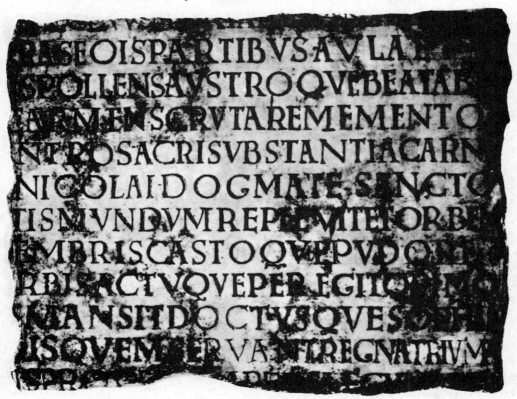

105. Rome. Epitaph of Nicolas I. Post 867. Monumental inscription.
Rome, Vatican crypt.
Square capitals with traces of Damasine titling and proportioned according to Gregorian standards. See pl. 73.
Silvagni i, pl. II. 7.

to countenance the divorce and remarriage of Lothair, brother of Louis II, and confirmed the right of bishops to appeal to Rome against their metropolitans. A fragment of his epitaph survives (see Plate 105), a powerful piece of work which recalls the inscriptions of Damasus; Gregory the Great would not have been ashamed of it.

It effectively symbolized the independent attitude towards the emperor which this pope was determined to maintain. Here and in the epitaph of his successor, Hadrian II (867-72), the antique leaf is observable. The latter inscription (Plate 106) is much less well engraved. Its style emphasizes the chronic instability of life in ninth-century Rome. The decline, partially arrested by the great Pope Nicolas I (858-67) and John VIII (872-82), continued. In 883 the Saracens destroyed Monte Cassino.

The vain attempt of John X (914-28) to organize an alliance against the Saracens was unsuccessful, but at least it lent some dignity to an office which,

106. Rome. Epitaph of Hadrian II. Post 872. Monumental inscription.
Rome, Vatican crypt.
Square capitals; slightly condensed.
Diehl 40a; Silvagni i, pl. II. 8.

by the middle of the century, was being bought and sold like any other job. But
if the authority of the popes continued to sink, that of the Western emperors
rose.

It had become evident that a policy for Western Europe could only become
possible if the Franks, now separated into French and German nations, should
develop sufficient cohesion. Eventually a sense of common danger compelled
the chiefs of the Saxons, Bavarians, Swabians, and Franconians to choose as
king Conrad, Duke of the Franconians, and after him Henry, Duke of the Saxons,
both descendants of Charles in the female line. Under Henry the Fowler Central Europe was given the chance of co-ordinating its strength, and only his
death in 936 prevented his claiming the rights of his position at Rome. His
son Otto I (936–73), with the consent of all the nobles of his diverse dominions,
was now in the position to create the greatest concentration of power since
Charles the Great. He was the man to accomplish this: he immediately chose
to proceed to Aachen, where he was crowned and anointed as the 'Elect of God'
by Hildebert, the Archbishop of Mainz, as, earlier, Boniface had anointed
Pepin.

Consolidation of his power enabled Otto I to raise himself to the position of
the first monarch in Western Europe. After completing his father's conquest of

the Wends, Magyars, and the Slavs between Elbe and Oder and in Bohemia and pacifying his own turbulent nobles, he descended upon Italy to rescue Adelheid, daughter of the king of Italy, from marriage with the new king, Berengar (951). Ten years later Otto again went to Italy and this time to Rome. He solemnly received the Imperial Crown in 963 from the hands of John XII (955–64), a vicar of Christ of some accomplishment outside even the usual criminal routine of popes in the tenth century. He was, however, effectively coerced by Otto.

The pope was eighteen when elected in 955. He was Octavian, son of Alberic, senator and in practice ruler of Rome, and he assumed the title of John XII, being perhaps the first pope to choose a new title. John was thus only twenty-five when he crowned Otto I, rightly called the Great, then about fifty. The emperor had little liking for the pope's tastes and none for his treacheries. In 963 he convoked a synod at St. Peter's at which John was generally accused of sacrilege, simony, perjury, murder, adultery, and incest. As a result of the case, Otto extracted from the Roman people an oath never again to elect or consecrate a pope without the consent of the emperor. In 965 John died.

It was a later pope of Otto's selection, John XIII (965–72), who on Christmas Day 967 crowned the emperor's son, the future Otto II (born 955) as joint emperor. By these acts the emperor with the pope reconstituted, as far as words and title could do, the Christian Empire of the West. Such an event could only put the Roman emperor at Byzantium on the defensive. But the peace was saved when, after unbelievable chaffering and the convenient murder of her father, Romanus II, Otto I succeeded in marrying his son to a Byzantine princess. She was Theophano, niece of the reigning Emperor John Tzimisces. They were married in 972 and Theophano was crowned empress by Benedict VI. Next year Otto I died.

Otto II was a born imperialist; he was the first to call himself (from 982) 'Romanorum imperator augustus'. He upheld Benedict VII and appointed John XIV in 983. In that year he died in Rome, and was buried in St. Peter's. The reordering in 1610 of the contents of the crypts as part of the completion of the new basilica of St. Peter's led to the reporting of numerous monuments including that of Otto II (see Plate 107). The sarcophagus is certainly a reconstruction and the inscription probably an original or a close reproduction.

Among the humbler Roman inscriptions of the later tenth century, a tablet recording the deposit of relics in St. Alexius on the Aventine may be noted. The engraver alternates Uncial (A, E, M, U) with excellent Square Capitals; Rustic (or Uncial) G is also present (Plate 108). The insertions and abbreviations (though he wastes space) are well managed, and the serifing is careful and constant. Another inscription of the same period, from SS. Cosma e Damiano, has the same good Square Capitals (see Plate 109). The R is classical; M and G have the same form as in the epitaph of Hadrian II (Plate 106); otherwise all Capitals are Square. The inscription is, however, well engraved and comparable with the Carolingian inscription for Hadrian I (Plate 104) in point of execution. The same might be said of an inscription dated 984 (see Plate 109), during the short

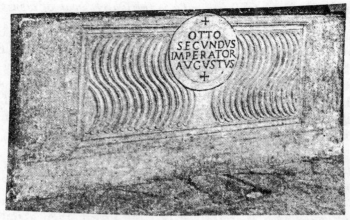

107. Rome. Inscription on Tomb of Otto II, post 983. Monumental
inscription. Square capitals of the Augustan type.

Rome, Vatican crypt. See P. E. Schramm and F. Mütterich,
Denkmäler der deutschen Könige und Kaiser (München, 1962),
pp. 145–6. For Otto II's seal see Fl. Philippi, *Siegel*
(Leipzig, 1914), no. 9.

Catholic Encyclopaedia xi, p. 356.

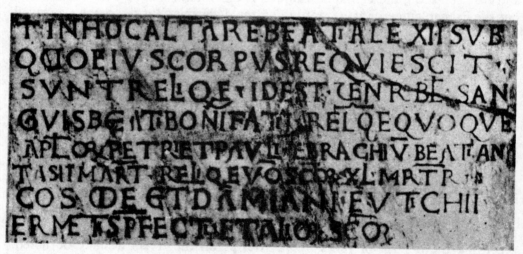

108. Rome. Record of relics in Church of S. Alessio. Documentary inscription. 10th century.
Rome, S. Alessio.

Square capitals with occasional neo-uncial characters; serifed.
Diehl 41c.

pontificate of John XIV (after a reign of only one year he was murdered by Boniface VII). Although there are a few Uncial forms and a mass of ligatures, the sweep of the tail of the R alone shows that the sculptors were looking back to Imperial standards.

At the turn of the millennium a distinct improvement may be seen in Roman inscriptions. The round ε and ɢ (ε and ɢ) are still in use, but the general proportion is square and the drawing is classical-Carolingian. In 996 the young cousin of Otto III, a member of the Imperial Chancery, became supreme pontiff by the will of Otto. He was the first German to be elected, and under the title of Gregory V it was one of his first acts, in 996, to crown his august relation Emperor. At the age of twenty-nine, after three years' reign, he died. He is buried in a fourth- or fifth-century sarcophagus with an inscription of sixteen lines, set out spaciously and terminating with a floral dash (see Plate 110). The Capitals are Square, mixed with round ɢ and spread ᴍ. Notwithstanding the open spacing, necessitated by the layout, itself dominated by the length of the sarcophagus, the letters reveal a certain antique inspiration derived from the Carolingian '*renovatio*'.

If the ninth and tenth centuries may be said to have witnessed what appears

109. Rome. Portion of record of vow taken by priests to say masses. Documentary inscription. 984. Rome, SS. Cosma e Damiano.

Square capitals with occasional ε and round ɢ; ligatures and insertions.

Silvagni i, pl. XVII. 2; Diehl 40b; Gray no. 148.

110. Rome. Epitaph of Gregory V. Rome, 999. Monumental inscription.

Rome, Vatican, crypt of St. Peter's.

Semi-condensed capitals, liberally spaced.

Silvagni i. pl. IV. 1; Diehl 41e; Montini, fig. 46; Gray no. 153.

to be a classical and Imperial revival it is in reality a Carolingian echo. There was little consistency in the calligraphy of Rome at this time. Nor was the German or Imperial policy sufficiently well established to create the necessary basis for a Western artistic movement. Yet such a policy existed in embryo. The conception of an Empire of the West was by no means extinct with the death of Otto II in 983, despite the fact that Otto III was an infant when, according to the legitimist beliefs of the Franks, he was elected emperor. Theophano, his mother, remained in sole charge as '*consors imperii*' of the Empire until her death in 991. Her son was then eleven, and his grandmother Adelheid took Theophano's place until 994, when Otto III, the half-Saxon and half-Byzantine, became sole ruler.

The secular and religious prestige of New Rome was widely recognized. Old Rome (and the West generally) was wholly unable to gainsay her rival's imperial, cultural, and commercial superiority. The organic unity of the Church was a conception that had over-long faded. Theological nationalism had taken its place and the situation became acute when the Byzantines pressed their customs upon the populations of South Italy. The poverty and impotence of Rome was more than obvious. In the arts the old City was destitute. In Rome there was no trace of the old tradition of fine books. No great Bibles, Lectionaries, Missals or other holy books were produced by the order of any pope of this period.

It is vain to speculate upon the form that, say, Sylvester II or Benedict VIII would have chosen for their alphabets had they possessed the means to produce books comparable with those executed for the Eastern or the Western emperors. It seems reasonable, however, to guess that those popes would have been obliged to consult Roman precedent and to decide for or against a Square Roman titling of the Gregorian type. Uncial or Half-Uncial would be considered for sub-titles; for the text, a minuscule would be compulsory, and it could hardly have been other than of the current Germanic-Imperial type. Whether Sylvester II would have judged Uncial by then to have become too Byzantine in association to be fitting in the main titles to a Roman book is very doubtful. What is less doubtful is that if the pope had admitted Uncial for titles he would have mixed it with Square Capitals. The choice before Rome at this time, granted a competent *atelier*, would have been either to look backwards to the old Gregorian standards, or to accept contemporary Imperial-German practice. But none of these problems was faced by the impecunious popes. Instead, they lay before the prosperous emperors.

In the tenth century, the Imperial ambition of the German kings led them to emulate the august example of Charles the Great. The new spirit is observable in the monasteries of Trier and Regensburg. These became the great artistic centres of the West and were destined to exert a continuing influence on the Continent. The unity of Europe, since the abortive effort of Otto III to re-establish Rome as *caput mundi* had not yet been made effective.

In 999 Otto III appointed as pope his former tutor Gerbert. The long weakness of the See of Peter was now to be arrested, and that to a degree that Otto's successors were to resist. The beginnings of the reform in Rome were stormy. Sylvester II (Gerbert's chosen title) significantly recalled the close relationship between Constantine and Sylvester I. The new pope found his relationship with the Emperor closer, even geographically.

Otto III built a palace on the Aventine and set himself to purify the city of the elements that had so long made Rome notorious for infamous living, and restore it as *caput mundi*. In 1001 the dissident elements forced the Imperial 'Servus Apostolorum' and the Papal 'Servus Servorum Dei' to flee from the City of Augustus and the See of Peter. Otto III died soon afterwards. He was less than twenty-two years old. Sylvester II died a year later. Otto's neo-Carolingian (and neo-Constantinian) vision of a united Church-State failed.

Sylvester, the most learned man of his age, a conspicuous book-collector, left few literary remains. His short reign had given him little opportunity to assist the arts of the book in Rome. The sepulchral inscription for him in the Lateran is a compromise (Plate 111). The capitals are Square in treatment but mainly Rustic in proportion. They comprise round E, mixed with Square E, and round G mixed with Square G. A is classical Latin; the M is spread in the Greek manner. The whole is monoline and unserifed, which are both Greek. It is an inscription which, taking the circumstances into account, has considerable quality. It admits Greek inflexions without enfeebling its Roman basis or its independence of Carolingian influence. A letter to be noticed is the round E and round G. These

111. Rome. Epitaph of Sylvester II. 1003. Monumental inscription.

Rome, St. John Lateran.

Semi-condensed capitals; unserifed.

Silvagni i, pl. IV. 2; Diehl 42a; Montini, fig. 47.

are Uncial forms. Their presence proves only that the historic script eked out a certain vestigial existence. But as the sequel will demonstrate, the round M and other Uncial forms would be deliberately revived for the Codices of Trier, Reichenau, and Regensburg.

Meanwhile, it is well to bear in mind Sylvester's epitaph and the presence of Uncial elements in a Roman inscription of the ninth century. These examples helped to keep historic Uncial alive in Rome while the great abbeys of the north were developing a novel Uncial, which later became one of the chief calligraphical symbols of the 'Gothic' age.

But Rome remained unable to give the necessary lead and the influence of Byzantium in Trier, Reichenau, and Regensburg was still paramount. For the present purpose it is only needful to reckon with the Byzantine factors in the pedigree of Ottonian art. It is well known that the art and skill of the great illuminated codices of this age are fully equal to any examples produced in the East. It may be remarked, too, that both Otto III and Sylvester II knew Greek.

An important difference may be remarked between the codices of the Carolingian and Ottonian periods, namely, in the source of patronage. After the grand Gospel-books of Charles, a new peak is reached in the tenth century with a set of splendid works attributed to the 'Master of the *Registrum Gregorii*', the superb manuscript made for the Cathedral of Trier. This Master was also responsible for the Morgan Golden Gospels and a Gospel Lectionary, the 'Codex Egberti' (Plate 112). These masterpieces were created during the last twenty years of the tenth century. Egbert was Archbishop of Trier at this time. He was an accomplished connoisseur and an energetic patron of every kind of craftsmanship that could contribute to the adornment of the churches in his diocese, after the devastation by the Northmen who ravaged the country at the end of the ninth century. To the churches that Egbert built Otto II contributed generously, though the emperor was not the prime mover in this large-scale and resolute plan to restore and decorate.

Egbert is one of the outstanding prelates of the age. During his rule of sixteen years he created at Trier a flourishing school of scribes, painters, goldsmiths, ivory-workers, and engravers of all kinds. It is probable, too, that the influence of his work spread outside his diocese, to Reichenau in particular. Before proceeding, it will be well to repeat that the commissions of Egbert were of great importance to the development of the Trier school, and that its influence was both direct and indirect. Egbert was, perhaps, the first prelate with the taste, means, and energy to create and sustain an impressive scale and range of talent and skill. His example in this respect was powerful in a circle in the West that was ambitious to equal, if not surpass, the finest books of the East, and, in doing so, to place the Ottos on a level, at least, with the Carolingians.

Otto III's successor and Benedict VIII's contemporary was Henry II (1002–24), who steadily consolidated his power over his dominions and also the Church. In 1146 he was canonized as Saint Henry: he might have been called the Autocrat. Bishops and abbots were created by his nomination. The See of Bamberg was founded in 1007, and Henry's wealth and energy were plentifully lavished upon the new cathedral as his personal creation. It marked Henry's preparedness to deal with any pressure from the Slavs who preponderated on the borders of the new diocese. The cathedral was virtually completed in 1012. To it the Emperor attached a magnificent library and commissioned a number of fine Sacramentaries, Gospel-books, and Lectionaries to which reference is made below.

Next, to restore his authority, Henry II marched to Rome, where in 1014 he was crowned Emperor of the Romans by Benedict VIII, in the now usual routine. Six years later the pope went to Germany to consecrate the Cathedral of Bamberg. The closer alliance of the popes and the emperors testified to their common dread of Byzantine pressure upon South Italy.

The lack of consistency, or, alternatively, the habit of freedom, noticeable in Rome at this period occurs also in the epitaph of Sergius IV. The E and G are classically shaped throughout, but the round D appears sporadically. The M has wide legs in the Greek style. The R is regular with a full Imperial tail. (Plate 113.)

Sergius's successor, a strong pope from Tusculum, was responsible for this epitaph (Plate 113), which is dated 1013. Benedict VIII (1012–24) was gravely troubled by the aggression of the Byzantines upon South Italy. One of its entailments was the forced conversion of Latin populations to the Greek rite. Benedict's lettering, not surprisingly, was purely Roman. Benedict VIII was succeeded by his brother, John XIX (1024–32). The state of the world in the eleventh century had hardly been worse since the chaos of the seventh century, from which Europe

IN ILLO TEMPORE· Cum esset sero die illo
una sabbatorum et fores essent clause ubi erant
discipuli congregati ppter metum iudaeorum·
uenit ihs et stetit inmedio. et dicit eis Pax uobis·
Et cum hoc dixisset. ostendit eis manus et latus·
Gauisi sunt ergo discipuli. uiso dno
Dixit ergo eis iterum Pax uobis Sicut misit me
pater. et ego mitto uos· hoc cum dixisset. insuf
flauit. et dicit eis· Accipite spm scm Quorum re
miseritis peccata. remittuntur eis Et quorum
retinueritis. retenta sunt

Thomas autem unus deduodecim qui dicitur
didimus. non erat cum eis. quando uenit ihs·
Dixerunt ergo ei. alii discipuli· Uidimus dnm
Ille autem. dixit eis· Nisi uidero inmanibus eius
fixuram clauorum et mittam digitum meum
inlocum clauorum. et mittam manū meām inlatus
eius. non credam. Et post dies octo. iterū erant
discipuli eius intus. et thomas cū eis· Uenit ihs ianu
is clausis. et stetit inmedio. et dixit Pax uobis·

112. Germany, Trier, Codex Egberti. (Gospel Lectionary.) 984-993. Late Carolingian or Ottonian minuscule.

Trier, Stadtbibliothek, Bibl. 24.

Orthodox minuscule, with German uncialesque elements.

Steffens 70a.

113. Rome. Epitaph of Sergius IV. 1013. Sepulchral inscription.

Rome, St. John Lateran.

Square capitals with a neo-uncial D; blunt serifs.

Silvagni i, pl. IV. 3; Diehl 42b; Montini, fig. 50.

had been rescued by Pepin and Charlemagne. The rule of southern Italy from Constantinople remained a main cause of strife, ecclesiastical and secular. As a strategical centre the abbey of Monte Cassino suffered from both its protectors and its benefactors. Connection between Monte Cassino and Byzantium dates from the end of the ninth century, when the Saracens had levelled the abbey. After the reconquest of South Italy by Constantinople the abbey came under the protection of the Eastern Emperors, and by the tenth century it was a centre of Byzantine uses in liturgy and hymnology. By the eleventh century the Normans formed an alliance with Italian rebels against Constantinople. The year 1018 saw a defeat of the Normans by the Byzantines so crushing as seriously to disturb the Germans.

In 1022 Henry II intervened in the south, with the intention of eradicating Eastern influence in Italy and imposing an abbot of his own choice. This policy being made effective, he lavished upon the abbey rich gifts, including books. Thus the Normans and the Germans together ended the power of the Byzantines in South Italy.

Henry II died in 1024 and was succeeded by Conrad, who also could trace his descent from Otto I. Conrad II was crowned emperor by Pope John XIX. Conrad's successor was the twenty-two-year-old Henry III, under whom Germany reached a high point of consolidation. He was a firm, studious, righteous ruler, and, like Pepin and Charles, saw himself as the successor of David, King of Israel, supreme over State and Church, the maker and unmaker of popes. He was not unmindful of the example of his penultimate predecessor, Henry II. In 1046 he appointed Suidger, Bishop of Bamberg, to the Papacy. Among other attempts to glorify himself, his position, and his dynasty, his saintly namesake had procured the writing and illumination of a grand Lectionary. As has been observed, it was by no means the first of such royal Gospel-books, but one of a new set which rank as the greatest monuments of illumination and calligraphy executed in the period from Otto II to Henry III, from, say, 980 to 1040. The motives for the commissioning of these sacred books were monarchical. It was necessary to remind the German nobles and the people that their kings were sacred persons. Secondly, it was desirable to demonstrate to the Byzantines that the Franks were no longer barbarians. The first efforts of this kind, it has been seen, were executed for Charles the Great by the artists of the Palace School of Aachen.

The creation of sumptuous works of art on such a scale by bishops and archbishops was a new development. Not unnaturally, the kings and emperors were ready to maintain their prestige by similar means. The Ottos were not less determined than their predecessors to rank themselves with David, King of Israel, and act as the sole fount of authority in Church and State. It was no longer enough protection for the German king to call himself *Novus David* as Charles had done, or to be content, as he was, to style himself Augustus. Otto III would claim the new title of *Servus Apostolorum*. Devotion to the holy books followed quickly upon these pretensions.

The Sacramentary (Plate 114), written and painted at Henry II's order, soon after 1007, for the Cathedral of Bamberg is a magnificent piece of Holy-Imperial and German propaganda. One of the illuminations depicts Christ in majesty bestowing the crown upon the head of Henry II, whose arms are upheld by SS. Ulrich and Emmeram, as Aaron and Hur supported Moses against the Amalekites. The same Sacramentary has a splendid opening to the Preface in the Canon of the Mass. Following a magnificent monogram of the V(ere) D(ignum) are five lines of Carolingian capitals treated in the Byzantine manner with Square G, ligatured NE, TE, NR, and other confusing contractions, abbreviations, and omissions made in the interest of the artist's conception of a pattern. Another Byzantinism is the insertion of vowels inside capital consonants, such as O in D. Also, the scribes wrote the old q as a capital. These, taken with angulated C and G, imply profound respect for the artistic authority of books brought to the West by Theophano.

More pictorial propaganda for the monarchy was to come. The provision of paintings which narrated serially, as in a modern strip-cartoon, the events recorded in the Bible had been limited in Carolingian times to the Old Testament. No doubt this was in whole or part due to the requirement of Carolingian statecraft for a Christianized Imperial equivalent to pagan emperor-worship, in addition to consecration, anointing, and other Jewish ceremonial and sacring. But the Ottos, in closer touch with Constantinople than the Carolingians, virtually

114. Germany. Regensburg Sacramentary of Henry II. *c.* 1007. Illuminated title-page.
Munich, Bayerische Staatsbibliothek, MS. Lat. 4456.
Roman capitals, mixed with uncial and Byzantine elements, and abbreviations.
G. Swarzenski, *Die Regensburger Buchmalerei* (Leipzig, 1901).

dropped the Old for the New Testament. They took not only the Church of Christ under their protection, but Christ Himself. They began the narration in serial form of the stories in the Gospel. The most splendid of all Lectionaries were those produced for the greater glory of the emperors.

It will be convenient, though once more out of chronological order, to make a few remarks about Henry II's Gospel-book. It was produced at Reichenau at the beginning of the eleventh century. In basic script it is an admirable Alemannic Minuscule of the slender type first seen at St. Gall, and it will be illustrated when we return to the Minuscule and conclude the discussion of the serif. Here only the display letters come under consideration. The titles are Rustic in proportion, with certain embellishments to be described later. The illuminations are a justly famous monument to Ottonian artistic ambition. An equally remarkable example of Imperial desire to impress is the superb gold altar frontal, made perhaps also in Reichenau, perhaps in Regensburg (Plate 115). Henry II presented it to the Minster Church in Basel, at the consecration of which, in 1019, he assisted. The frontal is now to be seen in the Cluny Museum. The scrollwork is of Eastern origin and the medallions in Ravennate style.

The lettering, with its capitals ligatured in the Byzantine manner, is interesting. More significant is the occurrence of right-angled C and G. This conjunction is common to both frontal and sacramentary, and is a sixth-century Gallican convention, though it can be found in exceptional use in Rome in the third century; it also has earlier Greek and later Irish parallels. It may possibly be a vestige of Insular influence, now almost at its end. Plate 116 shows a detail of the centre figure. The Christus is adorned with the legend REX REGVM DNS DOMINANTIVM. The Capitals are Square and even include a Square G. The text is reminiscent of the legend that Justinian II introduced on the Byzantine coinage, IHS CRISTOS REX REGNANTIVM, which was often used after the end of the seventh century.

Henry II's gold frontal was a spectacular object. The power resources of the German kings made it easy for them to assume the leadership of the West in every aspect of art, and thereby to give prestige to calligraphical expression. While no startling innovation distinguishes their book-scripts, their array of Biblical and liturgical manuscripts crystallized tendencies that had hitherto enjoyed only a measure of toleration arising from respect for antiquity.

The Gospels of Henry III (1039–56) were the most magnificent presentation of writing and painting that had so far been accomplished. Superb in every respect, Henry III's Golden Codex is a truly Imperial book. The large, plain, Carolingian Square Capitals are accompanied by ornamental initials of the same basic design; all of which are Roman as Alcuin would have understood the term. With these are employed as alternate characters a Majuscule (or rather Capital) Uncial written between two parallels (Plate 117). According to Boeckler and Goldschmidt, Henry III's Gospels was completed *c.* 1043–6. This was about the time when the king was looking forward to being crowned emperor.

The scale of the enterprise in terms of painting was unique at the time, which was obviously the intention. We have to attend only to the lettering. There are

115. Germany. Reichenau or Regensburg, 1019. Inscription on the gold altar frontal given to Basel minster by Henry II.

Paris, Musée de Cluny.

Square capitals with Byzantine ligatures.

R. F. Burckhardt, *Der Baseler Münsterschatz* (Basel, 1933); *Der Basler Münsterschatz*. Katalog der Ausstellung in der Barfüsserkirche zu Basel, 1956, pl. 1; H. Jantzen, *Ottonische Kunst* (Hamburg, 1959), fig. 38.

two reasons why the titling Capitals should occupy our attention. First, they depart from the Alcuinian canon, and, secondly, this departure was followed elsewhere so widely that Reichenau may be said to have developed the formalized version of Uncialesque that was to become the medieval Capital Script *par excellence*. That the Imperial approval was responsible for its acceptance in Italy and elsewhere cannot be in doubt. The remarkable skill of the scribes and their exalted patronage were together responsible for the canonization of this special type of Majuscule, particular to this type of book at this period of time. The antecedents of this Capital Script and its descendants will be noticed in the next chapter.

The location of its best mature practice may be placed first at Reichenau and later at Regensburg. As will be seen in the next chapter the elements of this Ottonian Capital Script are encountered before Henry's time. Insular and other non-Carolingian influences may have contributed to it. Nevertheless, the

189

116. Detail of Christus from preceding plate. Capital inscription on the central arch reads REX REGVM D(OMI)N(V)S DOMINANTIV(M). The Chi-Rho on the orb shows Alpha in the forked form.

formality given to the Capitals exhibited in Plate 117 seems to occur first in Reichenau. The abbey was the halting-place of emperors on the way to Rome. A paragraph about it is justified, in fact necessary, as it will be best at this point to return to and end the long discussion of the serif, and make some concluding observations about the Minuscule.

The abbey is situated on the western arm of Lake Constance. It was founded in 724. Charlemagne visited it in 780. Between 786 and 806 the library rose to eminence, largely as the result of the labours of Abbot Waldo from St. Gall. This abbey produced many fine and pure calligraphic Lectionaries in the icono-clastic period, but Reichenau was to ex-cel in miniature-painting. The influence direct or indirect, of Irish and Anglo-Saxon scribes on ornamentation is trace-able both at St. Gall and Reichenau. Immediate Insular influence seems to be more evident in the general orderliness and competence of the script than in any peculiar treatment of individual letters. Neither the wedge serif nor the rounded base of b and l appears in Minuscule as practised at St. Gall or Reichenau. The basic form at both abbeys, as at Tours, was Carolingian. The great Alcuinian Bibles, produced

117. Germany. Echternach Gospels of Henry III. 1043–6. Mixed capital and uncial titling.

Escorial, Vitimas 17.

The titling throughout Golden uncialesque, ligatured, serifed; D, E, G, M, U are often uncial; A, T, H are always capital, though uncial H occasionally appears as the initial letter to a verse. The minuscule is of the late Ottonian–Carolingian type.

A. Boeckler, *Das goldene Evangelienbuch Heinrichs III* (Berlin, 1933), pls. 126, 130; W. F. Oakeshott, *Classical Inspiration in Medieval Art* (London, 1959), p. 66; pls. 88, 90.

there, according to Kohler, under Fridugisus (807-34) and Adalhard (834-43), show no Irish or Anglo-Saxon scriptorial peculiarities. The wedge does not appear.

Indeed, if that appendage were to be accepted as symbolizing a connection with either Patrick or Columba (as the present writer has been bold enough to guess) it would not be found as appropriate in every Benedictine house as it was in St. Willibrord's foundation (698) at Echternach near Trier, where canonical Insular was practised as a matter of course. Apart from this consideration, the essential artificiality of the wedge was bound to prejudice its chances of survival in non-Insular houses, which lay outside the range of the sacrosanctity with which the wedge was respected by the Celts (and their English pupils). Its life was protracted in Irish and Anglo-Saxon houses, under the kind of authority that protected it.

As has been argued above, it may have been adopted in St. Patrick's time, and it was certainly used by St. Columba a hundred years later, about 560. Any weakening of the convention that may be perceived in the script of Dorbbene two centuries later is only slight. Although the wedge may be seen in all its strength at Echternach it had no place in the work of the great neighbouring school at Trier, where a particularly fine serif was practised under the Archbishop Egbert, already mentioned. Other factors may derive from the tradition begun by Dagulf, the scribe of the Golden Psalter commissioned by Charlemagne as a gift to Pope Hadrian (Plate 90).

Reichenau during this period, i.e. the first half of the eleventh century, produced for Henry II the great Lectionary now at Wolfenbüttel. His Sacramentary has been noted above (Plate 114). In Plate 118 it will be seen that the ascenders of the Minuscule are headed with serifs which, though not sharp, are regularly made and consistently disposed. In the absence of any specialized study of the history of the serif, it is only possible to chance the guess that it is to Reichenau that we must look for the incorporation of the serif into the canon of Carolingian Minuscule, that this process dates from the tenth century, and that it may be seen, in the plates collected by Anton Chroust, to be proceeding in the eleventh century towards crystallization.

118. Germany, Reichenau. Henry II's gospel lectionary. About 1012.

Wolfenbüttel, Herzog-August-Bibliothek, MS. fol. 84. 5 (2870).

Ottonian minuscule, regularly serifed. Alphabets of titling and text extracted by Lerche.

Das Reichenauer Lektionar, ed. Otto Lerche (Leipzig, 1928), p. 10.

Λ C D F G H J I M H Q R I V

λ ƌ ᴆ C E h ħ ᴆ ᴎ q

a b d e f g ħ l m n p q r ſt x ⲅ

An example of early Continental serif, in a form having some affinity to Insular, occurs in the famous German and French forms of Oath taken at Strasburg in 842 by the two Frankish successors of Charlemagne, and written, according to Lauer, towards the end of the ninth or the beginning of the tenth century (Plate 119). A better organized piece of script, showing the triangular serif fully absorbed and conventionalized within the Carolingian pattern, is to be seen in Sigebert of Gembloux's autograph codex of the *Gesta Abbatum*, written between 1101 and 1106.

The form the serif assumed in the twelfth century, whence it was first copied by Poggio, according to Ullman, and became incorporated in typography by Aldus (who was followed by Garamond, Granjon, and Caslon), is to be seen in Plate 120, which shows a fragment of a St. Augustine written at Worcester. This brings to an end the present discussion of the serif. It will not again call for attention—and the assurance will certainly please the reader—until this survey reaches the fifteenth century. Comment has been made upon the motives which led the German kings at the turn of the tenth-eleventh century to create the great set of Gospel-books for which they are, as they intended, famous. The calligraphical peculiarities of the Capital Script employed in these codices will be offered in the next chapter.

Meanwhile, it may be well to restate the conclusion that the effects of the Carolingian authority behind the decree of 789 continued to be felt long after Charles and Alcuin had passed from the scene. The Carolingian Minuscule was in use by the Papal Chancery of Clement II (1046-7), once as Bishop Suidger of Bamberg a member of the Imperial chancery. By this time the Irish and Anglo-Saxon scripts were wholly disused on the Continent.

It would have been a *tour de force*, anticipating the continental calligraphic experience of four hundred years, if, in the eighth to ninth century, the Irish, to save space, had condensed laterally the script of the Book of Kells. It is evident that they understood before anybody else that a broad script like Continental Half-Uncial could be improved by narrowing the body and sharpening the stroke. It is done with a masterly hand in the eighth-century Stowe Missal. But though its scribes achieved the result they did not create the style, or even establish the principle of saving space by condensation. Instead, they adopted the worst of all solutions—economy by abbreviation. The opportunity to contrive an economical, condensed, black, serifed Half-Uncial was missed. Thus the Irish failed to anticipate a black-letter. This, however, is not a topic for us.

It is necessary, rather, to return to Henry III's Gospel-book (of, say, 1046 at latest). The novelty is the formalization of a Capital Script which incorporated an Uncial element. It is so well organized, unlike the paintings, that none of the titles in Henry III's book is Byzantine or in any way influenced by Byzantine calligraphic detail, such as ligaturing. On the other hand, the attachment of the legends to the pictures is an Eastern convention. The Western novelty lies in the peculiar way in which Uncial had been amalgamated with Roman Capitals. This had long been the practice on the Eastern Imperial coinage, where the

cuidã presbitero nomine diruiso in uilla
mosomo pximo cõ manena hoftenfe.
Remis incorta. fãe marie follépnitate omiũ
fcon ũ. quidã dui contractus cuius corue
cruribus inteferant. iuncte poplitum
neruis ita retractas uirtute diuina
folutus & erepuf eft.

Anno . d cccc xxv . Redintegrante.
    Ragenoldus cũ suis Nordmã
nis burgundiã depopulabantur . cũq̃
vuarnerius & manaffes comites . anfegif
& gozcelinus pfules . congreffi apud
montê calaũ . nordmannoru plusquam
dccc fternunt . vuarnerius comes ibi
aequo cui salebat occa so . captus & inter
emptus ÷ . & anfegisus trecaffinę urtf
epf uulneratus ẽ Quo rodulfusrex
cõpto inburgundiã cũ quib: dã oefran
cia militibus falicet remensis aecclie

119. Frankish, Strasbourg 'Serments'. 842. Carolingian minuscule.

Paris, Bibliothèque Nationale, Lat. 9768.

Minuscule; serifs with Insular traits.

L. Delisle, *Le Cabinet des Manuscrits de la Bibliothèque Nationale* (Paris, 1881), iii. 265 and plate 30; Ph. Lauer, *Histoire des fils de Louis le pieux, de Nithard* (Paris, 1926); M. Enneccerus, *Die ältesten deutschen Sprachdenkmäler in Lichtdrucken*, Frankfurt, 1897, pls. 34-6; G. Eis, *Altdeutsche Handschriften*, Munich, 1949, no. 14.

120. England, Worcester. Augustini Enchiridion. 12th century. Romanesque minuscule.
Oxford, Bodleian Library. MS. Lat. th. d. 33, fol. 3ᵛ.
Later Carolingian, English minuscule; showing fully-developed triangular serif.

characters had always been monoline and unserifed. In the West, under the Germans, the serif was obligatory even on coins, and the same rule applies to the Capital Script here described as Uncialesque.

The script was originally used in the last quarter of the ninth century, and long afterwards limited to the titles of sections and the legends to pictures in the regal Gospel and liturgical codices of the Ottonian period. Although the sanction of the script came gradually, by way of example and not by authoritative precept, its adoption was a purely German act corresponding with the motives stated above. That the neo-Uncial had Gallican precedents will be seen in the next chapter. It remains that the inspiration of the calligraphy and painting that culminated in Henry III's sumptuous Gospel-book was essentially an affirmation of German nationalism and a manifestation of Western self-consciousness. These far-reaching ambitions, apparent as tendencies more than two generations before Henry III, were powerful enough in his time to create a masterpiece calculated to command the respect of the Eastern Imperial representatives for the skill attained by the Western and German scribes and artists hitherto rejected as uncouth.

That the Western scribes and painters had in the Carolingian and Ottonian periods reached very high standards of writing and illuminating was undeniable. By the first half of the eleventh century the chief centres of both halves of the old Frankish Empire were fully capable of producing work of unsurpassed magnificence in scale and excellence of craftsmanship. In richness of materials the Germans were foremost. This is obvious in both the painting and the writing.

To trace the pedigree of the models which inspired the painters is the task of the art historian. The calligraphic inspirations lying behind the forms distinctive of German fine manuscript production in the eleventh century will be discussed in the next chapter.

5

FROM THE EASTERN SCHISM, 1054, TO THE
END OF THE WESTERN SCHISM, 1417

THE eleventh century initiated changes in writing of maximum importance. The principal development was directed more by stylistic ambition, independent of dynastic, economic, or political necessity. The most significant of these changes lay in the gradual condensation of the Minuscule. The round, almost circular (or square) basis of the Minuscule practised at Tours in the tenth century may be seen submitting at St. Gall to a consistent attenuation which by the eleventh century became almost standard in Alamannic scriptoria. There is no evidence of the intervention, on either side of the Rhine, of authority, religious or secular, in this development towards a condensed version of the Carolingian Minuscule written with a slightly broader pen. The early Carolingian tradition of Rustic may have influenced the practice of condensation at Tours and St. Gall during the ninth and tenth centuries. It is well to notice, however, that while Uncial never died out in the Gallican regions, Rustic was the stronger element in the titles and colophons of the tenth century. It had its effect also on the contraction of the Minuscule during the eleventh.

There are two diverging styles, having opposed origins which require to be noticed in some detail since both were created and developed by the need for personal and national prestige. First, certain parallel developments in the Majuscule and Capital concern the present chapter inasmuch as they are to be seen in the luxurious royal and imperial manuscripts commissioned by or for the Germanic kings and emperors and because the books in which they are used initiated a tradition of great vigour and length of life. The importance for us of these books lies rather in their superb illumination and vigorous painting than in their distinctive lettering and script.

It is the present business to outline the process by which Uncial succeeded in maintaining itself as a distinct and dignified element in both Eastern and Western Romanesque calligraphy, and later became absorbed as a constituent 'Gothic'. The establishment of the Augustan Capital by Charlemagne and Alcuin involved the suppression of the mixed letterings used as titles at Luxeuil, Corbie, and elsewhere. To appreciate what happened it is necessary to glance, retrospectively, at the position of Uncial. In Alcuin's time few would ask whether, in a world long dominated by Half-Uncial, which had initiated the elevation of Augustan Capitals to the top position, Uncial could assert itself sufficiently even to rise above the occasional position of dignity as, for example, the initial line of a chapter or a single initial letter to verses. But could such a superb script, with such a positive Christian sanction, be destined to be rendered utterly obsolete? Many noble books so written were still being read and would continue to be read. Moreover, Uncial as a script for text had been majestically written in Metz in the middle of the ninth and also in Fulda in the tenth century. Yet it was virtually extinct as a text-letter everywhere in the eleventh century. Was none of it ever to be revived? Would, for example, the round Є made in two strokes be for ever suppressed by the square E made in four strokes?

The answer is that Uncial, while not destined to be continued or revived in the tenth century for the body of a text, was transformed for use as a canonical display letter over the written text and to the illuminated picture. The old Uncial, written between four lines, was succeeded by the neo-Uncial set between two. In other words, the old Uncial was always a Majuscule but never a Capital, while the new Uncialesque, which was never a Majuscule, was given new life as a Capital. As such it took priority in the great royal and Imperial Evangeliaries and Lectionaries over the Augustan or even the Gregorian capital. It is necessary to be careful at this point to note a technical development. At Reichenau in the ninth century, scribes were practising a Square Capital of Gregorian breadth and weight, with strong serifs only slightly bracketed. The contrast between the thicks and thins is accentuated. As such Capitals were less imitative of the Augustan proportions and more frankly written, it is well to remember them and at the same time to observe that the fully tailed Imperial R is preserved. It would appear that a broader pen was becoming customary at Reichenau and Regensburg.

In order to combine the late Uncial with this modern type of Capital constriction certain adjustments become necessary. As a principle this was nationally apprehended rather than logically applied in the great Gallican scriptoria during an earlier century. How did this originate?

Two noteworthy pieces of script from the late eighth century now need mention. The first is a specimen of Square Capital mixed with Uncial. Pre-Alcuin, it is found among the titles of the books of the Maurdramnus Bible mentioned in the previous chapter. These titles exhibit a wide variety of lettering, possible only to a powerful abbot having ample finance and access to expert scribes to whom was given abundant space and full freedom enabling them to display forms of whatever pedigree.

Among them occurs the title of Ezechiel shown in Plate 121 set out in splendid large formal Square Capitals mixed with equally large Uncial elements. The Square Capitals are pre-Alcuinian in form, in origin closer to Gregory than to Augustus. The Uncials and the Capitals are aligned in order to bring both categories between two parallels. Let the two braced-together last lines be observed. Significant is the h at the end of the penultimate line. This is the difficult letter of the design, for its perpendicular does not project above the normal top line, as may be appreciated from the ruling—which is perceptible in the plate. It demonstrates the inability of the scribe to maintain consistency by fitting the orthodox projecting Uncial Majuscule h into the framework of the Square Capitals. The scribe could not abridge the ascender without making the Uncial H unrecognizable. This was a problem that faced later scribes elsewhere, who found themselves forced back to H. The problem was not made easier in the

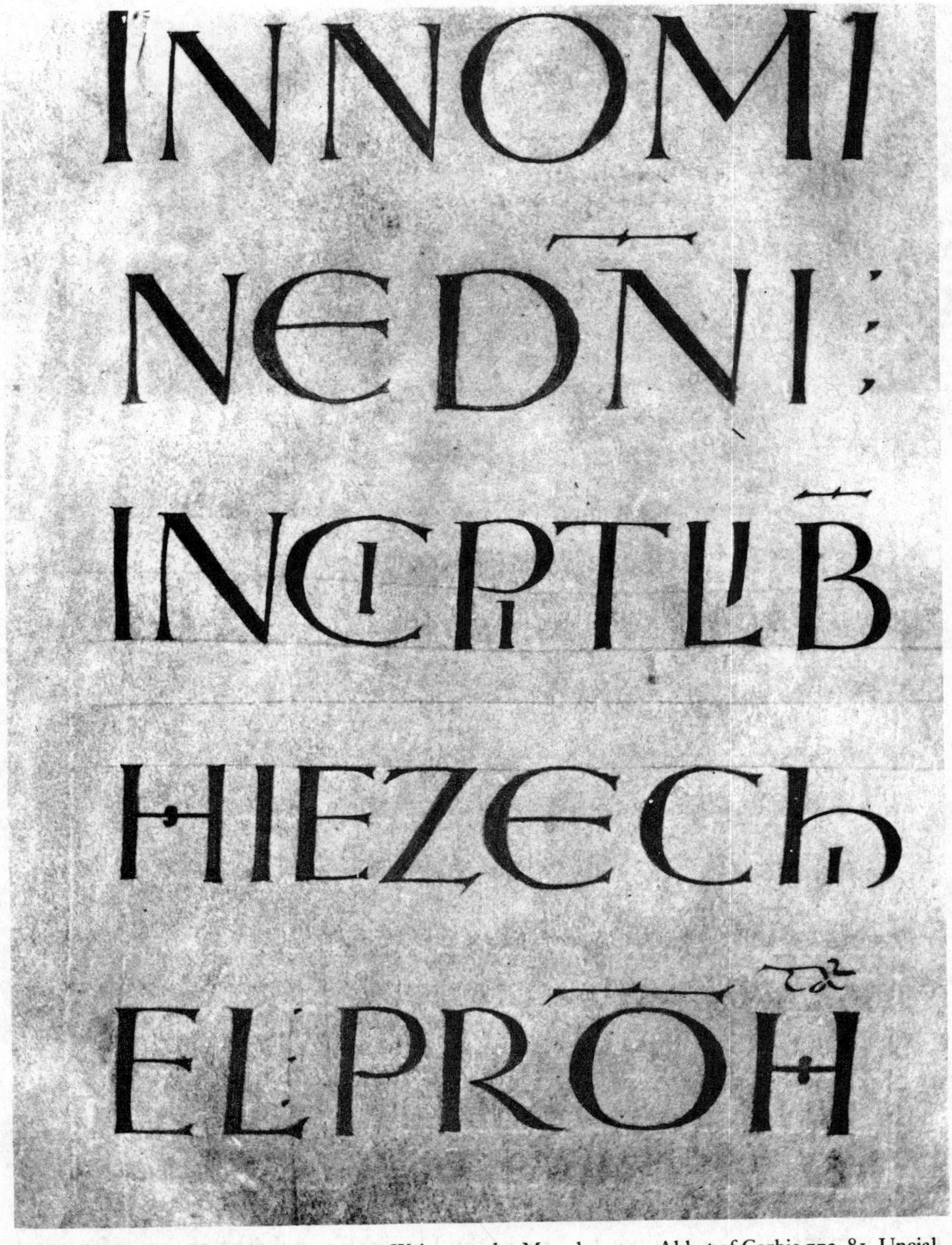

INNOMI
NEDÑI:
INCPTLB
HIEZECH
ELPROH

121. France. Corbie Bible, Old Testament. Written under Maurdramnus, Abbot of Corbie 772–81. Uncial-capital lettering.

Amiens, Bibliothèque municipale, MS. 8, fol. 9ᵛ.

Square capitals mixed with uncials.

C.L.A. vi, no. 707.

122. England (Southern). Gospels (Codex Bigotianus). End of 8th century. Uncial script.

Paris, Bibliothèque Nationale, MSS. Lat. 281 and 298.

Large uncial with strongly contrasted strokes. Byzantine style of initial A.

E. A. Lowe, *English Uncial* (Oxford, 1960), plates XXX, XXXI; *C.L.A.* v, no. 526.

eighth century by the habit of readers accustomed to the Half-Uncial h. The variety of skill manifest in the titles to this Bible is so considerable that if all were reproduced and studied they would probably reveal the antecedents of other later Capital scripts.

We now turn to a second late-eighth-century specimen which exemplifies a text of the Gospels written throughout in Uncial; in southern England, according to Lowe.

The Uncial of the Codex Bigotianus (Plate 122) is relevant here because, as a printer would say, it is 'big on the body'. It looks larger actually than it is in view of the space it occupies. This is a tendency that may be seen much earlier. In the Bigotianus it is formalized and standardized. That it is also blacker than the normal is also interesting and much might be said upon that point since Lowe argues that the quill here used is cut rather for writing Greek than for Latin. This hint of Lowe's deserves to be followed up.

The Greek element, indeed, is curious. Notice the T: which foreshadows old Slavonic or even modern Bulgarian. The Maurdramnus T is relatively less heavily serifed. Lowe's plate of the Bigotianus shows an initial A in the forked form, but having also a descending taper broadening as it reaches the base-line. This is a Byzantine creation. Both main strokes of this A are equally thick, which is un-Latin. However, interesting as this may be, it is necessary to remember that the shortening of the projectors marks the transition from the Uncial which is Majuscule into the Uncial which is Capital. This is probably in origin a continental development; yet, according to Lowe, the Uncial Gospel text above referred to is, by evidence of abbreviation, manner of pricking, and kind of membrane, an English product. There is no evidence that the book was ever in Corbie though it does have a late ex-libris of Fécamp.

Whether or not connection between the Western and the Eastern Frankish scriptoria was close in the tenth century, the reputation of Corbie remained high and precedents set by that house, the Palace School, and the Abbey of Tours will have been respected where they were known.

In any case Egbert and his circle were ambitious to surpass equally the Western Franks and the Eastern Romans. In other words, the calligraphic authority enjoyed by the Western Franks responsible for the striking productions of Corbie, Aachen, and Tours was to be challenged by more striking productions of Trier, Reichenau, and Regensburg. Works of splendour rivalling and if possible surpassing those executed under Charles the Great, needed similar Church–State collaboration. The degree of skill and the mass of talent required and secured were accompanied by intense care and thought in the choice of subject of the illuminations and, by no means least, the drafting of the lettering pieces and titles.

The basic reason for the departure, at the end of the tenth century, from the precedents set by Aachen at the end of the eighth century was due not so much to an artistic trend created by a conspicuously gifted scribe, as to a dynastic and nationalistic force created by indoctrination. Lowe, in pointing out that only one of the scribes of the Morgan Golden Gospels (written at Trier during the regime of Egbert in the last quarter of the tenth century) uses q in the place of Q, says that it was done by 'inadvertence'. This is a high compliment to the degree of consistency achieved by the other scribes, including those responsible for the lines of display. The capitals in all the Egbertine codices are occasionally Rustic, frequently Gregorian, consistently non-Augustan, and hence in larger measure Christian. When the mature, Uncialesque Capital was perfected by the scribes working in the Egbertine style and made symbolic of their nation, it must be presumed that they knew what they were doing and why they were told to do it. The great codices of the eleventh and twelfth centuries typify the strengthening of a desire for a modern native style and freedom from dependence upon what had become an old and alien tradition. The tendencies in the direction of local autonomy were given national expression by the ambition of a new German dynasty.

The last of the Carolingians of the German line was Lewis the Child. He died in 911, when the East Frankish Alamannic, Saxon, and Bavarian leaders elected the Franconian Duke Conrad, who reigned as king until 918. Conrad I did not essay to support his prestige by the patronage of art. He did not possess the resources to follow the cultural example of the great founder of the Carolingian dynasty. That time was now at an end east of the Rhine, and Conrad had failed to found a Franconian dynasty in its place. On his death-bed he affirmed that the future of the realm lay with the Saxons.

His successor was Henry I, later nicknamed the Fowler (919–36), a Saxon strong enough to reverse the anarchy which had weakened the monarchy during the second half of the ninth century, and to found the new dynasty known to historians as the Ottonian, which was eager to sponsor works of illumination and calligraphy comparable with those created by Charles the Great and his dynasty. There was not, therefore, in Germany a reaction against the Carolingian Imperial idea, though it is arguable that the use of the symbolic Augustan Capital was rejected as inconsistent with the idea of a Christian Empire. On the contrary, the emphasis was upon continuity; with reason, for a repetition of a Western Imperial-sacral coronation of the new dynasty was being premeditated.

In effect, therefore, between Otto I the Great (d. 973) and Henry III (d. 1056) there was created and canonized a Capital-Uncial alphabet having a Christian, Graeco-Roman, and Imperial basis fit to take prime position in the scriptorial hierarchy.

The essential novelty in the revised Uncial design lies in the abolition of the ascenders to h, l and of the descenders to g, f, p, in order to accommodate the alphabet between two lines. The Uncial a was given a crossbar, E remained the historic Greek Uncial form, G is Uncial, M is Uncial, N is sometimes capital, R and U are Uncial. The rest, B, C, D, I, L, O, Q, R, S, are Roman capitals. In the course of time long serifs were added to all the characters in the 'fount'. The two-line system was not new, for, following the example of the ancients, Alcuin achieved the same result with titles in Augustan capitals and with colophons in Rustic capitals. Again, while Verona and Luxeuil showed a partiality for titles, with ascenders and descenders, i.e. for four-line scripts, both houses also used two-line titles.

A main difference between Corbie in the eighth century and Reichenau in the eleventh is that the latter house seldom follows the Byzantine practice of saving space by inserting vowels in the body of consonants. In sum, the canonization of Uncialesque was a German or Alamannic act; yet, although this is so, it is necessary to repeat the statement that to mix Square Capitals with Round Uncials has Gallican precedents. When the hoped-for study of the design of medieval display lettering is available, it will be possible to trace the course of development of all the titles of the Carolingian and Ottonian Evangeliaries, Lectionaries, and Sacramentaries.

It should be emphasized at this point that the late Corbie examples of standard Carolingian script infrequently reveal direct Byzantine influence, while early Corbie examples do so frequently. The title in Plate 123 is an obvious Latin attempt to rival the intricacies of a Greek title. While nothing so complex appears under the Ottos it is obvious that scribes of this period were open to Eastern influence and that the painters were even more dependent upon Byzantine inspiration.

The growth in German self-consciousness led to a reaction against Aachen and the increase of Imperial ambition to an emulation of Constantinople. The Byzantines never forgave Charlemagne for his inroads across the Adriatic, and the Germans could not stand the presence of Greeks in Italy. The popes stood between both, and the descent of the Normans bedevilled everybody. The power of the German kings alone could keep peace in the West. The consecration of Bamberg Cathedral in 1020 by Benedict VIII, and the writing of the liturgical codices to be used in it, marked for the Eastern world the seriousness with which the German monarchs took their Christian duty.

Henry III's Gospels were completed, according to the best opinion, not later

O ni time & mandata eius obserua · hoc est
enim omnis homo · &cuncta quae fiunt
adducet dñ in iudicium : pro omni erra
to · siue bonum · siue malum sit ⁊

EXPLICIT LIBER
ECLESASTES ⁚⁊
INCIPICNT CANTI
CA CANTICORVM

123. France. Corbie Bible, Old Testament. Before 781. Capital titling.
Amiens, Bibliothèque municipale, MS. 12, fol. 68ᵛ.
Large condensed capitals with uncial E; ligatured, serifed with Byzantine C.
C.L.A. vi, no. 707.

than 1043, when the king was showing independence and even antagonism towards the Byzantium of Constantine IX (1042-54). In 1043 the feeble paralytic emperor committed the error of appointing the aggressively ambitious Michael Cerularius as patriarch (1043-58) only to find in his former familiar friend an implacable and insatiable competitor for power.

In 1045 the situation in Rome was intolerable to the emperor. The successor of St. Peter was a disciple of Epicurus in the person of a youthful libertine, Benedict IX (1032-45). He sold the tiara in 1045 to Gregory VI, who was next year forcibly deposed by Henry III. In his stead a good German from Bamberg was appointed. He reigned as Clement II for a year from 1046, and his first act was to crown Henry III as emperor. His successor died after a year. Thereupon came to the throne, also by the choice of Henry III, a notable reforming pope, a close relative of the emperor; one intent, nevertheless, upon rescuing Rome from servitude to the emperors.

Rome found in Leo IX (1049-54) a typical German though a former Cluniac. He was resolved to restore the authority of the successors of Peter and the prestige of the See of Peter. His match at Constantinople was Cerularius, who was determined to increase the power of the See of New Rome. The Patriarch of New Rome was as rich as the Patriarch of Old Rome was poor. In 1053 Cerularius closed all the churches of the Latin rite, and excommunicated those who refused to adopt the Greek Liturgy. Leo IX replied that no Latin thought of disturbing the custom of the Eastern churches in the Western Patriarchate; and next he sent a special embassy. Even while the legates of Rome were in the city with their missals, the Patriarch of Constantinople denounced all Latin deviations from the Greek liturgy.

What Cerularius thought of Latin calligraphy may easily be guessed. No doubt he would have denounced the Square Capitals of the Carolingian type as pagan and Frankish, of a detestable and bastard pedigree. He might have viewed the Uncialesque basis of the Ottonian titles and display lines with some measure of toleration as being Greek in origin.

Yet the kind of lettering with which the patriarch was familiar was the peculiar Byzantine hybrid Latin-Greek Capital. The legend on the coinage of Constantine IX did not differ materially from that of his predecessors except that he followed the example of Constantine VIII (1025-8) in spelling his name with an omega. Was this an accident? He kept the text REX REGNANTIUM that Justinian II had introduced in 685 rather than the IESUS CHRISTUS NICA which had been employed sporadically since Constantine V used it in 761. But the aversion from Augustan capitals first manifested by Constantine the Great was continued by his successors. The possibility that the Eastern Romans would always accept a pure 'classical' Latin alphabet for their coinage never really existed; it was bound to be superseded.

Cerularius was the man to accelerate the speed by which the mixed Greek-Latin legends would be supplanted by pure Greek (Plate 124). In the circumstances, the evolution in book-script of the East Romans was unlikely at any time after the eighth century to take a direction similar to that of the Western

124. Constantinople. Coins, sixth to eleventh centuries. Numismatic lettering.
British Museum.
Byzantine coins before and under Justin II, Constantine VIII, Isaac, and Romanus IV.

Romans or 'Franks'. It should be emphasized, however, that although the two halves of the nominally single Empire differed, both East and West possessed Uncial in common; the script was differently used in titles to books and legends to coins. There was little chance of the extension of the Uncial basis for an East-West alphabetical or scriptorial reciprocity as long as the Eastern patriarch held to its anti-Latin policy.

On the other hand, the Eastern emperor was less anti-Western, or, at least, not so anti-papal. Constantine IX, like his predecessors and successors, was well aware that the popes were anxious to neutralize the pressure upon Rome of the Western emperors by an appropriate understanding with Eastern emperors. Leo IX, troubled as he was by the Normans in South Italy, weakened by Henry III's refusal to intervene, was still determined on action. A papal-East-Roman alliance did not materialize. Yet its mere possibility was enough to alarm Cerularius. The negotiations in Constantinople worsened rapidly as the legates demanded precedence in the name of Rome over all Eastern bishops. Meanwhile, Leo's army was routed by the Normans and the pope made prisoner. Soon after his release, the pope died, 19 April 1054.

This event gave Cerularius the chance he had longed for, and he promptly refused, as he was entitled to do, to recognize the legates of a dead pope and overruled the emperor's objections. The legates of Leo's successor (Victor II, 1054–7) answered by excommunicating Cerularius, and that, apparently, on their own authority. Cerularius had already struck the pope's name off the diptychs. On 15 July 1054 the legates laid their bull on the high altar of St. Sophia. After consecrating some new places of worship of the Latin rite they left for Rome.

It was supremely unprovidential that Leo IX should have died in the middle of the negotiations between his legates and the Patriarch of Constantinople. Leo's successor, Victor II, was one more German. He was, however, the choice of Hildebrand and acceptable to Henry. Victor II was consecrated on 16 April 1055. On 5 October 1056 there died the great emperor of the West whose title was 'Henricus (III) Dei Gratia Romanorum Imperator Augustus'. He left his dominions to his son Henry IV.

Victor II died on 28 July 1057. His successor was Stephen IX, another German, one of the legates of Leo IX at Constantinople and one who excommunicated Cerularius. In the interval the patriarch had increased in pride and power, and dominated the emperor. But Cerularius overreached himself. Under Isaac Comnenus, emperor from 1057, he was tried for high treason, sentenced, and on his way to exile he died. This was the end of Cerularius, though not of the schism. In 1057, under Isaac Comnenus, Latin was banished from the Imperial coinage. In 1058 Stephen IX attempted to resume negotiations with Constantinople but died in the same year before progress could be made.

It would seem strange, or unexpected, if, after the excommunication, inscriptions in Rome should continue to show any sign of Byzantine infiltration. Yet Rome even then maintained her position, consistently held after Gregory the Great, of not objecting to Greek customs. The origins of the Latin alphabet as a borrowing from the Greek, told against any intolerance of Byzantinisms. On the other hand, no doubt, the barbarian invasions of the West, the political impotence and moral decadence of the popes, the rise of the Franks and the aspersion of the upstart Charles as the self-created Augustus of the West, alienated the Byzantine emperors. The alliance of the Franks with the popes was certain to maximize Greek ecclesiastical ambition to secure autonomy.

If anything like such autonomy were obtained there could be little future for the idea, less still for the fact, of a single Graeco-Latin alphabet as could have been brought to exist in the sixth century. So it would seem that as the Greeks became more Greek, the Roman Church would become more Roman. The distinction of the alphabets would become formal and symbolize the excommunication of 1054. Yet the excommunication of the Patriarch Cerularius by the papal legates did not immediately and automatically signify in Rome that there had been effected a permanent breach between East and West. It was the individual patriarch who was excommunicated and not the entire Patriarchate. Future emperors at Constantinople and the popes at Rome would try to heal the breach.

Under Pope Nicholas II (1058–61) Rome became less unsure of herself. At a Council held in the Lateran in which 113 bishops took part, the cardinals were empowered to elect the pope and thereby the anarchy of the Roman factions was practically ended, and the policy of Imperial domination set aside. This was in 1059. Meanwhile, Roman recognition of Norman power over the former Byzantine provinces of Calabria and Sicily rendered reconciliation with Constantinople still more difficult. An inscription from this time is in Square Capitals and of a high level of craftsmanship (Plate 125).

125. Rome. Epitaph of Pope Nicholas II. 1072. Sepulchral lettering.

Rome, S. Silvestro.

Square capitals; with no Byzantine elements (notice forked and straight A).

Diehl 430.

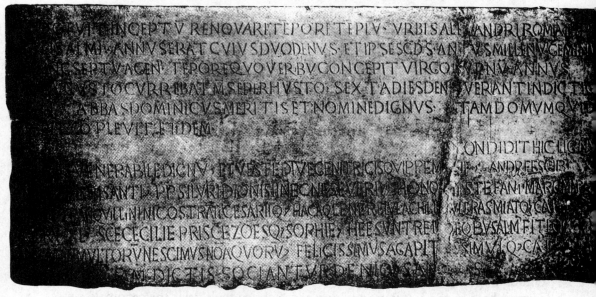

126. Rome. Commemoration inscription for Alexander II. 1070. Monumental capitals.
Rome, St. John Lateran.

Square capitals freely designed and hence permitting condensed form at line-endings. Archaic A and Rustic G.

Ph. Lauer, *Le Palais du Latran* (Paris, 1911), fig. 58.

In 1061 the Emperor Constantine X endeavoured to influence the election of a successor to Nicholas II, who should be pledged to an alliance with Constantinople. The plan failed. Instead, the Normans took Bari in 1071 and expelled the Byzantines from Italy. In view of Turkish pressure in the East, the emperors were more obliged than ever before to look for aid, not territorial dominion, in the West.

Rome in the hands of the reformers was now exercising a steady and unfamiliar influence. Alexander II (1061–73), who succeeded Nicholas II, reigned twelve years, which period was longer than that of several of his predecessors added together. The policy begun by Leo IX in 1049 began to bear fruit. Alexander II deserves recognition for choosing and elevating Lanfranc of Bec in the See of Canterbury. He was also the restorer of the Lateran. The inscription in the cloister which commemorates his benefactions is of interest (Plate 126). The G is always round as in Rustic and E occasionally occurs in the Greek form, otherwise the inscription ranks as good freehand Roman lettering with some archaisms as in A. The importance of the engraving is that it reflects a higher degree of craftsmanship, of the form that, although the mason is permitted to condense the words at the ends of lines of an inscription of this dignity, the practice may not thereby be said to have been canonized for first-class work.

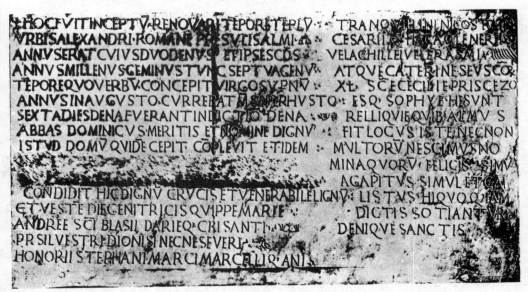

127. Rome. List of relics in S. Biagio. Alexander II, 1072. Documentary inscriptional lettering.

Rome, St. John Lateran.

Condensed capitals with Rustic vestiges.

Silvagni i, pl. XX. 2: Diehl 43b.

The inscription of the time of Alexander II shown in Plate 127 shows a regular compromise between the Square and the Rustic Capital style. However, that it should have been tolerated in the Lateran inscription does not yet prove the existence of so much as a permissive tendency in Rome to bring the old Square and Rustic proportions into the same line and provide a condensed alphabet. This was to come later.

In the last quarter of the eleventh century the most significant Roman inscriptions are naturally those of the reign of Gregory VII, 1073–85, (Plate 128). The

128. Rome. Decree of Gregory VII, 1072–85. Monumental lettering.

Crypt of St. Saba on the Aventine.

Finely cut capitals of admirable Roman design, having uncial A, ε alternating with E and Rustic G. In scale the lettering is not square; nor is it condensed.

Silvagni i, pl. XX. 5.

greatest man of the age began his official career unwillingly. He was a monk of St. Benedict when Gregory VI made him a secretary, since when he had filled many diplomatic posts. Like Leo IX, the policy of Gregory VII would be to reform the Church in its head and members.

The unfinished decree of Gregory VII shown in Plate 128 shows a remarkably high degree of artistry. The letters are consciously Roman, almost classical, for, while there is an archaic A and the round Rustic G there is only one round Greek E. Other legal inscriptions of Gregory's time incorporate the abbreviations invented by notaries. In all instances the capitals are less square than the classical scale would allow, though not consistently Rustic. As a whole this inscription is by far the most elegant that Rome had produced for centuries, and a superb symbol of the great Hildebrandine renaissance which, in justice, should be said to have been initiated by Leo IX.

While the tendency towards condensation of the letters was plain in the twelfth century it may be said, on the evidence of the available material, to have become dominant later. There are, it seems, many surviving inscriptions in capitals which are intentionally Square. During the time of Leo IX and Gregory VII, while the round Uncial or Greek E is found (though not customarily) and the Rustic G, there are contractions, but no Byzantinesque ligatures occur. There had hardly been any use of these since the tenth century, and then only in the meaner sort of inscription. The only one common denominator between Old Rome and New Rome, so far as it can be said to exist, in the inscriptions of Alexander II is that they are both narrow or condensed. It does not follow that in this respect Rome was dependent upon Byzantium. Both are rooted in Rustic. Rome, too, was in such poverty that the condensed form was an inevitable economy. It has been seen in an earlier chapter that the Byzantines standardized the proportions of Roman Rustic Capitals and permanently abandoned Square Capitals, whereas the old Roman practice of using these remained general. Even so, Rustic never entirely disappeared. A relatively economical, narrow-bodied proportion will almost maintain itself. That such a letter-form can be elegant was proved at Reichenau, which never knew poverty.

The Uncialesque Capitals that Henry III had canonized in Germany had yet to be accepted in Rome. An account has been given of the ceremonial use at Reichenau *c.* 1046 of Square Capitals treated in an Uncial manner but heavily serifed. This Capital script, made in Germany, was destined to spread in the West, but not even the round E was in current use in Rome a quarter of a century later. We may say that from 1072 to 1085 the official style was reminiscent of the fourth and fifth centuries, when Old Rome for mere conservative and prideful reasons kept to the old models and looked not to New Rome. What was to be the relation of the East to the West after the reign of Alexander II, and the action of his mighty successor, Gregory VII?

In 1073 the Eastern Emperor Michael VII (1071-8) sent an embassy of two monks to congratulate Hildebrand upon his election. In 1074 talks between East and West were continued, and the pope urged all Christians to help the East in their struggle with the Turks. But the West was disunited, with King

Henry IV at critical variance with Gregory VII over the secular investiture of clerics. In 1076 the pope excommunicated the king. Henry, facing diplomatic isolation, submitted, and after a spectacular act of penance at Canossa, was absolved by Gregory in 1077. Had King Henry IV been more like his father, it is possible that the West would have come to the rescue of the East and that after an alliance against the Turks, the Latin and Greek Churches would have been reconciled, and that the *rapprochement* might entail an assimilation of Eastern and Western scripts. But the chaotic conditions of the time were against anything of the kind. In 1078 when the Emperor Michael VII was deposed, Gregory excommunicated the intruder Nicephorus III Botaniates. Later East and West resumed negotiations, which amounted to nothing.

Two inscriptions surviving from Gregory's time remain to be noticed. Both are handsomely drawn and well engraved. The first is from the church of St. Pudentiana and commemorates its restoration by the pope (Plate 129). The A

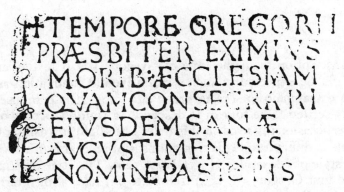

129. Rome. Recording of the renovation of S. Pudentiana.
Gregory VII, 1073. Monumental capitals.

Rome, S. Pudentiana.

Square capitals; serifed; with Rustic G.

Diehl 43d.

is classic, as are the rest of the characters except G, which lapses back to the Rustic round form. There are now the usual ligatures such as AE, AR, HE, MV, NE. A notable combination is UL, UR. There are also insertions of vowels such as O within the body of consonants such as C. This is a Byzantine convention —the kind of thing that the first Gregory (the Great, 590–604) had taken care to avoid. Curiously, there is no round E. The inscription as a whole is in Square Capitals, serifed. There are two lines at the foot in condensed capitals, serifed—this is a fifth- and sixth-century Roman convention. It is apparent, therefore, that this inscription is neither Augustan nor Carolingian. Nor is it Imperial. In other words, the appearance of early Byzantine and early Roman conventions may be deliberate. If so, it is one more proof that in Rome there was no discrimination against Byzantinisms. The date of this inscription is 1073.

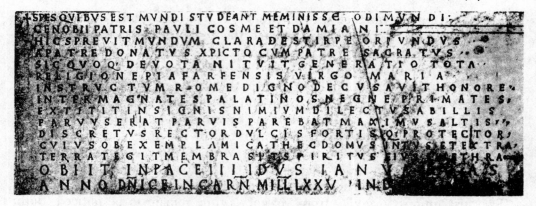

130. Rome. Epitaph of Bishop Odemund. Gregory VII, 1074. Ceremonial inscription.
Rome, SS. Cosma e Damiano in Trastevere.
Semi-condensed capitals with 'antique' mannerism; serifed and widely spaced.
Diehl 44a; Silvagni i, pl. XX. 4.

Our other inscription from the time of Gregory VII is in the 'antique' style as perhaps might be expected in such a primitive old foundation as the church of SS. Cosma e Damiano in Trastevere (Plate 130). It is composed of Square Capitals, finely serifed. The fork in M descends; a round E occurs once. Round, i.e. Rustic, G is occasionally used in this text. The slight intrusion of Uncial and Rustic elements is difficult to explain in an inscription that is otherwise so closely similar to the style of Alexander II (see Plate 126). The style of Square Capitals revived by the first Gregory (d. 604) (see Plate 73) had, with interruptions and corruptions, maintained only a tenuous existence until the time of Gregory VII. The inscriptions in St. Pudentiana and SS. Cosma e Damiano are neither Augustan nor Carolingian; nor Byzantine. They are decisively Roman in a distinct style, more spacious and deliberate than that favoured under Sergius IV (1012). It has been said above that the letters in the Gregorian Decree (Plate 128) appropriately symbolize the policy followed by the pope. It is not datable. The inscription in SS. Cosma e Damiano is dated 1074 and Gregory VII was elected in 1073. (Plate 130.) At this time the so-called 'Dictatus Papae' was compiled. One of its articles lays it down that the pope may depose emperors and that he only may use the Imperial insignia. The claim to monopolize for the Papacy the old Roman insignia including the Square Capitals may not have been explicitly maintained by Gregory VII but that an approved and zealous canon lawyer should realize that consistency would require the restriction is more than likely. If so, it follows that the adoption of the classical form of Square Capital is less an artistic or antiquarian essay than the symbol of the papal claim to Imperial sovereignty so far as Rome and the Roman Province was concerned. This is the meaning of Article 8 of the *Dictatus*: 'that he (the Roman Pontiff) only may use the Imperial insignia.'

In a few years Gregory VII's policy was decisively checked. The contest between King Henry IV and Pope Gregory VII remained acute. The humiliated king was eager to pay off old scores against the independent pope. In 1081 Henry was in Italy with a force strong enough to impose an anti-pope of his nomination. In 1084 Gregory was deposed and Guibert, archbishop of Ravenna, enthroned with the name of Clement III. Gregory's appeal to his vassal (the treaty was the act of Pope Nicholas II) had fatal consequences. When the Normans duly came, Henry withdrew and left Rome to the savagery of Guiscard's army.

Rome, which had been fired, besieged, devastated, and ruined over and over again since Alaric's outrage on the proud city in 410, had been largely restored between 1061 and 1081. It met with its worst disaster when the Normans gutted the city in 1084 to spite Henry IV. The flames swept away everything except the walls, leaving the place hardly habitable. The Normans carried off Pope Gregory VII and left the anti-Pope, Clement III, in possession of the See of Peter, while the Curia and Chancery were moved to Salerno where the pope died in 1085. Rome remained in ruins, and the idea of Gregory VII (or his Chancery) to give new and independent authority to the Roman Imperial precedent was buried under the rubble.

Gregory VII's successor (his choice) was Victor III, formerly Desiderius, abbot of Monte Cassino since 1058. The basilica he raised there was the most brilliant architectural achievement the West had yet seen. The men that Desiderius attracted from Byzantium and elsewhere wrought so superbly that the Eastern emperor, Michael VII, gave the monastery an annual grant of gold. Traces of the impact of its design upon neighbouring and distant churches and monasteries are still to be found. The magnificence of the basilica would have exerted an influence even greater and more rapid had the times been propitious. Even so, the great shrine of St. Benedict was destined to be the inspiration of much other construction in Rome and the West; and, as mentioned below, to influence the form of letters.

Desiderius was unsurpassed as a librarian. According to Lowe, 'the most beautiful eleventh-century manuscripts in Beneventan script owe their existence to the impetus given by his zeal and love of letters'. The scribes of his period show 'a consciousness of skill, a joy in the employment of it, and at the same time a masterly restraint and fastidiousness', which render their performances the finest of all the scriptorial triumphs of the epoch.

And so, when Gregory VII lay dying he named Desiderius as the most fit to succeed him. Hildebrand had been present on the memorable occasion fourteen years earlier when the great basilica was consecrated. Now, in 1086, Desiderius as Victor III, upon whom, as abbot, the purple was forcibly thrust, was one of the most tragically unwilling popes in history. He could do nothing for devastated Rome—except flee from it. He never had good health; and when, once more, Rome was in a state of siege, the enfeebled Desiderius returned to his abbey.[1]

[1] In 1727 the abbot of Monte Cassino was given leave to keep his feast on 16 September, the day of his death in 1087.

The claim of Desiderius upon the attention, if not the affection, of bibliographers lies in the manuscripts which Lowe lists as having been written by his orders. The survivors among the great books written at Monte Cassino in his abbacy are his monument. No Roman inscription to his memory survives. The great golden altar frontal adorned with gems and enamels which this great abbot obtained from Constantinople has not descended to us. Plate 131 is from the Lectionary written by the scribe Leo and dated 1072. Lowe says it shows the Beneventan script at its highest point of development. The display script and the decoration are important for our purpose.

Desiderius had made the basilica of Monte Cassino the wonder of the West. Its relations with Constantinople were very close. Yet the distinctive script of the abbey is unaffected by oriental influence and it seems fair to see in the characteristic decorative elements a striving for occidental association. Undoubtedly the impulse and style of the basilica was architecturally Byzantine in origin and inspiration. Even so, that of the scriptorium was Western; and, furthermore, northern.

This need not be surprising. Any artistic leadership that Rome might give could only wait upon settled times. The city had known every kind of devastation. For two centuries and a half the Roman factions, German armies, and Norman invaders had fought in turn for control of the papacy and the city, battering and destroying everything that lay in their path. The recovery of Rome waited upon the arrival of a pope who should have the opportunity and command the means of rebuilding the principle edifices, sacred and secular. In the north, after the year 1000, much construction had been completed. Bamberg Cathedral had been built and consecrated by a pope. The rebuilding of St. Mark's at Venice had been begun, so had the duomo at Pisa. Cathedrals were being raised at Mainz, Ely, Winchester, and Durham. Great abbeys such as Gloucester and Cluny had been erected.

The inspiration for this increased architectural activity and interest in the decorative arts had its source in the north, largely in the Île de France. The dynastic impetus for its development, notably at St. Denis, continued to exercise a powerful influence over the new style of what became known as 'Gothic', and is recorded below. In Italy the Ottonian style continued to exercise a powerful influence. The Lectionary written by Leo at Monte Cassino in 1072 (Lowe, *Scriptura Beneventana*, I, xvii = Monte Cassino MS. 99) is only one example of German precedent. The ornamental treatment traditional in Monte Cassino gave way before outside inspiration. The initial letters and some of the displayed titles are plain evidence that a great German manuscript had been seen by the Cassinese monks. There is good reason to believe, as Bloch points out, that the Gospel-book of Henry II, which is now in the Vatican, was a gift made to Monte Cassino between 1022 and 1024 (see Plate 132). This may well be the example by which the neo-Uncial mentioned above, as fashioned at Trier, Reichenau, Regensburg, and elsewhere, for titles is to be seen in Italy. The Henrician title, here shown, is in the early, light style. The latter style is heavily built. Ultimately, as will be seen, it appeared in Rome. The

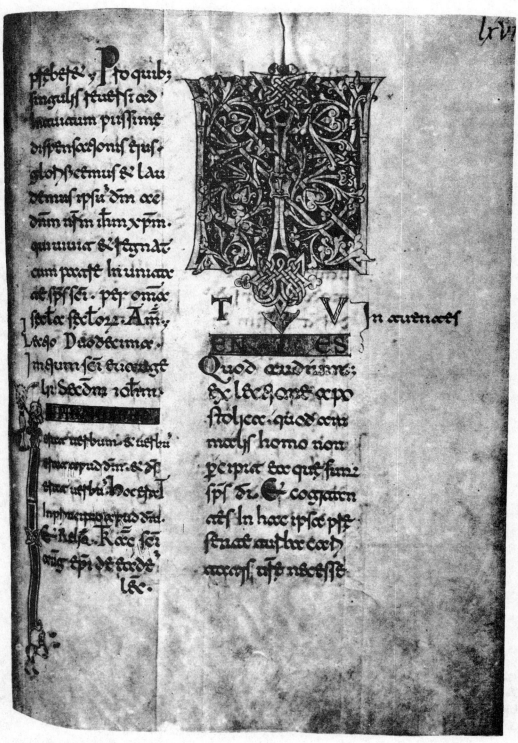

131. Monte Cassino Lectionary. 1072. Liturgical script.

Monte Cassino, MS. 99.

Beneventan minuscule in its finest state.

E. A. Lowe, *Scriptura Beneventana*, pls. LXVII-LXVIII.

132. Regensburg. Gospels of Henry II. 1022–4. Titling capitals.
Vatican, MS. Ottob. Lat. 74.
Uncialesque title in the early, light, Ottonian style.
G. Swarzenski, *Die Regensburger Buchmalerei* (Leipzig, 1901), pp. 123–32, pls. XIX–XXI.

new life given to the historic Christian script is the probable reason why the Uncial E reappears in the inscriptions of Gregory VII in SS. Cosma e Damiano.

It is, in fact, very possible that the Gospels of Henry II rank as the authoritative precedent which resulted in the establishment in Italy (as well as in its native Germany) of the Ottonian Uncialesque Capital and its continuous use for titles, inscriptions, and in combination with textual Minuscule until the fifteenth century, when it was superseded by the humanistic propagation of the classic Roman Square Capital. It will be noticed, in due course, that the strength of the Ottonian Uncialesque was not weakened by the emergence of 'Gothic' or Black-Letter but that it allied itself with this minuscule which rapidly attained such vigour from the thirteenth century as to become in its own day the 'modern' form, as opposed to the minuscule that had been in use for half a millenium.

We need at this point, however, to return to the early eleventh century and the successors of Desiderius. Pope Victor III was another Gregorian. Urban II (1088–99) also continued the struggle for spiritual independence, clerical discipline, moral reform, and ecclesiastical unity. Important in his pontificate was the Council of Bari, held in 1098, at which 185 bishops, among whom was Anselm of Canterbury, discussed the unity of the Church in relation to the *filioque* clause in the Creed. The material basis for this Council was the request of the Greeks for help against the Turks. It was Urban's conviction that a Western war against the Moslem would seem to unite the Church. As we know, the Eastern emperor did not give all the help that was expected by the Western armies marching on Jerusalem. Urban listened to the complaints of the crusaders but did not live to hear the news of their entry into the Holy City on 15 July 1099.

Urban's successor was yet another of the Gregorian school, the tragically weak figure of Paschal II (1099–1118). He could do nothing for ten years or more and only then after an abject surrender of all that Leo IX and Gregory VII had stood out for. It was only in 1112 that Paschal could set about the rebuilding and re-decorating of churches. For this he deserves credit. What was to develop into a considerable Roman school of art now began on the craft basis of the old and curious, father-to-son system. The names of some of these families have, in a few instances, come down to us. Paulo, whose sons are known to have worked in 1147 on the ciborium of S. Lorenzo fuori le mura. As Paschal's efforts were necessarily restorative, they were inevitably archaistic. It was incumbent upon him to provide for the basilicas such as S. Lorenzo in Lucina and S. Maria in Cosmedin and, certainly, S. Clemente, of which he was titular Cardinal. The style of lettering these ancient edifices required was, of course, archaic. Paschal II's reliance upon the inspiration of an earlier style is worth marking. It may have been a personal interest—since his seal, bearing the inscription PAS/CHALIS/ pp II, is a superior piece of engraved, serifed, Roman semi-quadrate Capital script.

An inscription of Paschal's dated 1112 should be admired as a fine piece of lapidary legality (Plate 133). The notarial M occurs once or twice, the round G always, but the remaining capitals are square though semi-condensed; they have an interesting, slight, right-to-left incline. A with its inclined crossbar is a curious vestige of the antique; and the more remarkable since it occurs here as a standard character in an inscription, otherwise very canonical, with only the usual AE and OR ligatures.

The style of Paschal II, therefore, is less a reproduction of the old Imperial lettering than an independent essay less in the style of Gregory VII than in that of Paschal's ninth-century namesake, Paschal I. He, too, had been a restorer— and, as such, an archaist. (There is a beautiful inscription of his over the portico of a chapel in S. Prassede). Paschal II, being in the same position, followed precedent. Nothing in the way of calligraphical innovation was called for, for, unlike the scribes at Monte Cassino in the time of Desiderius, the sculptors at Rome in the time of Paschal were given no incentive to imitate anything German. In 1111 Paschal had been made prisoner by Henry V who forced the pope to crown him emperor of the West. Thereupon the emperor of the East, Alexius I Comnenus, wrote to Paschal protesting against this treatment and professing a desire himself to come to Rome, rescue the pope, and himself be crowned Western emperor. Upon this an embassy left Rome for Constantinople. There is no need to say more of these negotiations than that they were prolonged. Another embassy was sent by Rome to Constantinople by Calixtus II in 1122. This was the year in which the pope and the Western emperor were reconciled and half a century of warfare between the Empire and the Papacy ended by the concordat of Worms.

That Rome continued to hope for reunion and had done so ever since 1054 may be inferred from an inscription in the church of the Greek quarter of the city: S. Maria in Cosmedin 'sive in schola Graeca' (Plate 134). A new collection of relics was inserted in the high altar, and it was reconsecrated under Calixtus II who caused an inscription to be set up in its commemoration. The date is 1123. This was the year of the first Council of the Lateran. Appropriately in the church of the Greek Quarter, the inscription is throughout in condensed lettering and the text highly abbreviated in accordance with Byzantine custom. The inscription is, in fact, a *tour de force* of economy in the use of space. Hardly a single word is left uncontracted. There are triple as well as double ligatures; contractions and insertions abound. The inscription also calls into use all the varieties of letters known to a versatile carver. Not all of these are ancient. Round G is present as a matter of course, and round E. The M occurs in half-a-dozen varieties including the notarial, cursive form derived from Uncial. This applies also to A, D, H, Q, and also T. Regular Capitals are also used, except that they are condensed equally with the rest. Most remarkable are the square C and the M with the fork terminating in a perpendicular. The latter is peculiar to Byzantine work. Finally, the tailed q may be seen in the last line as the initial for *quorum*.

The value to notaries of compacting the lettering required for legal, ceremonial, or commemorative (ranking below first class) purposes is obvious. The practice was already established by the tenth century in Greek scriptoria, and earlier in the ateliers of mosaic workers. A manuscript of the sermons of St. John Chrysostom, designed for Imperial use, illustrates this point.

PONTIANI·EVSEBII·VINCENTII·ETPB
EGRINI·QVEINDE AVFERENS SVIS
VMSOCIIS IN HANCÆCLAM TRAN

RESACTAFVERAT FIDELITERINTIMA

133. Rome. List of relics. Paschal II, 1112. Lapidary capitals.
Rome, S. Lorenzo in Lucina.
Condensed capitals in the square Roman 'antique' style. The A is the only Byzantine exception.
Silvagni i, pl. XXII. 3; Diehl 45a.

134. Rome. List of relics inserted at rededication of altar. Calixtus II. 1123.
Rome, S. Maria in Cosmedin.
Condensed capitals with Byzantine contractions.
Silvagni i, pl. XXV. 1; Diehl 45e.

Plate 135 exhibits two verses in three lines each of titling capitals, set over a painting of Nicephorus III Botaniates (1078-81), to whom the manuscript was presented. It was thought possible by Omont that it was originally executed for his predecessor, Michael VII Ducas (1071-8). It will be appreciated that the shape q in line two of column one and the first and last lines in column two is a vertical sigma-tau ligature. The serifs—which are affixed also to the flourished tops of tau and gamma—are to be noted. According to rule, the Greek titling Capital is serifed, but the Greek Minuscule never. The Greek canonization of Rustic proportions and the regularization of Rustic serifs is a sign, probably the only one, of Latin penetration into Greek. Latin influence upon Greek Minuscule cannot be traced.

The Byzantine and Latin Chancery-hands continued to remain distinct. Perhaps this is not surprising. According to Sir James Reid, the Roman Secretary-ship of State even under Claudius (d. 270) was divided into one side dealing with dispatches in Latin ('ab epistulis Latinis') and the other in Greek ('ab epistulis Graecis'). The development of the Eastern Minuscule out of the Byzantine Charter-hand, parallel (though later) as it was with the Western process, produced for the same purpose a different script, with different proportions. There is a common tendency in both scripts for the ascenders to taper downwards. This is a habit whose beginnings need more study than they have received. Apart from this practice in early Greek and early Latin Minuscule, there is little evidence after the Ottonian period of consistent Byzantine pressure upon Latin script until the new lavishly endowed church rising in the eleventh century at Venice was being decorated. Byzantine example upon S. Marco was all-powerful.

Building seems to have been started in 1063 and according to the Venetian chronicler the decoration of the church began in 1071, but it is thought that few examples of early work survive. Pietro Toesca believes that the mosaic of the Translation of the Body of St. Mark is one of the more ancient. Its inscription is brief in text and Roman in lettering (with M for MARCVS) and Square in proportion. Probably the older work was similarly treated. As time proceeded the lettering changed, whether as a matter of policy it is impossible to say. Little is known of the reasons why Venice committed itself to the plan of creating the greatest monument of Byzantine art and architecture ever to be seen in the West apart from Monte Cassino. The importance (which was increasing) and the closeness (which was variable) of the city's trading relations with Constantinople, do not by themselves explain the substitution of the Greek cross for the early Roman plain cross for the new basilica.

The great doges of the Orseolo family, from the end of the tenth to the twelfth century, maintained a regular pro-Byzantinism. The policy towards San Marco was also consistent. From the beginning it was decided to build upon the model of the Church of the Apostles in Constantinople. More and more artists were imported from the East and as they worked the inscriptions became longer and the Capitals less Roman and hence less Square. A vast variety of hybrid alphabets for display (they differ so widely in style as to deserve a monograph to themselves) were developed, some more and some less fundamentally Greek; most of which

135. Constantinople. St. John Chrysostom, *Sermons*. 1071–8? Byzantine titling script.
Paris, Bibliothèque Nationale, MS. Coislin 79, fol. 2ʳ.
Condensed capitals; ligatured; serifed; Nicephorus Botaniates with his officers of state.
H. Omont, *Facsimilés des miniatures*, pl. LXIII (Paris, 1920).

are later than the twelfth century and therefore become contemporary with the mosaics of the great churches in Palermo and Monreale erected by Roger II, Duke of Sicily from 1198. These, too, testify to the overwhelming prestige of the Byzantine artists. The lettering of the inscriptions on the Sicilian mosaics resemble the Venetian. It must be added that, following the example of San Marco, numerous other churches were built to serve neighbouring cities, which were also decorated in Byzantine style.

The just conclusion may be that the doges of Venice, like the dukes of Sicily, responsible for the grand design of their churches, were moved to imitate Constantinople less by the political and commercial opportunities than by their appetite for self-aggrandizement and admiration for the prestige of the uniquely beautiful capital, and for the artists who were its creators. In the case of Venice there was present the additional motive of impressing the emperor of the West. The great Doge Pietro Orseolo (perhaps the originator of the great design for S. Marco), was host to Otto III in 996.

The coexistence of the German type of Uncialesque on great codices, and the Venetian type of Uncialesque on great churches should not be overlooked, although, in spite of the fact that both the Byzantine and Ottonian scripts have a common denominator in Uncial, they exhibit differences. While the plan of S. Marco was a decorative scheme, the letterings as a whole were deliberately Byzantine. The inscription from the great series depicting the Creation (Plate 136) displays a type of lettering, reminiscent in point of heaviness of stroke of Byzantine script which the scribes of biblical and liturgical codices elaborated in the tenth century. This oriental, so to say, 'Black-Letter' had no contemporary equivalent in the occident. The capitals in this series while Greek are essentially Roman; being, for example, much more Square and less Uncial than the later capitals as in Plate 137. The persistence of Uncial, however, was not to be withstood. Why should the originally so definite Byzantine strain in the Venetian inscriptions give way during the first half of the thirteenth century before the northern style in which the Byzantine element was relatively so slight? The answer will be postponed for the present.

The Ottonian example is found by no means ineffective in Rome. In a regularized form it is plainly seen in an ill-cut inscription commemorating Innocent II (1130-43), the pope who crowned Lothair as emperor in Rome in 1130 and was deeply indebted to the Germans for their support against the anti-pope Anacletus. The inscription, dated 1148, was erected when Innocent's remains were transferred to S. Maria in Trastevere from the Lateran after a fire ruined an earlier monument (Plate 138).

If the masons attached to S. Maria in Trastevere are not to be congratulated upon their craftsmanship it may have been that they were cutting forms with which they were unfamiliar. The lettering itself, probably the handiwork of a notary in the apostolic chancery under Eugenius III (1145-53) is well designed in the canonical Uncialesque style. It will be noted that all the characters are round and not condensed as they became under Innocent III (1198-1216). The round H and T should be observed since their existence proves the expertness

136. Venice. San Marco. Mosaic of the Creation of the World. Early 13th century. Inscriptional capitals.
Condensed Roman capitals with heavy strokes to the Byzantine script.
Sergio Bettini, *Mosaici antichi San Marco a Venezia* (Bergamo, 1944), pl. LII.

and logic of the calligrapher responsible. The Roman H and T had been kept at Reichenau and were general in Ottonian work. Here it is to be seen co-ordinated with Uncial, a surprising but abortive precedent. There are other inscriptions of the pontificate of Eugenius III which use the round E and other Uncial forms but retain the H and T. It was not until the next century that sculptors in Rome were found competent to cut inscriptions in neo-Uncial.

Simultaneously Byzantine customs existed. This is further evidence of Rome's toleration of rites and customs other than her own; also some acknowledgement of political considerations may have been present. The door for the East would remain open, as the emperors, if not the patriarchs, were aware. The reigning emperor in the middle of the twelfth century was especially anxious to heal the breach with Rome.

The balance of power being what it continued to be, Rome had no alternative but to attempt a policy of independence and neutrality as between East and West, while bearing in mind the ecclesiastical and political significance of Byzantium and taking into account the determination and striking force of the German kings. There are calligraphical reflections of this situation. It has been mentioned that

137. Venice. San Marco. Mural of St. Peter and St. Mark, Byzantinesque. 12th century. Inscriptional capitals in mosaic.

Venice, S. Marco, Cappella Zeno.

S. Bettini, *Mosaici antichi di San Marco a Venezia* (Bergamo, 1944), pl. XCVII.

the Ottonian example was already becoming dominant in Venice. Much of the lettering on the mosacis shows the Ottonian style gaining over the Byzantine as the twelfth and thirteenth centuries progressed. Thus it was that the example, if not the authority, of the later German emperors prevailed over the intention and probably the instruction of the earlier Venetian doges.

During the same time the strokes of the scripts became heavier. Reciprocity between inscriptional architectural lettering and displayed titling script is, of course, ancient and consistent. In the twelfth century, an age of great building, it is specially evident. One finds instances of the increased freedom taken by artists and sculptors, as will be noticed presently.

The Byzantine and Uncialesque inscriptional work at S. Marco made familiar new capital lettering of superb artistry. Such an example of Venetian–Byzantine–Ottonian inscriptional craftsmanship could not fail to be impressive upon other Italian cities and, last of all, upon Rome herself.

The Byzantinization of early S. Marco was more thorough, perhaps, than had been the case even at Monte Cassino. It was too complete to be followed

138. Rome. Commemorating Innocent II, pope 1130–43. Dated 1148 (under Eugenius III, 1145–53).

S. Maria in Trastevere.

Informal (even casual) round, highly uncialesque capitals.

R. U. Montini, *Le tombe dei papi* (Rome, 1957), plate no. 59.

anywhere else. Rome's wide tolerance of the Greek rite and of Greek monasteries and liturgical customs would, of course, continue, but the resort by Rome to Byzantine models on the Venetian scale would not occur even if the city could acquire the money. After the settlement with the emperor, Rome was still the independent and primary see of Christendom and would conduct herself accordingly. It was not the fault of the Eastern emperors that the union of the Churches made no progress. Some Byzantines dreamt that as the question was more territorial than ecclesiastical repair of the schism would succeed the achievement of political fusion. The situation for the Eastern emperor was certainly growing more anxious. The Turks had gained a new leader, Saladin (1138–93), a profound Islamic theologian and brilliant warrior.

Manuel I Comnenus (1143–80) was a convinced pro-Westerner. His mother was Hungarian. He had married twice; and on both occasions to Latins. He had filled many of the principal offices of state with Italians and even Germans. He continued to hope that the divisions of the Western powers would improve the Eastern position in Italy. Manuel, therefore, determined to revive the project of Alexius Comnenus to buy the Western Imperial crown by offering ecclesiastical submission. The opportunity came in 1167 when Orlando Bandinelli, Pope Alexander III (1159–81) strove for the emperor's aid against the aggression of Frederick Barbarossa, indicated by his annexation of the title 'Sacrum' to the name of his Empire.

Thus Manuel more than once proposed to Alexander III reunion with the Eastern Church in exchange for the Western Imperial crown. It was given out by the pope that such a solution could only be made feasible if the emperor left New Rome and made Old Rome his residence and capital—an eminently sensible demand from a pope who knew his Germans and knew that an Eastern emperor whose seat was so far distant as Constantinople could not be relied upon to defend the papacy against a Western emperor whose force was much closer. But conditions forced Manuel to stay in the East. The Turks were becoming more menacing than ever before. In 1176 they inflicted upon Manuel a blow so crushing that the Empire never recovered from it: Saladin conquered Syria. All possibility of an Eastern-Western *rapprochement* vanished.

Manuel himself died in 1180 and there lay before the Eastern Empire a period of unsurpassed and uninterrupted degeneration. The anti-Western elements in the capital took their revenge. The ascent of Andronicus I Comnenus was a signal for a slaughter of the Latin community in Constantinople. This was one of the events which prepared the way for a Western reprisal. But it is not for us to dwell upon these happenings. It is more profitable at this point to revert to the scheme of Manuel I and speculate as to what could have happened if he and Alexander III had consolidated an agreement, considering 1167 as the last occasion upon which reunion between East and West was at all thinkable. Had it occurred under Alexander's terms and the Eastern emperor been soundly consecrated with the Western crown, and taken up residence in Rome, at least for part of the year, what description of building would the Eastern and Western emperor have commissioned, and what sort of Imperial inscriptional lettering would he have authorized for its identification? What script would have been employed by the Western and Eastern mints for the new coinage?

The schism of 1054 had ended the use of Latin legends on Byzantine coinage. The mints had henceforth used Uncialized Greek in varying degrees of inconsistency, as had been done for Latin before the schism. Thus East and West possessed one common alphabet during the reigns of Frederick Barbarossa and Manuel Comnenus.

Whether or not Barbarossa, who had procured from an anti-pope the canonization of Charlemagne, would have placidly accepted a concordat, political and religious, between Rome and Byzantium is not our question; only the fact that a common Imperial alphabet existed is what needs to be accepted. For us, it is the continuity of Uncial, already possessing an authoritative status in the West equally with the East, that is involved. It was not destined to be reinforced with Byzantine support. It is a pity the opportunity did not come.

Had the bureaucracy sought a precedent, and had the lettering on the ancient Imperial coins been considered, the characters chosen would have been comparable with those on the cross presented by the Emperor Justin II to Rome in the time of Pope John III (561–74). This Graeco-Roman Capital-Uncial alphabet for the Latin language was then regarded as appropriate to two ecclesiastical and political bodies in communion and friendship with each other (Plates 71–2). Such an alphabet could have been no obstacle in the Rome of Alexander III. In the course of time Latin inscriptions in Rome might have been engraved in a style of letter not differing greatly from many of certain of the early inscriptions in St. Mark's, Venice; half-Latin and half-Byzantine. Rome, in that event, would not have absorbed the particular style of Uncialized lettering that symbolized the prestige of the German emperors and was fated to be swept away by the humanist reactionary movement of the fifteenth century.

Thus, in the twelfth, thirteenth, and fourteenth centuries the Ottonian Uncialesque Capital remained throughout central Europe authoritative. It was by then Imperial and papal.

Simultaneously with the weakening in the East, and the consequent lessening of Byzantine prestige, there occurred a strengthening of power in the West— especially in northern and southern, rather than central Europe. There was a quickening of national unity which carried a new spirit into social, economic, legal, intellectual, architectural, and administrative standards. All these led to a great increase in the volume of writing and variety of style in script which, particularly in the northern European thirteenth-century form, will be noticed later. It is necessary first to notice a development that took place in northern Italy.

In Bologna Gratian lectured and compiled between 1139 and 1150 his vast but methodical *Concordia discordantium canonum*, later known as the *Decretum Gratiani*, which became the primary text in the schools; and in the expanded official text approved in 1179 at the third Council of the Lateran under Alexander III it was invested with the title of *Corpus Iuris Canonici*. The establishment of an additional faculty in the universities of Bologna, Paris, Oxford, and elsewhere carried with it an expansion of the legal profession which required the services of scribes, notaries, and other practitioners of legal hands of diverse and varying formality. The basic letter in which the text of a standard copy of the *Codex Iuris Canonici* (as distinct from commentaries upon it) was originated by and for the professional Bolognese legists and known later as the 'Scriptura Bononiensis'. It is a round and plain design evidently thought out and drafted for its specific purpose. As it is given shorter ascenders and descenders it has a correspondingly tall x-height. This minuscule, written with a broad pen in small size to narrow measure, makes no small contribution to a text whose volume exceeded that of the Bible. Apt for a lecturer's use it possesses that functional weight of stroke, and therefore appears to those habituated to modern typographical standards as related to what is currently termed the 'Gothic' style. Also, its strokes were unserifed. In its early state the 'Scriptura Bononiensis' is as rational a small minuscule as the extremely beautiful large-scale boldly designed liturgical hand practised at Verona and Padua from the twelfth century. It is notable that this bold script is unserifed at the feet; from which practice it is argued that the later and still larger round 'Gothic' was developed.

The utility and efficiency of the 'Scriptura Bononiensis' quickly won for it widespread acceptance in the papal Chancery, and its use for literary as well as legal texts became general in southern and other parts of Europe during the thirteenth century until it, too, was swept away by the humanist revolution.

The chief novelty in the writing of the script lay in the use of a pen broader in cut than had been employed earlier. This produced a thicker and therefore blacker stroke. The broad pen came into gradual use also in the north of Europe where, indeed, the practice may perhaps be observed earlier than in the south. This is a doubtful point to which reference is made below.

This, therefore, was the staple script used in the south for the texts of Justinian, the Decretals of Gratian, the Commentaries of Gregory IX, with all manner of other Summas, Digests, and bread-and-butter work.

Nowhere was this suitability appreciated so much as in Bologna, the first and greatest centre of juristic studies, powerful as early as the beginning of the twelfth century. A neat round heavily stroked Minuscule was evolved by the publishers to the University at the middle of the thirteenth century. The 'Littera Bononiensis' was so well suited in proportion and weight that it became the typical literary script of the fourteenth century. It may correctly be categorized as the first example of a utilitarian script backed by the authority of a university.

Side-by-side with this plain Bolognese book-script there flourished, even for literary purposes, a decorated notarial script. The Bolognese script is familiar enough but an early specimen may be of interest (see Plate 151). No doubt the influence of the legal hands upon sculptors and calligraphers was responsible for much of the uncanonical variety present in inscriptions and titles. It was a professional convention, long cultivated, that diplomatic scripts must be written with a deliberate and unbookish complexity. Such documents, by their nature private, were not subject to the laws of legibility, but some of their contrivances nevertheless affected documents intended for literary use.

The main distinction between the diplomatic and literary hands was that the royal Chancery (following the papal Chancery) developed a very condensed minuscule with exaggerated ascenders and descenders. What began in both chanceries as a stately version of the old, round, Carolingian Book-hand was, doubtless for security reasons, transformed into a new, normal diplomatic hand distinctive of, and reserved for, diplomatic use.

The desirability of such treatment of letter forms is obvious when it is understood that the texts of these documents related to property rights, titles, privileges, grants, and concessions having the force of law. The writers of such royal diplomas were highly efficient masters of their art and many of their performances are of interest to connoisseurs of calligraphy viewed as an art. The apostolic clerks in Rome became not less expert than those who served the Imperial chanceries at the invention of distinctive styles of titling. The Imperial form seems to have been dominant in Rome in the twelfth century. Even under Alexander III the diplomatic script resembled that of the German monarchs. Under Gregory VIII, as Alberto da Morra a former notary and chancellor, the efficiency and style of the Roman Chancery improved. Alberto became head of the Chancery in 1178 and as pope in 1187 (only) he instituted new rules for the style of curial Latin which necessarily influenced the style of Chancery script.

The election of Celestine III (1191–8) marked a return to the low standards of the papacy before Leo IX. Celestine was eighty-five years of age, and on becoming pope made it his first duty to crown Henry VI as emperor—as bloodthirsty a German as ever came south. Slaughter began forthwith. The aged Celestine afflicted the Church for seven years. His predecessor's inscription giving the title to the church of S. Giovanni a Porta Latina (Plate 139) is a stylish,

139. Rome. Dedication of a church. Clement III (1187–91). Inscriptional capitals. 1190.
Rome, S. Giovanni a porta Latina.

Square, mixed with uncialesque capitals; well serifed and the whole stylishly finished. See especially A, H, M; the square E is unexpected and the N is a freak.

Diehl 46c; Silvagni i, pl. XXVII. 3.

well-serifed piece of work cut after a calligraphic model made, surely, by a clerk who, trained under Alberto da Morra, was capable of creating a synthetic alphabet designed to be peculiar to his office. He reverses N and gives it the Byzantine short diagonal, while keeping the Rustic round G. Most important is his inclusion of Uncialesque A (in several varieties), M, and N. A Byzantinism is H which retains its Minuscule form, with single long perpendicular. Thus we have such a shape as hONORE. The text is highly contracted. This inscription ranks as an early specimen of notarial Roman penmanship in the finely engraved form. The Uncialesque characters are no doubt drawn ultimately from a German source. As such, it is evidence of persistent northern influence. This was not the only style practised at this time, as may be seen from a consecration tablet of the year 1195 in the church of S. Salvador de Cupellis.

Plate 140 shows an interesting example of a vertical inscription in highly condensed, abbreviated and ligatured lettering. It is quite as good a piece of engraving as that of Plate 137 but its style is wholly different and must then have been viewed as 'old-fashioned'. The design is canonical and quasi-quadrate, but the proportions are so condensed that the cramped tail of R is gothicized. The G is of the round type. Yet this was not the general tendency, which remained one of *renovatio*. There are several good inscriptions in the Square Capital style, but it is evident that while novelties were not welcomed by the clerk responsible, the trend was running against him, though at this time it was probable the new style was little more than a fashion. In other words, it had no authority behind it.

That the Uncialesque inscriptional style was strengthening is proved by two examples in the Lateran of Celestine III's reign. They are both engraved upon bronze doors, of which one is shown in Plate 141. The lesser inscription is of greater interest. It runs as follows: 'UBERTUS MAGISTER PETRUS' 'EI[US] FR[ATER] PLACENTINI FECERUNT HOC OPUS'. The second pair of doors adds to the similar 'credit line' a statement by another artist jealous for his city's reputation that Uberto and Pietro were from Siena (and not from Piacenza). More will be said later of such 'Magistri'. The insistence by the Sienese artist that the 'Magistri autem SENENSES fuerunt' was a highly deliberate and conscious act may be inferred; so, too, was the choice of Uncialesque lettering.

It should be noted that the Uncialesque capitals designed by the Magistri are canonical Uncialesque and that they differ only in point of artistic rendering from the forms that were contracted in the legal and other inscriptions which were drafted and supervised by the papal Chancery. The Uncialesque was at this time respected by the Magistri as authoritative. It was, indeed, the official Roman lettering for such purposes. It will be seen below that Magistri of the next generation, such as the Cosmati, departed from this convention.

The death of Celestine III in 1198 was an infinite relief to the College of Cardinals, to judge by the way they reacted. One who had chosen to live in retirement during this pontificate was now made to accept the tiara. Thus Innocent III (1198–1216) aged 37 succeeded Celestine III aged 92. He was lucky from the start. Innocent's immediate great fortune was that the Imperial throne

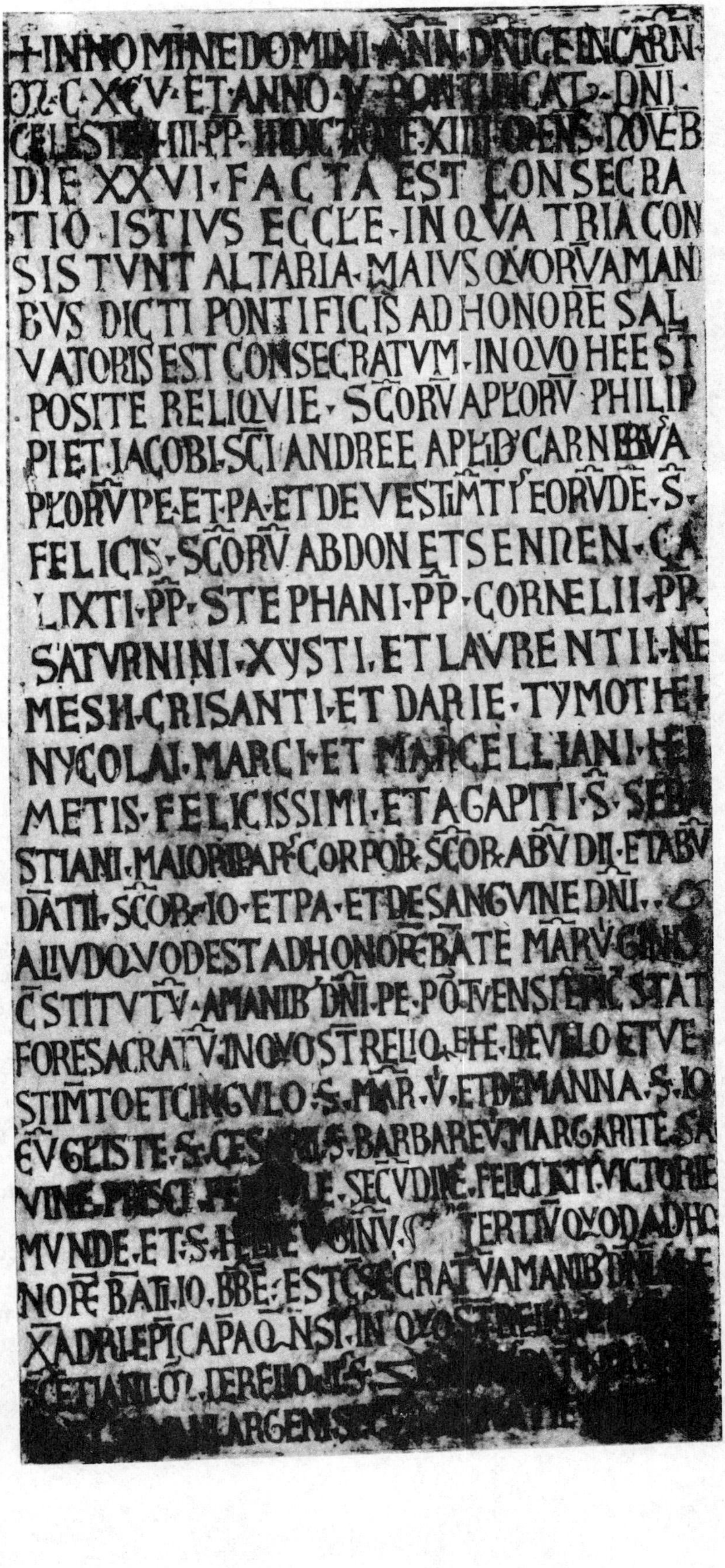

140. Rome. Record of
consecration and list of
relics. Celestine III. 1195.
Inscriptional capitals.

Rome, S. Salvatore alle
capelle.

Formal capitals condensed
with ligatures and
contractions; well serifed
and strongly stressed.

Diehl 46d; Silvagni i,
pl. XXXVII. 4.

141. Rome. Inscription naming donor and artists. 1196. Inscriptional capitals and bronze.
St. John Lateran.

Condensed uncialesque capitals signed by Uberto and Pietro Placenti.

Mann, x, p. 426. See also another inscription, Lauer plate XV.

was vacant. Henry VI died suddenly in the previous year. The new pope took full advantage of every available means to assert the right of the Church to govern herself, and to secure respect for something new in that world: the conscience of Christendom. Much vexed by the forgery of bulls and other papal diplomatic documents he strengthened the security regulations of the Roman Chancery, a measure which carried with it increased supervision of the official scripts; the pope also lavished care and money upon the churches. He became, in effect, a generous patron of architects, artisans, and their workmen, including sculptors and engravers and inscriptors. Among these were the Cosmati family, to be mentioned later. Some mosaicists and masons had already arrived at the stage when they were publicly known as 'stars' of their *métier* and permitted to affix their names to their work, as the brothers Uberto and Pietro had already done to the Lateran doors.

In the time of Innocent III Rome was tolerant and neutral. The Holy See neither encouraged nor discouraged Byzantinism. The situation in Venice had radically changed. It has been seen that the definite Byzantinization of the inscription in S. Marco during the late eleventh and twelfth centuries was succeeded by a wave of Ottonization. What was the authority for this? Was it purely 'artistic'; a reflection of the social aggrandizement of highly skilled workers in the building and ancillary trades?

A more probable cause may be the changed situation that came out of the consequences of the Fourth Crusade preached by Innocent III. Organized to start from Venice, it was perverted by the Serene Republic to the lowest of selfish motives and sailed first to Constantinople. On the pretext of returning an exiled pretender to his throne, they sacked the richest city in the world, imposed a new emperor, and installed a Latin patriarch. The effect was to enforce ecclesiastical union, with an ascendant Latin element.

The circumstances of 1204 were hardly those in which Venice could consider it appropriate to continue the policy of Byzantinizing the inscriptions of San Marco. The way was open therefore for a westernization of capital script; to be exact, for the adoption of the Ottonian Uncialesque. The vigour of the same script in Rome has a more commonplace explanation. The long-standing acceptance of Bolognese and Roman notarial elements in inscriptions restrained to some extent the influence in the early years of the thirteenth century of northern calligraphical example. When Innocent III, soon after his election, conferred by bull a high privilege upon the Benedictines of Subiaco, an impressive commemorative portrait fresco was painted of the pope by Magister Conxolus (Plate 142). The pope is seen in the act of donation of the bull, the text of which comprises upwards of a score of lines, alternately in red and black, painted in condensed lettering which is Uncialesque in several characters, notably (though not invariably) D, E, G. The rest of the characters are Roman with the exception of Q which is throughout of the Byzantine Ч type. The degree of condensation is marked, due to the limitations of space which become extreme in a legal lapidary bull, when the order was given that contractions must be reduced to the minimum. The retention of the roman characters in a majority position may be deliberate. The fully Ottonian inscription for Innocent II (Plate 138), therefore, was then acceptable, but the Uncial element was kept to a minor position under Innocent III. The Subiaco bull is of interest as an example of the slowness with which the German script made its mark in Rome.

It may have been that Uncial was regarded in Rome rather as an Imperial than as a Christian element, which is less surprising since the theory responsible for the establishment of Capital Uncial was originated more than two centuries before the pontificate of Innocent III. This should be borne in mind when the so-called 'Gothic' scripts are given consideration, as will be attempted below.

For the present it should be observed that while in the bull of Innocent III the Uncialesque capitals are in the main canonically Ottonian, they are narrow in the body; the stroking is heavy, and the effect in mass correspondingly 'black'. The adoption of a broader pen by the Bolognese law schools had been noted. The later use of a broader-nibbed pen, making an unprecedented stroke so heavy as to produce a 'black' effect, was a significant stage of a protracted development.

The general term 'Black-Letter' is as confusing as it is convenient. There is, for example, early medieval heavy 'Black' uncial. The particular term 'Gothic'

142. Record of Papal Bull: fresco by Magister Conxolus. Subiaco, *c.* 1200.
Condensed uncialesque; with 'lower case' q.

is equally confusing and equally convenient. There is, again, medieval 'Gothic' Uncialesque. It has been seen that the majuscule titles typical of the Ottonian regime are uncials treated as capitals. It has also been pointed out that these titling capitals obtained use all over Europe, including Venice (for one reason) and Rome (for another), and it has been shown that ultimately it became the standard Western calligraphical and inscriptional capital practised in the chanceries, including that of the pope. It was combined with the varying local types of contemporary minuscule. In late medieval times the minuscule preferred in northern Europe preserves a considerable, though only partially evident, residue of Uncial. The reason why the Uncial element is rather dormant than dominant is not because it has been 'blackened' but because it was subject to 'Gothicization' an extremely complex process which will involve the reader in some art history. It has been made clear that the present inquiry is limited to the elucidation of the social, national, ecclesiastical, and political causes underlying changes in the material shaping of Graeco-Latin scripts, irrespective of any artistic value that may be imputable to their form. However, in the instance of 'Black-Letter' it is impossible to consider its political authority if any, without regard to its deliberate aesthetic basis.

Accordingly, something must now be said about the design and formative career of 'Black-Letter' and 'Gothic'. Both terms are currently treated as signifying the same category of scripts, since they are equally black. In comparison with their Carolingian predecessors they are seen to be related inasmuch as they are created by a similar pen. How close the relation was between the scripts practised in the chief northern and southern writing schools of the late twelfth, thirteenth, and fourteenth centuries raises a point of technique too complex to be obtruded upon the present reader. It is only necessary here to say that in the north during the fourteenth and later centuries, the penhold is new and specifically related to the creation of a new form involving a new substitution of angles for curves. Where, why, and when this script was created, and how it secured authority, are the questions now to be considered.

First, as to the place of its origin. The popular impression, derived from the form of printing type used for the first Bibles printed at Mainz in the fifteenth century, is that the so-called 'Gothic' style is peculiarly Germanic. In fact it is to be classed rather as un-Germanic—or even as anti-Germanic. To say the obvious, 'Gothic' is anti-Romanesque. At the time of the invention of 'Gothic' the current Romanesque style was rightly seen to be essentially East Frankish in spirit.

In any case, whether or not the impulses that brought 'Gothic' into existence were anti-German, they were undoubtedly anti-Carolingian and took their origin in the ambition of the new West Frankish dynasty of Hugh Capet. In the context of north European history 'Gothic' architecture is recognizable as a by-product of the schism between the Franks, while 'Gothic' script is a delayed manifestation of the same national self-consciousness which eventually transformed the region of the West Franks into the nation-State of France. The political evolution was slow.

By the original partition Treaty of Verdun, negotiated between the two Carolingian dynasties in 843, the regions guaranteed to Charles the Bald were already described as 'Francia Occidentalis'. The treaty, which left unresolved grievances, felt by both wings of the Carolingian dynasty, set a seal upon the competitive nationalism which newly animated and separated the Franks east and west of the Rhine. The prospects for peace between them did not improve when the Carolingian dynasty petered out among the East Franks with the death of Lewis the Child in 911, and when the Saxon King Henry I (919-35) founded the succeeding Ottonian, Imperial dynasty.

Vital challenges between the neighbours arose when Otto III became King of the East Franks in 983 and Emperor of the Romans in succession to Charlemagne in 996. How Lothair, King of the Western Franks (964-86), invaded Lower Lorraine in 978, seized and plundered the symbolic-Carolingian capital of Aachen, sacked the Palace, and nearly captured Otto II, how Otto retaliated by attacking Paris, may only be mentioned here.

It has been seen that the Carolingian dynasty had already ended east of the Rhine in 911. The death of Louis V in 986 without heirs ended the direct Carolingian dynasty among the West Franks. The significant point for us is that the dynasty founded by the succession of Hugh Capet in 987 brought with it a basic revision of many existing political concepts and the reorientation of the power relations which the West Franks had shared with the East Franks during and since the time of Charles the Great. Hence the change of dynasty among the West Franks in 987 created for the following generations a climate which encouraged desire for more changes as between the two nations.

The direction given to West Frankish policy by the Capetian kings differed necessarily and fundamentally from that followed by their great neighbours. The Ottonian kings were also kings of Italy; they were all set, like Charles the Great, on becoming Roman emperors as well as being German kings. Hence they eagerly followed the precedents established by the Carolingians. As the Capetian kings had nothing to gain by challenging the Ottonian-Carolingian claim based upon precedent they laid emphasis upon continuity with the Merovingians, and therefore looked not to Charles but to Clovis as their patron. Consequently as time proceeded they resigned the Carolingian artistic inheritance to the East Franks, while they made themselves ready and free to dignify their nation by adopting an independent style of art when it could be formed. A rival architectural order, however urgently required for reasons of state, could not be rapidly organized. A fresh West Frankish or French style could not be created in advance of political and social consolidation or of technical and artistic capacity. The process occupied upwards of a century after Hugh Capet. His successor in 996 was his son Robert II who was crowned in the year of Otto III's march to Rome when he made his cousin Bruno pope who as Gregory V forthwith crowned Otto emperor. France's necessary policy under Robert II (d. 1031) and his successor was bound to be one holding Germany in check.

The precedent obtained by Charles the Great gave the German kings a special responsibility under papal consent for the protection of the Holy See. By the end of the tenth century the power of Germany overshadowed that of France to a degree that naturally caused her anxiety. A feeling of national insecurity is automatic when a relatively small kingdom is following a custom and speaking a language differing from the neighbouring empire. The feeling became the more acute when the Empire, already much more extensive, was exhibiting every indication of adding to its territory, maximizing its authority, and emphasizing its Germanic might. While this was the situation in the eleventh century, France steadily strove to increase her resources. It was achieved mainly by increase in administrative efficiency. By the time of Louis VII (1137-80) the West Frankish monarchy had acquired the prestige necessary so to impress the magnates that they tacitly accepted the father-to-son succession for which his predecessors had striven. The policy, foreign and domestic, of the Capetians became firmer and assured itself of continuity of family and consistency of aim.

Strong as it was, the French desire to become independent from the Carolingian system spent nearly a century and a half in finding the technical basis for an architectural and graphic art form vigorous enough to challenge the Carolingian-Romanesque style developed by the emperors on the other side of the Rhine.

Organized to supersede the existing Romanesque, the new so-called 'Gothic' style made its first effective appearance in the new choir of the Abbey of St. Denis between 1140 and 1151. It was erected and apparently directed by the most powerful personage in the kingdom, himself for years regent of Louis VII. This was the Abbot Suger.

The chief structural novelty in Suger's choir was the adoption of the pointed arch in place of the familiar semi-circular arch. A second innovation was the enlargement of window-space in order to increase the measure of light which Suger required for the illumination of his other novelty—stained glass, something known only in Byzantium. Finally, an innovation with great calligraphical eventualities lay in the admission of a strong decorative element. Whereas the Romanesque style was sparing in the use of ornament the new style was relatively lavish with it. Such ample use of decoration had been seen in the West only in Islamic Spain. This principle of ornamentation for its own sake was in due course applied to the ancillary arts and crafts and with them forms of lettering.

The construction and harmonization of the new structural factors deriving from numerous sources within and without the Île de France, joined to an equally new and generous element of decoration, became the spur of French ambition. The French could now hope to equal if not to surpass the Germans as the leaders of Christian culture in Western Europe.

The Capetian-French ambition was to establish a style completely different from and wholly superior to that of the Carolingian-Germans. Also the French would make their style demonstrably new. It has been noted above that the Capetians emphasized their continuity with the Merovingians. They did not for this reason essay to revive contemporary architectural (or calligraphical) features. The choice as the French saw it in the twelfth century was either to modify the German or Romanesque style or to invent something new. That they chose the latter alternative with all its particular consequences was due to Suger.

It is acknowledged (by Panofsky) that the abbot was aware that what he was doing was new, while what he had designed was to be congruous with its Carolingian surroundings. Moreover, while it does not follow that Suger built in accordance with a fully fledged theory, it appears that his 'invention' was no mere accident or whim. The 'invention' consisted of a synthesis of all the latest methods and techniques then being used by 'advanced' masons or draughtsmen wherever they might be working.

How far Suger foresaw that this concentration of all the talents was bound to inaugurate what modern men call the 'Gothic' style is a question not to be discussed here. Panofsky mentions that Suger was acutely conscious of the stylistic difference that existed between his own 'modern' structures which he designates *opus novum* and even *modernum* and the old Carolingian which he calls *opus antiquorum*. Suger, too, understood that what he was building was intended to possess, in the words of Panofsky, 'distinctive aesthetic qualities'. Here, in effect, lay the essence of the then 'modern' style whose conspicuous quality was a fresh and conscious aestheticism at the time peculiar to St. Denis. The lavish ornamentation of the up-to-date portion of the abbey is described in such graphic detail by Suger himself that his reader cannot but ask if the motive of building *ad majorem Dei gloriam* suffices alone to account for the colossal effort involved. It can hardly be doubted that Suger was also building for the greater glory of France.

Another part of his programme was to centralize administration in Paris and encourage the townsmen in return for their support of the monarchy against the feudal barons. Suger's 'modern' style, whatever its intended mystical significance, was, equally, a propagandist device for the aggrandizement of the Capetian monarchy. It was designed to support their nationalistic ambition to achieve a political supremacy and cultural precedence over Germany and a hoped-for French territorial domination of Burgundy.

Such a policy, buttressed by architectural, artistic, literary, and intellectual measures, would, it was conjectured, establish in time unity between the northern and southern regions, and a superiority of the *langue d'oïl* over the *langue d'oc*. The measures of Louis VI and Louis VII and Suger would transform a royal feudal domain into a distinct nation separate, self-sufficient, and inspired by an artistic style of her own.

This conception of a new course for the arts was an integral measure of the French policy of centralized nation-wide administration. Suger's innovation broadened beyond St. Denis. In 1220 the north transept of Chartres was begun. Amiens was begun in 1228. Work on Beauvais, Laon, and Paris (Notre Dame) soon began, and Reims was rebuilt. It cannot be doubted that the adoption of the so-called 'Gothic' style for all these capital edifices originated with Suger and the backing of royal authority. Hence, if justice were done this style of architecture and that of the lesser arts bearing similar principles of form would be known by us not as 'Gothic' but 'Capetian'. It was certainly French. More has to be said about the German failure to match the French in arms, art, or script.

By the time of Philip II (not for nothing surnamed Augustus) the Capetian policy had sufficiently achieved its purpose as to fit his kingdom to challenge the Empire to battle. Philip Augustus was king from 1180 to 1223. Otto IV was emperor from 1198 to 1216 and Innocent III pope from 1198 to 1216; they watched Philip Augustus rising to the primacy of power. Otto IV, unable to hold the Germans together, was challenged by the Hohenstaufen, Frederick II. In 1212 Frederick was crowned king at Mainz by the archbishop, the expense of the operation being met in large part by Philip Augustus. In 1214 Philip defeated the coalition armies of Otto IV and John of England at Bouvines. The battle was decisive in every sense and the greatest personal success for the king. Philip Augustus had the supreme satisfaction of seeing his knights chase the emperor off the field. The way was now open for Frederick II to be recrowned in Aachen in 1218. Otto IV died friendless, leaving Frederick undisputed as present and future king of the Germans. His death conveniently marks the beginning of the end of the Romanesque style in Carolingian Germany and the opening of a new stage in the progress of Capetian-'Gothic'. The old and familiar Imperial and Ottonian Capital Uncialesque was destined to hold its position in Germany, Rome, and Italy for a few generations. In France it was destined to be superseded by large 'Gothic' majuscules and minuscules. The Capetians continued to supply the momentum for change.

Philip was no less active domestically. He followed the policy that Suger had indicated. In 1200 the University of Paris was established by royal charter. It was an important step in the centralization of the administration in Paris and in the creation of an efficient and loyal bureaucracy. This was an organ necessary for the control of the townsmen, or bourgeoisie, whose expansion as the rising commercial class had been growing since the end of the eleventh century when the legal term 'bourgeois' is first encountered. For Philip it was essential to the royal programme to increase the legal and social reorganization of the bourgeoisie as a check upon the feudal baronage. The communal prosperity and cultural prestige of France rose rapidly to an unprecedented height, and the respect for her military strength and political capacity gave powerful support outside France to the 'modern' style, and elaborated by succeeding generations of French builders. The long dependence of the artists of the West upon the masters of the East was now ended in France, who, while not able to claim the status of the Empire, had created a 'modern' style independent not only of Byzantium and Aachen, but of Rome itself. It soon spread to the Burgundian regions and soon took root across the Channel and eventually beyond the Rhine.

The successor of the great Philip Augustus was the even greater Louis IX, known as St. Louis, king of France from 1226 to 1270. The gathering strength of French power earned corresponding respect everywhere in the north for all forms of French endeavour, and especially for the 'modern' building style.

Frederick II, for his favourite seat at Foggia, built in the 1230s a castle which according to Kantorowitz exhibited Gothic windows. The earliest German building in Gothic style was Cologne Cathedral, begun in 1248. Many cathedrals and abbeys set up east of the Rhine followed the examples of Cologne and Strasburg.

Developments in French script moved rapidly in the north parallel with the building of new cathedrals. It has been contended in these pages that the Uncial-esque capital essentially symbolized the Christian character of the German Imperial power. It was for centuries, even in France, a sign of the cultural prestige claimed by the German kings, who used to represent their claim to be the Imperial successors to Charles the Great. The claim was not lost sight of when the Hohen-staufens succeeded. As has been seen, the merging of the Augustan Square Capital, revived for Charlemagne, with the Uncial transformed into a Capital, created the characteristic Ottonian–Christian titling, and automatically took its place among the Germanic Imperial insignia.

The elevation and merging of the Uncial element with the Capital staple made the resultant combination 'Holy'. The coexistence of Uncial with the Capital made the whole scriptorial system 'Roman'; while its use for the great Gospel-books of the Ottonian kings, made the script Imperial and appropriate for an Empire that was Holy and Roman and therefore became an apt index for those who, since the coronation at Rome of Otto I by Pope John XII in 962, had sought recognition as the heads of the Holy Roman Empire. Its international reputation, as unique in the northern region of the West, and its artistic eminence was signifi-cantly raised in 972 when the Emperor Otto II married the princess Theophano in 972.

In the eleventh century the prestige of the Ottonian German Empire was paramount in Europe and so remained until it was challenged by the Capetian-French kingdom from St. Denis in the twelfth century. It has been argued above that the Ottonian patronage of art and the use of Uncialesque in the Gospel-books were in intention and effect aspects of propaganda for the Holy Roman Empire. It has been seen that under an impulse of august patronage the range of Uncialesque was bound to be wide and its example contagious among the painters, sculptors, and scribes of the entire north-west and, of course, Italy as a German dependency.

In terms of script, this could not permanently satisfy the expanding Capetian bureaucracy. The concentration of the government departments and university faculties of Paris in the late twelfth and early thirteenth century gave the city an importance no French city had ever before attained, and no German centre was destined to equal. It was this primacy which created for Paris the possibility to perfect the final stage of 'Black-Letter'. This was angular and above all decora-tive book-script commonly known as 'Text' or 'Textura'.

Although tendencies such as angularizing the curves and pointing the joins are observable in small-format book-production in some northern regions in the first three-quarters of the twelfth century on either side of the Rhine, there existed no style of script so set as to be, or even prefigure, a radical departure from the Carolingian standard. Naturally regional variants of the Carolingian Minuscule and the Ottonian Majuscule were bound to appear in some centres at some time during the late Carolingian period. But such as they were, these amount to nothing more than a number of variants, some related, and others independent, but all mere occurrences and divergences within the Carolingian canon.

The changes that took place between the twelfth and the mid thirteenth centuries on this side of the Rhine evolved into a revolutionary departure from the hallowed canon. It served as a positive sign of a dynastic, political, and cultural ambition only fully explicable by the slow but pregnant shift in the balance of power as between the Eastern and Western Franks which was completed in the thirteenth century.

In the thirteenth century Italy, while detached from the German-French rivalry, continued to use the Ottonian Uncialesque. The Subiaco inscription of Innocent III has been described (see Plate 142). These capitals thickened in their mainstrokes and, used with the Bologna Minuscule, combined to produce a workmanlike, bold, round, and legible script free from the superfluous decoration by which the French would indicate artistic superiority over their Imperial neighbour. In Italy there had so far been no regional movement in art. The Byzantine conventions in painting were paramount in Florence and remained so until the second half of the thirteenth century. The Roman or Romanesque convention remained the norm in building until later. It was a context with which the Bologna Minuscule and Uncialesque Majuscule fitted perfectly. The Romanesque style, whether Italian or German, was rational and so too were the scripts of Bologna and Reichenau.

This round and legible Bolognese and Uncialesque hand became the canonical Roman script in the second half of the twelfth century. It is important to note that the mainstrokes are markedly thick in contrast with the substrokes which are thin; secondly, that the capitals are narrow. Briefly, they are heavy and condensed. This combination is an instance, not the only one, of notarial influence upon inscriptional lettering. It has been mentioned that the influence of sculptural lettering upon diplomatic practice seldom appears. Any correspondence between the two had long been mostly accidental. In the thirteenth century, however, a degree of assimilation between the Book-hand and the Charter-hand is noticeable for the first time since the eighth century. This, in turn, took the place of Uncialesque capitals as a normal basis for sculptured lettering. Evolution at Luxeuil of the Minuscule Book-hand out of the Cursive Charter-hand has been described above. It needs now to be observed that at Paris, Rome, and elsewhere in the thirteenth century writers of liturgical and literary texts came under the influence of the scriveners of charters and other legal instruments.

These professionals, included perhaps for 'security' reasons as well as for aesthetic effects, were apt to introduce flourishing and the practice is to be seen gradually establishing itself in inscriptions. There are to be found, therefore, both plain and decorated versions of the Uncialesque capitals and the Bolognese Minuscules. In both instances the practice of flourishing may be seen to spread. In Latin texts it was firmly restrained in comparison with the unbridled striking of curves permitted in vernacular writing. It is possible that one of the reasons which safeguarded the position of Uncialesque in Rome was that some of the antiquarians remembered that the Ottonian Capitals originated in the historic premier Christian letter-form, native to Rome: the Uncial.

If in the thirteenth century a pope or a cardinal of erudite character should have seen one example of the pointed or angular script what would he have thought of it? In all probability he would have judged it as an irrational innovation to be respected, if at all, in terms of the great and effective loss of power by the Germans to the French, a development by no means insignificant to the Romans. It remained that the now weakened German State, as successor to the Carolingian Empire, inherited the protectorate of the Holy See, and although the popes had encouraged relations of special intimacy with France, the realities of decreased German power needed to be recognized.

For this reason, also, the Ottonian Uncialesque continued as the Canonical Majuscule in Rome, and was used in association with a variant of the Bologna Minuscule. The combination was another example of the structural change notable in the late medieval period and of the organization of the majuscule and the minuscule into one duplex alphabet which, when regularized, corresponds to the upper and lower case of the printer's composing room. For our purposes, however, it is only necessary to consider calligraphical developments in so far as they may have a political *raison d'être*. For this reason we do not need to tabulate the several aesthetic varieties of 'Black-Letter' or 'Gothic' or 'modern' script which originate in the French *Textura*. However, to understand the nascent Italian semi-nationalistic anti-'Gothic' and anti-'modern' movement of the fifteenth century it is necessary to summarize the French fully nationalistic 'Gothic' and 'modern' movement of the eleventh, twelfth, and thirteenth centuries in so far as both movements affected calligraphy.

The impulse of the new non-Carolingian and a new Capetian nationalistic programme encouraged in France, between the eleventh and thirteenth centuries, a gradual ousting of the hieratic tradition of a simple, abstract, and rationalist alphabet of ancient pedigree in favour of a secular, complex, artificial, and ornamental alphabet of units designed according to a consciously unhistorical system. The old calligraphical system possessed the permanent virtue (it has others) of being a medium of legibility; the 'modern' design exhibits the then interesting merit (it has no others) of a work of art.

The assimilation of the 'modern' minuscule with the 'modern' majuscule made possible by the garnishing of both with hair-strokes and flourishings, brought to completion the process of destroying the Roman basis of the antique majuscule. The cursives (Bastardas) followed the same course. This seemed wholly satisfactory. It exactly suited the politics of the situation since none could guess that the form of the 'modern' majuscule owed anything to the Roman Uncial or the Augustan Carolingian. This was new and followed the general course of building then being pursued with great enthusiasm in every diocese of France, and it was precisely what was required by the policy of Philip Augustus and St. Louis. From, say, 1250 there had developed the particular Gallican book-script from which all signs of the rational Carolingian ancestry had been eliminated. The 'Gothic' ideal was rather to create a distinctive work of decorative art.

Its immediate regulative authority was the craft-guild, who gave tacit licence for its creation by experts in handwriting. As an alphabet, the *Textus* is afflicted with the professional disease of over-designing. It was too elaborate to be practical, and the cursives derived from it were even more over-decorative. With the reflection that such a departure from legibility as the 'Textus Quadratus' and its derivatives created some generations later a 'neo-Carolingian' reaction, the subject may be dropped for the present. We may conclude by saying that without the backing of France, at last the greatest power in Europe, the use of 'Textus Quadratus' for general literary purposes would have been discontinued, even in the north, long before Poggio led his pro-antique Roman and Florentine 'calligraphical' movement.

The Western protectorate over the papacy, as has been seen, began with Charles the Great, and later had outgrown its inclusive Frankish origin and become an exclusive Germanic trusteeship. Under the Ottos the papacy was a protectorate of the Germanic Empire, and although the popes endeavoured to effect a balance of power by themselves protecting the Capetians, they were at all times exposed to the pressure of the emperors. The long struggle between the Church and the Empire which began in the eleventh century over the investiture of bishops and abbots did not seriously weaken the attachment of Rome to the Ottonian Uncialesque.

A lapidary bull of Gregory IX (1227-41) may be cited because its script represents a gesture of papal independence. It was not cut in an interval of concord between the papacy and the Empire. Had it been so, one would expect a notarial version of the Ottonian capitals. This was not the fact. Ugolino da Segni, a nephew of Innocent III, had not idly assumed the name of Gregory. If the cardinals who unanimously elected this octogenarian expected a quiet time they were disappointed. He became a highly militant defender of the patrimony of St. Peter. Hence, Gregory IX's inscription is in the style favoured by Gregory I and Gregory VII: the old Roman Square Capitals. They are monoline but well serifed. Unlike most lapidary documents of the century the shape is horizontal. Usually, engraved bulls are in the vertical proportion, which encourages condensed letters, just as the horizontal layout encourages quadrate capitals. And this may not, in Gregory IX's case, be an accident of layout choice such as might arise from the mason's desire to exploit the shape of the stone given him (Plate 143).

On the contrary, the Roman precision and consistency of Gregory IX's inscription seems so deliberate as to imply that the script, example, and prestige of the Ottos and Henrys had been rejected by the successor of Innocent III. The reversion accompanied the pope's evocation of the names of Constantine and Valentinian as emperors whose example should be followed and, more important, Gregory's claim, advanced against Frederick II, that when Constantine left Rome 'he handed over the Empire to the perpetual care of the Roman Pontiff, with the Imperial insignia and sceptres'. Such language was fully in the sense of the *Dictatus papae* of Gregory VII. Thus had Gregory IX written to Frederick II on 23 October 1236.

It may, therefore, not fetch it too far if we say that the Roman papal-Imperial characters of the bullatic inscription in S. Sabina were deliberately chosen to symbolize the pope's policy towards the emperor. It should be added that although

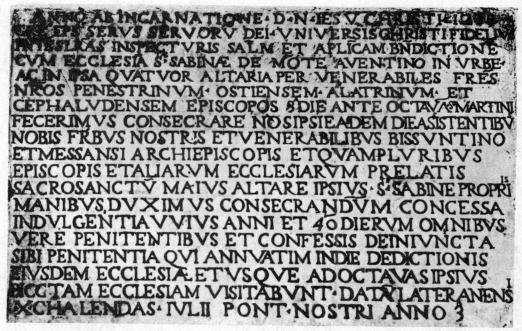

ANNO AB INCARNATIONE · D · N · IES V CHRISTI · 1229 ·
EPS SERVVS SERVORV DEI · VNIVERSIS GHRISTI FIDELIV
PNLICAS INSPECTVRIS SALM ET APLICAM BNDICTIONE
CVM ECCLESIA S · SABINÆ DE MOTE AVENTINO IN VRBE
AC IN IPSA QVATVOR ALTARIA PER VENERABILES FRES
NROS PENESTRINVM · OSTIENSEM · ALATRINVM · ET
CEPHALVDENSEM EPISCOPOS 8 DIE ANTE OCTAVA MARTINI
FECERIMVS CONSECRARE NOS IPSI EADEM DIE ASISTENTIBV
NOBIS FRBVS NOSTRIS ET VENERABILIBVS BISSVNTINO
ET MESSANSI ARCHIEPISCOPIS ET QVAM PLVRIBVS
EPISCOPIS ET ALIARVM ECCLESIARVM PRELATIS
SACROSANCTV MAIVS ALTARE IPSIVS · S · SABINE PROPRI
MANIBVS, DVXIMVS CONSECRANDVM CONCESSA
INDVLGENTIA VVIVS ANNI ET 40 DIERVM OMNIBVS
VERE PENITENTIBVS ET CONFESSIS DEINIVNCTA
SIBI PENITENTIA QVI ANNVATIM INDIE DEDICTIONIS
EIVSDEM ECCLESIÆ ET VSQVE AD OCTAVAS IPSIVS
ECCTAM ECCLESIAM VISITABVNT · DAT LATERANENS
XCHALENDAS · IVLII PONT · NOSTRI ANNO 3

143. Rome. Bull of Gregory IX of 1229, engraved in 1238. Inscriptional capitals.
Rome, S. Sabina.
'Gregorian' square capitals, otherwise neo-antique monumental capitals.
Diehl 46e.

the indulgence was conceded in 1229, the inscription was not engraved until 1238, when the pope was at the height of his struggle with the emperor. Frederick II, it is relevant to observe, used for his title on the great seal a finely engraved version of the Ottonian Capital consistently and logically set out, canonically except for v which is Roman. That Frederick kept to Augustan capitals for other purposes is also to be borne in mind. The 'SEMPER AVGVSTVS', having been excommunicated three or four times by Gregory IX, was in no mood to allow the popes of Rome to appropriate the alphabetical insignia of the creators of the Empire.

It was of the essence of the ninth Gregory's political claim, upon which he relied for the spiritual freedom of the papacy, that the final spiritual authority was also a supreme temporal ruler. This claim culminated in Gregory's unilateral calling of a General Council to assemble at Easter, 1241. Upon its assembling Frederick II marched upon Rome to overawe these presumptuous fathers. He intercepted a hundred of the bishops, bagged a couple of cardinals, reached Grottaferrata, and was preparing to invest Rome when Pope Gregory died just before his hundredth birthday. What happened then was much more exciting than anything calligraphical, to which, notwithstanding, it is our duty to attend.

The events were such as to encourage the expectation that the successor of

144. Rome. Dedication inscription by Innocent IV on an altar. 1248.

Rome, Church of S. Sabina.

Decorated semi-uncial; note the two different forms of forked A.

Silvagni i, pl. XXVIII. 5.

Gregory IX in 1241 would contrive a change of policy. But Celestine IV died within seventeen days. The confusion in Rome was indescribable, Frederick II being still in the neighbourhood. Finally, Innocent IV (1234-54) was elected. His title was enough to indicate what type of pope he would strive to be. Sinibaldo de' Fieschi was anxious for peace, but remained essentially of the school of Innocent III and as the struggle continued the pope found himself more dependent upon the king of France. Innocent IV did not continue the Imperial insignia of the old Roman Square Capital as used by Gregory IX in 1238.

The dedication of his, carved in vertical layout upon an altar dated 1248, is in Notarial Uncialesque, similar in style to the inscription reported from the beginning of the reign of Celestine III of 1195 rather than of Innocent III's Subiaco bull of 1200. Innocent IV's inscription is individualistic, like himself, but it is too decorative to be practical—unlike himself. In Rome the canons of script, whether of Square, Square-Condensed-Imperial Capitals, or of Uncial-esque, had all again been compromised, as was inevitable during the undecided struggle between the Empire and the papacy.

Frederick died in 1250, and Innocent IV could feel a sense of relief, accompanied by some abatement of claim. The ancient canons were not destined to be recovered even by the best Roman sculptors of the thirteenth century. The disuse of the old Augustan or Gregorian canons may not have been wholly due to the conditions accompanying the dispute with the Empire. The classical or Imperial Capitals, it has been seen, had been used by Gregory IX. It is to be noted that all the Gregorys since the first of the name had used them among their 'insignia'. Innocent IV may not have felt himself equally committed.

Alexander IV (1254–61), whose rule was one of hardly unrelieved disaster, is appropriately memorialized in the church of S. Agnese fuori le mura by an inscription recording the consecration of certain relics. Here the Square Capitals are bastardized with notarial Uncialesque; h and M are constant (Plate 145). The papacy was indeed in a dubious position.

Successive and permanent defeats imposed upon papal policy resulted in the urban inscriptional alphabet virtually ceasing to bear any resemblance to what would be classed in our vernacular as 'Roman' lettering. By the time of John XXI (1276–7) the standard Roman alphabet was a debilitated version of the original vigorous alphabet evolved, as has been mentioned, two centuries before at Reichenau for the Ottos. This lettering is an authentic symbol of the degenerate and dependent situation in Rome at the last quarter of the thirteenth century.

145. Rome. Consecration of altar and relics. Alexander IV, 1256. Inscriptional capitals.

Rome, S. Agnese fuori le mura.

Square capitals with mixed Rustic, uncial, and uncialesque elements.

Diehl 47a.

The outlook was certainly not hopeful for the re-establishment of the Gregorian Square Capital as the calligraphic symbol included within the regalia of Rome, whose government was transferred to its bishop when Constantine in 330 removed the capital of the Empire to Byzantium. Equally there was no greater hope for the establishment in the East Frankish regions of a reinvigorated neo-Carolingian script. The effect of the modern Capetian script upon the whole of the north and upon parts of Germany was far too powerful. In the thirteenth century the situation of script had changed too radically to permit of the kind of direct regulation hitherto possible. The mass of writing had multiplied everywhere on the mainland of Europe to an immeasurable degree. The growth of legal studies during the latter half of the twelfth century has already been pointed to as a primary force in the creation of a new professional class needing books and commentaries. The spread of literacy, the secular professionalization of handwriting, the expansion of universities, academies, and schools had brought a large measure of autonomy to the scribes. North of the Alps they shared fully, for the reasons given above, in the enthusiasm felt by all craftsmen and technicians for the modern or 'Gothic' style. It was inevitable, given the international constitution of the Church, that the political, intellectual, and artistic prestige secured by the Capetians should win respect south of the Alps. The acceptance of 'Gothic' style south of the Alps was partial and temporary. It could hardly be otherwise; it might be taken for granted in the Peninsula where Roman styles were indigenous and long practised. The northern pointed and angular minuscule did in fact make but a slight impression upon Rome and Italy—despite powerful patronage. There appears more than one reason for this failure in the South of a movement so powerful in the North, above all in France.

Its introduction began with the arrival of the French Dominican order. In 1219 Honorius III (1216–27) presented the fifth-century basilica of S. Sabina to St. Dominic. There are four inscriptions in that church which date from the second half of the thirteenth century. The revival for the fifth-century basilica of the old Gregorian alphabet may be thought to have been historically appropriate (supposing that the medieval sense of history corresponded to any extent with our own) at that (or at any other) time. Such a course did not suit the Black Friars, then, as since, impatient with the repetition of what was familiar and eager for the recognition of what was new; or, as we should say, 'contemporary'. The contemporary building and lettering for the time of St. Dominic was the 'modern' Gothic design as it had been elaborated by the thirteenth-century successors of Suger. In 1280 the resources of the Dominicans in Rome enabled them to begin their great 'Gothic' church of S. Maria sopra Minerva.

The Dominican repudiation of architectural and other forms of archaism was an essential element in the spirit of the Order. But the particular modernism in architecture sponsored by the sons of St. Dominic received but a temporary welcome in Rome and Florence, although the Order itself continued to be given exceptionally strong support. The successor of Honorius III did not take kindly to the latest lettering. The eventual appearance of the modern minuscule for an inscription in S. Sabina could only have given a severe shock to the vast majority of conservatives, including the clerks in the Chancery who were responsible for the drafting of papal inscriptions.

The Roman Chancery had been in the habit, since at least 1203, of keeping their registers in a minuscule of the Bolognese type, generally left plain, but occasionally elaborated with notarial swashes. The titles were in the Ottonian form.

The habit of thickening the strokes was an indifferent matter. Neither the 'Gothic' nor 'Roman' practice assists legibility and is a rational element, as has been seen above in the passage about books on canon law. It is not impossible that this tendency may have been assisted into Rome by the successor of Alexander IV, Urban IV (1261-7), a Frenchman. Although Charles of Anjou never visited the city, it was during Urban's reign that he was appointed Senator of Rome. Urban's successor Clement IV (1265-8) was also a Frenchman. It was he who invested Charles of Anjou with the kingdom of Sicily. This was in 1265. From this point there is evidence of French architectural influence in Rome.

There was also at work in Rome another professional body, from time to time and place to place, who engaged in lettering independently of the calligraphers, clerks, and notaries. These were the 'Magistri'. Families of talented sculptors whose initial work in Rome can be traced under Paschal II (1099-1118) made contributions to inscriptional lettering that deserve appreciation. Of these families, who worked in Rome and the neighbourhood between the reigns of Alexander III and John XXII, i.e. from 1159 to 1334, some details are known. The principal names are those of Laurentius, Vassalectus, and Cosmas. According to the tables of Frothingham and Hutton there were three notable representatives of the Vassalectus family, from 1150 to 1260. The most prolific in the architectural sense was the branch of Cosmas II, whose grandson, Cosmatus, had three sons: Jacobus Petrus (1296), Johannes (1296-1303), Deodatus (1295-1332). These families were sufficiently respected, as the fine builders and decorators they certainly were, to be permitted to sign at least some of their work. Notwithstanding, Venturi says, it is impossible to separate the individual Cosmati and their families or to distinguish with certainty their sculptures and decorations. In consequence, their work is often referred to under the somewhat misleading collective title of 'Cosmatesque'.

The 'Cosmati' were responsible for architectural and inscriptional work of the greatest beauty and significance. The cloisters built by these artists which bear inscriptions only concern us. The earliest of these to which a date may be assigned are those at the convent of S. Scholastica at Subiaco. It is the work of three generations of craftsmen of the same family. There are two inscriptions (Plates 146 and 147). In the first, over the arch on one side of the cloister, the builder gives us his name:

ϯ MAGISTER IACOBVS ROMAN'(VS), FECIT HOC OP'(VS)

Jacobus I was the second son of Laurentius. He was born *c.* 1180 and died in 1218.

Jacobus uses a headed A though without top cross-bar; C is serifed at foot and

146. Subiaco. Inscription in cloister signed by Magister Jacobus, before 1209.

Subiaco, S. Scolastica, terzo chiostro.

Artistic sculptured uncialesque capitals signed by Jacobus.

Edward Hutton, *The Cosmati* (London, 1950); Arthur L. Frothingham, *The Monuments of Christian Rome* (New York, 1925).

147. Subiaco. Inscription in cloister. 1231–5.

Subiaco, S. Scolastica, terzo chiostro.

Artistic sculptured antique capitals with Byzantine ligatures.

Edward Hutton, *The Cosmati* (London, 1950).

148. Detail of Plate 147.

the G is round. The whole is condensed (which includes R with short vertical tail), and beautifully and regularly serifed. In ROMAN' Jacobus ligatured the MA, which is a Byzantine habit. But for the round Uncial G the shapes are quadrate, though the proportions are Rustic or Byzantine.

The completing three sides of the cloister are similarly signed by Cosmas, the younger brother of Jacobus, and his sons Lucas and Jacobus II:

Ⰱ COSMAS ET FILII L̄V̄C̄(AS) ET
ĪĀC(OBVS) ĀL̄T̄(ER) ROMANI CIVES IN
MARMORIS ARTE PERITI HOC OPVS
EXPLERV(N)T ĀB̄B̄(AT)IS T(EM)P(OR)E LANDI

The date of this inscription is between 1225 and 1235, during the pontificates of Honorius III and Gregory IX. The lettering is again quadrate in form but Rustic or Byzantine in proportion. The ligature MA recurs. G is not required by the text (Plate 148).

Its greater length brings in a number of ligatures and abbreviations in the Eastern manner, such as AB, AR, AN, MA. A curious pseudo-Byzantine invention is the abbreviated form of ET. The inscription as a whole has an individualistic air. It is altogether worthy of its splendid cloister setting. The Lando mentioned was abbot of S. Scholastica from 1227 to 1243.

The most exquisite example of Roman cloistral architecture of the period is thought to be that of the Lateran (Plate 149). The name of Magister Vassalectus

149. Rome. Inscription in the cloister of St. John Lateran. 1220–30.

Hutton, pl. 8, pp. 9, 10, 46; Lauer, pl. xvi.

appears in one of the inscriptions. It is known that he was at work on the cloister from 1220 to 1230. The capitals of the filled-in inscriptions that surround the inside of the square are slightly condensed Roman versions of the Augustan Square Capitals, again more or less Gregorian in form, with some occasional ligatures such as ET. But there is a marked difference in G, N, and R. These are in the Uncialesque. The ligatures AR, ET, and other combinations are Byzantine. As a whole the Vassalectus inscription is a Roman-German-Byzantine synthesis.

A more distinct example of late Byzantine influence upon an individual style exists in the Duomo at Parma. Here exists one of the finest works of Benedetto Antelami, architect and sculptor. His Deposition from the Cross is signed and dated in a syncretic lettering that betrays the inspiration, among other centres, perhaps of Monte Cassino, or rather of Palermo (Plate 150). Its numerous

150. Parma. Duomo, Battisterio. 1178. Artistic capital uncialesque (the first line retouched). Sculpture of the portion of the inscription on the Deposition by Benedetto Antelami.

Enciclopedia Cattolica i, s.v. Antelami; Kurt Forster and Leonard von Matt, *Benedetto Antelami : der grosser romanischer Bildhauer Italiens* (Munich, 1961); see also the special issue of *Du* (Zurich, Feb. 1960), with many large illustrations of sculptures, including inscriptions; G. de Francovich, *Benedetto Antelami* (Milan, 1952), tavv. 107–10.

Uncialesque elements are individualistically treated, or even it might be said, egoistically fashioned. Most remarkable is the fact that the artist dares to sign his name, not upon the mere façade of a cloister, as the Cosmati did, but upon a sacred pictorial object. This is highly significant.

It was seen above that the flowering of art under the Ottonian emperors took place under the direction of the state-supported abbeys of Trier, Reichenau, and Regensburg which, principally, but by no means exclusively, employed monks as the monasteries' scribes and painters who were at times assisted by laymen. In Rome under the popes while the initiative came from ecclesiastics, the builders and scriptors were exclusively laymen. The final stage of the transition, from the anonymous monastic scribe to the professional lay 'artist' desirous of personal publicity hitherto given to emperors as patrons, is well seen taking effect in Rome from the mid thirteenth century. The city was at last able to organize and support a school of master-builders, sculptors, and decorators eager to arouse the admiration of the whole wide world.

In the thirteenth century the long influence of Byzantium upon the West was drawing to a close. In the late twelfth century besides great architects and builders there were, as Garrison has liberally proved, expert painters and scribes collected in Rome. Some were born Romans, others came from Venice, Monte Cassino, and, no doubt, from Constantinople. In the 1270s Rome made one more determined effort to end the schism and, as always before, it failed. Success went only to Islam. Every turn of the continuing crisis of invasion that loomed before Constantinople brought another appeal from the Eastern emperors to the popes, and more negotiations followed. In 1270 the one monarch, Louis IX of France, who might have led a united Christendom, died in camp before Tunis. Its spectacular consequence, the General Council of Lyons in 1274, was the most gigantic of these failures to achieve unity. A signature given in the West was always repudiated in the East. In Greek ecclesiastical judgement and popular opinion the united if menaced East would survive without the disunited West. However great might be Islam's territorial gains they had not lessened Byzantine confidence. Her populace had unbounded faith in her destiny. Constantinople possessed supernaturally effective relics of the Incarnation such as no other Christian city, certainly not old Rome, could parallel. These, with the protection which the Holy Virgin herself bestowed upon Constantinople, the city of the Thirteenth Apostle, were its guarantee against invasion. In the popular estimation, help from the West was never regarded as essential to any final survival of the Eastern capital.

The Greeks remained devoted to a policy of separation from the Latins. A theological, political, or social or artistic authority or sanction might theoretically exist for the revival of an assimilated alphabet. But too many centuries of schism had parted East from West to allow this. It was tacitly understood on both sides that although the two alphabets had characters in common, Greek should look like Greek and Latin should look like Latin. Apart from architectural-artistic lettering such as that practised by the 'Magistri' the normal Latin majuscule used in Italy in the thirteenth century was the Ottonian Uncialesque. Linked

151. Bologna. Bible dated *c.* 1267.

Paris, Bibliothèque Nationale, Lat. 22.

'Littera moderna', the rounded Italian gothic minuscule.

B. Pagnin, 'La Littera Bononiensis', *Atti del Reale Istituto Veneto di Scienze, Lettere ed Arti*, XCIII (1933-4), ii, pp. 1631-2 and plate 19.

with the efficient minuscule produced in Bologna at the end of the thirteenth century (Plate 151) the combination enjoyed an unequalled popularity for 300 years. It was to hold its position easily against the Capetian 'Gothic'.

Soon after the middle of the century, the Italian peninsula in her own way was about to rival France in intellectual and artistic activity. In 1260 Cimabue, the last great Florentine painter in the Byzantine style, completed his Madonna for the church of the Trinità and worked steadily until towards the end of the century. Dante was born in 1265. He was to write in the *Divina Commedia* (composed 1314-21) that the splendours of Cimabue were obscured by the innovation of Giotto who, according to Lorenzo Ghiberti, was the pupil of Cimabue. For the first time there appeared from Florence a native artist who was not attracted by Byzantine antecedents nor even Romanesque precedents, but sought, rather, classical inspiration. His lettering is in the frescoes in Padua (completed, it is thought, in 1306) and is in fine Ottonian Uncialesque. Giotto closed the long period of Italian subjection to Byzantine formulas, but inevitably the change was not immediate.

An instance of the transition at Rome is seen in the works of Pietro Cavallini, the great mosaicist, pupil of the Cosmati and teacher of Giotto. He made a remarkable contribution to S. Maria in Trastevere. Plate 152 is from the mosaic Cavallini completed in 1291 at the commission of Cardinal Bertoldo Stefaneschi. Cavallini, revered as he was in his lifetime, did not reflect any change of attitude towards lettering as such, though he may well have stabilized its style. It is Ottonian, not Byzantine. In his frescoes Cavallini reduced the use of the inscription to the briefest of legends; this had been for some time the custom in the

152. Rome. Mosaic by Pietro Cavallini. 1291. Mosaic capitals.

Rome. S. Maria in Trastevere.

Text in condensed uncialesque capitals accompanying the Blessed Virgin, SS. Peter and Paul with Bertholdo Stefaneschi.

A. Busuloceanu, 'Pietro Cavallini e la pittura romana del Ducento Trecento', *Ephemeris Dacoromana* 13, 1925, p. 303.

West. In the Scrovegni Chapel at Padua Giotto revealed (in his design to commemorate the proclamation of the Jubilee of 1300 by Boniface VIII) his powers as a fresco artist. The painter elsewhere assumes that the topic of every scene in some thirty-seven panels was so familiar as to need no explanatory lettering. This is a non-Byzantine or even an anti-Byzantine gesture.

From what has been seen, it is clear that any relation of script to an overriding Christian conception of world order had gradually and surely weakened, almost—by the twelfth, and certainly by the thirteenth century—to a point of disappearance. That Rome should have preserved its own ancient classical standards was out of the question. The Magistri, the painters and craftsmen, were now their own authority and patrons were happy to confer it upon this or that Magister. The fine Roman school of whom Cavallini was an example flourished under Nicolas IV (1288-92) and Boniface VIII (1294-1303). They were natives of Ancona and Rome respectively.

But nothing long remained stable in Rome. Whereas Boniface VIII, pope and dictator, was able to welcome two (it was said) million pilgrims to the Roman Jubilee of 1300, and, following it, promulgated in the highest terms the claims of the papacy to universal and independent supremacy, Boniface's policy towards Philip the Fair (grandson of Louis IX) suffered a catastrophic defeat. France was now more than ever animated by nationalistic emotion.

At Anagni in 1303 Philip had Boniface seized. The pope escaped but soon died. This event closed the long epoch of Church and State rivalry, with French nationalism triumphant. Boniface's successor was the Dominican Master General. As Benedict XI (1303-4) he sought the restoration of peace between the papacy and France, but his sudden death was an advantage to Philip, by whose diplomacy the Frenchman Clement V (1305-14) was elected. He refused to come to Rome and his coronation took place with particular pomp at Lyons in the presence of Philip, his absolute master. After sojourns at short stages at various places in France, the pope was installed in Avignon, where seven successive popes, including Clement, all French, resided until Pierre Roger de Beaufort, Gregory XI (1370-8), returned to Rome in 1377. He died next year and was succeeded by the Italian Urban VI (1378-89).

This, however, is to anticipate. A political influence upon lettering, doubtless indirect but not to be underrated, became apparent in the middle of the century. It was one aspect of a secular *renovatio* of the antique glory which gathered force in Rome during the absence at Avignon of Clement VI. But the decade from 1343 when Rome and the cities of the peninsula felt this new impulse laid too insecure a foundation to provide a permanent basis for it. The vacuum in Rome created by the withdrawal of the popes to Avignon did, however, create the opportunity for the passionate expression of a new Roman, or rather Italian, nationalism fed and led by Cola di Rienzi (*c.* 1313-54).

This dynamic personality, of singular precocity and force of will, began his career as a notary and Latinist. His study of the historians of ancient Rome inspired him to revive the spirit of the constitution of the Roman Republic, restore the sovereignty of the Roman people, and, in particular, its organs.

That Rienzi's effort failed does not mean that it was without effect in Rome, Florence, and other parts of Italy. It is to be observed that his campaign was for a political restoration of the Roman Republic as head of the other republics in Italy. The restoration of the Empire was another matter, and might come later, if ever. The immediate objective was to revive the old Republican constitution.

Such a crusade was welcomed by Petrarch. It also pleased those in Florence who had reasons of their own for wanting to consolidate a Republican constitution. Those movements may not delay us, though the Republican principle will need to be referred to in the next chapter. Our present point is that Rienzi's Roman patriotism answered to the hopes of many Romans, and though he failed in the end, there remained long after his death (by stabbing in 1354) a vivid interest in antique Rome. This, indeed, was his permanent achievement. It had calligraphical consequences. Rienzi, as a professional notary, recognized a piece of classical lettering for what it was. This is clear from his reference to the bronze tablet of the reign of Vespasian which he describes as a 'tabula magna aerea litteris antiquaris insignia' (Price 293). Rienzi's dream of a united Italy headed by Rome was, of course, an anti-foreign gesture. Even without him some such emotion was inevitable in the political conditions.

It was natural during the Avignon period that the papal registers should be kept in scripts that superseded the Bolognese model by the 'Gothic'. Thus there are to be found formal *Textus* and cursive *Bastarda*. Inevitably, also, the clerks reverted to the Bolognese script when the Chancery was re-established in Rome.

Since Boniface VIII Rome had been no city for artists. Until the election of the Italian Urban VI there had been no reigning pope in Rome from 1305 until 1377. By force of custom the old German-Roman Imperial Uncialesque remained the canonical and Chancery style for inscriptions and other 'display' lettering. This is as it had been under Boniface VIII. Inevitably there would be little copying in Rome of the 'modern' Gothic, rightly described in Italy as the 'lettere Francese'. Rome, left to herself, reverted to habit. In Rome and elsewhere in Italy it was becoming something more than a settled disposition to use a certain kind of lettering style. One effect, the German-Imperial, exercised since Charlemagne, had been to give the Ottonian Uncialesque the status of a habit native to Italy. As the Avignon experience inspired in Rome and beyond a new feeling of local patriotism, if not Italian nationalism, 'Gothic' lettering became repugnant. This feeling in Rome at this time is most probably explained by relating it also to the more immediate Rienzi experiences. Interesting indications of a retreat in Rome from modern Gallican example is to be seen in the inscriptions to be found in S. Maria sopra Minerva.

It has been noticed that the Dominicans had been provided in 1219 with the fifth-century basilica of S. Sabina. The church had been much damaged and frequently restored. But it was not a new or 'contemporary' change such as the Order desired to build. It is necessary to record the design and erection of the church of the Minerva in the full French modern or 'Gothic' style. The enviable site was given to the Order by Nicolas III in the last year of his pontificate.

Building began immediately. The troubles in Rome lengthened the process and the church was not completed for a century. As may be expected during so long an interval, upon the walls and side chapels of so large a church are found numerous inscriptions and monuments. These are of interest.

The early (thirteenth-century) inscriptions vary in detail, but remain basically Uncialesque during the late thirteenth and early fourteenth centuries. This is the Canonical style. The popes from John XXI (1276-7) to Boniface VIII (1294-1303) are all commemorated with inscriptions in the Roman Uncialesque, the style of lettering originally contemporary with the style of building described by modern art historians as 'Romanesque', which had also been adopted by the early generations of workers in the style known to historians as French 'Gothic'. It is significant that the formal 'Gothic' Minuscule (referred to above as 'Textus Quadratus') is not employed in the Minerva. This was no accident. The inscription for St. Catherine of Siena (d. 1350) is of considerable interest as indicating a 'trend' in which Roman Square Capitals predominate, but certain 'outside' characters, such as A with forked crossbar, occur. This, too, is no accident.

It was St. Catherine of Siena who persuaded Gregory XI to return to Rome despite the protests of the French king and the majority of the cardinals, most of whom were French. The attitude of the Italians and the French, whether in Avignon or Rome, was one of reciprocal hatred. Nothing French, therefore, would be welcome in Rome. No other church in Rome would be built there in the modern French or 'Gothic' style.

A large and curious inscription of the previous generation deserves mention. The Vatican grotto of miscellaneous inscriptions preserves a memorial tablet recording a benefaction of Benedict XII (Plate 153) who had rebuilt the roof of a basilica (unspecified). The pope was formerly a French Cistercian and the Uncialesque was an appropriate choice for him. The work was done and the tablet signed by Master Paul of Siena. It is unlikely, on the appearance of it, that the master himself cut the letters or that they were even cut by one familiar with any script. That such a low standard should have been accepted for such a high purpose proves that the Roman Chancery had been in the time unable to restore its command on a high quality of lettering. Benedict XII himself was buried at Avignon in 1342.

The calligraphic customs of Avignon do not appear to have influenced the established canonical style of Rome at the end of the fourteenth century. A surviving lapidary bull of Gregory XI is of interest. It confirms the primacy of St. John Lateran over all the churches of the world and was given at Avignon on 23 January 1372 (Plate 154). It is, as might be expected, in Uncialesque lettering of the established type. It is clear from this example that Uncialesque was the official, authorized version of legal lettering in Rome at the end of the century, though it would not have been seen particularly appropriate for a pope who had taken the name of Gregory. But the eleventh Gregory's time in Rome was brief and torn by rebellion in his own cities who feared new papal alliances with their hereditary enemies.

The Lateran inscription is a notably fine piece of carving. It was engraved,

153. Inscription on marble. Vatican Grotto.
Uncialesque capitals, dated 1341.

says Diehl, under the pontificate of Boniface IX (1389-1404). He was very different from the other popes of the period. Obviously it required courage to take the name of Boniface and thereby evoke memories of his forebears of that name —generally execrated by the Imperialists and the French. This, however, must not detain us. It may be that it was Boniface IX who in 1403 appointed to the Roman Curia a young man whose literary scholarship and calligraphic artistry were later to make his influence very powerful in his own day and his name famous in ours: Giovanni Francesco Poggio Bracciolini (1380-1450). His major contribution to the arrangement of what is called the 'littera antiqua' is described in the next chapter. At the beginning of the fifteenth century Poggio was writing the 'littera moderna' in the *Bastarda* form, and it is tempting to think that through Boniface IX Poggio had some responsibility for the excellence of the Uncialesques of the Lateran bull.

No evidence appears at the time to suggest that Poggio was in a position to influence the official scripts in Rome in any way from the established style. Any departure from the Uncialesque was not the result of official direction. Instead, the use of Roman Capitals in the Minerva implies that neither the old German-Imperial or the French-modern lettering would correspond to the mood of the contemporary Dominican.

It was remarked above that the trend away from Uncialesque seen in the inscription for St. Catherine of Siena is no accident. The same tendency is to be observed in the inscription for the tomb in the same church commemorating Fra Angelico (*c.* 1380), whose text is in serifed Capitals which are less than square.

154. Rome. St. John Lateran. Confirmation of primatial status.

Bull of Gregory XI dated 1372. Engraved 1390.

Diehl 49c; Lauer, p. 269.

It is improbable, however, that this inscription owes much to Byzantine inspiration. It may be concluded, indeed, that any direct non-Italian inspiration in the lettering of Rome was fading. In other words, the inscriptions in the new and principal Roman church were becoming more Roman. The most tolerable outside influence might be Byzantine. The 'Gothic' *Textura* was not merely not native; it represented France, a power inimical to Rome. It is more than possible to believe that the tendency, noticeable in the Minerva inscriptions of this period of a return to old Roman standards of letter-structure, suggests something different from sentimental antiquarianism. Nor, on the other hand, did it represent Gregorian-Imperial symbolism.

It has been seen above that Augustan Capitals appear, carefully serifed, on the inscriptions of Gregory I, and that Gregory VII explicitly claimed the Imperial insignia as the patrimony of the pope. The second Gregory (715–31) is found using the same square capitals carefully serifed, as also Gregory III (731–41). The same formation of capitals may be seen in the inscriptions of later popes bearing the name of Gregory. This fact, it may be accepted, points to a pious respect towards the great Gregory I. It does not necessarily mean that all six of the popes of that name from 590 to 1045 severally appropriated the old Roman Square Capitals and carefully serifed them because in their minds they were Augustan and were given imperial as well as papal authority.

It was otherwise with the sixth Gregory's successor, Hildebrand. It has been seen at page 212 above that Gregory VII regarded the old Roman capitals as part of the insignia proper to the popes. The eleventh of this name had not the opportunity to memorialize his reign in terms of lettering. He arrived in Rome on 14 January 1377. His death on 27 March 1378 prevented his return to Avignon, and his tomb, when erected, only in 1584, naturally bore an inscription in typical late Renaissance Capitals. The chronically unsettled condition of Rome after the death of Gregory XI, together with the confusions engendered by the irreconcilable ambitions of the European powers, created an international political situation leading to the ecclesiastical chaos which Christendom was to endure from 1378 to 1409. This, the Great Schism of the West, marks the end of the Gregorian attempt to pacify the West by the Roman, papal, theocracy.

The Western Church had been in schism in the East with the Byzantine Imperialist theocracy since 1054. The Great Schism within the Latin patriarchate arose from a rebellion of a faction of cardinals against Urban VI (1378–89), the pope elected in 1378, in succession to Gregory XI. The Western Church found herself governed by one pope (Clement VII) at Avignon, and an anti-pope (Urban VI) at Rome. Something similar, or worse, was destined to continue in the West for some thirty years. It may now be asked what the situation was in the East, and what were the relations between the two main divisions of Christendom. In 1281 Michael Palaeologus was excommunicated by Martin IV (1281–5), a Frenchman dependent upon Charles of Anjou. There then began a new Greek-Latin schism. In the reign of Andronicus II Palaeologus (1258–1328), which coincided with the victories of the Turks that assured their eventual triumph, unavailing ecumenical efforts were made under successive popes.

The beginning of the fourteenth century marked the end of Byzantinism in the West. Receptive of Eastern inspiration and example, as the Roman and Florentine schools of the twelfth and thirteenth centuries had been, their artists showed only slight dependence upon Byzantine lettering. The time had passed for close approximation of the form of the Greek and Latin alphabets that had perhaps been possible seven or six centuries earlier. The configuration of the world had so changed since 1054, and with it much more had waned than the possibility of an alphabetical approximation between Eastern and Western Christendom.

Thus the Romano-Judaeo-Christian-Imperial theocratic conception of a society made prosperous by divine blessing at the expense of its neighbours, was patently irreconcilable with Saladin's conquests. As a constituent of the Byzantine State theory, and the basic sanction for its political constitution, it held un-diminished force long after the continuous and irreversible victories of the Turks and the chronic and suicidal schisms with the Romans brought closer complete disaster to the entire Byzantine Empire and endangered the Western powers. By the thirteenth century the position was hopeless. Yet the overruling belief in the military power of the orthodox armies remained a popular as well as imperial conviction in orthodox Byzantium. The historic device of the Empire, IESUS XRISTOS NIKA, was accepted in all literality. Even so, during the fourteenth century the emperors, if not the patriarchs, understood that Old Rome could be a useful ally to New Rome.

An East-West *rapprochement* after the Second General Council of Lyons (1245) and the similar effort in 1339, were both abortive for the usual run of theological, racial, economic, and territorial pretexts. The break was too complete to be materially affected by a literary or intellectual attempt at understanding, though these were not lacking. Soon after 1360 Leontius Pilatus was persuaded by Boccaccio, his pupil, to teach Greek at Florence. In 1369 John V Palaeologus (1341-91), under the usual pressure from the Turks, visited Rome during Urban V's temporary sojourn (1367-70). No accord was attained or even approxi-mated. It was not Urban's fault. While a patriotic Frenchman, he was a pious Benedictine. His reasons for abandoning Rome were not discreditable. He returned to Avignon in 1370 and died in the same year. Meanwhile the Byzantines were left to look after themselves.

Western conventions were also studied in the East. Something was done in Constantinople to explain the Latin mind when Demetrius Cydones, the Imperial secretary (no less), translated into Greek the *Summa contra Gentiles* of Thomas Aquinas. However, disunion in the West and the misuse of resources in the East continued to obstruct another Western expedition against the Turks. Had religious appeasement been successful and Western military and naval help been given in time, the chances for a Graeco-Latin ecclesiastical union and the survival of the Eastern Empire would have brightened.

Had this been so, once more some calligraphical approximation, even slight, might have accompanied a common theological understanding. Rome would probably have shown once more her willingness to absorb Greek liturgical customs; certainly calligraphical habits. Not since 1054 had there existed any possibility of a common Greek and Latin alphabet. It has been reported that the coinage current in Byzantine regions exhibits legends in mixed Latin and Greek characters, for example, ıhsus xristus nica and that these were supplemented by wholly Greek legends about the time of Romanus IV (1067-71). Under the Latin emperors Greek predominated (for example, ıc xc nika) and the restored Greek emperors naturally used pure Greek legends. During the Great Schism the one script possessing authority was that on the Byzantine coinage. A parallel to such authority did not and could not exist in the newly nationalistic West with its consequent ecclesiastical divisions. The emperor, kings, and princes desired the council of the Church and of the pope to be committed to a council managed by themselves. This was the situation faced by Boniface VIII between 1294 and 1303.

It is not our business to discuss the exalted claims put forward in the several famous bulls of which Boniface VIII was the author, or the fierceness of the repudiation they encountered from the Imperial and monarchical sides. As the time had long passed when France would allow the emperor to impose upon Rome a pope of his choice, and other nations such as England would abate their claim to a voice in the nomination, it became clear, at the death of Gregory XI in 1378, that Europe had reached a new stage of development. But the trend was not towards unity.

If the European princes could agree upon a personality, his canonical election might bring into the West an agreed *modus vivendi* between the popes and the monarchs and make Rome once more a centre of unity, strong enough to override national jealousy. Christendom, Eastern and Western, might be saved from the worst effect of the oriental schism of 1054, still continuing, and the Western, that began in 1378. At the end of the century there was still no practical basis for a league able to reverse the victories of the Turks and their continuing menace to Byzantium.

If, too, in the course of events, Rome were to reform her bureaucracy, one of the results might be the revival of her old authority over at least the capital lettering and bring, perhaps, simplicity and legibility into the correspondence scripts of Western Christendom. The presence of a man like Poggio in Rome at the end of the fourteenth century guaranteed the possibility of a new lead to Europe in calligraphy. No sign of any such developments was then manifest. To all appearances Rome would remain severed from Constantinople by the eleventh-century Eastern Schism, and be rent by the fourteenth-century Western Schism. Thus was Christendom ecclesiastically divided, and the scripts left with nothing more than local guild-sanction.

The attempt of the Church under Boniface VIII to enforce unity by obedience to himself and its acceptance of one sovereign authority in Europe, was inevitably met by the challenge of the princes who continued to prefer the rules of a competitive independence to the safeguards of an order imposed by one not of their sort. The bond of union between the princes was opposition to the papacy as existing in the terms of its thirteenth-fourteenth century self-definition. Thus was Western Christendom politically divided. The old Carolingian or German-Imperial-Christian lettering had lost both its ideological basis and its international prestige. Henceforth, script developed upon national and social lines.

Independently of Church and State there increased in power a third force which required by its nature a mechanism of social cohesion. This was the community of bankers and traders. But the scripts used in their counting-houses, like those used in the chanceries of princes and dukes, were subject to local professional preference, though all bore signs of their origin in the sophisticated schools of the Paris scriveners. Thus the rapidly expanding commercial world of the fourteenth century was scriptorially disunited.

In the same century, there had developed, independently of the two swords of the Church and the State, and of the gold of the bourgeoisie, a new fourth force. This was humanism, which was destined in the fifteenth century, by its alliance with the bourgeoisie, to cause a profound and momentous shift in the entire spiritual, philosophical, and social structure of Western European society. The new fourth force, intellectually distinguishable and often independent from Church and State, was emerging. Simultaneously, continued pursuit anywhere of the Christian theocratic ideal as re-established by Charlemagne and continued by the German kings, was consistently slackening. The idea of world unity had already faded. Theodosius I's and Innocent III's 'One flock, one shepherd' was no longer looked for and still further from reality.

The confused state of lettering in the half-century or more after Boniface VIII (d. 1303) authentically reflects the condition of Church, State, and society. Authority over every estate and every script had already drifted out of the control of emperors and popes, into the hands of princes and dukes, with attendant chanceries and corps of intellectuals, poets, littérateurs; even architects, masons, artists, and, of course, lawyers intervening; next also painters and scriveners. From among this unco-ordinated corps of princes, dukes, guilds of book-scribes, and legal scriveners there was to arise, in the early part of the next century, an agreed style wholly different from that sponsored by the 'modern' or French Gothic Court which had so long dominated Europe.

The anti-modern or pro-antique style was an archaeological by-product of the political movement led by Cola di Rienzi. It gathered force from the reaction against French pressure for ascendancy after the Council had, for the time being, ended the Great Schism. The calligraphic changes that followed the settlement achieved at Constance, and the kind and degree of authority which became attached to them in the new situation must now be inquired into.

6

FROM MARTIN V, 1417–1431, TO SIXTUS V, 1585–1590

AFTER an unhappy opening, the fifteenth century witnessed a pacification of the ecclesiastical antagonisms. When the aged Alexander V, formerly Archbishop of Milan, died in 1410, the Roman cardinals elected John XXIII. At this point there were three claimants to the chair of St. Peter. John, encouraged by the Emperor Sigismund, summoned a General Council. It met at Constance in 1414. Ten months later John XXIII took flight, was arrested by the Council, tried, deposed, and imprisoned. In 1415 Gregory XII obliged by abdicating. Two years later the Council deposed Benedict XIII. Thus the Holy Seat was vacant.

As the Council of Constance continued, it became for the time being the sole authority in the Church; also the longest in duration of all her councils. A new pope, unanimously elected by the Council thus constituted, was seen by all to be the one necessity. This they finally did in 1417. The Great Schism was ended. The restoration of some sort of centralized Christian authority, acknowledged by all the European powers, was now a legal fact and with its accomplishment we may turn away from ecclesiastical affairs to consider the changes in script which accompanied the restoration of papal authority, the growing Italian supremacy in thought, literature, learning, and the coincident decline of French prestige and power.

The formative influences upon script and lettering in the fifteenth century did not derive from Cola di Rienzi as they might have done had he lived. But, it needs to be borne in mind, while the collapse of Rienzi's political ideas ended the possibility of a re-establishment of the Respublica Romana, their archaeological and philosophical associations remained vigorous not only in Rome but elsewhere in the peninsula.

If Rienzi had been less of an actor and more of a writer he would without doubt have won for Rome the title of the primal city of the Republic of Letters, and for himself the position of the elder and leading inspirer of the great revolutionary intellectual movement begun, as it happened, by Petrarch, and so powerfully influenced by his circle of followers in Florence.

Thus it was that Florence, in a state of warfare, took the lead and Rome was left in second place. Nevertheless, the artistic role of the papal city, so long delayed by the Great Schism, in due time became highly significant, even calligraphically. The calligraphical development was uneven in both centres, subjected as it was to interruption in Rome from the continuing conflict between the ambitious families on the one hand, the secular powers on the other, and, in Florence, by civil strife. Furthermore, while the principles of the chief instigators of the calligraphical change were consistent, they varied in important detail.

It follows that to separate the origins and to define the sanctions of the fifteenth-century calligraphical revolution in the scriptorial changes of the time involves consideration of the authority under which foremost artists effected them. The personages responsible for the ideas and doctrines that underlay the whole of the epoch-marking intellectual and artistic change drew their inspiration principally from Petrarch, who died in 1374, and to some degree from Rienzi, who died in 1353.

As this fourteenth-century movement gathered strength as a Florentine intellectual-literary force, it adopted a calligraphical symbol known as 'humanism'. The term is not documented in Latin before the first decade of the sixteenth century, though it is very probable, Augusto Campana argues, that 'umanistica' occurs much earlier in Italian. The basic *raison d'être* of the new Florentine intellectual trend was its lay outlook. The medium of transcription sponsored by the most influential adherents of 'humanism' is correspondingly known as the 'humanistic script'. The 'humanists' themselves called it 'anticha' or 'antiqua' in the sense in which the term was understood by Rienzi: the use of Rome's heroic ancient past. It was the opposite of the term 'moderna' as it was understood by Suger and his northern contemporaries. The new age of humanism is said to have been born in Vienna in 1348 when Petrarch discovered Cicero's letters to Atticus, the text of which had not been known in the Christian centuries.

The history of the epoch known to historians of art as the 'Renaissance', which the humanists created, is so well known as to not need the slightest recapitulation here. That the leaders of the movement in thought and art refashioned the script usual for literary transcriptions of Latin authors in the eleventh and twelfth centuries is a commonplace. It is unnecessary therefore to tabulate here the evidence available in B. L. Ullman's original and exhaustive studies relating to the origins and early development of the 'humanistic' script. Nor is it needful to retrace the steps of Millard Meiss's clarification of the origins of later calligraphic refinements, or, finally, Giovanni Mardersteig's detection of the modifications that mark the inscriptional work of the second half of the fifteenth century.

It does remain necessary, however, to reconsider some of the reasons for the scriptorial practices of these few men of learning and laic spirit who bred in Italy and thence dispersed to the world a taste for the 'antiqua'. In the time of Petrarch the authority over script could be said to consist in the custom obtaining in the equivalent of the modern University Press and learned publisher, in particular at this time the University of Bologna.

In the circumstances already described the University had developed and given its sanction to an economic, round, plain, and legible book-hand. Beside it there were produced a host of cramped, flourished cursive hands considered fit above all for correspondence and vernacular texts. In addition, there were the special hands developed by the diplomatic and Chancery clerks for whom security was a greater virtue than legibility. This was the general situation south of the Alps. In the north the 'modern' or Gothic book-hand and its cursive derivatives dominated the writing schools. The script now to be considered is that used in the texts of Latin authors, and this book-script only in so far as it gained authority and from whom.

It has been seen that the new interest in archaeology and the revived cult of the antique began with Cola di Rienzi and that the disillusion in Rome after his death in 1353 did not greatly favour the extension in the city of his general philosophical, as distinct from his specific political ideas. The Great Schism was a further obstacle to Rome's ability to forward a new philosophical movement.

Petrarch, disillusioned by the Rienzi episode, was not incommoded by the Great Schism, and his work continued in various places. It is not to be overlooked that his birth took place in Arezzo because his father was banished from his native Florence. Petrarch died (reading Virgil) in 1374 and Boccaccio died the next year. In 1375 Florence appointed as its Latin secretary Coluccio Salutati (1330–1406), one of Petrarch's associates, whose ideas inspired Salutati who, in turn, inspired Niccolò Niccoli (1363–1437) and Poggio Bracciolini (1380–1459). These men were the learned but private persons who guided the new calligraphical trend. Niccoli and Poggio, as the younger men, also practised the new hand. Poggio, it has been seen, was a Chancery clerk from 1403 in the Curia of Boniface IX. It was Poggio who gave professional form to the new 'antique'. The nature of the authority by means of which the revived 'antique', commended by Salutati, practised personally by Niccoli, and professionally by Poggio and established in Florence, now needs to be inquired into.

It is certain that at the beginning the script had no institutional support. Although Salutati was a power in the republic of Florence, he made no step to obtain official support for a new hand, then in its infancy and, by definition, apt only for the transcription of a specific class of Latin literature. How, then, was it that a new script of strictly limited purpose, possessing no authority, became accepted in what was, as a fact, a very brief interval of time? Did it establish itself? And by what date?

Although Niccoli, as the organizer and commentator, made the initially important contribution to the recovery of classical literature, Poggio as the researcher and transcriber must be given pride of place in the designing and giving calligraphical form to the new 'antique' script deemed appropriate at this time (*c.* 1399) for the transcription of ancient Latin texts. Poggio's journeys in search of manuscripts outside Italy are well known. The details of his life do not concern the present purpose, but a few dates need to be set down.

Poggio was born in 1380. His professional training at Bologna included calligraphy. He emerged a qualified notary, expert in all the legal, literary, and diplomatic hands. Any book-hand he may have practised in his early days would have been of the customary plain, round, Bolognese type such as Petrarch practised. Among the hands practised by Poggio was an exceptionally fine version of the 'modern' (or 'Gothic' to us) cursive. He was evidently fond of this hand, since he practised it for non-literary purposes all his life, and even to the extent of using it at least once for a transcription of the text of Cicero. Poggio always used it for his marginal glosses in classical works.

After service as secretary to the Cardinal of Bari he began his professional career as a Chancery scribe under Boniface IX (1389-1404). He was appointed 'litterae apostolicarum scriptor' in 1403. He wrote very elegantly the Gothic cursive then prescribed for the new class of papal document known as the 'Breve'. Simultaneously he privately practised the new majuscule and minuscule, the theory of which he had learnt from Salutati and Niccoli. He became attached as a principal copyist to these two employers shortly before 1402. Niccoli employed other scribes in Florence certainly after and perhaps before the date (*c.* 1402) at which Poggio left Florence for Rome.

Poggio was 22 when he transcribed for Salutati his treatise *De Verecundia* which, according to Ullman, is 'actually the very first *datable* example of humanistic script'. It was completed, Ullman argues, between 1402-3. He was not thirty when he transcribed in 1408 his first dated text. This was Cicero's Epistles to Atticus, written in formal 'antiqua' (now Berlin, MS. Hamilton 166). Plate 155 is from Cicero's *De Oratore* written by Poggio some time between 1423 and 1431.

The so-called 'Gothic' *bastarda* like any other cursive is written with greater ease, and therefore speed, than any formal hand. Consequently the humanistic hand requires greater effort and therefore more time; and the proper execution of this then revolutionary hand, required from the scribe his highest discipline and his best skill. After Coluccio's death in 1406 Poggio became dependent upon Niccoli, and with his continued support became the dominating figure in humanistic calligraphy during the pioneer period. There were others, also, good scribes,

155. Cicero, *De Oratore*. Well-formed minuscule with square capitals of general inscriptional form; unserifed. Written by Poggio, 1423-31.

Florence, Laur. 50, 31.

Morison, pl. 12; Ullman, pp. 35-6.

who transcribed manuscripts of Cicero dated 1405 and 1406 (Ullman 40, 41). They followed Poggio's best style. Poggio was unique because he was the only practitioner who was a first-class scholar as well as a first-class scribe. He also held a first-class position in the Roman Curia. He consolidated his status when, at the end of the Great Schism in 1417, he was appointed secretary to Martin V. In all his calligraphy Poggio formed his letters with the utmost strictness according either to the canons which the Roman Chancery approved for diplomatic business or, equally, for the nascent literary canons approved by the select Florentine intelligentsia.

It follows that the majuscules, which Poggio consistently used with his humanistic script for a period of twenty-five years, represented the consensus of preference on the part of Niccoli and other scholars anxious to find the letter-form most correct for their purpose. Thus, in Poggio's script there was nothing that was imposed by his own personal fantasy. Hence, the use by him of a specific capital is likely to have been the recommendation implicitly agreed of Salutati, Bruni, Niccoli, and Biondo. No doubt Poggio, as an archaeologist intimate with Rome and a collector of antiquities, had much knowledge of inscriptional lettering to contribute. Without assuming some such consensus among the leaders of the new school, it is difficult to account for the high degree of consistency with which Poggio for so long practised his capitals (also his minuscules); secondly, the high degree of agreement among the best esteemed contemporary sculptors to follow the same model.

It is to be borne in mind that all his life Poggio's instrument was the quill, used purely as a scribe. He was never a painter, carver, engraver, or miniaturist. Consequently his work is to be judged as calligraphy not as lettering. Despite the strictness with which he wrote every letter of the new medium, he ever respected the liberty of the quill to produce according to its proper character. Hence, while he keeps his hand under strict control he permits it a degree of liberty, ease, and spontaneity lacking, as will be seen, in the script of later self-conscious artistic practitioners of the humanistic hand. The humanistic script of Poggio and others of his time was a controlled free-hand appropriate to a work of exact scholarship, plainly written for a man of learning. The script of later artists such as Antonio Sinibaldi was a supreme performance appropriate to fine work decoratively written for a rich patron. It may be contended that while Poggio was also an artist, he was primarily a scholar.

Irregularity of line or serif that may occur in either humanistic alphabet is due to Poggio's settled free-hand style and not to a weakening of his strong consistent sense of exactitude. The absence of serifs in Poggio's capitals is intentional and proof of his fidelity to a canon believed by him to be theoretically, historically, and archaeologically justified. Moreover, though, it is wholly important that Poggio is alone in this archaeological approach to the form of the new script. As a design of majuscules and minuscules, Poggio's 'antiqua' is consistent with history, but not with itself. The significant difference is that whereas the majuscules are not serifed, the minuscules are.

It is a commonplace that the school of which Poggio was a member drew inspiration for the design from the old formal Roman sculptured or carved inscriptions. But there are two kinds of such classical inscriptions; those unserifed and others serifed. Was the refusal to admit serifs to the capitals a reflection of Petrarch's objection to superfluous ornament expressed to Boccaccio in 1366? If so, why were serifs allowed in the minuscule?

Petrarch's prescription of a letter-form was the general one that writing was a medium of visual communication by reading, and it should be '*castigata et clara*'. This prescription was certainly in the minds of his friends. Poggio became almost puritanical in his attitude towards textual transcription and never made the slightest attempt to become an illuminator. His prime and sole object was to devise a plain, legible, and classical duplex (capitals and lower case) alphabet whose constituent letters corresponded with clearly understood and firmly held archaeological and philological, philosophical and literary convictions and principles, preferences, and precedents. The artistry of the manuscript lay not in the script but in the text. This being so, the reason for the absence of serifs in the capitals may lie in the prose, of which it was the chosen medium. It is not, however, to be thought that the use of unserifed capitals would be limited to one certain author and one kind of text.

Poggio's capitals may earlier be seen on monuments in Florence. Besides these notable Florentine examples, the large-scale lettering on the erections by Leon Battista Alberti at Rimini about 1450 should be remembered. It has been necessary to comment on this style of lettering precisely because it was a pattern paramount in use among sculptors most famous in their day, and still more famous today. They obviously regarded it as an authoritative pattern set for them. The degree of consistency cannot otherwise be explained. It is too strongly reminiscent of the Rome of, say, 150 B.C. to be an accident. As the originators of the idea of using it as their symbol were not mere ignorant enthusiasts, it must be assumed that they were aware of this. Many of the political philosophers of the movement were specially devoted to the Rome of the Republic. On the other hand, for the Empire they had no such feeling. For them, in the direct line of Rienzi and Petrarch, Rome was the Rome of Cicero. They revered him as their political as well as stylistic ideal. Accordingly it was the discipline of the Republican inscriptions that the successors of Petrarch and Salutati imposed upon their script, and this is the reason why it was accepted as their norm by the great Florentine artists. To be precise, the sans serif (to use a northern term) capitals occur in Poggio's Cicero of 1402, and on an inscription for John XXIII, whose tomb is in the Baptistery at Florence. Baldassare Cossa was forced by the Council of Constance to abdicate in 1415, and died in 1419 as Cardinal-bishop of Tusculum. He was magnanimously treated by Martin V and a magnificent sepulture was made by Donatello and Michelozzo.

The reason for this demonstration was that John had been, from before his election in 1410, given wholehearted support by the Republic of Florence. The text of an inscription for the tomb of an anti-pope required tact, as H. W. Janson points out. He accepts 1427 as the year of the completion of the work, and it is likely that the text with its controversial wording QVONDAM PAPA was the last

AMMIANI · MARCELLINI · RERVM · GESTARVM · LIBER
XIIII · INCIPIT · FELICITER ·

POst emensos insuperabilis expeditionis euentus: Languentibus par
tium animis quas periculo$q$ uarietas fregerat & laborum non
dum tubar$\bar{u}$ cessante clangore: uel milite locato per stationes hibernas
fortunae saeuientes procellae tempestates alias rebus infundere com
munibus: per multa illa & dira facinora caesaris galli. qui ex
squalore immo miseriarum in aetatis adultae primitiis ad prin
cipale culmen insperato cultu prouectus ultro terminos potestates de
latae procurrens asperitate nimia cuncta foedabat: Propinqtate
enim regiae stirpis genitalitateq$:$ etiam tum constantini nominis
efferebatur in fastos si plus ualuisset ausurus hostilia in auctorem
suae felicitatis ut uidebatur: cuius acerbitati uxor graue accesse
rat incentiuu$m$ germanitate augusti turgida supra modum quam
anniballiano regis fratris filio · Ante hac constantini iunxerat
pater · megera quaedam mortalis · inflammatrix saeuientis ad
sidua humani cruoris auida · Nihil mitius $q\bar{m}$ maritus · qui pau
latim eruditionis facti processu temporis ad nocendum per clande
stinos uersutosq$:$ rumigerulos compertis leniter addere quaeda$m$
male suetos falsa & placentia sibi discentes adfectati regni uel ar
tium nefandarum calumnias insontibus adfigebant · minuit
aute$m$ inter humilia supergressa iam potentia fines mediocriu$m$ de
lictorum nefanda clematii cuiusdam alexandrini nobilis more
repentina: cuius socrus c$\bar{o}$misceri sibi generum flagrans eius amo
re non impetraret ut ferebatur per palatii phts pseudotyrum
introducta: oblato pretioso reginae monili id adsecuta est · ut ad

Nam faciunt homines plerumque cupidine caeci
Et tribuunt ea quae non sunt his commoda vere
Multimodis igitur pravas turpisque videmus
Esse in deliciis summoque in honore vigere
Atque alios alius inrident Veneremque suadent
Ut placent quoniam foedo afflictentur amore
Nec sua respiciunt miseri mala maxima saepe
Nigra mell chrus est immunda et foetida acosmos
Caesia palladium nervosa et lignea dorcas
Parvula pumillo chariton mia tota merum sal
Magna atque immanis cataplexis plenaque honoris
Balba loqui non quit traulizi muta pudens est
At flagrans odiosa loquacula Lampadium fit
Ischnon eromenion fit cu vivere no quit
Pnemarie rhadine verost iam mortua tussi
At tumida et mammosa Ceres est ipsa ab Iaccho
Simula Silena ac Saturast Labeosa philema
Cetera de genere hoc longum est id dicere coner
Sed tamen esto iam quantovis oris honore
Cui Veneris membris suis omnibus exortatur
Nempe aliae quoque sunt nempe hac sine viximus ante
Nempe eadem facit et scimus facere omia turpis
Et miseram taetris se suffit odoribus ipsa

---

156. Niccolo Niccoli:

(a) Ammianus Marcellinus, *Rerum Gestarum Libri XXXI*, semi-formal humanistic cursive, 1423.

Florence, Naz. Cent., Conv. Soppr. I. V. 43.

Morison, pls. 8, 16; Ullman, p. 63.

(b) Lucretius, *De Rerum Natura*, informal sloping humanistic cursive, c. 1425–9.

Florence, Laur. 35. 30.

Morison, pls. 9, 15; Ullman, pp. 64–6.

157. Florence. Tomb of Pope John XXIII, by Danatello and Michelozzo, *c.* 1427.
The Baptistery, Florence.
Unserifed stressed Roman capitals.
H. W. Janson, *The Sculpture of Donatello*, 1957, pp. 59-65 and plates 85-92.

157. *Detail.*

detail. As Plate 157 shows the inscription is brief and the letters are sans serif. It is probable that the inscription ranks as the first datable public presentation in any city of sans-serif Roman lettering of Poggio's type. That he had any responsibility for it is highly improbable.

The lettering itself is of an 'artistic' and primitive experimental type, such as might have been sketched by Donatello himself. The letters are inferior in design to those on the tomb at Siena of Giovanni Pecci, dated by Janson as *c.* 1428-30. It would appear, therefore, that the lettering for John XXIII might be classed as the sculptured 'antiqua' in the early experimental stage. There are in Florence inscriptions by Luca della Robbia dated 1431-7. While these are usually mono-line and always unserifed, their shapes are less controlled by authority and logic, and in this respect are comparable with the precedents set up at Subiaco and Rome by the Cosmati family half a century earlier. At this time it seems that the Florentine artists felt the use of antique Roman capitals of the sans-serif type was obligatory if their patrons were to be pleased, but obviously their understanding of it was limited. They did not understand at this time the importance of proportion and spacing of the letters.

In sum, the first private appearance of the revived 'antiqua' in manuscript is Poggio's transcription of Coluccio's *De verecundia* completed in Florence *c.* 1402-3, while the first datable public appearance of the Roman 'antiqua' is Donatello's inscription on the tomb of John XXIII *c.* 1427.

The *De verecundia* was commissioned by or for Cosimo de' Medici, who, as will be argued below, was a consistent supporter of the movement represented primarily by Niccoli. That Cosimo de' Medici was fully consulted by the executors of John XXIII about the tomb may be safely assumed, although he did not become *de facto* ruler of Florence until 1424. The private or public use of the revived 'antiqua' in Florence was not the object of an even semi-official instruction. None was required in a republican city which believed profoundly in the principle of popular liberty. There were many good artists in equally good standing with the guilds in Florence at the time who continued to use Uncialesque. Hence, Florence neither accepted nor conferred any authority for the adoption of the revived 'antiqua', other than the permissive *placet* of the craft guilds of Florence. Its progress was gradual.

The contemporary situation in Rome needs now to be considered. It has been noted above that Poggio was made an Apostolic Secretary in 1406, under Boniface IX, and became principal secretary to Martin V in 1423. Martin V died in 1431 and was buried in Rome. The tomb (Plate 158) and its lettering are of interest. The tomb was designed by one Simone Ghini, whose identity is in dispute. The first point of significance in the lettering is its distinction from that of Martin's predecessor, Gregory XII (1406-13), who was buried at Recanati in a very handsome tomb decorated with a long inscription in what palaeographers might call 'formal Gothic *Textura*'. It is the first papal tumular inscription of the kind, and it is also the last. It departs equally from the Square Roman Capital and from the Franco-German Uncialesque. Gregory's 'Gothic' monument in Recanati does not, by any means, mark the end of that style. A tomb of considerable splendour, decorated with pseudo-fenestration in the full 'Gothic' style of the Minerva, was erected in the Lateran to the memory of Cardinal Casato (d. 1500) but an inscription is carved in orthodox Uncialesque. The 'Gothic' style was by no means unsupported in the highest quarters at the time when Poggio was active.

The tomb and the inscription for Martin V, however, departs almost sensationally from precedent, and that in more than one respect. According to Panofsky it is the sole example of a papal monument in only two dimensions. Significant is the fact that Simone Ghini is believed by experts to have cut the lettering for the pope's tomb. The vested figure of Martin V, surmounted by floral and conventional ornament, is seen to correspond with the modern notion of 'renaissance', just as his predecessor's ornament and script corresponds with Vasari's notion of 'Gothic' and our notion of 'medieval'. The contrast is, indeed, striking. Martin's inscription is in sans-serif Square Capitals, in the style of Poggio. This is obvious. What is not obvious is the date of the inscription and it would be convenient if one could be confident of the date of the first appearance in Rome of sculptured capitals of the Martin-Poggio type.

It must be repeated that the dating of sepulchral monuments is conjectural. Furthermore, it is not to be assumed that a new style of capital deemed fit for a privately commissioned manuscript would be considered appropriate for the inscription on a public monument such as the tomb for a pope—especially one of the stature of Martin V.

158. Rome. Tomb of Pope Martin V, by Simone Ghini, post 1431.
S. Giovanni in laterano.
Unserifed monoline Roman square capitals.
E. Panofsky, *Tomb Sculpture* (Princeton, 1964), p. 72; figs. 309-10.

It could be argued that as the antiquities of Rome comprised inscriptions in antique Square Capitals, they were specially appropriate for members of the Colonna family. Also, it could be claimed that the sculptors found it easier to carve unserifed rather than serifed capitals. Were they chosen and authorized for Martin V as Oddo Colonna because his line reached back, it was believed, to pre-Christian Rome?

To account for the presence of Square monoline sans-serif Roman Capitals on the tomb of Martin V it is well to look further than the Roman Chancery. It might be guessed that artists in official employment were following the lead of Poggio. It is possible that, as he was certainly in a position to draft and design the inscription for his late master, he did so in fact. Yet this seems unlikely; no Chancery official could have seen the artist's working sketch of the text with such errors as appeared on the finished tomb, 'FEBRARII' for FEBRUARII and 'FILICITAS' for FELICITAS. However, bad as the spelling may be and bleak the prose, the working of the engraving is excellent. The modesty of the tomb and the brevity of the inscription testify to the condition of Rome after the pontificate of Martin V. The death of this tyrannical nepotist on 20 February 1431 precipitated manifold difficulties for any successor. Gabriel Condulmaro was elected on 3 March 1431 and took the title of Eugenius IV. On 31 May 1433 the pope placed the crown of gold upon the head of Sigismund and made him head of the Holy Roman Empire. A year later after an outbreak of violence in Rome the pope disguised as an Augustinian friar fled to Florence. This event concerns us in so far as the resulting confusion made impossible any important artistic work in Rome either on the tomb of Martin V or any other work of significance.

The Colonna family were deeply involved in this rebellion against the Pope and the probability is that Simone's work on the tomb of Martin V was suspended until Rome could settle down. A further probability is that the tomb of Cardinal Crivelli in the Roman church of S. Maria in Ara Caeli was completed by Donatello in 1434 in Square sans-serif lettering. It may be well, therefore, to accept a date after 1434 as that for the first papal tomb to be lettered in this type of script. This precedent was never reversed. No papal tomb since Martin V has been lettered in Gothic or Uncialesque script. This was less than a century after the death of Rienzi, who, it has been suggested above, might, had he lived beyond his birthday in 1353, have then accorded official Roman recognition to a revival of the antique capitals; while in Rome sometime after 1434 that degree of public recognition was accorded to them. The degree is difficult to define, but it soon became clear that it was accorded the authority of precedent.

Thus the capitals which Poggio had been consistently writing for private purposes at least since 1408 were engraved for a public purpose in Rome a quarter of a century or so later. The length of the interval in Rome may safely be charged to the continuance of disputes between the popes and the councils. In consequence the revival of the engraved and sculptured antique was slower than one would have expected. However, that the lettering was followed by the sculptors of successive popes is proof of a sanction greater than that of the accidental wish of their respective executors. By the time of Nicolas V (1447–55) the revived 'antiqua' was apparently less of a novelty in Rome.

Before leaving the matter of the papal lettering it is relevant to ask why, if the popes decided to abandon Uncialesque or Gothic lettering, they did not revert to an earlier papal precedent. It may well have seemed to popes and the emperors that, with Martin V's successor Eugenius IV in exile at S. Maria Novella in Florence, Rome had finally ceased to function. The future *caput mundi* would be Florence. Such a destiny must have beckoned Cosimo de' Medici from 1429, when his father's death made him the wealthiest and ablest dictator that the city had ever known, and the most lavish and consistent supporter which the humanists, and those who worked for them, could imagine. Papal Rome, having no such protector, no longer had any meaning.

The later Imperial capital lettering, designed to aggrandize emperors and appropriated by the popes, had also ceased to possess meaning. After the flight of Eugenius IV the old symbolism of the Gregorian capital could not be regained. Never again was the claim to be made that the Bishop of Rome, besides bearing the universal spiritual authority of the Apostle Peter, also inherited the temporal sovereignty of the emperor, after Constantine had taken his capital to Byzantium.

Thus the future of lettering in Rome lay in the revival of a symbol of secular Rome, in fact pagan Rome, specifically of the Republic and not of the Empire; of the time of Cicero and not of Augustus. This is a point to which we shall return. Meanwhile, there is another point to be noted: the degree to which the neo-'antiqua' of the humanists was affected by the presence of the Greeks at the Council of Ferrara–Florence.

A highly interesting specimen of the application of the sans-serif alphabet is to be seen in the large bronze portrait medal of the Eastern Emperor John VIII Palaeologus made by Pisanello (Plate 159). It will be observed that both Greek

159. Antonio Pisanello, portrait medal of John VIII Palaeologus, Florence, 1438–9.

G. F. Hill, *A Corpus of Italian Medals of the Renaissance before Cellini* (London, 1930), i. 7, no. 19; ii, pl. 3, no. 19.

and Latin legends are, like the portrait, engraved in bold relief (for bronze castings) and, it must be inferred, the cutting is by the hand of the artist himself rather than by that of an independent professional engraver of metal letters. The medal is datable as of 1438-9. In any case Pisanello signed the work and it became his custom to use unserifed capitals as, for example, his medal for Sigismondo Malatesta. This is dated 1445. In this connection it may be noted (though we need not spend time on the priority of their respective dates) Leon Baptista Alberti and Matteo de' Pasti were working for Malatesta in 1454 and that their lettering is quadrate in proportion, sometimes monoline, sometimes with contrasted strokes, and only later adding serifs to similar architectural letters.

The Pisanello lettering in the two languages is consistently shaped and regularly spaced. The portrait is superbly drawn and perfectly engraved. It is a worthy essay to achieve an ecumenical alphabet fit to symbolize the reconciliation of the Greek and Roman divisions of the Church. The use of the Square sans serif lettering for the Greek legend recalls the Athens of the fifth century B.C. and not that of the Byzantium of the fifteenth century A.D. The commissioning of the best available artist-craftsman for the portrait work intended to gratify the personage concerned according to protocol described on the medal as BACILEVC KAI AVTOKRATωP RωMAIωN must have been considered by its sponsors in terms of high diplomacy. Was the archaic Greek lettering selected, not contemporary Byzantine, as the result of a politico-ecclesiastical decision? The question may well be asked, but less well answered. The selection may have been purely artistic or technomorphic. Again, it followed the Florentine-Roman precedent set by Donatello and Ghini. It is possible that the shape of the Greek letters depended entirely upon the artist, who signed his name in both languages. If it was Pisanello's personal decision he must be credited with having perceived the historic fact that the Latin alphabet is a Greek derivative. There were available many learned Greeks willing to advise the artist. It was not thought desirable for Pisanello to make the Greek numismatic capitals conform to the Greek manuscript capitals. The lettering on later Byzantine coins is also sans serif but roughly executed. The latter was familiar to the circles in Florence.

Others of the scribes retained by the first generation of humanists are even to be found writing a hybrid Byzantine-Latin capital script. Commanding though the example of Poggio's script was (and, doubtless, the force of his oral exposition), there were other influences and other scripts which, while humanistic, were less Roman in Poggio's sense. The most important of the scholars responsible for approximating Greek to Roman calligraphy was Ciriaco di Pizzicolli of Ancona, who represents for us the last manifestation of the contact so constantly evident, so frequently negligible, sometimes powerful, but never paramount, of old Rome with new Rome. The recovery and eventual disappearance of Byzantinisms which Latin script had harboured intermittently over a thousand years needs now to be summarized, however briefly.

It has been seen that the influence, impossible to exaggerate, of Petrarch carried with it a dependence, particularly evident in the minuscule of Poggio, upon central European scriptoria. The pedigree of his capitals has already been traced.

Much could be said of the descent of his minuscule, but all that is necessary here is to say that Poggio collected and copied in the libraries of St. Gall, Fulda, Cologne, and other northern houses, in which or for which was practised the national round Carolingian minuscule as it was written before the thirteenth century when contraction, thickening, and decorating forced it into a highly artificial contracted and perpendicular design. Poggio's neo-Carolingian humanistic minuscule was a Western script and for the reasons given above it cannot be doubted that to safeguard its purity as a Western script signified in the eyes of the humanists that it was essentially a pure Latin 'antiqua' script, apt as nothing else was or could be, for the transcription of noble Roman philosophers.

The alternative system of transcription employed by Ciriaco of Ancona represented a distinct standpoint. The man himself was of a wholly different type from Poggio. He was born in 1391. About 1420 he studied Latin literature systematically and learnt Greek in 1425. Business took him to Dalmatia, Greece, Asia Minor, and the islands of the Aegean, also Egypt. He visited Constantinople and was often in Rome. There is no evidence of this born traveller going further north than the emperor's court at Siena. His acquaintance was appreciated by the Emperor Sigismund who in 1433 kept court at Siena; but Ciriaco remained a westerner who never lost his admiration for the easterners, and as such he was an influence for Graeco-Latin ecumenism. He was an enthusiast and could afford to be.

Traces of Byzantine influence upon Latin script before the time of Ciriaco are noticeable though not numerous. Manuscripts written outside Florence can be pointed to. One example is a Statius (once in the collection of Major Abbey) written in 1419 at Pisa by Niccolò da Camogli. A later example which may owe something to Ciriaco's influence (though this is doubtful) is the Aulus Gellius (now in the Newberry Library, Chicago), written in Milan in 1445 by Milano Burro. Pisa, in addition to a well-nourished hostility to Florence, enjoyed a long-standing trade pact with Constantinople, and it was trade that connected Ancona with Constantinople.

Business had made Ciriaco rich. His importance is that, though more than a 'collector' in the modern sense and well able to read and write, he remained less a man of letters than a man of business. His tastes were archaeological and his means ample for its indulgence. As a merchant he travelled and exchanged goods; as a connoisseur he copied inscriptions and collected manuscripts, which, when at home, he diligently studied and accurately copied. Ciriaco generously communicated his ideas and discoveries to like-minded amateurs among his friends as well as to professionals like Poggio and amateurs like Niccoli. As a man of business who had a passion for books, he resembled in a small way Cosimo de' Medici; as a competent freehand scribe he resembled Niccoli; as an indefatigable archaeologist he surpassed Poggio.

As a scribe Ciriaco was self-taught. As a rapid worker his scripts varied from the very formal to the veriest scribble. None was first class of its kind. His mind was far too curious and experimentalist for his hand to be constant to a single script. His earliest datable autograph is the Ovid *Fasti* which he transcribed in

1427 in a moderately formal humanistic upright hand with some cursive elements. There are, also, at this early date some slight Byzantine symptoms. Of more interest to this present investigation is the mixed Graeco-Latin script which he created later. Although the first dated autograph of this kind is as late as 1442 it is more than likely that he was practising it by 1431 (Plate 160), when the first Greek delegations began to arrive at Ferrara.

As a philo-Byzantine Ciriaco was active behind the scenes in the preparations for what became known as the Council of Florence, the greatest of all efforts of old Rome to heal the breach with new Rome, and the culmination of all hopes for the creation of a Christendom united against Islam. Some recapitulation of certain events which followed the end of the Council of Constance and the election of Martin V are desirable at this point.

Against all advice Oddo Colonna, Martin V, a Roman of the Romans, went to Rome and found exactly what had been described to him; a place of anarchy, ruin, starvation, and pestilence. Forthwith, however, he set himself to establish order, rebuild public edifices, organize food and medical services. For the restoration of the churches and chapels he fetched architects and artists from Tuscany; builders to renew the bridges and aquaducts. Gentile da Fabriano, Vittore, Pisanello, Tommaso Masaccio, and Fra Angelico were among the painters that this pope attracted to redecorate the desolate city. Thus Rome's artistic enrichment was mainly and necessarily dependent upon Florence. The Colonna revenues were the strong reserve that Martin V had at his disposal.

Five years after Martin's election the Turks mounted a fresh and serious attack on Constantinople. The threat produced a crisis which, however, passed for the time being. But it was clear to the Byzantines that the relief was temporary. In 1431 John VIII Palaeologus (1425–48) sent an embassy to Rome to persuade Martin V to call forthwith a General Council which the Greeks would attend. The pope agreed. The emperor wished the new Council to assemble in Constantinople, but gave way when the pope promised to put up in the West the whole Greek delegation on his own expense account. At the point of agreement upon the preliminaries and the assembling of the Council in Basel Martin V died. His successor was Eugenius IV (1431–47). The Council at Basel, dominated by the secular powers, though sparsely attended, anticipated the pope by dispatching an embassy to take to Constantinople a message that if the Greeks would come to Basel their gesture would be recognized with good Latin money—in the form of a bill drawn upon Cosimo de' Medici. The emperor expressed deep interest in the Council's suggestion of his going to Basel. At the same time he sent envoys to the new pope. It suited John Palaeologus best to get both delegations to appear before him, and the Basel emissaries duly arrived in Constantinople bearing with them the promised bill on the Medici bank. That was in September 1435.

In the following March the Roman delegation instructed by Eugenius IV waited upon the emperor with a still larger sum. So far so good. The place at which the great General Council of East and West should congregate was not so easily settled. No pope would choose to situate the Council in an imperialist stronghold such as Basel; the last country to which any good Greek would go

160. Thucydides, annotated by Ciriaco d'Ancona, possibly not before 1434.
Bodleian Library, Oxford, MS. Canon. Gr. 48.
Heavily ligatured, contracted, and accented Greek cursive.
Ruth Barbour, *The Bodleian Library Record*, v. 1, pp. 9–14.

would be France, the home of the abominated Franks. Italy was the nearer country and they knew it better; so the Byzantines plumped for the pope of Rome against the Council at Basel. As Rome believed that Basel had become schismatical in tendency, this was satisfactory to Eugenius IV. At loggerheads, then, with Basel, Rome was more dependent upon Constantinople; which was exactly what the Eastern emperor most desired. The year was now 1437, which was hardly a good time for Christians of any party, papalist or imperialist. The Turks already had Macedonia, Thessaly, Thrace, Bulgaria, and Serbia. Everybody, including Basel, knew that Constantinople was their immediate objective. New Rome now desperately needed old Rome, and the pope needed the emperor as never before. The Council was an urgent matter. Eugenius IV sent a fleet to collect John VIII Palaeologus and his bishops. The General Council was to be assembled at Ferrara.

The cultured Greeks sought suitably to impress the barbarous Latins by using the fleet of Eugenius IV to transport an immense variety of ecclesiastical gear, including extensive wardrobes of golden, jewelled, and brocaded vestments. The magnificence of this equipage was unequalled in all the annals of politico-ecclesiastical diplomacy. Carrying also a huge bulk of secular luggage, the fleet bearing the emperor and patriarch left Constantinople on 27 November 1437 and landed at Venice on 6 February 1438.

The emperor was accompanied by a select court of advisers, court officials, and Chancery clerks. Their overriding secular motive was proper to Byzantium: to prepare the way for an Oriental-Occidental naval and military alliance against the Turk. The patriarch was supported by more than a score of metropolitans, numerous bishops, with their retinue of theologians, monks, scribes, and notaries. Unlike the emperor, the patriarch and his clergy having come West, were less sensitive about the extreme pressure from the Turks. Their national motive was to defeat the errant Latins on urgent theological points of difference, such as the single or dual procession of the Holy Ghost, and the nature of the pains of purgatory. Some seven hundred Greeks whose expenses were paid on a royal scale by the pope arrived at Ferrara early in 1438. Some delegates also arrived from Basel. To help forward the discussions, the pope soon moved the Council to Florence. The emperor secured the pope's agreement to financial provision (guaranteed by three banks in Venice, Florence, and Genoa), military guarantees (a permanent guard, two ships to be maintained and more ships in case of emergency), and if a land army for defence became necessary the pope was to use all endeavours to persuade the Western princes accordingly. The agreement on material points thus being achieved the settlement of spiritual differences was next achieved. The decree of union was published in Greek and Latin on 6 July 1439, and the assent of the Armenians, Syrians, Copts, Chaldeans, and Maronites was received in the course of the next three years. The emperor, John VIII, had returned to Constantinople in 1439.

What, at this time, was the epigraphical or calligraphical situation in those years? First it may be presumed that Ciriaco was very active behind the scenes in forwarding the arrangements for the General Council, and he was certainly influential with the pope.

Martin V was 63 when he died in 1431 and Eugenius 48 when he succeeded. He was himself a 'buon scrittore' according to Vespasiano da Bisticci who may be believed on this point, and had written out his personal office-book (which may be questioned). That he shared some of the preferences of the leaders of the new antique Florentine movement cannot be doubted, and he certainly felt sympathetic towards architects, sculptors, and painters. He welcomed Donatello to Rome in the second year of his pontificate. At this time the sculptor was employed on the tomb of Giovanni Crivelli, Cardinal Patriarch of Aquileia, who died in 1432. The work set up in the church of S. Maria in Ara Coeli is signed by the artist who, it may certainly be presumed, was responsible also for the form of the long inscription. Though the recumbent effigy itself is laid out in 'Gothic' style, the lettering is square capitals unserifed. Donatello left Rome in 1434, the year when Eugenius fled to Florence from the outbreaks organized by the Colonna.

In 1445, two years after he returned to Rome, Eugenius IV reorganized the papal Chancery. For the improvement of discipline he created the 'Scriptores litterarum apostolicarum' into a separate 'Collegium'. He also extended the use of the new class of expeditious diplomatic instrument which had been originated during (possibly before) the pontificate of Boniface IX. Eugenius IV appointed as his Apostolic Secretary Flavio Antonio Biondo (1390–1463) a worthy successor to Poggio and himself an enthusiastic archaeologist and the future author of *Roma Instaurata*. At a time not at present determinable but not later than 1434, a particular cursive version of the script now known as humanistic was first given official diplomatic use in Rome under the authority of Eugenius IV and over the signature of Flavius Blondus (Plate 161).

Biondo wrote a handsome humanistic cursive (of which more below) and about this time developed out of it a purely Latin semi-cursive, free from Byzantine elements. The fact is worth noticing, since the pope was so eager to placate the Greeks at the Council of Florence, and especially as he had become intimate with Ciriaco, the philo-Byzantine who had evolved a Graeco-Latin script, and had

161. Brief of Eugenius IV, dated 8 June 1446, signed by Flavio Biondo.

Paris, Archives nationales, L. 325.

Humanistic cursive, as adapted for use in the papal chancery.

W. Arndt and M. Tangl, *Schrifttafeln zur Erlernung der lateinischen Palaeographie*, vol. iii (Berlin, 1907), pl. 99c; *Recueil des facsimilés à l'usage de l'École des Chartes* (Paris, 1880), pl. 68.

presented a specimen to the pope. It is a remarkably hybrid experiment. The effect of the East was, for theological reasons, fated to be transitory. It might have been otherwise if the Act of Union reached in Florence had been ratified in Constantinople. However, as during the pontificate of Eugenius IV it ranks historically as the final impact of Byzantinism upon Western calligraphy, something must be said about it. Its origin and impulse was purely Western, literary, and archaeological; philosophical also, and in so far as it symbolized the desire deeply felt for Greek and Roman ecclesiastical unity it was theological.

Ciriaco wrote Latin in the cursive style peculiar to the Byzantine Chancery. It was adopted in the twelfth century and later became the common correspondence hand of the educated classes in Constantinople and elsewhere. This singular but highly deliberate choice by Ciriaco brought into his Latin such typical Byzantinisms as vertical ligatures, unknown in any script in Latin. There were also combined capitals such as EV in DEVOTVS and PR in PROFANO. Ciriaco's Greek script, naturally was a highly ligatured cursive.

Secondly, even for his transcription of Ovid's *Fasti*, he created capital horizontal ligatures and would incorporate Byzantine sorts, such as M, with its centre terminating in a vertical stroke. Admittedly people who had seen this done in the mosaics at Cefalù for Greek inscriptions and at Palermo and Venice for Latin, but it was unprecedented to incorporate such an M in the Book-hand for a Latin author. Ciriaco when he wrote a Latin inscription took pains to reproduce as accurately as an untrained amateur could, square Roman capitals with serifs of the Imperial type. This is well shown in the dedicatory page to his *Itinerarium* addressed to Eugenius IV and autographed by 'Kyriacus' (as he here signs himself) in 1441. This consistent application of the serif by Ciriaco signifies his belief that it was appropriate in a Latin address to the august personage who was no less than the sovereign of Rome (Plate 162).

Florence never accepted Ciriaco's Byzantine perpendicular ligature in her minuscule. What, then of the majuscule? Did those in the Council of Ferrara-Florence exercise any influence, direct or indirect, upon the form of capitals? The Council was, it has been seen, in session until 1445. An incidental memorial of the Council and of the Act of Union signed by all but one of the delegates on 3 July 1439 is (Plate 163) to be seen in a work of Antonio di Mario. This talented scribe flourished between 1417 and 1456 and was employed by Niccoli among others. The long colophon to his Pliny, finished in 1440, specifically mentions the Act of Union (Plate 164). It will be observed that, unlike Poggio's capitals, Di Mario's are regularly serifed. He had been using this style at least since 1419, when he transcribed the *Historia* of Q. Curtius Rufus while Poggio was still faithful to sans serif, as he shows in the Cicero which he transcribed in 1428 (Plate 155). Di Mario had the support not only of Niccoli but of Cosimo de' Medici. In 1440 di Mario completed a second Pliny which also has a long colophon commemorating the unity of the Greek and Latin Churches. Here, it might be thought, was an opportunity for the use of a Graeco-Roman alphabet which should write the script of the two Patriarchates. The text being a Pliny obviously required a Roman Capital for its titles to accompany the neo-Carolingian hand

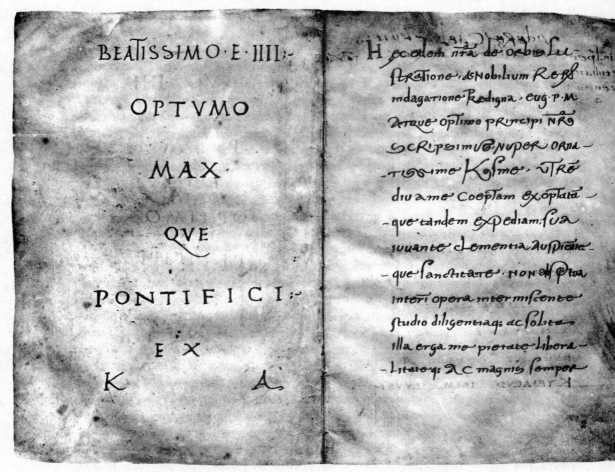

162. Ciriaco d'Ancona. Letter to Eugenius IV. Current humanistic cursive, 1441.

Florence, Bibl. Laurenziana, Gadd 90. inf. 55.

Heavily ligatured Latin in the Byzantine style. Title in Rustic and square capitals.

Baudini, *Cat. Codd. Lat.* iii. 740.

employed for the text. Rightly, the colophon of the second Pliny of 1440 is dominantly Roman but it has as alternative characters, the Greek or whole Uncial round A, E, M, V, while F is flourished at the head as if it were Rustic as written in the twelfth century. G is Roman but bearded. The point at the centre of the perpendiculars of I, P, T is to be seen occasionally in Latin manuscripts of the ninth century; but not in combination with Uncial. On the other hand, it is a regular device in Byzantine Greek. In the Florence of Di Mario's day it may rank as a reflection, though faint, of Byzantine custom. The main point to be noticed below is that his capitals are serifed. The Byzantines did this too. The question is whether this was or was not a mere coincidence. Traditional Byzantinisms were not easily extinguished. The prestige of Constantinople still lingered.

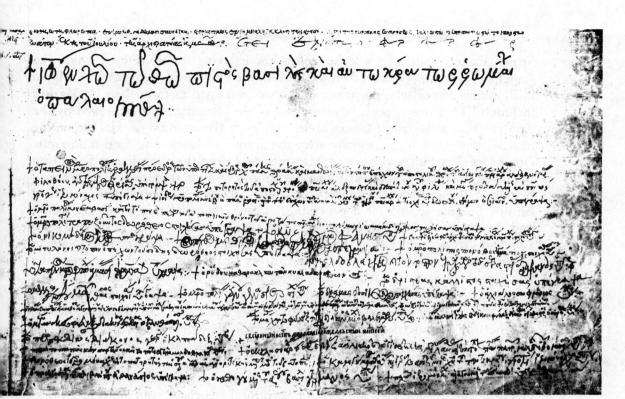

163. Decree of union of the Council of Florence 1439. Signatures of the Greeks.

Florence, Bibl. Laur. Cassetta Cesarini No. 1.

See J. Gill, *The Council of Florence*, Cambridge 1959, pp. 295-6.

164. Antonio di Mario. Colophon to his Pliny. Humanistic capitals. 1440.

Rome, Vatican, Cod. Urb. Lat. 245.

Square capitals with A, curved E, Rustic F, pointed I, curved M, low diagonal N, and other uncial–Byzantine elements.

Morison, pl. 19; Ullman, p. 102.

ANTONIVS·MARII·FILVS·FLORENTINVS·CIVIS·ATQ;
NOTARIVS·TRANSCRIPSIT·FLORENTIAE·X·KLD·IVNII
·M·CCCC·XL·QVO·TEMPORE·GRAECOR·ECLESIA·RO
MANE·ECLESIAE·DEI·OPE·SVMOQ;·STVDIO·AC·LABORE·IN
DICTA·CIVITATE·VNITA·EST·VIRTVTE·ATQ;·SAHCTISSIMOR
ATQ;·PRECLARISSID·VIROR·EVGENII·PP·IIII·SVMMI·ROMA
HOR·PONTIFICIS·ET·IOSEPH·PATRIARCE·CONSTANTINOPOL
TAHI·AD·LAVDEM·ET·GLORIAM·DEI·ET·HONOREM·NOSTRE·REI
PVBLICE·FLORENTIHE.

VALEAS·FELICITER·Q·LEGIS.

Strong Eastern influence is to be seen in the lettering to the frescoes which Fra Angelico (1387-1455) painted on the walls of the Dominican convent of S. Marco in Florence. His letters, narrower and more restrained in form than Di Mario's include ε. That this is not a reminiscence of the Ottonian style is proved by the painter's occasional use of Uncial abbreviations in Byzantine style. His Florentine frescoes date from 1443, shortly after the accord of Rome and Constantinople. Other Greek impulses at work at this time arose from the attention and curiosity bestowed upon the graphic art. The beginnings of modern connoisseurship may be traced in the thirteenth century. It could only be a matter of time, provided Europe became settled for a generation or two, that Hellenistic culture would find, as in Ciriaco, its Western interpreters. It is curious that he never practised a regular Greek literary Book-hand of the type, say, of the Plutarch now (Vatican Urbin. grec. 100) written in 1402 by Andreas Leantinus. A bridge between the two alphabets existed in the capital titles with the short, heavy serif they had inherited from Latin Rustic. In their Minuscule they placed no serif upon the heads of the ascenders or at the tails of the descenders, and this practice obtained whether the Minuscule was formal or informal. The descenders stopped at the pear-shaped terminal that the West had not practised in Latin since the flourishing days of Luxeuil and Corbie.

The ninth-century Byzantine formal, upright minuscule is a fine austere practical and legible creation apt for scriptural, patristic, and liturgical work. It is much superior to the informal and deceptively elegant cursive script used for the mass of Byzantine literary work after the twelfth century—but the latter, being a cursive, is much more quickly written. It deliberately encourages the complex ligatures, convolute abbreviations, and dazzling artificialities that so naturally corresponded with Byzantine ideas of courtliness, etiquette, and sophistication.

When Ciriaco was addressing Eugenius IV in 1441 he used the style to be seen on Plate 162. It may be inferred that westerners having Greek connections, commercial and cultural, were accustomed to the decorated and flourished Byzantine cursive. And this presented the less difficulty, since it was normal for Italians to write in flourished Gothic cursive both for Latin and the vernacular. And, also naturally, people could read what they wrote. Hence, neither Greek nor Latin cursive was more 'illegible' to contemporaries than English scribble is to us.

It is certainly easier for all of us nowadays to read any formal more rapidly than informal writing, just as typewriting is easier than either. Greek cursive may well have been difficult for the early pupils of Leontius Pilatus, who taught Boccaccio in the years 1361-4, or Chrysoloras, who later taught Guarino, and no doubt they found it beneficial to teach them a semi-formal script. This, any-how, is what Aurispa, Guarino, and others wrote, and perhaps they were never at their best at cursive. With Ciriaco it was different; he knew the Byzantine cursive perfectly and liked it extremely. In the Thucydides, discovered a few years ago by Miss Barbour, Ciriaco writes a cursive, admirable in flow, as may be seen in Plate 160 which exhibits Ciriaco's heavily ligatured, cursive Greek, like his also heavily ligatured Latin. A word may be said later about the Latin. Meanwhile, though far out of chronological order (as the convenience of this chapter requires), a portion of a decree of the Council of Florence on the union of the Greek and Roman Churches needs to be noticed. This decree was drawn up and signed in 1439 (Plate 163). Evidently the Greek theologians wrote in cursive, and Latin theologians able in Greek wrote nothing but the cursive. There can hardly be any doubt, therefore, that had the union become effective, the cursive would have been the normal medium of diplomatic communication between East and West, and that Rome would have trained a number of clerks to be expert in reading and writing it; thereby giving a measure of authority to it, without prejudice to the use for other purposes of a formal hand.

Whether, had this happened in Rome, and numbers of Greek ecclesiastics had made a habit to visit the city, or the emperor to maintain an embassy there, Latin script would have gradually approximated to Greek, is not impossible. Since the sixth century East and West had become so accustomed to a distinct grouping of symbols that they could reasonably wish to elevate such a distinctive convention. The independent development of the minuscule in both languages made it almost inevitable in the fifteenth century that the two languages should look in future what they were in the ninth century—two related languages expressed in related scripts; and as they were not identical in language they would be dissimilar in script. It has been pointed out that even in the days of Diocletian the Roman Chancery decided that it was administratively convenient to make visible the distinction between the two languages.

The influence of Byzantine conventions upon Latin script so far noticed has been incidental. No reconstruction of the minuscule was involved and all that can be pointed to in the scripts of Ciriaco of Ancona or Antonio di Mario is a certain imitativeness in the design of capitals and the use of ligatures in the capitals.

Inevitably Byzantine influence upon Latin script lessened after the fall of Constantinople and the death of Ciriaco. As suggested above some approximation of the Roman to the Greek alphabet might have been expected to follow the Act of Union. This consummation of the union, however, was not realized; and what was realized instead came less for calligraphical than for typographical reasons.

The last calligraphical instance of a Greek and Latin text designed with a script designed to serve both languages was inspired by Joannes Basilius Bessarion (c. 1400–72). Bessarion was a man of great character and prodigious learning. In many respects he was one of the greatest men of the age. He—great Greek theologian from Trebizond—who accompanied John VIII Palaeologus to Ferrara contributed largely by his learning to the acceptance of the Decree of Union. It was he who read out the Greek text of the Decree in the cathedral of Florence on 6 July 1439. In January 1440 Eugenius IV created Bessarion a cardinal (with Isidore, Metropolitan of Kiev). As the cardinal changed to the observance of the Latin rule he earned thereby extreme unpopularity in Constantinople by abandoning the Greek rite in favour of the Latin. He made matters worse for his reputation with the Greeks by abandoning Constantinople in 1440 to live in Venice. As Mahomed II could not afford Greek ecclesiastic union with the West because he knew what that would lead to, the Orthodox patriarchs comfortably repudiated the Act of Union.

To return to Bessarion: he became a lavish benefactor to the University of Bologna where he had been sent by Nicolas V as his legate and with the civic rank of governor. He attracted many first-class professors to the University and rebuilt its halls and schools and fostered the study of the Greek and Latin classics.

Bessarion used all his endeavours, though unavailingly, to get the Venetians to expel the Turks from Constantinople and to help Pius II in a crusade for that purpose. Disappointed, Bessarion abandoned himself to studies and the society of scholars, who joined with him in founding in Rome the first Academia. He eagerly assisted the plans of Sixtus IV to organize a crusade and as legate journeyed north to interview the kings of England and France, the duke of Burgundy, and others. At Ravenna on 18 November 1472 the great man died. His body was taken to Rome and he was buried in his titular church of the Twelve Apostles. His collection of 800 Greek manuscripts was bequeathed to the Republic of Venice and became the nucleus of the Marciana Library. Among them is the splendid Ptolemy of Ioannes Rhosos, written presumably at Bessarion's commission. It begins with an epigram composed by Niccolo Perotti which the scribe wrote in Greek and Latin. The capitals on the page (Plate 165) had a particular interest. Both sets of capitals are of the customary narrow, Byzantine form, and both are slightly serifed also in accordance with Byzantine tradition. It should be noticed that round, Uncial E is standard in the Greek, while square E is retained in the Latin. The fork of M does not fully descend. The diagonal to N terminates above the bottom of the right-hand stroke. These traits are Byzantine.

As the text of the body is written in a script inspired by the traditional ninth-century pattern, it follows that its assimilation by Latin in the fifteenth century suggests a new principle. There are, of course, precedents of scribes having before them the problem of writing Greek and Latin with the same pen. The Laurentian Homer which was written for Filelfo under the eye of Theodore Gaza, the grammarian who also participated in the Reunion Council, is one of these.

Whether the Florentine and Venetian scribes should make these Latin Capitals square and unserifed as Poggio did or condense and serif them as the Byzantines did was the calligraphic problem facing Bessarion and his scribe. But both Bessarion and the scribe of the Ptolemy were Greeks and the problem for them was trivial. They chose to write Latin in the Greek style. It would be natural if a distaste for 'Byzantine art' in Rome and Florence followed the action of the Orthodox Patriarch Gennadius in establishing affectionate relations with Mahomet II. No new architectural foundation in the West comparable in style, if not in scale, to S. Marco can be pointed to. What is now called the Italian renaissance would itself make such a building impossible in Florence or Rome. With the exception perhaps of Venice, the trend of thinking in learned Italy was insular. The Serene Republic, so far from being in the mood to engage in any

Ἐπίγραμμα ὅπερ ἅπε πτολεμαῖ εἰς ἑαυτὸν

ΔΙΛΟΤΙ ΘΝΗΤΟΣ ΕΦΥΝ ΚΑΙ ΕΦΗΜΕΡΟΣ ΑΛΛΟΤΑΝ ΑΣΤΡΩΝ
ΜΑCΤΕΥΩ ΠΥΚΝΑC ΑΜΦΙΔΡΟΜΟΥC ΕΛΙΚΑC
ΟΥΚΕΤΕΠΙΨΑΥΩ ΓΑΙΗC ΠΟCΙΝ ΑΛΛΑ ΠΑΡΑΥΤΩ
ΖΗΝΙ ΘΕΟΤΡΟΦΕΟC ΠΙΠΛΑΜΑΙ ΑΜΒΡΟCΙΗC

EPIGRAMMA PTOLEMEI
MORTALEM VITAM PERITVRA Q̃ MEMBRA DEDERE
FATA MIHI & SVMVM PRESTITVERE DIEM
SED IOVIS AMBROSIA VESCOR TERRAM Q̃ RELINQVO
INGENIO CVRSVS DVM NOTO SYDEREOS

165. Ptolemy, *Geography* (epigram on Ptolemy by Niccolò Perotti). Not after 1453.

Venice, Bibl. Marc., gr. 388.

Greek and Latin capitals in Byzantine style.

See M. C. Ferrari, 'La Geografia del Zolemeo fatta miniare dal Cardinale Bessarione', in *La Bibliofilia* 40 (Florence, 1938).

crusade, looked instead to increasing her trade with the new government of Constantinople and, incidentally, to exploit some of the old Oriental decorative arts that were now in the Occident.

Bessarion presented his collection of Byzantine manuscripts to Venice in 1464, the year when Sweynheym and Pannartz were on the verge of completing their rendering of Cicero's *De Oratore*, in a number of identical copies, by the novel art of typography, never before practised in Italy.

Before looking forward to certain consequences of the introduction of typography in Greek and Latin which are relevant to the present investigation, it is necessary to look backwards to an aspect of the early development in humanistic script which has, so far here, been left out of account: the capitals used by the scribes and the sculptors at work during the first four decades after, say, 1402 until 1445. The humanistic calligraphy has hitherto been discussed in terms of formal capitals and formal minuscule. The revolutionary script was not limited to these two constituents. An alternative script with the same constituent of capital and minuscule began a career whose vigour until the present day justifies more than mere mention.

It has been made clear in a previous chapter that the minuscule is a stylized cursive and that cursive minuscule is, by its nature, easier to write than the formal minuscule; also that the informality essential to cursive minuscule may vary in degree but does not in any case require that it must be written at an inclined angle. In other words, a cursive minuscule does not always slope though it usually does. Similarly, it does not always join letter to letter, though it often does. A dual tendency was in fact inherent in cursive minuscule, towards faster writing, and towards slower. The former is observable at Luxeuil in the eighth century and the second at St. Gall in the ninth. It is abundantly possible, though far from established, that when Poggio was at St. Gall and other northern libraries he secured in addition to manuscripts of classical authors written in formal Carolingian Minuscule some written cursive minuscule of the same period. This seems certain. The facts remain that whereas the formal humanistic minuscule made its original appearance not later than *c.* 1402 the cursive minuscule cannot be dated, only as of a much later date. There are several manuscripts in the hand of the writer (he can hardly be called a scribe) all in cursive in several degrees of currency. The writer was Niccolo di Niccoli, who came under the influence of Coluccio Salutati and after his death in 1406 seems to have taken his place as the leading Latin scholar in Florence. He seems, nevertheless, to be a professor. Probably he received from Cosimo de' Medici a stipend more than sufficient for his personal needs and other money as more or less necessary for expenditure upon the collection of manuscripts and their transcription by Poggio and other professional scribes and writers. It is obvious that the humanists were bound to need a script which, while corresponding with the requirements of the group (see p. 268) was less expensive in terms of writing time. Poggio never responded to this need, perhaps because as a professionally competent and trained scribe he would reduce the hours of transcription even of a Cicero by writing in the orthodox Gothic cursive and at the same time lessen the cost of material by using paper.

Niccoli's humanistic cursive corresponds to the necessary degree with the Petrarchian requirements. This is admirably shown in his transcription of the *De Oratore* and Lucretius. He eschews all the flourishing which might tend towards the '*vaga ac luxurians*' and maintains all the discipline which preserves the quality of '*castigata et clara*'. He contrives a speedy but unhurried letter, temperately written in conformity with its function, as a medium for the efficient transcription by scholars of texts they desire to preserve. While being a non-professional he was an active scribe. While being active he never copied hastily. Niccoli seems to have begun copying a section of Plutarch before 1415 and continued until after his Chrysostom of 1432. During this period he transcribed upwards of ten substantial codices the writing of which, all in cursive, is singularly regular, always unhasty and therefore habitually uncasual. That he made other transcriptions which are lost (and therefore unrecorded by Ullman) is certain. Equally it is certain that such a mass of writing by such an eminent scholar, supported as he was by such a powerful patron as Cosimo de' Medici, the texts of which were of such importance as, for example, the Brutus and the Lucretius, exercised a commensurate influence upon the extensive contemporary book trade of Florence. In due course Niccoli's style was followed, adapted, and modi-fied by the professional scribes and notaries whose services were available to the booksellers.

Inevitably some increased the currency of the humanistic cursive while others decreased it. As will be seen, a later generation committed the absurdity of formal-izing the informal. The degree of informality essential to Niccoli's style needs comment.

While Niccoli was careful to preserve all the essentials, as he thought them to be, of the ancient script, especially the ligature ct which the formal humanistic took over from the twelfth-century original they used as exemplars, he made a notable and unprecedented departure in his treatment of the serif. In fact Niccoli set up a canon of his own and from this he allowed himself no departure. In all his work the heads of his ascenders (b, d, h, l) partake so completely of the cur-sive nature of the whole script as themselves to be cursive. In other words, the heads of these characters begin with a slight curve and are not serifed as in the formal humanistic script of Poggio. In fact Niccoli reverses Poggio's scheme and while leaving his minuscule without serifs made it a rule to give them to his capitals. This is another instance of the humanists' disdain of logic. Consistency with precedent did not require co-ordination between minuscule and majuscule. Unlike the scribes of Gothic, the scribes of humanistic did not relate the two alphabets. It has been pointed out above that a thirteenth-century Gothic scribe would have rejected the fifteenth-century humanistic scribe as lacking in co-ordination. The minuscules and the capitals are not written as one integrated design but as two. Petrarch, Salutati, Niccoli, or Poggio were without any know-ledge of the pedigree of Latin script though they were not so naïve as to think that Cicero himself wrote in twelfth-century style. It is more than doubtful if any of these founding fathers of the Renaissance and creators of the letter forms we use today realized that the thirteenth-century script they rejected was an advance in point of design upon the twelfth-century script they revived. Had they ever considered the matter in these terms it might be supposed that they would have contended that while it may be desirable from a designer's point of view to create one duplex script out of two basic alphabets, their solution was no solution. The 'Gothic' scribes devised a series of structural tricks and decorative embellishments which fused the two originally distinct alphabets into one single harmonious design, thus producing a true work of art. The humanists were, in fact, at pains to put a brake on the tendency inherent in cursive towards a degree of curving that carried with it a temptation to flourishing and decoration which are opposed to the canons of legibility. As later history proves, as the years passed the plain hand which Niccoli invented for the service of scholars was transformed into a decorative script for the pleasure of collectors.

With this type of aesthetic writing the present chapter does not concern itself. It is relevant, however, to observe that Niccoli's cursive humanistic met a permanent need felt outside his immediate circle which judged it unsuitable for the general transcription of classical authors, though it could be used in exceptional circumstances. That Niccoli himself shared this standpoint is clear from the neatness and regularity of his minuscule and the simplicity and plainness of his capitals. His style of serifing the capital is to be noted. Niccoli gave them at the same time a slight slant regular with the minuscule and, as has been already reported, he serifed all of them. The serif is elementary and it is evident that he esteemed it as a fitting terminal stroke and not as an embellishment. Niccoli thus conformed to the spirit of the calligraphical reform.

It was pointed out by A. Hessel in 1933 that Giovanni Aretino, a professional scribe, was practising a humanistic cursive in 1415. This was an upright version. As the manuscript was written for Cosimo de' Medici it may reasonably be assumed that Niccoli approved and perhaps inspired its transcription. In other words, it is not to be assumed that Niccoli insisted that his personal cursive should be followed in detail by the trained writers in Florence.

From the technical standpoint, a cursive does not necessarily slant. In the early career of this 'second class' the literary manuscripts written in humanistic cursive during the first half of the fifteenth century testify to the effect of the support in Florence given to this style by the private patronage of Cosimo de' Medici. More important still was the support given by its public use by Rome.

It has been seen above that one of the first acts of Eugenius IV was to reorganize the Roman Chancery. At some time after 1432 the Apostolic Secretary, Flavio Biondo, successor to Poggio, secured the pope's approval for the use of a cursive humanistic for the engrossing of the 'Breve', the humblest diplomatic instrument under the secretary's seal. This was the beginning of the humanistic cursive's career as one Chancery script in the place of the Gothic cursive which had been the rule since the time of Gregory XII. The change is a significant indication that the papacy under Eugenius IV was prepared to go further in the acceptance of humanism than it was under Martin V. The prestige and publicity given to a humanistic cursive by the Roman Chancery and probably by its Secretary, whose character was esteemed, and his script admired even by those who regarded Poggio with suspicion. Blondus's new Roman diplomatic cursive humanistic script was an upright version of Poggio's literary formal humanistic. It conveyed only a faint reminiscence of the old Gothic cursive and possesses an overall elegance lacking in the book script of Niccoli.

In the competition between the upright and the slanted versions of the humanistic cursive it soon became obvious that as the slanted version proved itself the speedier the majority of professional scribes preferred it. Blondus was an exception but his successors in the Roman Chancery adopted the slanted cursive for the Brief. As this type of papal document was extensively used for all types of major and minor indulgences and dispensations its script became familiar to courts and personages other than secretaries and notaries. Inevitably the papal Chancery script became professionalized and in the last quarter of the fifteenth century it was elevated to a degree of formal elegance which was as fully time-consuming as any formal humanistic. As early as 1460 in Florence the book-sellers were employing first-class miniaturists to decorate sumptuously classical texts in the second-class humanistic script written with all the care of a first-class humanistic script. Side by side with this service to rich customers the booksellers provided a service of third-class current humanistic cursive as the medium for plain texts in which speed of writing and economy of price were the only consideration.

Thus the scriptural revolution, so far as Latin literature was affected, was complete by the second half of the fifteenth century. At some time during the pontificate of Paul II (1464–71) or of Sixtus IV (1471–84) the Roman Chancery adopted the slanted humanistic cursive. This was a simple plain script of the Niccoli manuscripts. It became the permanent standard script for the Brief, although its plainness was marred by over-professionalization in the sixteenth and later centuries.

By the last quarter of the fifteenth century the humanistic script in its several degrees of formality was established for Latin letters and it was only a matter of time before it was used for the vernacular. The continuing example of the Roman Chancery was followed not only in the chanceries of princes and dukes for their Latin letters but by syndics and merchants for their vernacular orders and correspondence. It may be said therefore that while the papacy did not initiate the use of what later became known as the Chancery cursive its use for so widely circulated a document as the Brief brought it a dispersal which it could hardly otherwise have achieved.

The suppression of Gothic cursive in favour of the Roman Chancery cursive was rapid. It must be understood that this revival of the Carolingian Minuscule, the greatest scriptural achievement of all history—was accomplished by the example but not by the authority of the papacy. It must be added that the script itself was always speedy in execution, economical in space, and, if required, graceful in form.

We have no information of the place, presumably in Italy, where Sweynheym and Pannartz succeeded in finding metal workers able to engrave the punches and cast the types. The pioneers of printing in the peninsula knew in advance how difficult it would be to find these new techniques available to them at a place so far from Rome as Subiaco. It is likely that the enterprise occupied much time. Sweynheym knew his business, if the accepted view is true that he was one of Fust and Schoeffer's staff that was dispersed by the sack of Mainz in 1462. If he and his partner spent some time in Venice they could have had access to greater technical assistance than could be available in Rome. If the punches were designed and cut within the shadow of S. Marco the Byzantine element in the capitals would be accounted for.

It is difficult to account for the change of design in both Greek and Latin when Sweynheym and Pannartz left Subiaco for Rome in 1468. Did they think that their first Latin showed too great a Byzantine dependence to be appropriate in Rome *post* 1453?

It is to be admitted that the Byzantine influence is noticeable, but it may be rightly argued that it is present only in capitals and not in all of them (though the alternative straight M with its high centre suggests a Venetian-Byzantine source). But if it were contended that the Byzantine element in the Subiaco type is too slight to be considered, is there any other sign of Byzantine influence in early Italian typography in the Greek language? Yes, Greek printing at Milan (D. Paravisi in 1476; B. Accursius, 1479), at Florence (de Libri 1488), Venice (Alexandros and Laonikos 1486), and Vicenza (I. Achates 1489), all are fully Byzantinized, with round Epsilon, and Mu with the extension from the centre. The lower-case of all of these is sans-serif monoline, formal, and therefore upright. These instances are all found outside Rome.

The Greek types just mentioned fall into two categories, eastern and western. The capitals in the Epitome of C. Lascaris (1476), of the Theocritus and the Etymology (1499), are both Venetian renderings of Byzantine originals (Plate 166). The lower case of the first two is upright Byzantine and formal; of the third, cursive. The first descended from an original formal Greek Minuscule Bookhand. The third was modelled on a later cursive, all-purpose, hand.

The next category is that of the Greek Anthology. It is composed in inscriptional serifed capitals, having contrasted strokes, the whole deliberately made serviceable for both Latin and Greek. Plate 167 shows first the state of the fount as used for Latin in the dedicatory letter to the Anthology of 1494. Next, the Latin capitals can be seen as adapted for Greek and completed with lower case of the cursive pattern for the scholia to the Apollonius Rhodius of 1496. The printer was Alopa of Florence, working under the direction of Ioannes Lascaris.

It is unnecessary to say more of these founts since they have been analysed by Proctor and described also by Scholderer. The only point it is necessary to make here is that the Florentine founts are the same in principle as those earlier used by the calligraphers and those later created by Aldus and thereby given unusual dispersion. His first Greek text type was in use in 1495. It is shown in *a*

ΠΕΡΙ ΠΑΘΩΝ ΤΩΝ ΛΕΞΕΩΝ ΕΚ ΤΩΝ
ΤΟΥ ΓΡΑΜΜΑΤΙΚΟΥ ΤΡΥΦΩΝΟΣ·

b

ΕΙΔΥΛΛΙΟΝ · Α ·
ΚΥΚΛΩΨ ·

166. (*a*) Constantius Lascaris,
Epitome.
Milan, D. Paravisinus, 1476.
Proctor, pl. I; Scholderer, fig. 8.

(*b*) Theocritus and Hesiod.
Milan, B. Accursius, *c.* 1479–80.
Proctor, pl. II; Scholderer, fig. 9.

Plate 168 from the Aristophanes of 1498. Here is to be seen the same combination of formal, upright, inscriptional serifed capitals, with contrasted stroke in Latin style, joined with informal, inclined cursive lower case in the contemporary Greek current hand. It is usual to heap abuse upon Aldus for having cut so many ligatures and contractions. A sounder reason for adversely criticizing him would be his combination of the formal and the informal as combined into one text, as shown in our Plate 169. This, however, was the standing convention among the scribes (and hence the readers) of the time. Aldus followed the same precedent with Latin in 1500, when he combined capitals upon a humanistic cursive descended from the hand of Niccolò Niccoli, first used about 1462 by the papal Chancery.

In Venice at the end of the century engravers of punches for the printing trade vied with each other in the production of intricately ligatured characters designed for Latin as well as Greek texts. Punch-cutting had made much progress in the sixty or so years since the great invention and simultaneously wood-engraving

295

RAM Pɪ LATINVM INDE DEDVCTVM PARVA DECLINATIONɛ
REFERRE VIDEATVR . AᴌTERIVS AVTEM FIGVRA QVOD ᴌɪ
VAE DEXTERAM LINEAE DEMITTIT AEQVAᴌEM. EX NOTIS Iᴌ
LIS CONSTARE POSSIT. QVIBVS ETIAM ANTIQVISSIME NV
MERI SIGNABANTVR. VT IN DECRETIS ET IN ANTIQVIS MO
NVMENTIS INVENTVM EST . Qᴠɪʙᴠꜱ ETIAM NOTIS Sᴏ ᴌO
NIS LEGES MEMORIA PRODITVM EST POENAS PECVNIARIAS
SIGNATAS HABVISSE . Iɴ ɪᴌᴌɪꜱ . ɴ . COMPERIO IN ANTI
QVIS ADHVC VOᴌVMINIBVS IN CAᴌꜱE OPERVM QVANDO
QVE SIGNATIS Πί ΔΈΛΤΑ MEDIVM IN SE CONTINENS. HOC
MODO. ⊞ . QVINQVAGINTA SIGNIFICARE . Iᴛᴇᴍ Γί Hᴛᴀ
MEDIVM IN SE CONTINENS HOC MODO. ⊞ QVINGENTA . Lᴵ
TEM Πί Χί MEDIVM IN SE CONTINENS. HOC MODO. ⊠ .
QVINQVE MILLIA . Πί ENIM QVINQVE SIGNIFICAT. ΔΈᴀ
TA DECEM. H ᴛᴀ CENTVM. Χί . MIᴌᴌE . QVAE Γί CONTENTA
IDEST QVINQVIES REPETITA PRAEDIᴄᴛOꜱ REDDVNT NV
MEROS . Sᴇᴅ HAEC Sɪꜱ HABENT. NON OMNINO PRAETER
REM HOC ᴌOᴄO INTERPRETATA. QVANDOQVIDEM ET NO
TAE SVNT ANTIQVISSIMAE. ET EAS ADMODVM PAVCIS EXɪ
STIMEM ESSE COGNITAS. Γί AVTEM TVNC FORTE DIᴄᴇTVR
AᴘTIVS ΔΕΛΤΑ . ᴇᴛ HTA . ᴇᴛ ΧΙ IN SE MEDIAS
CONTINERE. SI LEVAE LINEAE PAREM HABVERIT DEXTᴇ́
RAM Qᴠɪᴅ QVOD ᴇᴛ ΘΗΤΑ FIGVRAM ᴌVGVBRIS
LITTERAE EX FABARVM FLORIBVS AVTORE Vᴀʀʀᴏɴɛ
VT REFERT Pʟʏɴɪᴠꜱ

⊞
⊠
Π
Δ
Η
Χ

---

167. Florence. *Anthologia Graeca*, Lorenzo di Alopa, 1494.
Latin inscriptional capitals with Greek capitals in Latin style.

Ὡς δ'ὅτε τίς κεράμω· ταῖς κεραμίσι καταστεγάζει· Ἀλλω δ'ἔμπεδον· ἄλ
λος δὲ ἄλλω φησὶ κέραμος ἀντίσαιαι ἀσφαλῶς ἢ σύμπηρμοσται. ἐπαμοι
βοὶ γ' ὄχοι ἀμείβοντ'· ἀλλ' ἐπικλλαμένοι τ' σύνδεσιν. Οἱ δὲ κλατ'· ὁ

ποῖα δὲ βοή ἐ-
νέλαι ἐν πλέ-
μω ὁπόταμ
ἀλαλαξαμτ
ξυνέρχωνται.
Ἐνναέται· κα-
τ'ἐξαίρεσιμ τ
.ι. ἰνὴ ἐνραι-
ται · κλημία-ς
Δὲ φησὶ ἢ τ
ναόν ητε οὕ-
τως ἐρηθ' αἰέν
ναιον διὰ τὸ ἐν
μαιὸν ἐν αὐτῶ
τοὺς θεούς·
Ἡμται ἀκημ-
καὶ θκν̃ται ἐνοῖ
κω ἐστι τρεφό
μενοι τ χωι-
μῶνοσ ἢ τῶσ
χαλάζης διὰ
τὸ ἐξηρτημέ-
μους αὐτους ᾶ
ναι· Μέλα
θρον τ' ὀροφήν·
κραιτης δ'τ̃ην

ΑΥΤΑΡ ΓΑΝΥΜΗΔΗΙ ΠΕΡΙΩΣΙΟΝ ΟΡΝΥΤ ΑΥΤΗΝ
ΑΘΡΟΟΙ. ΟΦΡΑ ΚΟΛΩΩΝ ΑΗΘΕΙΗ ΦΟΒΕΩΝΤΑΙ
ΝΕΥΟΝΤΑΣ ΤΕ ΛΟΦΟΥΣ ΚΑΙ ΕΠΗΟΡΑ ΔΟΥΡΑΘΥΠΕΡΘΕΝ.
ΕΙ ΔΕ ΚΕΝ ΑΥΤΗΝ ΝΗΣΟΝ ΙΚΩΜΕΘΑ, ΔΗ ΤΟΤΕΠΕΙΤΑ
ΣΥΝ ΚΕΛΑΔΩΙ ΣΑΚΕΕΣΣΙ ΠΕΛΩΡΙΟΝ ΟΡΣΑΤΕ ΔΟΥΠΟΝ.
ΩΣ ΑΡ ΕΦΗ. ΠΑΝΤΕΣΣΙ ΔΕΠΙΡΡΟΘΟΣ ΗΝΔΑΝΕ ΜΗΤΙΣ.
ΑΜΦΙ ΔΕ ΧΑΛΚΕΙΑΣ ΚΟΡΥΘΑΣ ΚΕΦΑΛΗΙΣΙΝ ΕΘΕΝΤΟ.
ΔΕΙΝΟΝ ΛΑΜΠΟΜΕΝΑΣ. ΕΠΙ ΔΕ ΛΟΦΟΙ ΕΣΣΕΙΟΝΤΟ
ΦΟΙΝΙΚΕΟΙ. ΚΑΙ ΤΟΙ ΜΕΝ ΑΜΟΙΒΗΔΗΝ ΕΛΛΑΣΚΟΝ.
ΤΟΙ ΔΑΥΤ ΕΓΧΕΙΗΣΙ ΚΑΙ ΑΣΠΙΣΙ ΝΗ ΕΚΑΛΥΠΤΑΝ.
ΩΣ ΔΟΤΕ ΤΙΣ ΚΕΡΑΜΩΙ ΚΑΤΑΡΕΤΕΤΑΙ ΕΡΚΙΟΝ ΑΝΗΡ
ΔΩΜΑΤΟΣ ΑΓΛΑΙΗΝ ΤΕ ΚΑΙ ΥΕΤΟΥ ΕΜΜΕΝΑΙ ΑΛΚΑΡ.
ΑΛΛΩΙ ΔΕΜΠΕΔΟΝ ΑΛΛΟΣ ΟΜΩΣ ΕΡΑΜΟΙΒΟΣ ΑΡΗΡΕΝ,
ΩΣ ΟΙ ΓΑΣΠΙΣΙ ΝΗΑ ΣΥΝΑΡΤΥΝΑΝΤΕΣ ΕΡΕΤΑΝ.
ΟΙΗ ΔΕ ΚΛΑΓΓΗ ΔΗΙΟΥ ΠΕΛΕΙ ΕΞ ΟΜΑΔΟΙΟ
ΑΝΔΡΩΝ ΚΙΝΥΜΕΝΩΝ ΟΡΟΤΕ ΞΥΝΙΩΣΙ ΦΑΛΑΓΓΕΣ,
ΤΟΙΗ ΑΡ ΥΨΟΘΙ ΝΗΟΣ ΕΣ ΗΕΡΑ ΚΙΔΝΑΤ ΑΥΤΗ.
ΟΥ ΔΕ ΤΙΝΟΙ ΩΝΩΝ ΕΤΕΣΦΕΔΡΑΚΟΝ. ΑΛΛΟΤΕ ΝΗΣΩΙ
ΧΡΙΜΨΑΝΤΕΣ ΣΑΚΕΕΣΣΙΝ ΕΠΕΚΤΥΠΟΝ. ΑΥΤΙΚΑ ΡΟΙΓΕ
ΜΥΡΙΟΙ ΕΝΘΑ ΚΑΙ ΕΝΘΑ ΠΕΦΥΖΟΤΕΣ ΗΕΡΕΘΟΝΤΟ.
ΩΣ ΔΟΠΟΤΕ ΚΡΟΝΙΔΗΣ ΠΥΚΙΝΗΝ ΕΦΕΗΚΕ ΧΑΛΑΖΑΝ
ΕΚ ΝΕΦΕΩΝ ΑΝΑ Τ ΑΣΤΥ ΚΑΙ ΟΙΚΙΑ. ΤΟΙ ΔΥΠΟ ΤΟΙΣΙΝ
ΕΝΝΑΕΤΑΙ ΚΟΝΑΒΟΝ. ΤΕΓΕΩΝ ΥΠΕΡΕΙΣΑΙΟΝΤΕΣ

δοκὸν ἐδέξατο· ὡς ἢ παρὰ τῶ ποιητῆ· Αἰθαλόεντος ἀνὰ μεγάροιο μέ
λαθρον· Ὡς πυκινὰ πτερά· χαλάζης πυκνότερα ἐφίεσαν αὐτ̃ πτερά

168. Florence. Apollonius Rhodius, L. de Alopa, 1496.
Proctor, pl. VI; Scholderer, fig. 20.

169. Venice. Aristophanes, Aldus Manutius, 1498.
The first Greek cursive text type; combined with Roman inscriptional capitals; in use by Aldus from 1495.
Scholderer, fig. 21.

had developed from the thick to a thin line; and calligraphy had manifested an increased fondness for refinement. This love of decoration and increase of technical efficiency, combined with added financial prosperity in the book trade, rendered possible accomplishments and experiments which were out of the question a decade earlier. The production of an upright Greek in elementary form apart from the accents and breathings, was no more difficult than an upright Latin. It was otherwise when Alopa and Aldus decided to produce in type the cursive script that most Greek scribes and most Greek readers wrote and read.

Thus the formal typography that had issued from the Venetian presses of Accursius and Zacharias Kallierges was discontinued after 1499 (Plate 170). The Western Aldine-Alopa cursive typography was destined to set the style for Garamond and Granjon, and for all the Italian, French, and Dutch presses until modern times. There were exceptions. The New Testament portion of the Great Alcalà Polyglot of Cardinal Ximenes is a work whose range and excellence of typography have yet to be duly appreciated. As to its Greek lower case: it is

170. *Etymologicum magnum*; portion of page. The headpiece is in red.

Venice; Zacharias Callierges for Nicolaus Blastus, 1499.

Proctor, pl. XXI; Scholderer, fig. 22.

composed in an upright, formal letter stated in the preface to have been directly derived from a manuscript sent from Rome for the purpose by Leo X. It is the last formal Greek or Byzantine letter to appear in Western Greek typography. The Polyglot was begun *c.* 1502 but the printing was not finished until 1517. The delay was due, Lyell says, to 'ecclesiastical reasons'—indeed the fact. The issue was serious; whether the Roman Church had or had not absolutely committed herself by the 1438 Decree of Union to the Greek Canon of Scripture. Pending the solution of this doubt, the publication of the Polyglot was held up. Plate 171 is from the Musaeus of 1510 which exhibits the type in complete state.

But, although the Spanish Greek represents the final appearance of a formal Byzantine model of the eleventh or twelfth century as opposed to the later informal script, there remains for notice one later manifestation of Oriental influence. The point has been made above that Ciriaco d'Ancona showed his love of the Byzantine flourish by writing his Latin cursive with similar exuberance. It may be observed in Plate 164, which illustrates the Byzantine style of ligaturing, that Ciriaco was happy to follow.

U

Εἰπέ θεὰ κρυφίωμ ἐπιμάρτυρα λύχμομ ἐρώτωμ,
καὶ μύχιομ πλωτῆρα θαλασσοπόρωμ ὑμεμαίωμ,
καὶ γάμομ ἀχλυόεμτα, Τὸμ ὀνκ ἴδεμ ἄφθιτος ἠώς,
καὶ σηστὸμ καὶ ἄβυδομ, ὅπη γάμος ἔμμυχος ἡροῦς.
μηχόμεμόμ Τε λέαμδρομ ὁμοῦ καὶ λύχμομ ἀκούω,
λύχμομ ἀπαγγέλλομτα Διακτορίημ ἀφροδίτης.
ἡροῦς μυκτϊγάμοιο γαμοστόλομ ἀγγελιώτημ,
λύχμομ ἔρωτος ἄγαλμα, Τὸμ ὤφελεμ αἰθέριος ζεύς,
ἐμμύχιομ μετάεθλομ ἄγειμ ἐφ᾽ ὁμήγυριμ ἄστρωμ,
καί μιμ ἐπικλῆσαι μυμφοστόλομ ἄστρομ ἐρώτωμ.
ὅτ̔ι πέλεμ συμέριθος ἐρωμαμέωμ ὀδυμάωμ.
ἀγγελίημ Δ᾽ἐφύλαξεμ ἀκοιμήτωμ ὑμεμαίωμ,
πρὶμ Χαλεπὸμ πμοιῆσιμ ἀήμεμαι ἐχθρὸμ ἀήτημ.
ἀλλ᾽ ἄγε μοι μέλ πομτι μίαμ ξυμάειδε Τελευτήμ,
λύχμου σβεμμυμέμοιο καὶ ὀλλυμέμοιο λεάμδρου.
σηστὸς ἔημ καὶ ἄβυδος ἐμαμτίομ ἐγγύθι πόμτου.
γείτομές εἰσι πόλπες. ἔρως Δ᾽ἀμὰ Τόξα Τιταίμωμ,
ἀμφοτέρης πτολίεσσιμ ἕμα ξυμέηκεμ ὀϊστόμ,
ἠίθεομ φλέξας καὶ παρθέμομ. ὄυμομα Δ᾽αὐτῶμ
ἱμερόεις τὲ λέαμδρος ἔημ καὶ πωρθέμος ἡρώ,
ἡ μὲμ, σηστὸμ ἔμαιεμ. ὁ δέ, πτολίεθρομ ἀβύδου,
ἀμφοτέρωμ πτολίωμ περικαλλέες ἀστέρες ἄμφω,
ἴκελοι ἀλλήλοισι. σὺ Δεῖ πότε κεῖθι περήσεις.

171. Alcalà de Henares. Musaeus. Arnold Guillen de Brocar, 1510.
The Complutensian Greek, also used for the New Testament portion of the Polyglot published in 1514.
Scholderer, fig. 24.

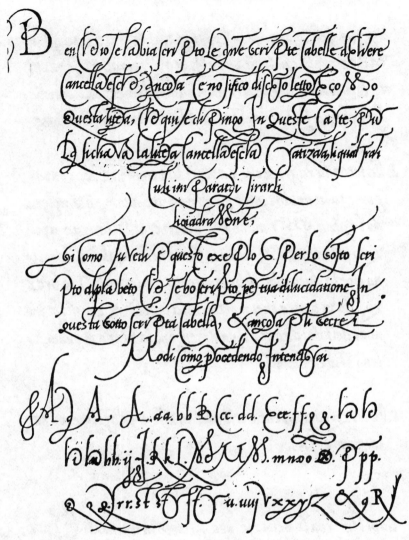

172. Giovanantonio Tagliente, *Opera . . . che insegna a scrivere di molte qualita di lettere intitulata Lucidario,* Venice, 1524.

A. F. Johnson, p. 26.

J. Wardrop, 'A note on Giovanantonio Tagliente' (*Signature*, N.S. 8 (1949), p. 59); see A. F. Johnson, 'A catalogue of Italian writing books of the sixteenth century' (*Signature*, N.S. 10 (1950), pp. 26-30).

Plate 172 is from the first edition (Venice, 1524) of Giovanantonio Tagliente's manual of handwriting which he called *Lucidario*. The plate shows a capital B of which the initial flourish is slightly trimmed. This matters not. The line reads 'Benche io te habia scripto le ante scripte tabelle de litere Cancellaresche'. Note particularly the *ch* in Ben*ch*e and in 'Cancellares*ch*e', as well as the overall exuberant flourishing. This is fully in the Byzantium Chancery style.

La penna del Cesano. ꝑ Eßer großa & dura, e adopera
ta da molti la quale te dico et si te affermo eßere, laudabi
le & maxime alle lettere mercadantesche & alle cancel
laresche, corsiue, et questo ti basta per tua dilucidatione.

Alla seconda ragione che e a tener la penna in mano con ra
gione tu la debbi tenere sempre ad uno modo, nõ ti uolgen
do la pena ꝑ mano & poi tenerai lo brazzo apo
zato su la tauola, & etiam le punte delli doi deti dilla ma
no cioe lo ditto minudello conzonto con laltro & lo braz
zo stia in altura chel non tocchi la tauola & etiam gli tre
nodi deli doi dita con li quali tengono la penna in mano, uo
leno stare releuati,

Alla terza ragione che e a sapere in che modo se die menar
la penna,

Sapi cte con la penna se puo scriuere in tre modi & non
con piui,

173. Lucidario. Venice, 1524.
Tagliente's highly ligatured italic.

Whereas Tagliente's script shown in Plate 172 is engraved as a wood-block, the succeeding plate (Plate 173) shows the script separated into alphabetical units, engraved on punches designed to be struck into matrices as the preliminaries to the casting of founts of type. No doubt Tagliente wrote out with great care the model for his punch-cutter to follow. The enterprise required a degree of craftsmanship exceeding that of Aldus's great punch-cutter, Francesco Griffo, who cut the pioneer italic of 1500. But the technical excellence of Tagliente's shows a philo-Byzantine temper, fully consonant with the long-standing Venetian policy of appeasement with the Turks and trade with Constantinople. Such a calligraphic practice as Tagliente's would hardly have been acceptable by the early humanists, or even by Aldus, tolerant as he was of Greek and Latin ligatures provided they were philologically orthodox. Granjon and the great punch-cutters who were to work for the leading publishers of Antwerp and Paris followed the Tagliente style because it was offered as a strong challenge to their craftsmanship. We do not continue the story of Greek since it can lead to nothing of significance for our speculations.

A more germane inquiry is: what would official Rome think of such an italic as Tagliente's? What italic was used by Antonio Blado, the official printer to the papacy who necessarily acknowledged the authority of the Roman Chancery? The 'cancellaresca' used by Blado was a pure Latin form uninfluenced by the schismatic East. This may not be merely an accident of the humanistic tendencies of Martin V and Eugenius IV: nor just a confirmation of the style set for the Roman Chancery by Poggio and continued by Bembo and their successors. Rome's rejection of 'Gothic' in accordance with Poggio's idea of humanistic consistency automatically excluded the Byzantine elements commended by Ciriaco. Had he become secretary things might well have been different. As it was, Rome was never again to embody Byzantine elements in its Latin script.

Were there no other Byzantine traces elsewhere in the West? A curious possible connection with Ciriaco may be worth notice since it may have been responsible for the appearance in northern Europe of certain Byzantine vestiges. About the time Hans Memling was born at Seligenstadt-am-Main, Sigismund the German king (1368-1437) was crowned emperor by Eugenius IV, who, it has been pointed out, was the friend of Ciriaco d'Ancona. In Rome during 1433 the emperor had with him one Gotzkircher, a doctor of medicine who was also an archaeologist with an enthusiasm for calligraphy. On the occasion when Sigismund was crowned he was conducted over the Eternal City by Ciriaco who expounded the history of the chief sights. It is at least likely that Gotzkircher secured a place in the party and talked with the antiquary. What is certain is that Gotzkircher made notes. He kept a scrap-book and years later copied out a considerable number of such letterings as appealed to him. Among them is the page shown on Plate 174. Here will be noticed numerous Byzantine characters that also occur in manuscripts of the period of the Council of Florence.

Gotzkircher may have circulated among his German friends specimens of these and similar pieces of calligraphy. If so, the Byzantine characteristics such as the M with vertical centre stroke that are to be encountered in the legends to Memling's paintings are thus explained. The M may be seen in the lettering of the Mystic Marriage of St. Catherine, and the Adoration of the Magi, both in the Hospital of St. John of Bruges. It may also be noted that Memling was esteemed in Italy and painted portraits of Milanese notables. There is nothing

INPRINCIPIO. ERAT. VERBVM. ET.
VERBVM. ERAT. APVD. DEVM. ET.
DEVS. ERAT. VERBVM. HOC. ERAT.
INPRINCIPIO. APVD. DEVM. OMIA
PER. IPSVM. FACTA. SVT.

174. Sigmund Gotzkircher, Miscellaneous Codex, c. 1435-6.
Munich, Universitäts-Bibliothek, 4°, 810.
Byzantinesque capitals and cursive sorts.
S. H. Steinberg, 'Medieval Writing Masters' in *The Library*, 4th series, vol. xxii, no. 1 (June 1941), pp. 7-8.

to report in the way of any later Byzantine impression upon formal (upright) Latin typography after 1499 (Kallierges) or informal (cursive) Latin type after 1522 (Tagliente). The Greeks were not interested in Western gadgets and made no contribution to the art of printing. Their Turkish masters esteemed calligraphy and believed in the Koran as a written book—and therefore gave no encouragement to any typographical deformation of Arabic.

The invention of printing was bound to have a determining influence upon the style of lettering that would be adopted for books for general reading, works, that is, that were not liturgical or legal in nature. In so far as market considerations were bound to take precedence over all other, the approaching authority for script in the West would be literary. The summit of literary authority was also the supreme typographic authority; the achievement virtually of one man whose unique and comprehensive authority reposed not so much upon the form of his editions, immensely significant as that was in certain instances, but upon their accuracy as Latin and Greek texts. Thus the authority for script lay with Aldus because of the soundness of his scholarship.

We may roughly define scholarship as the documentary medium by which the present faces our past. In the sense that no agreement on meaning is possible without an agreed text, typography gave scholarship a broad social potentiality instead of keeping it a conventional or private amenity. This was the accomplishment of Aldus Manutius. He bestowed upon the world a philological, classical, and literary heritage in terms of Greek and Latin literature, in multiple editions from folio to pocket size. Nor was it his intention to limit his activity to secular, humane works. Unfortunately his Polyglot Bible projected *c.* 1501 never materialized beyond the specimen page in Hebrew, Greek (cursive), and Latin.

Aldus died in 1515, nearly 65 years of age. His example of exactitude was applied to Biblical learning by Ximenes at Alcalà, Robert Estienne at Paris, and Christopher Plantin at Antwerp. The authority of these printers was equally based upon the accuracy and depth of their collating and editing. The most meritorious of all the productions of the period was Ximenes' Polyglot Bible, which was initiated in 1502. The reasons for the delay in publishing have been noted above. Plantin's Polyglot, completed at Antwerp in 1572, is a magnificent rival at once to the Polyglot of Ximenes and the texts of Estienne. The techniques required in the production of critical texts had immensely improved in the first half of the sixteenth century.

As has been pointed out above, the lettering preferred by intellectual leaders of the period 1450-1550 was that of men who were neither statesmen nor theologians, but littérateurs, artists, sculptors, and painters. Archaeologists, philologists, and stylists also played a role. The preferred Latin alphabet symbolized a philosophical attitude. It was the adoption of their point of view by Pope Nicolas V which gave a degree of prestige that amounted to authority to the revived antique alphabet and led to its now universal use in books.

The practical and versatile values of the combination of classical capital and Carolingian Minuscule seem today to be a complete justification of the choice then made. Its impulse came from a coterie of dilettanti, whose chief preoccupation was the study of antique culture, literature, and monuments. It began as a private expression of preference. It was secular, though its leaders were in good standing with the Church and eminent ecclesiastics favoured it, especially popes like Eugenius IV and Nicolas V. It was not, however, a Christian movement. Rather, it ranks as the only instance of a society held together by an intellectual attitude which was held in common by laymen and churchmen.

While remaining unformulated it was by implication a criticism of terrestrial life viewed from the standpoint of human experience and observation unconditioned by divine revelation or established tradition. It followed that any scriptorial medium devised by the pioneers of this activity could not be conditioned by the Christian past. It was the pre-Christian past which inspired them. Moreover, even had they wished otherwise, the mere idea of a Christian script had long utterly dissolved. The latent vestiges of Uncial in the contemporary codices were unrecognized for what they originally had been. Again, the papal regime, even under Martin V, was too vexed by divisions to direct lettering and Sigismund the German king (1411–37) was not the personage to see the point of devising a script that would symbolize his power.

But the career of any script cannot begin without the backing of authority, ecclesiastical or political, and preferably both. Even the highest authority has often been insufficient to protect the integrity of a script. The main reason for relating the accidental changes in script has been the insecurity of its protection. It is always necessary, but too often impossible, for authority to protect itself. As it is of the nature of authority that it shall attract challenge, and of the nature of power that it cannot be self-perpetuating, change in script may follow expansion of authority. The shrinkage of preferences exhibited in Florence by Poggio and Niccoli in the first quarter of the fifteenth century would have been short-lived indeed had the void of papal or imperial patronage not been filled by a third force upon which the other two powers were becoming increasingly dependent.

It was in the highest degree fortunate for Poggio and Niccoli and those who stood with them that they should have been active precisely when Cosimo (1389–1464), the founder of the power of the Medici family, was disposed to train, through his bookseller Vespasiano da Bisticci, the finest calligraphers, in considerable number, to copy the classical and other Latin texts in the chosen script. Cosimo bestowed vast sums upon libraries and scribes. As early as 1408 he was employing Poggio to transcribe Cicero's Letters to Atticus.

That Cosimo de' Medici correctly understood and fully approved the plans of Poggio and Niccoli cannot be doubted. As it was not in his nature to be half-hearted, once Cosimo had decided to support by his example, his wealth, and by every other means the copying of Latin literary texts in the novel script which he knew under the title of 'littera antica', he kept the traditional script for biblical, legal, and theological works, in the provision of which he was also interested.

It is to be borne in mind that as a merchant-banker Cosimo was independent of the territorially tied nobles, and needed no authority but that of his wealth to patronize whom he would, including artists who should work as he and they thought fit. As a Florentine he would gladly see the city play a role superior to that of Rome, and help the peninsula to challenge and if possible surpass the cultural achievement of France. Cosimo would therefore make Florence and not Rome or Paris the cultural capital of the civilized world.

As to the 'antique' script: the point here to be emphasized is that without Cosimo the new script, first fashioned by Poggio and Niccoli, and later developed by such fine scribes as Antonio di Mario, would never have emerged from the narrow circle which gave it birth. There would not have been produced by Vespasiano any of those lavish illuminated manuscripts which presented the 'littera antica' so magnificently.

The circulation of printed manuals of calligraphy brought into existence a new kind of pseudo-authority, that of the specialized teacher of handwriting. While the writing masters were glad to advertise their skill by giving numerous and superfluous specimens of fanciful, exotic, and ornamental scripts, a number of them gave prominence to the Roman Chancery hand, and propagated it in specimen books.

In 1501 Aldus printed a Virgil composed in a printing type fashioned on the model of the Chancery cursive and, later, two, perhaps more, practising writing masters found craftsmen able to engrave punches and cast the type for a highly elegant typographical version of the Chancery cursive. No interposition of authority was necessary to forward the career of the humanistic script, formal or cursive. The utilitarian simplicity of its form was enough to provide the momentum required for this practical letter. The case of Black-Letter, however, was very different. It enjoyed certain advantages that the 'antique' letter lacked. Its majesty had long given dignity to so much general literature, and its four centuries of use so great a familiarity, that it could not but seem to have the sanction of authority.

The competition, at least in terms of Latin belles-lettres, was undeniably powerful. But after 1465, when typography in the 'littera antiqua' was introduced in Italy, the position of Black-Letter for Latin literature was effectively weakened. The backing of some sort of authority needed to be given it if the four centuries old Black-Letter was to hold its position. Such support was at length given to it by the Emperor Maximilian. Some account of this last Imperial gesture in favour of a selected script needs now to be given.

Maximilian, a very self-conscious traditionalist, interested himself in the production of the *Theuerdanck*. This knightly work he wrote and caused a sumptuous edition to be printed, also by Schönsperger (who had removed from Augsburg to Nuremberg in 1517). This is composed in a different type of the same category, but more strongly cursive and equipped with flourishes and swashes. The text is German.

We leave aside the reason why, later, these types of Maximilian were reserved by custom to the German language, in order to emphasize the fact that but for the patronage of Maximilian the form of letter known as 'Fraktur' would never have taken such deep root in Germany. It should be added that the influence of Dürer, who stood, between 1512 and 1519, very close to Maximilian (and was on his salary list), was above all a German of the Renaissance, and was deeply interested, probably inspired, and certainly approved the types. Maximilian's interest in such details was notorious. There is extant an engraving of Maximilian as a calligrapher seated at his table engaged in writing a specimen for the admiration of his courtiers. The great *Proba scripturarum diversarum* executed by Leonard Wagner, monk of SS. Afra and Ulrich at Augsburg, was probably completed and presented to Maximilian about 1510, three or four years before the *Liber Horarum ad usum Maximiliani Imperatoris*. Few of Wagner's specimens are significant book-scripts; they are almost all Chancery inventions; cursive as they had always been. The calligraphic pedigree of the type of Maximilian's *Horae* may be traced in Wagner's *Proba*. This, however, is not our business. It is necessary here only to lay stress upon the fact that it was the authority and example of the emperor that established the peculiar 'baroque' Gothic (a needed term) which gave Black-Letter a form which was destined to become the paramount national book-script and printing type of Germany.

Maximilian's Black-Letter was, however, originated for Latin. It was, as H. Fichtenau points out, his individual version of the Burgundian *lettre bâtarde*, which he was taught as a youngster. The latter was a cursive of markedly vigorous character, apt for Chancery use and also for vernacular romances and other subordinate literary purposes. Maximilian's *Horae* type is more formal, yet cursive. It is regularly perpendicular but ostentatiously calligraphic to a degree avoided in the great Bibles of Gutenburg, and the sumptuous missals of Petzensteiner. Maximilian's intended personal monument, the *Horae*, was appropriately a private issue, made not for sale but for presentation to nobles (Plates 175, 176).

The *Theuerdanck* mentioned above was similarly conceived by the emperor. A new type, based on a slightly less formal Chancery-hand, was cut. Maximilian contributed all its details, but did not live to see its completion. As already mentioned, the text of the *Theuerdanck* is in the vernacular. The types of the *Horae* and of the *Theuerdanck* quickly obtained a dominance in the expanding German printing industry. After the neo-medieval letter had been invented for classical Latin, it became permanently reserved in German, but the reason for this need not detain us. It must be emphasized, only, that the establishment of this cursive upright Gothic in typography was due to the authority and example of Maximilian. The industrialization of the design of the so-called 'Fraktur' types, by cutting them with narrow bodies, thereby making them more economic in space for long words so common in German, inevitably gave it an advantage over the Roman. The design more than held its own against Roman until 1941 when Hitler denounced the 'so-called' 'Gothic' type as a Jewish invention.

It has been seen that the types of Maximilian were cast upon his initiative and directive. They were used in accordance with his design. Had he lived and had the Reichstag provided the money Maximilian would have been the greatest patron of the press in all history. The emperor drew up a list of 150 books that would glorify the Habsburgs, and especially himself. The emperor was sixty when he died in 1519.

175. Augsburg. *Liber Horarum.* Johann Schönsperger.

Maximilian's individual version of the Burgundian *bastarda*. The Latin ancestor of the German *Fraktur*.

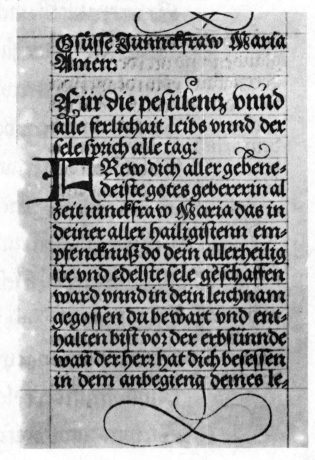

The French King Francis I distinguished himself and France as a patron of Greek literature, and caused the founding of three sizes of letters to be cut for the use of Robert Estienne, the *imprimeur du roi*, in the production of fine editions of Greek texts. The patronage, however, was comparatively indirect and limited to the granting of honorary patents or titles.

The French monarch showed no personal initiative in the form of script and appears to have had no desire to alter or modify the letter-designs that had the approval of such an artist as Geoffroy Tory and a scholar like Guillaume Budé. The royal Greeks were first used for a text of Eusebius published in Paris in 1544. The example of Aldus was all powerful in the learned circles of Paris and the printers of the city were encouraged to surpass him in exact scholarship and typographical technique.

Renaissance Italy had overwhelmed Gothic France. The great triumph of Parisian book-design owes everything to Venice and the authority for the stylistic changes in France was the royal example rather than the legislative decree. The

Er wer ye nit kßomen daruon

In den danncken/sach Er hergon

Gegen Im den tewrlichen Held

Zu dem Er sprach herr Eüch erwelt

Billichen mein fraw zu der Le

Dann Ich der gleichen sach nit mee

Gehöret hab von eim sagen

Bey allen meinen lebttagen

Vnnd dieweil Ichs selbs hab gesehen

So mag Ichs mit warheit iehen

Vnnd öffnen der edlen Künigein

Die wirt darab vol freuden sein

Mit den worten Sy hin kßamen

Widerumb ßußaus vnnd namen

Von einannder ein gutte nacht

Fürwittig sich weyter bedacht

Wie Er mocht durch subtilig weg

Den Held bringen/das Er niderleg

176. Nürnberg. *Theuerdanck*. Johann Schönsperger. 1517.
Maximilian's *Fraktur* in the German language.

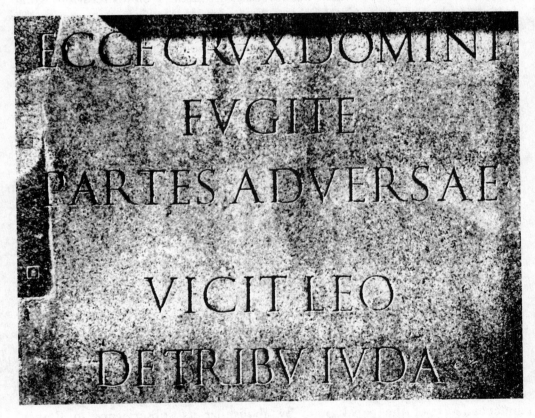

177. Inscriptions from the base of the obelisk erected by Sixtus V, after lettering by Luca Horfei. The classic Roman capitals, never better designed or engraved (note the characteristic R). Photographs by James Mosley.

religious sanctions did not explicitly enter into the question of Gothic v. Roman. Luther kept to Fraktur because he was more a German than anything else, while Calvin supported Roman because he was a humanist as well as a Protestant. As will be seen in the next and final chapter, the France of Louis XIV originated a royal and significant rationalist alphabet a hundred years after the Roman and papal standardization of a rationalist and Christian letter-form appropriate to the Rome created by Sixtus V. This now needs to be examined.

The readiness of Rome to conciliate Byzantium has been frequently mentioned in these pages. The aftermath of the Venetian devastation of the city in 1204, unforgivable in its savagery and greed, made virtually impossible any Eastern rapprochement. The repudiation in 1443 in Constantinople of the agreement reached in 1439 at the Council of Florence and the subsequent capture of the city and the conversion of Sancta Sophia, so long the greatest of all Christian cathedrals, to the requirements of Islam presented Rome in the sixteenth century with many problems. Among them was the question of rebuilding St. Peter's. The immediacy of this particular decision lay in the general requirement of the rebuilding of the city which was forecast by Martin V on his return to Rome in 1420 at the end of the Great Schism. Eugenius IV, Martin's successor, unable to proceed with Martin's plans, bequeathed the problem to Nicholas V, a pope in a position to put forward plans to rebuild Rome in accordance with the new task which Martin V and Eugenius IV had viewed tolerantly in Florence. Nicholas V was more than tolerant of the new Florentine ideas. He was an enthusiast for them. As to the new St. Peter's, the pope was resolute.

In 1450, three years after his election, he held a jubilee at Rome, and upon the offerings of the pilgrims who flocked to Rome, his new programme was launched, 'to strengthen the weak faith of the people by the greatness of that which it sees'. He restored the walls and the churches, improved the water supply, and began the rebuilding of the Vatican and St. Peter's. Paul II (1464–71) and Sixtus IV (1471–84) continued the work of Nicholas V in very different ways. Paul, a conservationist and antiquarian, sought to preserve the ancient monuments; he continued the work on St. Peter's. The aim of Sixtus, a vigorous upstart, was to make Rome a modern defensible city. The old winding streets came down. The approaches to the Vatican were strengthened and simplified, and the first Vatican library and the chapel that bears his name were built. Sixtus IV was Francesco della Rovere. He effectually assured an Italian majority in the Sacred College by the nomination of an all but unprecedented number of cardinals, no fewer than four of them his relations. The common bond between them was less Italian national feeling than Roman and Latin patriotism. Among the immediate creations was Giuliano della Rovere, like Sixtus himself a Franciscan in his late twenties—destined to be elected pope some thirty years later as Julius II (1503–13). The cornerstone of his policy was to restore the independence of the papal State by abolishing its subservience to France. Incidentally the pope's programme for the building up of a modern Rome would give encouragement to the Gothic style of architecture. Rather, Julius was the man for Bramante, Michaelangelo, and Raphael. Much of the old design for

St. Peter's was swept away in his haste, and the great new designs of Michael-angelo and then Bramante, which so appalled the Romans, went up apace. But much was left to do when Julius died, and the times were not apt for building. The disastrous diplomacy, political and religious, of the twenties culminated in the sack of Rome in 1527. A generation passed before building could be resumed, and it was not until the end of the century that the programme begun by Nicolas V was resumed.

A more direct authoritarian interest in the formation of letters became mani-fest in Rome at this time, and a change in the proportions of the inscriptional alphabet was made by the will of Sixtus V (1585–90). He inherited the task (to him decidedly congenial) of completing the restoration of Rome and St. Peter's. The pope was resolved to rebuild the Eternal City and adorn it with inscriptions of his own devising. Much of the classical and therefore pagan deposit of the new wave of culture that had been welcomed by early Renaissance figures such as Nicolas V and Eugenius IV was displeasing to Sixtus V, a truly 'baroque' pope. For him the capitals of Augustus and Trajan, so painstakingly revived by Feliciano and the antiquarians, were living symbols of paganism that was not now as thoroughly dead as Christians should wish. The Franciscan pope had not forgotten the lesson learnt by his Dominican predecessor (Pius V, pope 1566–72), that the pursuit of antique culture can lead to the imitation of antique morals. The loss of a vast number of pagan monuments and their classical in-scriptions destroyed in the execution of his grandiose plans meant nothing to him.

The lettering designed for Sixtus V was consistent with the plan to present old Rome as the supreme Christian capital in place of new Rome, and St. Peter's as the supreme Catholic basilica in place of Orthodox Sancta Sophia. The Sixtine letters were different in proportion and form from those of pagan Rome. For the same reason the pope crowned the re-erected columns of Trajan and Marcus Aurelius with the statues of St. Peter and St. Paul respectively. The triad of inscriptions on the main face of the base of the obelisk which the pope caused to be re-erected in front of the façade of St. Peter's repeated the theme. It has been pointed out by Ernst Kantorovicz that Sixtus V caused to be engraved on his coinage the text with which the Catholic Church superseded the acclama-tion by which the old Roman Senate saluted the Imperial name. Sixtus saw the obelisk as a monumental witness to the martyrdoms of the Christians under Nero, and the words used on his cross were appropriate: 'CHRISTUS VINCIT, CHRISTUS REGNAT, CHRISTUS IMPERAT.'

Of all the ecclesiastical achievements of this pope the most impressive was his completion of St. Peter's with the splendid dome. At last the conception of Nicolas V and Leo X was realized and since Sancta Sophia, the great church of new Rome, remained the possession of Islam, the Christian primacy in architectural terms was taken by old Rome. The great cupola with its inscrip-tion by Horfei was successfully placed in position on 14 May 1590, three months before the pope died on 27 August following. His inscriptional alphabet is the one direct papal contribution to letter-design. Unsupported by legislation or Chancery authority, the Sixtine alphabet derived its capacity to supersede the neo-classical (or as Sixtus would have it 'neo-pagan') capitals because of its superior rationality of proportion. Its distinction as a Christian form graced its beauty of execution, and the number and splendour of its public displays throughout what was virtually a new city, was created in five years by the unique combination of engraving talent and architectural genius secured by Sixtus V.

The rational proportions of the Sixtine alphabet entered into the conventions of Roman sepulchral and other monumental lettering. The antique or neo-classical lettering was little seen in or out of Rome from the beginning of the seventeenth century.

It should be noticed that when, simultaneously with the completion of the cupola the façade was finished, the builders incorporated the ancient epitaph commemorating Pope Hadrian I (d. 795) which Charles the Great sent to Rome. The inscription in Carolingian-Augustan Square Capitals (see Plate 104 above) is still to be seen in the position given it by Sixtus V, the distinction of whose own capitals, as compared with those on the base of the obelisk in front of the façade, points to the contrast in proportion between the shapes which Charles for one motive and Sixtus for another respectively sponsored.

After the Sixtine example Rome never returned to the neo-classical inscriptional convention. Henceforth, however, one effect of the Reformation was to restrict if not obstruct any authoritative Christian leadership from Rome even in such neutral matters as the Kalendar or the alphabet. The result was an impetus towards humanism or secularism, and nationalism. The initiatives in script taken by Florence and followed by Rome were adopted by Paris. France was, when she had reached a settlement of her religious question, once more able to make a new bid for the broadest cultural supremacy which should show an authorization or renovation of all the fine and industrial arts including that of letter-design.

7

FROM THE FRENCH ACADEMY TO THE INDUSTRIAL REVOLUTION

IN seventeenth-century France the principal influence over script was the Ministry of Finance. The authority of the Paris Parlement for the distinctive hands used in the service was local and departmental, though nationally it spread to the provinces. A more significant development arose from the application of the critical method to the verification of charters, diplomas, and other documents upon which claims are based.

Herbert Rosweyde (1569-1629), the originator of scientific investigation of hagiographical tradition, had as his successor Johann Bolland (1596-1665). Daniel van Papebroch (1628-1714) was Bolland's pupil and companion in his travels in search of manuscripts, and after his death was suspected of heresy and prosecuted by the Inquisition. One of his books, the *Acta Sanctorum* for April, included a dissertation entitled *Propylaeum antiquarum circa veri ac falsi discrimen in vetustis membranis*. It amounted to a critical examination of diplomas and other manuscripts and an attempt to formulate the rules for distinguishing the authentic from the spurious. It was the first sketch of a scientific classification of scripts and of the establishment of the criteria of comparison. Papebroch's investigation was not only critical, but sceptical. Among the diplomas impugned were some of St. Denis. The defence of the Abbey's diplomas was conducted by Dom Jean Mabillon (1632-1707) who brought out in 1681 a great book. It is dedicated to Colbert and is lavishly illustrated. *De Re Diplomatica* ranged much further, and in far greater detail, than Papebroch's pioneer sketch and, incidentally, demonstrated the authenticity of the characters and diplomas he had challenged. The result of this controversy, which ended in the graceful withdrawal of Papebroch, was the creation of the new science of the comparison and historical development of scripts which, after Mabillon, was called 'palaeography'.

In 1704 Mabillon provided a Supplement to his great treatise of 1681. The stimulus that he gave to the historical study of script was bound to lead to the application of the new knowledge to contemporary scriptorial practice and typography. Colbert's interest in the machines used in manufacturing was taken up by the Académie des Sciences founded by Richelieu in 1635. Investigation was made of the printing types used in the Imprimerie Royale, founded at the instance of Richelieu in 1642. A committee of members of the Academy assembled in January 1692 and promptly set to work to devise a scientific letter-form appropriate for use in the Royal Printing Office. Every trouble was taken to see that the new forms were thoroughly studied. Large patterns were superbly engraved

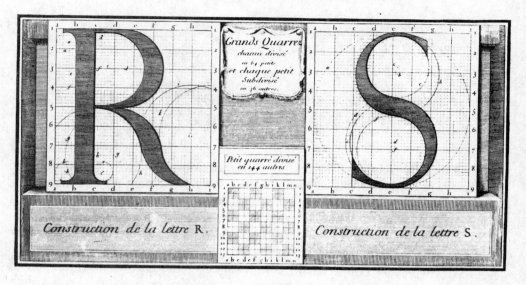

178. Paris. Roman capitals as geometrically constructed by Louis XIV's Commission of the Académie des Sciences.

Engraved in series by Luc Simonneau from 1690.

André Jammes, *La Typographie royale. Le Grandjean* (Paris, 1963), which prints the series from the original copper plates.

by Luc Simmoneau on copper (Plate 178) for the guidance of Philippe Grand-jean, the cutter of the punches from which the matrices were to be struck and the type cast. The first size was finished and proved in 1699. The details do not concern us, further than to point out that the letters were drawn upon a square of $2\frac{3}{4}$ in., sub-divided into 2,304 squares, and that the whole series of alphabetical patterns was rationally designed and geometrically controlled. The Academy's scheme is the first and only attempt to create, under authority, a norm of letter-ing for a governmental department of typography. It was, to the best of the Academy's belief, free from individualism, personal taste, or artistic originality. Having before them the mass of documents collected by Mabillon, Jaigeon, and others, the Commission decided first to accept the discipline of geometry, and secondly to render the shapes consistent with one another. They therefore abandoned the calligraphic basis that had hitherto underlain typography.

It was suggested in the first of these lectures that the reason for the bias in the stress of o is due to the scribe's difficulty in holding the pen directly in line with his shoulder. Confirmation of this statement was adduced from the earliest example, the Ambrosian Iliad. It was also noticed that the inclined or biased stress-line was 'canonized' by the artists and engravers of the Emperor Augustus when they designed and cut the lettering for his first-class inscriptions. The artists of the fifteenth and sixteenth centuries took care to preserve the bias in their geometrical rendering of the epigraphic alphabet. The vertical stress in

316

the new French norm amounted, therefore, to a considerable change; one that might be expected from a system which ignored long tradition and practice, and concentrated on a mathematical theory of letter-design.

There is one highly significant point at which the mathematicians and logicians departed from their principles in the construction of the 'Romain du roi'. While in all the circular (such as O) and semi-circular characters (such as D) which occur in the 'Capitales' and the variations of semi-circular characters which occur in the 'Lettres courantes droites' (the Commission's term for lower-case 'Roman') and 'Lettres courantes penchées' (their term for lower-case 'Italic') they standardized the rational and therefore vertical stress and maintained the age-long calligraphic tradition in all Latin lettering, epigraphic and manuscript, of differentiating the originally pen-made up (thin) and down (thick) strokes.

It is clear that this was never the practice of the Greeks, for whom every stroke being equally essential, it was necessarily equally thick. The Greeks had fewer fully curved characters than the Latins and the stroke of their inscriptional lettering was less than that universal in Latin. The width of the mainstroke in the 'Romain du roi' is eight times that of the substrokes. In the instance of G (which the Greeks do not have) it is obvious that to make an elegant design of this character, whose stroke shall throughout be equally thick, is not an easy matter. That the scientific commission was interested in the aesthetic quality of the 'Romain du roi' is obvious from the attention paid to the layout and engraving of the patterns. These are superb and far superior in allure to the geometrical projections of the Latin alphabet made by the artists and archaeologists of the Renaissance.

It is obvious, too, that the Latin convention of varying the width of stroke enables the designer to increase the visibility of his letter, whether in sculpture or script, or print, by thickening some of the strokes, while using the thin strokes to prevent coarsening the alphabet as a whole. That the Commission bore in mind such calligraphic amenities is obvious from their decision to incorporate the serif. This alone makes difficult the designing of a pleasing monoline letter whose high visibility is achieved by solid thickness of stroke. It was pointed out in the first chapter that when the Greeks adopted the serif in the third century B.C. they appended it to what the Latins later regarded as being too weak a stroke to be sufficiently commanding for an Imperial inscription.

The Imperial capital as constructed under Augustus was larger in scale than that of Alexander, and the Latin pen created a distinct difference between the thick down-stroke and thin up-stroke. As the thin related to the thick stroke, the thick stroke was related to the height of the letter. These relations were adopted in principle by Louis XIV's commission; the result was a new canonization and consequent perpetuation of the historic Latin letter with contrasting stroke for the composition of all literary and other texts. And thus the capital alphabet which the West had inherited from ancient Rome, and the minuscule which had been accommodated to it in the eighth century, was confirmed by the authority of Louis XIV's commission.

With one exception, no alternative to this purely Western script existed. As has been seen, Greek and Byzantine calligraphical influence is traceable in the sixteenth century but not later. Black-Letter was used in Germany for the vernacular. Elsewhere in the West from the eighteenth century it was employed only for ceremonial purposes. The alphabet originally invented *c.* 1400 by Salutati, Poggio, and Niccoli for Latin literature had long since been adopted by all the vernaculars except German and some of its derivatives. The humanistic term 'Antiqua' was, and is, still used in Germany to distinguish the script from 'Fraktur', the national Black-Letter which had been in use since its inspiration in 1519 by Maximilian for his *Theuerdanck*.

During the seventeenth and eighteenth centuries formal calligraphy passed out of use except for limited ornamental purposes. The primary model of the Western alphabet became typographical towards the end of the fifteenth century, when Griffo cut for Aldus the punches of the finest of all printed versions of the humanistic Roman (Bembo, *De Aetna*, Venice 1495) and the humanistic cursive (Virgil, Venice 1501). The Aldine roman maintained its position until the implications of the 'Romain du roi Louis XIV' were worked out by the commercial typefounders in the second half of the eighteenth century, and Baskerville began his innovations (Virgil, Birmingham 1757). The end of the century brought to the front G. B. Bodoni (Virgil, 2 vols., Parma 1793) and Pierre Didot (Horace, Paris 1799). The latter was given official support by the Imprimerie Nationale, as the institution founded at the Louvre by Richelieu in 1642 had been renamed in 1791.

There was nothing revolutionary about the luxurious editions printed after 1789 by Pierre Didot (1761-1853) except the paper which was close to Baskerville's. The types reflected the inspiration, if not the authority, of Louis XIV's commissions. By utilizing art, skill, and scholarship the Revolution conferred prestige upon the Didot family, and began the process of stabilizing an official lettering which is familiar in the wall-legend of DEFENSE D'AFFICHER.

The end of the eighteenth century (also the approaching finish of this book) suggests a recapitulation of the most significant changes in script pointed to in these chapters. The most primitive (and as will be seen, also, the most modern) of ancient Greek letter-forms (and nowadays current in contemporary Europe), is the square monoline unserifed capital seen in an inscription from the island of Melos (Plate 1), where it was cut in the fifth or sixth century B.C. There follows (Plate 2) the square monoline serifed capital from an inscription in Priene where it was cut in the fourth century B.C.

Next is the oldest surviving papyrus of any Greek text; also of the fourth century B.C. It is square, monoline, unserifed (Plate 8). There follows the earliest square, monoline, serifed script—a portion of the Bible—which is of the second century B.C. (Plate 9).

We now turn to Rome. An inscription of the first century A.D. is square, monoline, and serifed. Next is the Latin inscriptional letter as canonized for Imperial use under Augustus. The structure tends to abandon the Greek monoline basis in favour of a stroke that is thick and thin. There are Greek papyri in which some slight contrast of stroke may be perceived; but in no part of Greece before the

Roman conquest does anything of the kind seem to have appeared in a public inscription. The systematized contrasted stroke was a Latin innovation. So, too, was the elongation of the serif which was consistent with the thickening of the mainstroke. The Roman inscriptional style also required a larger scale than had been seen in truly Greek lettering. After standardizing the thick and thin stroke, the Romans increased the weight of the stroke, thus creating a thicker stroke than had been used in Greece and a longer serif. This was, so far, the extent of Latin innovation in Imperial capital lettering. The basic design, and its square proportion, were Greek.

The one absolute Latin script invented in the heathen period is shown in Chapter 2 (Plate 35). It is a half-square, speedily made, serifed capital. As has been said above, it is the sole originally Latin letter that was continued by the Byzantines. Both the square and the half-square capitals may be compared in this plate. It will be seen in its largest scale in the lower part of Plate 36. They complete our set of the main varieties of Greek and Latin scripts that were developed between, say, the sixth century B.C. and the fourth century A.D. These eight or nine hundred years comprise the pre-Christian period. The authority that lay at the basis of these forms was that of a guild, of a local municipality, or a central Imperial chancery. The Virgils of the fourth century (Plates 38–43) had behind them the prestige of fashionable booksellers. It was they who bestowed a dignified literary function upon a letter whose origins were those of a humble wall-script.

We now turn to the script which was deliberately contrived as a symbol of the change of religion. It is square and contains characters to be found in pre-Christian Greek Uncial. The Latin Uncial was the medium by which the Church set out to present Christian writings in a Christian script. (Plate 48.) The new script was practical in the sense that it was calculated to be recognizable to both Christian communities—Greek-speaking and Latin-speaking—living side by side in Rome and elsewhere. At this period, at least, there seems to be evident a certain interest on the part of the emperors and the bishops in an alphabet that would be understood in both Rome and Constantinople. Thus the lettering on the Byzantine coinage and on the processional cross which the nephew of Justinian presented to Old Rome (Plates 71-2, 124) shows the extent of this assimilation, probably deliberate. It was a calligraphical policy that Old Rome, herself conscious of her debt to the Greek Fathers of the Church, was more than ready to follow—if, indeed, she did not initiate it.

This policy was reversed by Gregory the Great. The present inscription shows the revival of the Square, Imperial shapes (Plate 73). The date is 604. It symbolizes Gregory's Roman-Imperialist anti-Byzantine position. It may have been the first papal intervention in script.

Gregory's policy was not destined to endure. His successors needed the support of the Byzantine emperors even while they resented the pretensions of the Byzantine patriarch. Nevertheless, the Eastern and Western diplomatic, commercial, and correspondence hands, the Cursives and the Half-Cursives, were set upon divergent paths. The present plate exhibits a letter-form that is purely Latin which reaches a formal development in the fourth century but did not attain prestige until later. This is the script now known as Half-Uncial. This, too, has a fair claim to be described as a Christian script.

On the Continent the promotion of inferior cursive hands into formal book-hands was carried furthest in Gaul. Plates 76 and 78 show the hand of the Mero-vingian Chancery clerks being promoted by contemporary monks into a liturgical hand in the seventh century. The same process applied to a script of higher degree is to be seen in Plates 82 and 83, both of which show the influence of the script of the books sent by Paul I, like the Hilary *De Trinitate* which is Half-Uncial. In sum, the authority of the Merovingian Chancery was translated into the authority of the Luxovian academy or monastery.

The Carolingian Official Minuscule partakes of a mixed origin: these are of the eighth century. The favouring of the old Square, Imperial, Augustan design by Charlemagne was, it has been suggested above, implied in his policy as the Augustus of the West. The authority for this script was formally royal.

But, although these developments took place on the Continent significant developments independently occurred in Ireland. The present Plate 95 is Irish of the sixth century, a local version of the Latin Half-Uncial. It has been sug-gested above that the authority which gave the Irish Half-Uncial its distinctive form was that of one of the founders of the Irish Church, possibly Patrick. More important in certain respects are these pages from the Bangor book of the seventh century (Plate 99) which were written between 680 and 691—which exhibit an earlier minuscule than that formed at Luxeuil out of the Merovingian Chancery Cursive. Thus the Irish have the credit of inventing the earliest minuscule. The authority for it was monastic. There is no evidence of its earlier use in any chancery. They are also to be credited with the triangular serif which, in a somewhat less conspicuous form obtained a firm lodgement in late Carolingian Minuscule, as may be seen in Plate 92. These Irish characters rank with those of Corbie and Luxeuil as distinctively West Christian. The Irish Half-Uncial survives in typography at the present day in its native country. The Irish-Carolingian style of serif was revived by Salutati, Niccoli, and Poggio and their followers in Florence in the first quarter of the fifteenth century.

The ninth century witnessed a significant East-Christian missionary activity. It entailed an alphabetical innovation that is used for a language now diffused over an area second only to that covered by what is so loosely called the 'roman' alphabet. Cyril and Methodius were two brothers born in Thessalonica in 826 and 827 respectively. About 866 they translated the liturgy of the Greek Rite into what is now called 'Old Slavonic'. Cyril is credited with the creation of the alphabet that corresponded with the sounds of the Slav language as then spoken by the Bulgars and Moravians.

Not unnaturally the use of the Slav language in the liturgy and the appearance of the new alphabet aroused the hostility of those accustomed to the Greek and Latin Rites in these languages and alphabets. There were not wanting theologians ready to argue that Hebrew, Greek, and Latin were the only languages that could properly be used in formal, liturgical, Christian worship. The Franks with their Imperial Minuscule behind them were especially hostile to the Slav innovation. It is unnecessary for us to enter into these quarrels, though it may be pointed out that Czech rule, as a vassal state of the Holy Roman Empire, was established in 895. The linguistic details are accessible in the masterly article contributed by E. H. Minns to the *Encyclopaedia Britannica* (Cambridge, 1911, s.v. 'Slavs') and in Alfred Senn, 'Slav Linguistics', in the *Handbook of Slavic Studies*, Harvard, 1940). But it is well to note, however, here, that in an appeal to Rome, John VIII (872–82) in 879 emphatically pronounced that 'we rightly praise the [Slavonic] letters invented by Cyril in which the praises of God are set forth'. The letters themselves are derived from upright Greek Liturgical Uncial, and have as their backing the highest ecclesiastical authority.

The paramount economic and political situation of Byzantium gave its artists a dominating prestige. In script and illumination the Eastern Christians by the eleventh century established a book-art luxurious to a degree not so far approached since the time of Charlemagne, by whose authority elaborately decorated Gospel-books were produced in his Imperial scripts.

Two centuries later the West acquired a new Imperial majuscular lettering. The titles and headings of the Gospel-books commissioned by the emperors between the tenth and twelfth centuries are written in what is essentially a Western, Uncialesque, Christian script. In combination with the heavily built and strongly contrasted minuscule which is characteristic of the twelfth and later centuries, the Ottonian Majuscule produced a majestic Christian-Germanic script.

Thus, the authority over script, which had never been so absolute as under Charlemagne, was exercised indirectly by his Germanic successors. Side by side with the luxurious Ottonian codices intended to rival the brilliant achievements of the Byzantines, the Church in the West was having an increased reading public, and the schools, having brought into existence a lay professional class competent to execute the books required, the authority over script gradually passed into the hands of the guilds, with the agreement of the regents of the academies. The script that we call 'Black-Letter', having begun its career as a design that conformed with the economic demands of the twelfth century, evolved in the hands of professional calligraphers, principally laymen, into what virtually became an art-form. When script became independent of the cloister its basic forms were overlaid by decoration, as in the small *Textura* used in the portable Bibles and texts produced in Paris in the thirteenth and fourteenth centuries.

Petrarch's complaints of unnecessary scribal luxuriance which reduced texts to illegibility, would have had greater justification in cisalpine countries. Italy never had to endure the excesses practised, for instance, in France. This was probably due to the authority of the University of Bologna, which ordained the use of the round, plain minuscule which, while primarily designed for juridical texts, was fit for literary work. Petrarch himself wrote the Bolognese hand. Salutati used it for most of his life. The 'Scriptura Bononiensis' ranks as an admirable example of direct academic authority over script. It is probably the most direct and practical example we have of academic legislation affecting script. It was also the last. The script of Bologna was vigorous, but lacked the power to resist the slow but finally victorious script of Florence. This, as suggested above, was the creation of a literary coterie and possessed only the authority of men of learning and taste. Its establishment owed everything to the patronage of Cosimo de' Medici.

One of the outgrowths of this neo-classical movement was a rediscovery of the geometrical basis of the Augustan inscriptions. After Leon Battista Alberti had adopted it, many artists followed the method. Later it was given exaggerated respect by enthusiastic antiquarians and professional calligraphers who successively, but not successfully, introduced the increased use of the compass. The highest and final absurdity was reached when Ferdinando Ruano applied the geometrical method to the Chancery Cursive, the 'lettera de' brevi', and published his treatise in Rome in 1554.

A slightly less absurd attempt was made by Albert Dürer in 1525 to form pointed Black-Letter geometrically. The same method had been applied by Sigismondo de' Fanti in 1514 to round Black-Letter. He was one of the first to print a treatise on the 'ragione geometrica' and his series of capitals is simple and practical. So, too, is Tory's *Champfleury* of 1529. The fact is that it is one thing to apply scientific measurement to an essentially architectural alphabet and another to apply it to an essentially cursive alphabet. Hence, geometry is necessary for the construction of large inscriptional letters for public use, and the Imperial Roman Capital proved to be the most practical form ever devised for administrative use all over the Empire. It is not surprising that Louis XIV's scientific commission should have used geometry for their projected 'Romain du roi'; nor is it surprising that the 'Premier graveur du roi', Philippe Grandjean, should have rejected the authority of the method while accepting the guidance of the patterns. This was naturally the end, reached in 1692–1702, of the use of the geometrical method, as applied to calligraphy or typography.

It needs now to be noted that the diplomatic cursive which had been so influential in ancient times as ultimately to give rise to the Latin Minuscule, thereafter pursued a different course of development. The professionalism of the Chancery notaries encouraged the invention, perhaps in the interest of security, of highly elaborate scripts whose great difficulty of execution made it impossible for the Charter-hands to influence the Book-hands.

The one exception was the cursive employed in the papal Chancery in the fifteenth and sixteenth century. This was the last instance of a diplomatic hand, written by authority, being adopted for literary purposes in calligraphy and typography. While it is true that the letter-form known to Aldus as 'cancelleresca' and to us 'italic', was invented for personal use by Niccolò de' Niccoli sometime before 1420, its public career began only when the papal Chancery adopted it in the second half of the fifteenth century.

It has to be said, however, that the authority of the pope was limited to the Roman Chancery. It was the simple elegance of the cursive, and its propaganda by print, that gained it widest acceptance and led to its ultimate triumph as the basis of all domestic and commercial scripts. With the protection of custom rather than by the exercise of authority, the Gothic hands lived on in the English and other courts of law until the end of the nineteenth century. With their supersession by the typewriter, the decorative Black-Letter kept a vestigial place in the initial sentence of indentures and other legal or quasi-legal documents.

The only exception, it has been seen, is in Fraktur, the German upright Gothic cursive which owes its position to the authority of Maximilian. Hitler's denunciation of this form of script is the last instance of the exercise of State authority in the field of script. What long had been respected as an admirable symbol of Nordic culture was denounced in 1941 as a Jewish abomination. 'The Führer has decreed that the roman type should be designated as the standard type.' It remains the fact that Fraktur is peculiarly adapted for the German language, and that despite the great number of experiments made during the past half-century no roman type has been designed in Germany which, as satisfactorily as Fraktur, produces the factors of economy, legibility, and suitability for the German language. It may safely be predicted that, at some time in the future, designs of Gothic derivation will be revived for purely national circulation. Thus the victory of the neo-Carolingian script invented and propagated by the humanists of fifteenth-century Florence cannot be said to be absolute in Germany despite the authoritative decree of Hitler.

There is, however, one other letter-form expressed in printing-type street signs and public buildings which competes with the humanistic script. The competition daily increases in vigour in all Western countries. Its rise to power, at the expense of the humanistic script, parallels in some respects the process which began in the fifteenth century.

Three centuries later, after Europe had settled down after great wars, and travel became a pastime for gentlemen, expeditions were organized by serious amateurs. Thus came into existence a new classical renaissance with architectural, and hence inscriptional, interests. The possession of wealth made possible the several volumes of James Stuart (1713–88), painter and architect, on *The Antiquities of Athens*. It began to appear in 1762. Its range and detail had a tonic effect upon artistic circles in Europe. In 1764 Richard Chandler, who had earned a high reputation as an archaeologist, was commissioned by the Society of Dilettanti (founded 1733), which comprised men with money and also a taste for classical learning, to investigate the antiquities in certain regions of Asia Minor. The work progressed over many years until its completion in four volumes in 1814. Chandler's *Ionian Antiquities* was published in 1769. James Stuart was a member of the Society of Dilettanti.

The new mood, the 'Grecian Gusto', was thus initiated. It culminated in England in the next century with the architectural work of John Nash (1752–1835). His building of the streets from Carlton House Terrace to Regent's Park is his best-known work. The model of Nash was not lost on the developers who followed him, and they soon discovered the need for an architectural letter that would reflect 'Grecian' styles. One such was W. H. Seth Smith, who was one of those associated with Thomas Cubitt in the development of Belgravia. In 1830 Seth-Smith built the 'Pantechnicon', a warehouse for goods of all descriptions.

179. London. Inscription on the façade of the Pantechnicon.
London, Motcomb Street.
Relief monoline unserifed capitals.
C. Hussey, 'Future of the Pantechnicon', *Country Life*, vol. 139, part i (1966), p. 714.

On an entablature above the fine colonnade of Ionic pilasters is the name of the establishment (Plate 179). The choice of letters for it, perhaps the work of Joseph Jopling, an architect of theoretical and mathematical tastes associated with Seth Smith,[1] is highly significant. They present an early architectural display in low relief sculpture of monoline sans-serif capitals in the Greek style, current, without exception, from the fifth to the second century B.C. The model is orthodox antique 'Grecian' except that the strokes are much thicker than would ever have been permitted by the ancients. What began *c*. 1820 as a choice of lettering based merely on 'taste' and 'feeling' representing a form which had never before been used in Western Europe, has now become established as an alternative version of the Roman alphabet.

Besides men of taste, the 'Grecian Gusto' made an appeal to the English Utilitarians. Was this enough to establish a letter-form that had been unknown in the West for so long? How long in fact was it that a sans-serif alphabet had been in use in Europe?

In considering this question it needs to be remembered that the Western alphabet, as stabilized in the eighth century, comprised capitals (majuscules) and lower-case or small letters (minuscules). These were all serifed and so remained until the process of contractions of the body and thickening of the stroke, which created the 'Black-Letter' style, reached in the twelfth century a novel point of development in the minuscule which will stand comparison with the nineteenth-century invention of sans-serif lower case.

[1] The origin, or revival, of the 'Sans Serif' letter is still obscure. James Mosley ('The Nymph and the Grot', *Typographica* 12, 1965, pp. 2–19) is inclined to give the credit to Sir John Soane, an ascription supported by subsequent research. Jopling may have known Soane's work. (On the Pantechnicon, see 'Future of the Pantechnicon', *Country Life*, vol. 139, part i (1966), p. 714.)

180. Psalter. English, thirteenth-century Gothic minuscule in the form of 'Textus prescissus sine pedibus'; nearly sans-serif.

New York; Morgan MS. 100. Formerly in the collection of William Morris. According to Sydney Cockerell probably written in the neighbourhood of Canterbury.

No. 45 in the *Exhibition of Illuminated Manuscripts held at the New York Public Library* (1933).

Adept professionals drafted during the twelfth century a highly artificial script for first-class liturgical work. It is a magnificent invention, carrying a most impressive presence on the page. The 'textus prescissus vel sine pedibus' (as it was called in the later Middle Ages), abolishes serifs of the Carolingian type, in favour of terminations of the perpendiculars which are slightly splayed. The 'textus sine pedibus' was a highly deliberate formation successfully realizing the scribe's intention to create a calligraphic work of art. Without doubt it is the finest of all the products of the scriptoria of the high Middle Ages. It may well be an English invention (Plate 180). It was succeeded in the fourteenth century by the 'textus quadratus' in which diamond-shaped terminals are applied to the perpendiculars. And this is the design of pseudo-serif, in a softened form, with which Maximilian finished off the Black-Letter printing type of his sumptuous *Horae* of 1513.

One other letter-form possibly foreshadows the nineteenth-century sans-serif lower case. This is the rounded Black-Letter which became dominant for liturgical work in southern Europe during the late Middle Ages. The Italian and Spanish 'Textus Rotundus' is a bold, round, Black-Letter designed for the large choir-books required for mass, matins, vespers, and other offices (Plate 181). The size resembles the wood letters used for the modern poster. It is capable of being formed geometrically and was so treated by the writing-masters of the sixteenth century. Certain perpendiculars, p, r, and others, terminate without a serif, but the script as a whole is not consistently serifless; nor is it truly monoline. Its immediate forefather was the 'littera bononiensis' of the fourteenth century

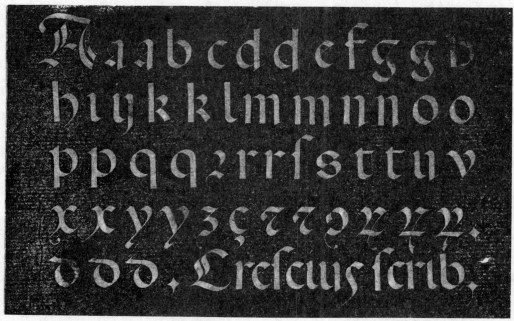

181. Alphabet from Giovan Francesco Cresci, *Essemplare di piu sorti lettere* (Rome, Antonio Blado, 1560). Johnson no. 10; Bonacini no. 415, Gothic minuscule in the form of 'textus rotundus'; almost completely sans serif. Cresci describes this alphabet as 'Lettera ecclesiastica'. It is an enlarged and formalized version of the 'Lettera bononiensis' in the version used by Petrarch. See his personal transcription of the *De sui ipsius et multorum ignorantia* (Ehrle & Liebaert, p. 45); see also A. F. Johnson and S. Morison, 'Two Letters of Petrarch to Boccaccio A.D. 1366', in *The Fleuron*, vii (Cambridge, 1930), with two facsimiles.

and, more remotely, the fine north Italian minuscule which was executed to perfection in the twelfth century at Verona. Here was written a singularly handsome minuscule which contrasted in boldness and roundness with the more utilitarian and slender minuscule practised at St. Gall. Moreover, the Verona minuscule was consistently serifed. While the later Italian 'Textus Rotundus' or Round Gothic further diminishes the role of the serif it does not suppress it.

As neither the Italian type of Gothic nor the Maximilian type is monoline, it follows that the nineteenth-century design, consistently monoline and consistently unserifed, is a novelty. Its range, extended in our time over both sides of the Channel and the Atlantic, gives it a position that needs consideration, and any authority it may have obtained merits examination.

It has been argued above that the neo-Carolingian Roman invented and espoused by the Florentine humanists would never have been established but for the use and support given it by Cosimo de' Medici, who bestowed upon it a quasi-authority. It was essentially different from that of the papal or Imperial chanceries. It is the only example of a script being established because of the accident that it corresponded with the taste of a merchant banker. Without him the then novel script would never have been more than the hobby of a society of 'literati'. In this sense the humanistic roman may be described as a capitalist script. Similarly, the neo-Grecian, monoline, sans-serif used by John Nash and others would never have been established had it the backing merely of the Society of Dilettanti or the Utilitarians. The neo-Grecian lettering had points of interest to others than the class of archaeologists and philosophers. A new class had arisen: the manufacturers and industrialists. This class respected it not as something old, but as something new. They found it appropriate to the changes they were, despite themselves, effecting in social life. In particular it brought into existence a new dimension of advertising. This social need and satisfaction had existed since the printed newspapers of the seventeenth century when, no doubt, small handbills and cards also made their appearance.

A uniquely strong impulse was given to outdoor placard advertising by the traction steam boom which followed upon the successful experiment of the Stockton and Darlington Railway in 1825 (Plate 182). The earliest innovations inspired by the new need for popular publicity were designs whose mainstrokes were thicker than any medieval black-letter. As the substrokes remained thin the contrast was stronger than anything Bodoni had contrived. The retention of historic tapered and bracketed serifs manifested the continuity of the design with book-typography. Even so, the English type-founders were the first to realize that, for appropriate use in publicity, the designs of the letters needed radical revision. The so-called 'fat-faced' romans were an irrational design, but they possessed visibility to a degree never before achieved.

The next step represented an attempt to solve the problem by a new and rational design. The 'fat-face' romans committed the absurdity of retaining the contrasted stroke and the tapered serif. By drawing a uniform or monoline stroke and standardizing a serif of a width equal to the stroke, an entirely new and rational design was brought into commission. Size for size the monoline stroke and serif design has the same visibility as the 'fat face', but has greater legibility in both capitals and lower case. The type then called 'Egyptian' was an instant success, and is still in great demand for not only typographical purposes but for architectural letterings.

The 'Egyptian' has not, however, attained the position now occupied by the contemporary monoline sans-serif (Plate 183) design mentioned above. Both were used by architects, sign-writers, and other craftsmen engaged in the vast amount of building required by the new Factory Age. The first appearance of the neo-Grecian monoline sans serif and the 'Egyptian' monoline serif cannot be dated more precisely than between 1816 and 1825.

Of the two designs, both equally typical of the early Industrial Age, the neo-Grecian monoline sans serif fitted more perfectly than any other design into the Industrial pattern because it is more easy and less expensive to make. This was not immediately understood by the type-foundry, printing trades, and sign-writing crafts. For them it was the new, heavy, capital which they had needed to replace the old black-letter. So far, therefore, the 'antique' had been only a revival, limited to capitals. Architects, of course, had no need for anything more. Nobody would commit the solecism of lettering a Nash terrace in upper and lower case.

Years passed before it was realized that the fount needed to be completed by

Stockton & Darlington
Railway.
The Company's
COACH

CALLED THE

EXPERIMENT,

Which commenced Travelling on MONDAY, the 10th of OCTO-BER, 1825, will continue to run from *Darlington* to *Stockton*, and from *Stockton* to *Darlington* every Day, [Sunday's excepted] setting off from the DEPOT at each place, at the times specified as under, (*viz.*):---

ON MONDAY,

From Stockton at half-past 7 in the Morning, and will reach Darlington about half-past 9; the Coach will set off from the latter place on its return at 3 in the Afternoon, and reach Stockton about 5.

TUESDAY,

From Stockton at 3 in the Afternoon, and will reach Darlington about 5.

On the following Days, viz.:---

WEDNESDAY, THURSDAY & FRIDAY,

From Darlington at half-past 7 in the Morning, and will reach Stockton about half-past 9; the Coach will set off from the latter place on its return at 3 in the Afternoon, and reach Darlington about 5.

SATURDAY,

From Darlington at 1 in the Afternoon, and will reach Stockton about 3.

Passengers to pay 1s. each, and will be allowed a Package of not exceeding 14lb. all above that weight to pay at the rate of 2d. per Stone extra. Carriage of small Parcels 3d. each. The Company will not be accountable for Parcels of above £5. Value, unless paid for as such.

Mr RICHARD PICKERSGILL at his Office in Commercial Street, Darlington; and Mr TULLY at Stockton, will for the present receive any Parcels and Book Passengers.

STOCKTON PRINTED BY ...TON.

182. Placard composed in a variety of the new display types known in the trade as 'Fat Faces' and 'Egyptians', 1825.

Heavily stroked monoline roman with serifs of equal weight (see 'EXPERIMENT') and heavily contrasted roman and italic (see 'Railway').

Railway Museum, York.

183. Cincinnati Type Foundry, specimen book, after 1830.
Monoline; unserifed capitals and lower case.

a lower case. Everybody who has worked in the business knows that it is never easy to establish a new typographical design. It was twenty years before a foundry produced what was, in effect, the most novel and permanent contribution to letter-design that had appeared on the printed page since the Aldine italic of 1501. The monoline lower case without serif was an absolute creation with the sole exception, perhaps, of the 'Egyptian' lower case. The priority has not been established. The earliest appearance in commercial use of monoline sans serif, so far noted, occurs in American advertising dated 1835.

The essential virtue of advertising is to attract attention by high visibility, which includes novelty of letter-form and arrangement. The first monoline sans serif in capitals and lower case was the greatest novelty in letter-design. Hitherto novelty had been avoided. Many changes in script had manifested themselves in history, but they made their way very slowly. There had been inventions, like the plain, nearly sans-serif capitals on the mosaics; the decorative capitals of Damasus I; the titling capitals of the Merovingian period; and the legends in St. Mark's at Venice and the capitals of Donatello. These however, despite the authority behind them, were intended only for specific and not for general use.

On the other hand, the nineteenth-century sans serif, like any other letter-design cast in type for the printing trade, was intended for the largest market obtainable. In the new manufacturing age, symbolized by advertising to the masses of the people, the novelty of monoline and particularly of sans serif, made certain their permanence.

In the twentieth century the industrial and commercial factors in society have hugely expanded sales-promotion, merchandising, and information services. It is believed that eleven thousand million dollars is spent each year on advertising in the U.S.A. and a third of that sum in Great Britain. The volume of lettering of all kinds needed to sustain the burden of all this advertising in all media can only be guesswork, but it must be enormously greater than is required by the total sum in any case of biblical, liturgical, literary, educational, journalistic, periodical, official, and traditional media.

In advertising the independence from tradition is total unless the nature of the commodity requires 'conservative' treatment. All advertising specialists are aware that unlimited choice of lettering is necessary to the business of setting that responds to the one and only test: its effectiveness. The advertising profession has therefore created innumerable varieties of script, both capitals and lower case. Of all the vast range of letters designed for display advertising during the past hundred years, the sans-serif upper and lower case is by far the most widely used in every part of the world and in every language where the Graeco-Latin alphabet obtains.

The monoline sans serif of primitive Greek origin now occupies a position which is unassailable. This is the more certain since it has been adopted and standardized by large public bodies. From the beginning, transport adopted it. The earliest standardization of sans serif was in the lettering adopted by the world's first subway or underground system—the District Railway of London, in the 1860s. Then followed a similar standardization by the German State Railways in the 1890s. The principle was extended in the 1920s by the London Underground Railways system (which incorporated the District Railway) to their surface transport, buses. The example was followed by the L.N.E.R. and since by the British Railways system. Today, as Plate 184 proves, the British Railways gives its authority to a sans-serif script.

Other powerful agencies support it. Certain sections of the public are regarded by journalists as being at certain times so specially responsive to the monoline sans serif as to regard the design as conveying a note of excitement. Whereas the newspapers published in the morning for the benefit of the more serious reader are headlined with serifed letters of the thick and thin Latin form, those addressed

As the 24-hour system for Railway Time operates on the Continent, it is used in this time-table thus :—12.00 noon, 18.00 6 p.m., 24.00 arrival midnight, 0.00 departure midnight.

LONDON—LISBON
PARIS—BORDEAUX—IRUN

Through Sleeping Cars from London to Paris indicated by dotted line.

Miles (n)	OUTWARDS			1 & 2 Cl. A	1 & 2 Cl.	1 & 2 Cl.	1 & 2 Cl. Pullmans B		1 & 2 Cl. C		1 Cl. D
—	London (Victoria)	...	dep.	9.05½	10.00	12.30	13.00	...	...		21.00*
—	„ (Waterloo)	...	dep.	...	...	...	...	...	19.30†		
72	Folkestone Harbour	...	arr.	...	...	14.25	14.38	...	...		
			dep.	...	...	15.10		...	...		
78	Dover Marine	...	arr.	...	11.32	...	...	...	...		22.40*
			dep.	...	12.00	...	...	...	...		23.25½
—	Newhaven Harbour	...	arr.	10.16½	...	...	...	...	...		
			dep.	10.45½	...	...	...	...	...		
—	Southampton Docks	...	arr.	...	...	...	...	...	21.44†		
			dep.	...	...	...	...	...	22.15†		
101	Calais Maritime	(Br.T.)	arr.	See Note "g"	13.20	16.40	...	...	...		3.05*
		(F.T.)	arr.		14.20	17.40	...	...	...		4.05
					1 Cl. E	1 F						4.23
			dep.	14.42	14.59	18.02	...	...	...		
—	Dunkerque (Ferry Berth)	(Br.T.)	arr.	...	...	...	...	...	...		
			dep.	...	...	...	...	...	...		
—	Dieppe Maritime	(Br.T.)	arr.	14.00½	...	...	...	...	...		
		(F.T.)	arr.	15.00½	...	...	...	...	...		
			dep.	15.30	...	...	...	...	...		
—	Havre Quay	(Br.T.)	arr.	...	...	...	...	...	5.00h		
		(F.T.)	arr.	...	...	...	...	...	6.00		
									Autor. 1 Cl.	1 & 2 Cl.	
—	Havre Ville	...	dep.	18.08	...	...	...	...	7.15m	8.40	
—	Paris (St. Lazare)	...	arr.		18.10	19.33	...	...	9.22m	11.34	
288	Paris (Nord)	...	arr.				21.41	...	...		9.00

				1 & 2 Cl. G	1 & 2 Cl. H			1 & 2 Cl. J	1 Cl. K		
293	Paris (Austerlitz)	...	dep.	21.20	22.45	...	...	8.00	13.35		
665½	Bordeaux (St. Jean)	...	arr.	3.35	7.00	...	...	13.59	18.34		
			dep.	3.52m	7.46	...	...	14.09	18.38		
799½	Hendaye (F.T.)	...	arr.	7.20½	11.42	...	...	17.15	20.50		
			dep.	7.50½	11.56	...	...	17.45	21.05		
802	Irun (Sp.T.)	...	arr.	7.55½		1, 2, 3 Cl.	...	17.50	21.10		
								1, 2, 3 Cl.	1 Cl.		
			dep.	...	19.00	...	...	19.00	22.15		
913½	Miranda de Ebro	...	arr.	...	22.55	...	...	22.55	1.35		
1070½	Medina del Campo	...	arr.	...	23.05	...	...	23.05	1.40		
			dep.	...	3.43	...	...	3.43	5.48		
			arr.	...	6.30	...	...	6.30	6.10		
1196½	Fuentes de Onoro (Sp.T.)		dep.	...	12.30	...	...	12.30	10.45		
			arr.	...	13.10	...	...	13.10	10.55	10.55	
1197	Vilar-Formoso (P.T.)		arr.	...	12.15	...	...	15.20	10.00	11.00	
			dep.	...	15.30	...	...	15.30	10.15	11.10	
1225½	Guarda	...	dep.	...	16.32	...	...	16.32	11.00	11.10	
			arr.	...	16.47	...	...	16.47	11.14	12.11	
1274	Mangualde	...	arr.	...	18.24	...	...	18.24	12.24	12.11	
1290	Oliv.-Cabanas	...	arr.	...	18.40	...	...	18.40			
1300½	Santa Comba	...	arr.	...	18.50	...	...	18.50	13.03	14.00	
1317	Luso-Bussaco	...	arr.	...	19.40	...	...	19.40	13.43	14.38	
1322½	Pampilhosa	...	arr.	...	19.50	...	...	19.50	13.53	14.42	
			dep.	...	20.18	...	...	20.18	13.56	14.58	
1331½	Coimbra-B.	...	arr.	...	20.30	...	...	20.30	14.07	15.00	
1343	Alfarelos	...	arr.	...	20.46	...	...	20.46	14.22	15.16	
1361	Pombal	...	arr.	...	21.10	...	...	21.10	15.10		
1400½	Entroncamento	...	arr.	...	22.06	...	...	22.06	15.44	16.36	
1470½	Lisboa (Santa Apolónia)		arr.	...	23.35	...	...	23.35	17.04	17.55	

For explanation of time indications see page 14   — 8 —   The times of trains in Spain and Portugal shown above are liable to alteration.

184. British Railways,
Continental time-table, 1957.

185. *Daily Mirror*, London,
3 May 1957. Popular 'morning'
journalistic layout. Three old sans-
serif headlines.

to the multitude are lettered in a heavy variety of the ancient Greek model, as
may be seen in any issue of the *Daily Mirror* (Plate 185).

It should not be thought, however, that the journalistic preference for bold
sans serif is made on behalf merely of the proletariat. The front page of the London
Evening Standard (Plate 186), a newspaper published for an educated, or at
least sophisticated 'class' readership, proves that it is believed journalistically
necessary to present an 'evening' in a style different from that of a morning
newspaper. The reader on his way home wants a change from the style of newspaper he read on his way to the office, and will buy a copy if it should be headlined
in heavy type. And this is the supreme virtue of the monoline sans-serif design:
it is possible to thicken it to a greater degree than the thick and thin serifed design.
The choice here is purely pragmatic. All the journalistic typographer requires
is maximum visibility on the newspaper stall.

Elsewhere, however, the effort has been made to find a philosophical justification for the choice by municipalities and public bodies to select the sans-serif
as a practical solution to their problem of naming their streets and giving direction to traffic. One of the early uses of this lettering was architectural and, as
such, an artistic element. It was no part of the plan of the Society of Dilettanti

186. *Evening Standard*, London, 29 May 1957. Middle-class evening journalistic layout. Bold sans-serif headlines.

to philosophize about the history of art, or to create a style of lettering for a new age. They were satisfied to discover the archaeological facts and evoke corresponding emotions. There is no evidence that the architects and engineers of the first half of the century (or later) set about to create a theory that would give the contemporary 'Egyptian' or sans serif an intellectualist basis.

A sanction of such an order was late in coming to formulation in the minds of the fifteenth-century humanists. A similar delay is manifest in the nineteenth century. While the advertisers of the 1850s were using the sans serif because they found by thickening all the strokes they could give the design more 'punch', the artists and poets treated it as if it were an industrial design unfit for respectable use. Artistic reaction against industrialism was typified in England by Ruskin and Morris, whose teaching and example took root abroad. An English artist who had an influence on the Continent, and particularly Germany, at least equal to that of William Morris, was Aubrey Beardsley, whose attitude towards calligraphy was more individualist and untraditional. The difference between Morris and Beardsley was that between the Arts and Crafts and the Art Nouveau movements.

When the illustrator of Wilde's *Salome* (London, 1893) incorporated sans-serif

333

capitals in his drawings, it was doubtless because he found the letters best suited to his personal style, as well as being perhaps easy for him to design. It was, however, a singularity of Beardsley's practice, and in no sense a symbol of the 'nineties' period. It was not otherwise when a German contemporary poet, Stefan George, well known in London pre-Raphaelite circles, designed a sans serif in capital and lower case. It was an individual fount in which the a, e, and t were of the uncial form. The type was used by its creator for his translations from Dante Gabriel Rossetti, Swinburne, Dowson, and others. Hugo von Hofsmannsthal also used what was known as the 'St. G. Schrift' (Plate 187). The

> Gedenke meiner wenn dein blick sich senkt
> Auf jeden gegenstand den ich berührt·
> Wann die gedanken sich dir trüben wollen
> Und leer wird deines herzens heiligtum!
>
> Gedenke meiner wenn in zarte arme
> Der reue meine bangen sinne fallen·
> Wann einsamkeit an ihre brust mich drückt·
> Verzweiflung über meinem haupte hinzieht!
>
> Gedenke meiner! himmlisch denke meiner
> Wenn meine hoffnung manchmal mich verlässt·
> Erinnerungen wie ein feindlich heer
> Herziehend mich zu schwerem kampfe fordern!
>
> Gedenke meiner wenn in schwäche ganz
> Den todesengel ich willkommen heisse
> Und wenn ich mit der allerbangsten stimme
> Ihn frage nach des sonnenaufgangs zeit!

187. The 'St. G. Schrift' from *Zeitgenössische Dichter übertragen von Stefan George* (Berlin, 1905). Literary sans-serif, monoline.

design was hardly used after the war. If it may have seemed too classical and archaic for the post-war contemporary purpose, it was not because of a reaction in Germany against sans serif as such. The contrary is the case.

The necessity to reckon with industrialism was felt by nineteenth-century critics, poets, and artists with differing emotions. Morris's lead was widely followed, and many believed that the only way to deal with industrialism was to destroy it by force. The next generation was disposed less to destroy it by violence than to redeem it by art. By the time of Henry van de Velde (1863-1951) and more especially his successor Walter Gropius (1883-1969), who reorganized his predecessors' creation, the Art School at Weimar, a significant transition had been completed. Art and Industry were reconciled and synthesized on the terms laid down by artists. The Bauhaus movement, supported as it was by the Grand Duke of Saxe-Weimar, attracted architects and painters whose number and prestige strengthened what became a world-wide movement.

From 1919 the School became an Academy under the leadership of Gropius and sought to lay a philosophical foundation for what has since become known as the 'modern' style or the 'contemporary' feeling. The effort in due course involved the shapes of the letters in which those associated with the movement printed in their manifestos. The early nineteenth-century sans serif was, by the deliberation of members of the Academy, adopted as the symbol of 'our time'. Thus the Bauhaus attitude towards the sans serif of John Nash in 1830, of Aubrey Beardsley on the one hand in 1893 and of Stefan George on the other in 1905, was wholly different from that of Wassily Kandinsky in 1924 and Paul Klee in 1925, and El Lissitsky in 1926.

In the Academy it was imputed to sans-serif lettering that it accorded in spirit so exactly with new contemporary building construction methods and materials, that it was pre-eminently the letter-design most fit for use in association with the new materials and ideas at the disposal of the architects working in the post-war period of 1919-25. Such new materials, iron and steel, concrete and, above all, glass, were then new to the theorists and practitioners at the Bauhaus at Weimar from 1919. The result of the discussions between the schools of art, applied arts, and architecture, was the formulation of a novel doctrine of universal application. Henceforth form should obey, express, and exploit function, material, and space. The doctrine was a reaction against the Arts and Crafts movement and the Art Nouveau group in favour of Industrialization and mechanization. The Bauhaus removed to Dessau in 1925 and occupied a new building designed by Gropius. Its inscription was in huge sans-serif capitals of corresponding thickness. Set vertically they read BAUHAUS from head to foot.

The Academy was suppressed by the Nazis in 1933 and its members dispersed into various parts of Europe and America. Within thirty years this doctrine has become so broadly welcomed in schools on the Continent and in Britain and America as to become the main impulse of its use by contemporary architects and graphic designers.

Thus, the sans serif which began *c.* 1820 as a by-product of a gentlemanly survey of the monuments of ancient Greece, next adopted by advertisers because it was a novelty, used by engineers and draughtsmen because it was easily thickened, finally progressed to acceptance as a norm by artists and intellectuals.

The increase of architectural and typographic use of sans serif is so great and so rapid that its future progress against the serifed roman must be taken as automatic. The use of sans serif is now so firmly established as a convention that the design may be held to possess the authority of architects and art workers. It is at least true to say that the contemporary industrial architect would think twice before using any other alphabet and that it would be second nature for the engineer responsible for the design of a Diesel locomotive to use it.

The argument is persuasive; sufficiently so to bring into existence a sort of artistic-bureaucratic, architectural-technocratic consent which has attached to itself responsibility for the form of such institutional building, lettering, and publicity. Over 65 per cent of general publicity and 100 per cent of transport publicity has abandoned the neo-Carolingian pattern. The justification given to upper- and lower-case sans serif by municipalities and other public authorities is a recognition of its proven up-to-dateness, practicability, legibility, and economy. This would nowadays seem to be all the authority that is necessary, or possible, or desirable. Most important is the fact, so it is believed, that it is 'modern'.

The sans-serif style for headlines (only) is preferred by certain journalists, not because it has any intellectualist or ideological significance, but because it it is black in colour and has associations different from those which for centuries have been considered proper to the relatively grey type of book-typography, and thereby rendered conventional and respectable for literature. To the publisher of ephemeral and popular reading matter, the sans-serif headline is appropriate precisely because it has no literary accent. Its only authority is that of the most powerful of all forces of modern society: the 'mass-market'. This may be, indeed is, the antithesis of the imperial, papal, literary, and artistic aspects of authority, which have been under observation in the preceding pages, but it would seem that there is today no higher sanction for the world's lettering as applied to popular commercial and printed matter.

It should not be overlooked that apart from such categories of typography as time-tables, guide-books, and textbooks of a technical kind, the bulk of composition in sans serif is reserved for printed matter that is distributed gratis for the 'consumer'.

The nearly unanimous consent thus given by industrial designers to the sans-serif design was bound to lead to the attempt being made to give it literary status. The composition of current literature in sans serif has not found a welcome from authors, printers, and publishers of works of learning or belles-lettres. The serifed, humanistic type of the Aldus or Didot model continues to monopolize the typography of the text of books intended as permanent possessions. It also monopolizes the text of newspapers, irrespective of headlines. And this is true, also, of nearly all books and of most periodicals offered for sale.

The gains of Gropius's sans-serif upper- and lower-case lettering, immense as they are, and greater as they promise to be in view of the authority now conceded, have not been made at the expense of Aldus's serifed typography. The true purpose of the Gropius letter is above all architectural, his mastery of a medium of which must be admitted, even if one tires of its glass and cube-sugar elements. It has been pushed by his pupils in the graphic arts into typography, a medium of which their desire to astonish, and striving for novelty, is more evident than their mastery of principle or breadth of experience.

The problem of devising brief public directions for instantaneous recognition by motorists and other itinerants is essentially different from that of providing long texts for continuous perusal and reference by generations of readers and students. The typographical sans-serif style adopted in 1916 by Wyndham

Lewis for his magazine *Blast* was certainly appropriate. A militant literary, artistic, or political group may sensibly adopt such a 'coterie' style. It would be unfortunate in work intended to approach the mind by the process of reasonable discussion. Despite the contemporary freedom and consequent relaxation of discipline in public alphabetical usage, less artistic whimsicality than might have been expected has made its way into the printing of books intended for the consideration of the literate public, not merely of one generation or of one country. This is the result of a proper restriction of typographical freedom and innovation to ephemeral matter, and a soundly based respect for convention and discipline in the production of literary matter.

The production of texts to be read more than once in the medium of a duplex (capitals and lower-case) alphabet has now been in progress, whether in script or in type, for a period of nearly a thousand years. The process has been that of trial and error. Only the chief survivals have been noticed in these pages and, in the main, those whose career was advanced by the exercise of authority. Some notice has been taken of the career of scripts which exemplify the desire for freedom. There is full justification for both authority and tradition, and for freedom and novelty in scripts, provided the permanent and ephemeral categories are separated and not confined. And this principle would appear to be firmly established. The inherent rationalism of individual forms of the Carolingian Majuscule and Minuscule, and the perception by Petrarch and Salutati of their superior legibility, led to the establishment by their followers, supported by Cosimo de' Medici, of the revived eighth–twelfth century script. This letter, it cannot be denied, retains and deserves to retain its position as the paramount medium for literary composition.

This position has been challenged. In 1921 the Austrian, Herbert Bayer, who had studied painting under W. Kandinsky, was placed in charge of the Typography Department at Weimar. He decided that it was unnecessary in writing or printing to continue the use of two alphabets. That the lower case should be suppressed had, on more than one occasion, been put forward in England and elsewhere. It is relatively new, however, to suppress capitals in favour of lower-case only.

Professor Bayer was 21 when he enunciated his thesis that the single alphabet was sufficient, and convinced his colleagues at the Bauhaus that in all the typographical productions of the Academy the composition, including proper names, should be composed in sans-serif lower case. Thus, there were no initial capitals after the full point, or to the paragraph, or to substantives in the German language.

But although capitals were never used with lower case, they were consistently used for placards and posters. Hence, the placards for the Kandinsky Exhibition of 1936 were designed by Professor Bayer in capitals only, sans serif of course. The Academy was suppressed by the Nazis in 1933 and the staff dispersed.

The novel ideas of the theorists at work in the Bauhaus typographical school have since been propagated in the schools of high repute in Germany, Switzerland, England, and the United States. Their application to matter which is printed to be read once or twice and then destroyed may be welcomed in the appropriate quarters. That Professor Bayer was 21 years of age when he enunciated these principles of typographical composition is a fact without relevance; his master W. Kandinsky was only four years older. They never pretended to any experience in the typography of books, and would probably have smiled at some of the capricious exercises of their disciples. Professor Bayer himself, who designed Siegfried Giedion's *Space, Time and Architecture* (Cambridge, Mass., 1941) and *Mechanization Takes Command* (New York, 1948), has returned to tradition except for the title-pages, whose main legend runs across the two pages of the opening. The composition is conventional, the body type being of late eighteenth-century 'classical' design. Thus the force of the Bauhaus doctrine of typography is to be seen to have declined since 1923-6, when it was first promulgated at Dessau.

The decline in the application of the doctrine to the typography of books intended for permanent possession and reading is the more striking in view of the remarkably inclusive exhibition of the whole Bauhaus accomplishment in architecture and the arts which was mounted in 1938 by the Museum of Modern Art in New York. The commemorative volume *Bauhaus 1919-1928* edited by Herbert Bayer, Walter Gropius, and Ise Gropius, is a characteristic expression of the school's typographical orthodoxy, save that capital letters are admitted in the first half of the text and abolished only in the latter half. The whole, it needs to be allowed, is in the nature of a manifesto and, as such, not necessarily to be taken as a pronouncement of irreformable dogma, though there are passages which suggest the opposite.

On the other hand, Professor Giedion's books were intended to be serious contributions to their subject. His *Space, Time and Architecture* is now in its fifth edition and sixteenth printing (1971); *Mechanization takes Command* has reached its second printing. Doubtless the Harvard University Press, and the Oxford University Press, New York, undertook responsibility for the publication of these volumes. No doubt the Presses wished these books to be given the attention which, in their opinion, Professor Giedion's writing deserved.

The two academic Presses might have considered it appropriate to dress both works of so notable a supporter of the School in accordance with orthodox Bauhaus teaching as enunciated by Professor Bayer. By so doing they would have earned the approval, and perhaps applause, of numerous graphic artists and designers whose tradition it is to be anti traditional.

But while Professor Bayer was retained to design the typography, and the fact is recorded in the verso of the title-pages, the designer chose, in this instance, to defer to the convictions of the academic presses throughout the world. These presses respect the authority of tradition, not because of any value that may be sentimentally imputed to it as a deposit of history, but primarily if not solely as the accumulation of past experience which is daily verified in present-day practice.

The respect for tradition, understood in this sense, may not be lessened in the typography of books without risk to the author's meaning and purpose, which it is the vocation of the printer and publisher to protect and assist. The degree of agreement among the academic presses upon the alphabet to be used for learned texts is virtually unanimous.

In sum, the equivalent today of the authority in any of its aspects as directly exercised over script in the past is found indirectly exercised by the institutional presses. Thus the State Printing Offices of France, Britain, Germany, and the U.S.A. are important in this respect. The existence of the Imprimerie Nationale in Paris (1640), Her Majesty's Stationery Office in London (1785), the Government Printing Office in Washington (1850), the Bundesdruckerei incorporating the Reichsdruckerei in Berlin (1879), is a factor that stabilizes the art of typography regarded solely as a medium of permanent record and of current documentation and communication. The Imprimerie Nationale has won also great prestige for its past and present contributions to learning in occidental and oriental founts.

A greater responsibility for the maintenance of the highest standards of typographical rationality, legibility, and orthography in all the numerous languages which employ the roman alphabet lies with academic presses. They are to be found in Rome, Oxford, and Cambridge. These three Presses are the Typographia Vaticana, founded by the illustrious pope and planner, Sixtus V (1585–90) in 1588; the press of the University of Oxford, founded under the will of the great bishop and printer, John Fell (1625–86) in 1690; the press of the University of Cambridge, founded at the instigation of that remarkable polymath and critic Richard Bentley (1662–1724) in 1698.

The productions of these presses in the biblical, liturgical, classical European, and oriental languages severally reach the highest degree of scholarly accuracy, literary excellence, and scrupulous typography. The complete technical equipment of the compositors, illustrators, and printers, directed by the commissioners, delegates, and syndics drawn from the respective institutions, libraries, and colleges have together, though independently, established a standard toward which important private offices throughout the world are glad to reach. There exists an effective universal consensus upon the principles that should govern the shapes and uses of the Graeco-Roman alphabet in all works addressed to the intelligence of mankind. This consensus is the result of a twenty-five-century process of evolution inspired by many scribes and sculptors working collectively and individually under the authority of emperors, popes, and patriarchs or abbots or masters of guilds. Hence, there is implied in this agreement a reconciliation of authority and freedom in relation to Graeco-Roman script which is the best guarantee against experiment or innovation or irresponsibility.

By irresponsibility is meant any reduction of the authority proper to the style of permanent literature addressed to the intelligence of man in favour of the freedom proper to ephemeral matter addressed to the emotions of man. The typographical tradition tested and developed by the infinitely numerous and expanding categories of literature printed and reprinted during the centuries since Gutenberg, Aldus, and Plantin is rightly judged to be secure in the hands of the successors of Sixtus V, John Fell, and Richard Bentley.

LAUS DEO

LIST OF WORKS CONSULTED

ANDREAS ALFÖLDI, *The Conversion of Constantine and Pagan Rome* (Oxford, 1948)
—— *Insignien und Tracht des Römischer Kaiser*, Kaiserlich Deutsches Archäologisches Institut, Römische Abteilung, Mitteilungen Band 50 (Rome, 1935)
R. P. AUSTIN, *The Stoichedon Style in Greek Inscriptions* (London, 1938)
A. M. BANDINI, *Catologus Codicum Latinorum Bibliothecae Mediceae Laurentianae*, 5 vols. (Florence, 1774-8)
RUTH BARBOUR, 'A Thucydides belonging to Ciriaco d'Ancona' in *Bodleian Library Record*, vol. v (1954-6)
V. BARTOLETTI, *Papiri Greci e Latini* (Florence, 1957)
Der Basler Münsterschatz. Katalog der Ausstellung in der Barfüsserkirche zu Basel (Basel, 1956)
STELIO BASSI, *La Scrittura Greca in Italia* (Cremona, 1956)
—— *La scrittura calligrafica Greco-Romana* (Verona, 1957)
C. H. BEESON, 'The Palimpsests of Bobbio' in *Miscellanea Giovanni Mercati*, vi (Vatican, 1946)
S. BERGER, *La Bible française au moyen âge* (Paris, 1884)
—— *Histoire de la Vulgate pendant les premiers siècles du moyen-âge* (Paris, 1893)
S. BETTINI, *Mosaici antichi di San Marco a Venezia* (Bergamo, 1944)
R. BIANCHI BANDINELLI, *Storicità dell'Arte Classica*, 2nd edition (Florence, 1950)
—— 'Schemi iconografici nelle miniature dell'Iliade Ambrosiana' in *Rendiconti dell'Accademia Nazionale dei Lincei, Classe di Scienze Morali* (Rome, 1951)
L. BIELER, *Ireland, Harbinger of the Middle Ages* (London, 1963)
A. BOECKLER, *Abendländische Miniaturen bis zum Ausgang der romanischen Zeit* (Berlin-Leipzig, 1930)
—— *Das Goldene Evangelienbuch Heinrichs III* (Berlin, 1933)
C. BRANDI, *Unsere Schrift* (Göttingen, 1911)
—— et al. (edd.), *Archiv für Urkundenforschung* (Leipzig, 1907-44)
—— *Ausgewählte Aufsätze* (Berlin, 1938)
H. BRESSLAU, 'Ein lateinischer Empfehlungsbrief' in *Archiv für Papyrusforschung*, iii, 2, pp. 168-72 (Leipzig, 1904)
A. BRÜCKNER and R. MARICHOL, *Chartae Latinae Antiquiores*, i-iv (Basel, 1954-68)
R. F. BURCHARDT, *Der Basler Münsterschatz* (Basel, 1933)
A. BUSULOCEANU, 'Pietro Cavallini e la pittura Romana del ducento e trecento' in *Ephemeris Dacoyomana*, 13 (1925)
F. CABROL and H. LECLERCQ, *Dictionnaire d'Archéologie et de Liturgie chrétienne* (Paris, 1907 etc.)
R. CAGNAT, *Cours d'épigraphie latine* (4th edition, Paris, 1914)
A. CALDERINI, Introduction and Appendix to *Ilias Ambrosiana* (q.v.)
AUGUSTO CAMPANA, 'The Origin of the Word "Humanist"' in *Journal of the Warburg and Courtauld Institutes*, vol. ix (London, 1946)
E. CARUSI and W. M. LINDSAY, *Monumenti paleografici Veronesi*, 2 vols. (Rome, 1929-34)
P. FRANCHI DE' CAVALIERI and J. LIETZMANN, *Specimina Codicum Graecorum Vaticanorum* (Bonn, 1910; 2nd edition, Berlin, 1929)

List of Works consulted

A. M. CERIANI and A. RATTI, *Homeri Iliadis pictae fragmenta Ambrosiana* (Rome, 1905)
—— see also *Ilias Ambrosiana*

E. CHATELAIN, *Uncialis Scriptura Codicum latinorum novis exemplis illustrata* (Paris, 1901-2)

ANTON CHROUST, *Monumenta Palaeographica*, ser. I-II (Munich, 1899-1917)

Corpus Inscriptionum Latinarum (Berlin, 1862-1936)

MATTEO DELLA CORTE, *Notizie degli scavi di Pompei* (Naples, 1911)

H. DEGERING, *Die Schrift*, 3rd edition (Berlin, 1954)

E. DIEHL, *Inscriptiones Latinae* (Berlin, 1912)

L. DUCHESNE, *Histoire ancienne de l'Église*, 3 vols. (5th edition, Paris, 1911)

J. EBERSOLT, *Orient et Occident. Recherches sur les influences byzantines et orientales en France avant les Croisades*, 2 vols. (Paris, 1928-9)

C. C. EDGAR, *Catalogue général des antiquités du Musée du Caire* (Cairo, 1925-31)

F. EHRLE (ed.), *Fragmenta et picturae Vergiliana Codicis Vaticani Latini 3225* (Rome, 1899)

—— (ed.), *Picturae ornamenta complura scripturae Specimina Codicis Vaticani 3867* (Rome, 1902)

—— and P. LIEBAERT, *Specimina Codicum Latinorum Vaticanorum* (Bonn, 1912)

V. FEDERICI, *Archivio Paleografico Italiano* (Rome, 1932)

M. C. FERRARI, 'La geografia del Zolemeo fatta miniare dal Cardinale Bessarione' in *La Bibliofilia*, xl (Florence, 1938)

H. FICHTENAU, *Mensch und Schrift im Mittelalter* (Vienna, 1946)

MAX FRAENKEL, *Inschriften von Pergamon* (Berlin, 1894)

ARTHUR L. FROTHINGHAM, *The Monuments of Christian Rome* (New York, 1925)

E. B. GARRISON, *Italian Romanesque Panel Painting* (Florence, 1949)

H. GERSTINGER, *Die griechische Buchmalerei* (Leipzig-Berlin, 1927)

—— *Der Wiener Genesis* (Vienna, 1931)

—— and P. BUBERL, *Die byzantinischen Handschriften*, 2 vols. (Vienna, 1937-8)

J. GILL, *The Council of Florence* (Cambridge, 1959)

A. GOLDSCHMIDT, *Die deutsche Buchmalerei*, 2 vols. (Florence, 1928)

N. GRAY, *XIX-Century Ornamented Types and Title-pages* (London, 1938)

—— *The Palaeography of Latin Inscriptions in the Eighth, Ninth and Tenth Centuries in Italy* (Rome, 1948)

—— *Lettering on Buildings* (London, 1960)

B. P. GRENFELL and A. S. HUNT, *Oxyrhynchus Papyri* (Oxford, 1904)

A. HESSEL, 'Die Entstehung der Renaissanceschriften' in *Archiv für Urkundenforschung*, vol. xiii (Berlin, 1935)

G. F. HILL, *A Corpus of Italian Medals of the Renaissance before Cellini* (London, 1930)

F. HILLER VON GAERTRINGEN, *Inschriften von Priene* (Berlin, 1906)

E. HÜBNER, *Exempla scripturae Latinae a Caesaris dictatoris morte ad aetatem Justiniani* (Berlin, 1885)

E. HUTTON, *The Cosmati* (London, 1950)

Ilias Ambrosiana [facsimile], *Fontes Ambrosianae*, vol. xxviii (Bern and Olten, 1953)

H. W. JANSON, *The Sculpture of Donatello*, 2 vols. (Princeton, 1957)

H. JANTZEN, *Ottonische Kunst* (Hamburg, 1959)

W. KAECH, *Rhythmus und Proportion in der Schrift* (Olten, 1956)

J. R. VON KARABACEK and R. BEER, *Monumenta paleographica Vindobonensia* (Vienna, 1910 etc.)

C. M. KAUFFMANN, *Handbuch der altchristlichen Epigraphik* (Freiburg, 1918)

F. G. KENYON and H. I. BELL, *Greek Papyri in the British Museum; Facsimiles II* (London, 1898)

OTTO KERN, *Inscriptiones Graecae* (Bonn, 1913)

A. KIRCHOFF, *Studien zur griechischen Alphabets* (4th edition, Gütersloh, 1887)

W. KÖHLER, *Byzantine Art in the West* (Cambridge, Mass., 1940)

—— *Die Karolingischen Miniaturen*, 3 parts (Berlin, 1930–60)

K. LAKE, *Codex Sinaiticus* (Oxford, 1911–22)

P. LAUER and C. SAMARAN, *Les Diplômes originaux des Mérovingiens* (Paris, 1908)

—— *Le Palais du Latran* (Paris, 1911)

—— *Histoire des fils de Louis le Pieux, de Nithard* (Paris, 1926)

H. J. LAWLOR, 'The Cathach of St. Columba' in *Proceedings of the Royal Irish Academy*, vol. xxxiii (Dublin, 1916)

O. LERCHE, *Das Reichenauer Lektionar* (Leipzig, 1928)

E. LESNE, *Les Livres, 'scriptoria' et bibliothèques du commencement du VIIIᵉ à la fin du XIᵉ siècle* (Lille, 1938)

W. LEVISON, *England and the Continent in the eighth century* (Oxford, 1946)

E. A. LOWE et al. (edd.), *The Bobbio Missal*, Henry Bradshaw Society, vol. liii (London, 1917)

—— *Scriptura Beneventana*, 2 vols. (Oxford, 1929)

—— *Codices Latinae Antiquiores*, 11 vols. (Oxford, 1934–66)

—— 'The Script of Luxeuil' in *Revue Bénédictine*, 1953, Nos. 1 and 2

—— *English Uncial* (Oxford, 1960)

W. LÜDTKE and T. NISSEN, *Die Grabschrift des Aberkios* (Leipzig, 1910)

J. P. MAHAFFY and J. G. SMYLY, *The Flinders Petrie Papyri*, 3 vols. (Dublin, 1891–1905)

J. MALLON, R. MARICHAL, and C. PERRAT, *L'Écriture latine de la capitale romaine à la minuscule* (Paris, 1939)

GIOVANNI MARDERSTEIG, 'Leon Battista Alberti e la rinascita del carattere lapidario nel quattrocento' in *Italia Medioevale e Umanistica*, vol. ii (1959)

—— *Felice Feliciano Veronese: Alphabetum Romanum* (Verona, 1960)

—— 'Aldo Manuzio e i carratteri di Francesco Griffo da Bologna' in *Studi di Bibliografia e di Storia in onore di Tammaro de Marinis* (Verona, 1964)

O. MARUCCHI, *Christian Epigraphy* (Cambridge, 1912)

E. MAUDE THOMPSON, *Introduction to Greek and Latin Palaeography* (Oxford, 1912)

MILLARD MEISS, 'Towards a More Comprehensive Renaissance Palaeography' in *The Art Bulletin*, vol. xlii, 2 (June 1960)

K. MENZEL, et al., *Die Trierer Ada-Handschrift* (Leipzig, 1889)

G. MERCATI, *M. Tullii Ciceronis De Republica* (Bobbio facsimile) (Rome, 1934)

H. J. M. MILNE and J. C. SKEAT, *Scribes and Correctors of the Codex Sinaiticus* (London, 1938)

E. H. MINNS, 'Big Greek Minuscule, Pembroke College, Cambridge, MS. 310' in *Annual of the British School at Athens*, vol. xlvi (1951)

C. MOHLBERG, *Missale Gothicum (Codices Liturgici I)* (Augsburg, 1929)

R. U. MONTINI, *Le Tombe dei Papi* (Rome, 1957)

S. MORISON, *The Art of Printing*, from *Proceedings of the British Academy*, vol. 23 (Oxford, 1937)

—— 'Early Humanistic Script and the First Roman Type' in *The Library*, 4th ser., vol. xxiv (1943)

FRANTIŠEK MUZIKA, *Krasné Písmo ve vývoji latinky* (Prague, 1958)

MEDEA NORSA, *Analogie e coincidenze tra scritture greche e latine nei papiri* (Rome, 1946)

343

List of Works consulted

W. F. OAKESHOTT, *Classical Inspiration in Medieval Art* (London, 1959)

H. OMONT, *Fac-similés de manuscrits grecs des XVe et XVIe siècles* (Paris, 1887)

—— *Fac-similés des manuscrits grecs datés de la Bibliothèque Nationale du IXe au XIVe siècle* (Paris, 1891)

—— *Fac-similés des plus anciens manuscrits grecs en onciale et en minuscule de la Bibliothèque Nationale, du IVe au XIIe siècle* (Paris, 1892)

B. PAGNIN, 'La "littera Bononiensis"' in *Atti del R. Istituto Veneto*, vol. 93 (1933-4)

E. PANOFSKY, *Tomb Sculpture* (Princeton, 1964)

PETRIE, *see* Mahaffy

F. PHILIPPI, *Siegel* (Leipzig, 1914)

H. L. PINNER, *The World of Books in Classical Antiquity* (Leiden, 1948)

R. PROCTOR, *The Printing of Greek in the Fifteenth Century* (London, Bibliographical Society, 1900)

E. K. RAND, *Studies in the Script of Tours*, 2 vols. (Cambridge, Mass., 1929-34)

J. S. REID, *The Municipalities of the Roman Empire* (Cambridge, 1913)

ERNEST RENAN, *Histoire des origines du christianisme*, 8 vols. (Paris, 1863-83)

E. H. J. REUSENS, *Éléments de Paléographie* (Louvain, 1897; 2nd edition, 1899)

C. H. ROBERTS, *Two Biblical Papyri* (Manchester, 1936)

—— *Catalogue of the Greek Papyri in the John Rylands Library* (Manchester, 1938)

—— *Greek Literary Hands, 350 B.C.—A.D. 400* (Oxford, 1955)

E. S. and E. A. ROBERTS, *An Introduction to Greek Epigraphy* (London, 1889, 1905)

J. B. DE ROSSI, *La Roma Sotterranea* (Rome, 1867)

R. SABBADINI, *Codicis Vergiliani qui Augusteus appellatur reliquiae* (Turin, 1926)

—— *Codex Vergilianus qui Palatinus appellatur* (Paris, 1929)

L. SCHIAPARELLI, 'Influenze straniere nella scrittura Italiana dei secoli VIII e IX' in *Studi e Testi* (Rome, 1927)

V. SCHOLDERER, *Greek Printing Types, 1465-1927* (London, 1927)

P. E. SCHRAMM, *Kaiser, Rom und Renovatio*, 2 vols. (Leipzig, 1920)

—— and F. MÜTTERICH, *Denkmäler der deutschen Könige und Kaiser* (Munich, 1962)

W. SCHUBART, *Papyri Graecae Berolinenses* (Bonn, 1911)

—— *Griechische Paläographie* (Munich, 1925)

A. SILVAGNI, *Monumenta epigraphica christiana saeculo XIII antiquiora quae in Italiae finibus adhuc exstant* (Rome, 1943 etc.)

FRANZ STEFFENS, *Paléographie latine* (Trèves, 1910)

—— *Proben aus griechischen Handschriften und Urkunden* (Trier, 1912)

S. H. STEINBERG, 'Medieval Writing Masters' in *The Library*, 4th ser., vol. xxii (1942)

G. SWARZENSKI, *Die Regensburger Buchmalerei* (Leipzig, 1901)

M. N. TOD, *Greek Historical Inscriptions* (Oxford, 1948)

PIETRO TOESCA and F. FORLATI, *The mosaics in the church of St. Mark at Venice* (London, 1958)

—— *Pietro Cavallini* (London, 1960)

L. TRAUBE, *Vorlesungen und Abhandlungen*, 3 vols. (Munich, 1909-20)

C. H. TURNER, *The Oldest Manuscript of the Vulgate Gospels* (Oxford, 1931)

B. L. ULLMANN, *Ancient Writing and its Influence* (New York, 1932)

—— *The Origin and Development of Humanistic Script* (Rome, 1960)

A. VENTURI, *Storia dell'arte Italiana*, 7 vols. (Milan, 1901-13)

L. VOELKL, *Der Kaiser Konstantin* (München, 1957)

A. DE WAAL, *Das Kleid des Herrn* (Freiburg, 1891)

—— *Roma Sacra. Die ewige Stadt in ihren Christlichen Denkmälern und Erinnerungen alter und neuer Zeit* (München, 1905)

L. WALLACH, 'Alcuin's epitaph on Hadrian I' in *American Journal of Philology*, vol. lxii (1951)

F. E. WARREN, *The Antiphonary of Bangor* (London, 1893–5)

K. WEITZMANN, *Illustration in Roll and Codex* (Princeton, 1947)

ULRICH VON WILAMOWITZ-MOELLENDORF, *Der Timotheos-Papyrus gefunden bei Abusir* (Leipzig, 1903)

H. A. WILSON, *The Calendar of St. Willibrord* (London, 1918)

W. W. WROTH, *Imperial Byzantine Coins in the British Museum* (London, 1908)

E. H. ZIMMERMANN, *Vorkarolingischen Miniaturen*, 5 vols. (Berlin, 1916)

INDEX

8147813	MOORHEAD John	Theoderic in Italy
8264259	MOORMAN John	A History of the Franciscan Order
8181469	MORISON Stanley	Politics and Script
9240582	MUSURILLO H.	Acts of the Pagan Martyrs & Christian Martyrs (2 vols)
9240213	MYRES J.L.	Herodotus The Father of History
8219512	OBOLENSKY Dimitri	Six Byzantine Portraits
8270259	O'DONNELL J.J.	Augustine: Confessions (3 vols)
8116020	OWEN A.L.	The Famous Druids
8131445	PALMER, L.R.	The Interpretation of Mycenaean Greek Texts
8143427	PFEIFFER R.	History of Classical Scholarship (vol 1)
8143648	PFEIFFER Rudolf	History of Classical Scholarship 1300–1850
8111649	PHEIFER J.D.	Old English Glosses in the Epinal-Erfurt Glossary
8142277	PICKARD–CAMBRIDGE A.W.	Dithyramb Tragedy and Comedy
8269765	PLATER & WHITE	Grammar of the Vulgate
8213891	PLUMMER Charles	Lives of Irish Saints (2 vols)
820695X	POWICKE Michael	Military Obligation in Medieval England
8269684	POWICKE Sir Maurice	Stephen Langton
821460X	POWICKE Sir Maurice	The Christian Life in the Middle Ages
8225369	PRAWER Joshua	Crusader Institutions
8225571	PRAWER Joshua	The History of The Jews in the Latin Kingdom of Jerusalem
8143249	RABY F.J.E.	A History of Christian Latin Poetry
8143257	RABY F.J.E.	A History of Secular Latin Poetry in the Middle Ages (2 vols)
8214316	RASHDALL & POWICKE	The Universities of Europe in the Middle Ages (3 vols)
8154488	REYMOND E.A.E & BARNS J.W.B.	Four Martyrdoms from the Pierpont Morgan Coptic Codices
8148380	RICKMAN Geoffrey	The Corn Supply of Ancient Rome
8141556	ROSS Sir David	Aristotle: De Anima
8141076	ROSS Sir David	Aristotle: Metaphysics (2 vols)
8141092	ROSS Sir David	Aristotle: Physics
8142307	ROSTOVTZEFF M.	Social and Economic History of the Hellenistic World, 3 vols.
8142315	ROSTOVTZEFF M.	Social and Economic History of the Roman Empire, 2 vols.
8264178	RUNCIMAN Sir Steven	The Eastern Schism
814833X	SALMON J.B.	Wealthy Corinth
8171587	SALZMAN L.F.	Building in England Down to 1540
8218362	SAYERS Jane E.	Papal Judges Delegate in the Province of Canterbury 1198–1254
8221657	SCHEIN Sylvia	Fideles Crucis
8148135	SHERWIN WHITE A.N.	The Roman Citizenship
9240167	SINGER Charles	Galen: On Anatomical Procedures
8113927	SISAM, Kenneth	Studies in the History of Old English Literature
8642040	SOUTER Alexander	A Glossary of Later Latin to 600 AD
8270011	SOUTER Alexander	Earliest Latin Commentaries on the Epistles of St Paul
8222254	SOUTHERN R.W.	Eadmer: Life of St. Anselm
8251408	SQUIBB G.	The High Court of Chivalry
8212011	STEVENSON & WHITELOCK	Asser's Life of King Alfred
8212011	SWEET Henry	A Second Anglo-Saxon Reader—Archaic and Dialectical
8148259	SYME Sir Ronald	History in Ovid
8143273	SYME Sir Ronald	Tacitus (2 vols)
8200951	THOMPSON Sally	Women Religious
924023X	WALBANK F.W.	Historical Commentary on Polybius (3 vols)
8201745	WALKER Simon	The Lancastrian Affinity 1361–1399
8161115	WELLESZ Egon	A History of Byzantine Music and Hymnography
8140185	WEST M.L.	Greek Metre
8141696	WEST M.L.	Hesiod: Theogony
8148542	WEST M.L.	The Orphic Poems
8140053	WEST M.L.	Hesiod: Works & Days
8152663	WEST M.L.	Iambi et Elegi Graeci
9240221	WHEELWRIGHT Philip	Heraclitus
822799X	WHITBY M. & M.	The History of Theophylact Simocatta
8206186	WILLIAMSON, E.W.	Letters of Osbert of Clare
8208103	WILSON F.P.	Plague in Shakespeare's London
8247672	WOODHOUSE C.M.	Gemistos Plethon
8114877	WOOLF Rosemary	The English Religious Lyric in the Middle Ages
8119224	WRIGHT Joseph	Grammar of the Gothic Language